WILLIAM LYON MACKENZIE:
A Reinterpretation

WILLIAM LYON MACKENZIE:
A Reinterpretation

William Dawson LeSueur

Edited and with an Introduction by
A. B. McKillop

The Carleton Library No. 111
*Published by Macmillan of Canada, Limited,
in association with the Institute of Canadian Studies,
Carleton University*

Canadian Cataloguing in Publication Data

LeSueur, William Dawson, 1840-1917.
  William Lyon Mackenzie

(The Carleton library; no. 111)

"The text reprinted here is that of the original
manuscript, written between 1907 and 1908, and of
the preface to the revised edition of 1915" (both
previously unpublished)

Includes bibliographical references.
ISBN 0-7705-1743-9 pa.

1. Mackenzie, William Lyon, 1795-1861.
2. Politicians - Canada - Biography.   I. McKillop,
A.B., 1946-   II. Carleton University.
Institute of Canadian Studies.   III. Series.

FC451.M3L4   971.03'8'0924   C79-094069-8
F1032.M148L4

*Printed in Canada for
The Macmillan Company of Canada,
Limited, 70 Bond Street,
Toronto M5B 1X3*

CONTENTS

	Page
Editor's Introduction	vii
Acknowledgments	xxxi
Preface by the Author	xxxiii

Text of the Biography

CHAPTER ONE: The Beginnings of Upper Canada   1
CHAPTER TWO: The Advent of Mackenzie   16
CHAPTER THREE: The Times and the Man   34
CHAPTER FOUR: The Criticisms of a Journalist   53
CHAPTER FIVE: Some Questions of the Day   68
CHAPTER SIX: The Germ of the Rebellion   88
CHAPTER SEVEN: Elected to the Legislature   104
CHAPTER EIGHT: The Tenth Parliament of
            Upper Canada   120
CHAPTER NINE: A Conservative Reaction   141
CHAPTER TEN: Mackenzie Expelled from
            the Legislature   157
CHAPTER ELEVEN: Mackenzie in England   178
CHAPTER TWELVE: A Faction-Rent Province   196
CHAPTER THIRTEEN: The Combat Deepens — Mackenzie
            First Mayor of Toronto   211
CHAPTER FOURTEEN: The Twelfth Parliament —
            A Wave of Reform   230
CHAPTER FIFTEEN: Sir Francis Bond Head and the
            Question of Responsible
            Government   246
CHAPTER SIXTEEN: Foreshadowings of Rebellion   266
CHAPTER SEVENTEEN: The Outbreak   285
CHAPTER EIGHTEEN: The Activities of an Exile   305
CHAPTER NINETEEN: Imprisonment and Other
            Vicissitudes   324
CHAPTER TWENTY: The Advent of Responsible
            Government   348
CHAPTER TWENTY-ONE: A Fighter to the Last   365

Notes to Text   391
Suggestions for Further Reading   427
Note on the Editor   430

EDITOR'S INTRODUCTION

William Lyon Mackenzie has always been an enigma in Canadian historical writing, and he has never quite been out of the public eye. In life or in legend, he has been praised and damned, seen as a political reformer and as an unprincipled demagogue, a defender of free speech and a practitioner of gutter journalism, a Jacksonian democrat and a British liberal. But he has never been ignored. His has been a special place in Canadian history, for he has meant many things to as many people.[1]

It may come as a surprise, then, to learn that there have been few book-length studies made of Mackenzie. One was published within a year of his death. It was thorough, but it was also written by his son-in-law and bore several of the marks of filial piety and few of scholarly detachment. Another, written almost a century later, was novelesque in form and substance. Admirable in the way it evoked the details and atmosphere of Mackenzie's age, it was less a full-scale biography than it was an attempt to use the fictional form to portray Mackenzie's part in the coming and course of the Upper Canadian rebellion of 1837.

Mid-way between the publication of these two books, Charles Lindsey's adulatory and official *Life and Times of William Lyon Mackenzie* (two volumes, 1862) and William Kilbourn's popular *The Firebrand* (1956), another study of the life of Mackenzie was written. This biography was by William Dawson LeSueur, one of Canada's foremost men of letters. It was written for a popular historical series entitled "The Makers of Canada," but its author intended from the outset that the book be a critical examination not only of William Lyon Mackenzie and his career but also of the chain of political and constitutional events and ideas with which the red-wigged rebel of 1837 had often been associated. LeSueur's "William Lyon Mackenzie" was never published, for it engendered so much controversy as a manuscript that it became the subject of no less than five court cases between 1908 and 1913. As late as 1945, LeSueur's son was told that only after another fifty years or more had passed would animosities have died down sufficiently for the book to appear in print.[2] The lapse of time suggests that this has proved to be only a minor exaggeration, for only now, more than thirty years later and seventy after the final words of the study were penned, has the book become available in published form to readers of Canadian history.

In that marvellous gem of historical detective fiction, *The Daughter of Time* (1951), Josephine Tey reminded her readers that truth was that daughter. The lapse of over half a century since W. D. LeSueur wrote the book that he hoped would constitute a permanent contribution to Canadian history has done little to undermine seriously that wish, for when viewed against the picture of Mackenzie provided in other accounts a new perspective – perhaps a greater approximation to truth – emerges. It is not the purpose of this introductory essay to compare LeSueur's judgements with those of later generations of scholars, but to place his work into the social and intellectual context in which it was written, and to examine it primarily against the tradition of historical writing from which it emerged. It is sufficient to state that LeSueur's radically different interpretation still provides a distinct and suggestive perspective on Mackenzie and his age.

I

Who was William Dawson LeSueur and what were the circumstances which resulted in the suppression of his book? Those who wish more thorough answers to these questions will find another volume in the Carleton Library Series of value. *A Critical Spirit: The Thought of William Dawson LeSueur* (Carleton Library No. 104, 1977), a collection of his nineteenth- and early twentieth-century writings, contains lengthy commentary on his life and thought. It reveals a man whose place in the intellectual history of Canada was a substantial one in his day, but who has largely been forgotten in ours. LeSueur was the first native-born Canadian to be committed to the spirit of critical intellectual enquiry as a means of self-improvement and social well-being. This belief demanded that he defend "the intellectual life" against the views of those who believed intellectual enquiry to be an activity that subverted accepted notions. It saw him become the major Canadian advocate of scientific evolutionary ethics. Comte, Darwin, and Spencer each found a popularizer and a defender in him, and for the last quarter of the nineteenth century he attempted to counter the simplistic reductionism of some of their Canadian critics. It demanded too, that he subject the political and constitutional process in Canada to a similar scrutiny. A number of his essays examined the relationship of morality, political practice, and popular political beliefs.

William Dawson LeSueur was pre-eminently a Victorian. He was born in 1840, three years after Victoria assumed the throne, and died in 1917, at the end of the Edwardian era. Professionally, he was an Ottawa civil servant of the higher ranks, but considered from the perspective of his many essays on a variety of subjects he may be seen as a barometer of some of the most fundamental and pervasive assumptions of the Anglo-American world. He was, to begin with, a moralist – a believer in the operation of a universal moral law that could help to harmonize the laws of the spiritual and material worlds. Secondly, he was a "progressivist" – one who thought that man could be progressively improved through the cultivation of his higher nature.[3] These elements remained central to his thought even in an environment of shifting convictions and belief in the twentieth century. His study of Mackenzie was shaped by their presence.

As noted earlier, however, the biography was never published. An advisory editor of the "Makers of Canada" series for which his "Mackenzie" was being written (as well as the author of a study of Frontenac for the series), LeSueur had submitted the sole longhand copies of his chapters to the publisher, George W. Morang, throughout 1907 and early 1908. He was aware that William Lyon Mackenzie King, Deputy Minister of Labour in the Laurier government and grandson of Mackenzie actively opposed him as the biographer of his grandfather and was lobbying to this effect. But he had been set somewhat at ease by Morang, who had consistently applauded and encouraged his work on Mackenzie, even though at times expressing some concern about the conclusions drawn by the author. Despite these hints of trouble, LeSueur was stunned when he received a letter from Morang notifying him that the biography had been rejected because it portrayed William Lyon Mackenzie in too negative a light, as a "breaker," not a "Maker," of Canada.

The author then sought to recover his manuscript. Morang refused to relinquish it, however, declaring that LeSueur's acceptance of a $500 cash advance had transferred ownership from author to publisher. (LeSueur had already offered to return the advance by certified cheque.) Legal action followed. First, author sued publisher for recovery of the manuscript; he won, and Morang appealed to a higher court. The original verdict was ultimately sustained and the manuscript returned to LeSueur. But this marked only the beginning of the courtroom proceedings faced by LeSueur, who by 1910 was in his seventies.

The heirs of Mackenzie, urged on by Mackenzie King, then proceeded to take legal measures to prevent LeSueur from either publishing his book elsewhere or making further use of any notes taken while he had consulted the Mackenzie papers in the possession of Mr. Charles Lindsey. The Lindsey appeal to the courts of Ontario, which rested upon the claim that LeSueur had obtained access to the family papers under false pretenses, was successful. An Ontario court injunction was granted in 1912 and upheld the next year, prohibiting LeSueur from publishing any book based upon materials found while consulting the Lindsey-Mackenzie papers. These court cases, held in Toronto, became a *cause célèbre* in late 1912 and early 1913. Journalists and lawyers, politicians and professors, daily packed the courtrooms to hear LeSueur, George Lindsey (son of the deceased Charles Lindsey, author of the original biography of Mackenzie), and Mackenzie King defend their respective positions by articulating their understanding of the course of Canadian history in the nineteenth century and its contemporary significance in the twentieth.

A much more detailed account of the "LeSueur-Lindsey Controversy," using such materials as trial evidence and the diary of Mackenzie King, is provided in another volume in the Carleton Library Series, *A Critical Spirit*. In addition, George Morang's letter of rejection and the author's long reply to it are reprinted in that volume. LeSueur himself wrote an extensive commentary on the controversy in 1915, in the form of a preface to a revised (but never published) version of the book. This preface sets forward LeSueur's own perspective upon the case and raises the legal and moral issues involved in the controversy. It has been included in the present edition of the original biography, for it is only fitting that the aggrieved author finally be given an opportunity to tell readers of his long-unpublished book his own side of the story.

It should be noted that there appear to be no factual inaccuracies in LeSueur's 1915 preface. Furthermore, his interpretation of the affair is borne out by evidence unavailable to him. This is especially the case regarding his suspicion that the suppression of the manuscript was due largely to the actions of Mackenzie King. Near the end of December, 1911, King read all available correspondence between LeSueur, Lindsey, and Morang. "It was quite clear," he confided to his diary, "that there was a conspiracy to which Morang, thro' the influence of Christopher Robinson & Leseuer [*sic*] thro' prejudice were parties to have Mackenzie written down instead of up."[4] This sentence accurately indicates King's attitude toward the prospect of LeSueur as biographer of his illustrious forebear.

The passage also suggests that from the outset LeSueur's biography held a significance greater than that of a simple study of the Upper Canadian agitator. The lapse of seventy years between writing and publication has expanded that significance, for while the book still adds to an understanding of Mackenzie it is now also a document that reflects certain aspects of the age of Laurier. LeSueur's critical assessment of Mackenzie became a matter of interest to press and public not only because it touched the raw nerves of Mackenzie King's sense of political identity, but also because it insisted upon an examination of the meaning and legacy of the constitutional heart of the political culture of English-speaking Canada, the idea of Responsible Government. Finally, as part of a biographical series of historical figures, LeSueur's book affords a glimpse into the state of historical writing in Canada as well as the place of biographical studies within it.

II

When William Dawson LeSueur first began serious research on his biography of William Lyon Mackenzie in 1906 he wrote to the Librarian of the Toronto Public Library to ask what materials relating to Mackenzie existed there. "I have already a general knowledge of the period and the characters that figured in it," he said, "but for the purposes of my book I want to get a very exact and comprehensive knowledge of the whole subject, which I do not think has yet been set in such a light as to do full and impartial justice to all parties concerned."[5] From the outset he was as much concerned with the age in which Mackenzie lived as with Mackenzie himself. This was not all, however, for the prospective biographer sought to write not only an impartial and judicious book, one which would "stand criticism from every point of view," but also "one that will really instruct the rising generation of Canadians as to the great issues of that period and with what degree of sincerity and good faith those issues were on both sides fought out."[6] Scholarly and judicious LeSueur may have meant to be to Mackenzie, his supporters, and his opponents, but it was clear from the outset that his study was intended as a tract of direct significance for its own times. In some respects, then, it says as much about the intellectual and political climate of Canada in the early twentieth century as it does about British North America in the nineteenth.

It is necessary to consider two strands in the political fibre of Laurier's Canada in order to understand fully the circumstances which informed the substance of LeSueur's "Mackenzie." First is the state of political life in Canada. Politics, by Laurier's third term in office, had reached an exceedingly low ebb. The tide of enthusiasm for his administrations had by then receded, particularly in intellectual circles. Differences in principle seemed no longer to exist between parties; each week seemed to witness new scandals; the press seemed incapable of offering a criticism of politics that could not be directly traced to political partisanship. The Conservative opposition under Robert Borden, especially between 1906 and 1908, emphasized the corruption of the Laurier ministry and not its own declaration of political principles and policy as set forward in its "Halifax Platform." "Failing rivalry in politics," O. D. Skelton could conclude by 1908, "we have fallen back on rivalry in billingsgate." In doing so, he summed up the general disaffection of Canadian intellectuals with the Canadian political process by the end of the first decade of the twentieth century.[7]

Given this rising judgment that Canadian politics had become morally irresponsible, LeSueur found it immensely ironic that Canadian historical scholarship had gradually articulated a "whig" version of the nation's past.[8] From the 1870s on, Canadian historians had concluded that the essence of the country's political accomplishment had been the triumph of "responsible government," the very apex of political freedom. It had also been construed largely as a Liberal achievement. This conclusion, understandably, increased with each successive electoral triumph of the Liberal party. By Laurier's second term in office, one popular history of Canada could suggest that even the Canadian literary imagination, like the country's political history, came to maturity as a result of the political concessions won by Canadian reformers in the 1830s and 1840s. "The real beginnings of a literary spirit in Canada," concluded Charles G. D. Roberts in 1902, "may be said to date from the triumph of Responsible Government. That struggle had broadened men's minds and taught them to think for themselves."[9]

For LeSueur, the ironic juxtaposition of morally irresponsible political practice with an historical "school" which told of the triumph of a theory of government that was called "responsible" merited examination. He had thought so for several years. In an 1895 essay entitled "Problems of Government in Canada" he had noted that sixty years earlier "responsible government" (in its late nineteenth century sense) had not been in existence, yet colonial governors and politicians had not necessarily been morally or politically "irresponsible" in their actions.[10] In the twentieth century the legacy of responsible government could be judged; LeSueur was not impressed with what he saw around him. In the wake of Laurier's compromise on the Autonomy Bills in 1905 he wrote to J. S. Willison, publisher of the Toronto *News*, offering advice on what it should say editorially:

Of course *party*, as I point out, is the only thing in the way; but whose fault is that? Not Sbarretti's. The point to emphasize is that party as we have it directly antagonizes the principle of government responsibility. . . . *Do* try to show the people where we stand in this matter, and tell them that where there is keen party strife and rigid party organization *there cannot be responsible government* in anything approaching the full sense.[11]

LeSueur's objection was not simply to political parties devoid of principle, but to parties themselves. He had long been suspicious of "party politics," for it led in his view to the politics of self-interest, in which the interests of the party were equated with those of the common weal. In giving voice to such sentiments, LeSueur was simply continuing what had been a constant strain in Anglo-Canadian social criticism since Confederation. As late as 1904, Goldwin Smith (who with LeSueur and Principal G. M. Grant of Queen's University had long been a critic of partyism) had suggested that parties should be eliminated, since they were "held together by the machine, within an organ of corruption, aided by blind passion and a party name."[12] For his part, LeSueur had seen nothing in the course of Canadian political life that should have caused him to alter his 1872 view that "party may . . . be defined with absolute correctness as a body of men whose interest in supporting one another is greater than the interest they have in giving a right direction at all times to public policy."[13]

In his earlier writings on politics, LeSueur's major aim had been to make the public aware of the ambiguities of modern political evolution. His hope had been that, thus enlightened, the public conscience would insist upon necessary corrective measures. He had therefore focussed upon the key words in contemporary political discourse – "representative," "democracy," "public opinion," and "responsibility" – and had insisted that they be examined in the light of actual political practice. When so viewed, "responsible government," a phrase uttered triumphantly to imply political freedom, actually meant popular self-government through the agency of parties. Yet parties, he concluded, subverted the ideals of freedom and progress by turning party interests into ends in themselves. From years of first-hand observation as a senior civil servant in Ottawa, LeSueur could state with some authority that the modern politician publicly pandered to "public opinion" yet privately belittled the intelligence of the average citizen. Local issues were given more attention than national needs. True leadership was abrogated, and its place taken by the self-definition of the politician as delegate. Parliament was in decline as a deliberative body, for it was beginning to become a mere forum where tin gods purveyed government favours to their particular constituencies.

By the early twentieth century, LeSueur, now retired, began to write editorials regularly for the Montreal *Star* and Toronto *News* in order to give his views a more public forum. "The thought I want to bring home to the people," he wrote to Willison, "is that they have a most serious proposition on hand in making a decent use of representative institutions, and that all the trouble and scandals of the political arena are due to their darn deficiency in public virtue and intelligence."[14] A few years later, when he was given the opportunity to write the biography of William Lyon Mackenzie for the "Makers" series, LeSueur realized that he had been handed a golden opportunity not only to demonstrate these views historically but also to examine the origins of the myth of responsible government. "What I shall make clear," he wrote to his publisher midway through the writing of his book, "is that 'responsible government' is a name that has been given to *party government*. The people have *party government*; there is no question about that. They choose to call it – having picked up the name from the politicians – 'responsible government.' Well and good – they can call it what they like. I have nothing to say about it except here and there as occasion offers, to indicate what it really is, and that, not by any expression of my own opinions, which will be kept discreetly in the background, but by simple exposition of facts."[15]

The completed biography contained far more than mere exposition of facts. Not only was it very critical, although nowhere libellous, of Mackenzie; it also committed the far greater offense of putting forward – as will be seen – a general interpretation of Upper Canadian history that ran counter to the whole orientation of the "Makers" series. More was involved than a simple criticism of William Lyon Mackenzie, more at stake than the biography of a political reformer and the examination of a political theory. Called into question was the political mythology of English-speaking Canadians, for no period had become more sacrosanct than that between the arrival in Canada of William Lyon Mackenzie and the advent of Responsible Government with Elgin's signing of the Rebellion Losses Bill.

"Probably nowhere else can that [constitutional] development be more admirably studied," the reviewer of Charles

Dent's *Story of the Upper Canadian Rebellion* had written in 1885, "than in the isolated colonial community of Upper Canada. Here can clearly be seen the stages by which

FREEDOM SLOWLY BROADENED DOWN.

It was not without much heroic effort that the liberties which we today enjoy were won for us by the constitutional reformers to whom Liberals and Conservatives alike acknowledge their debt of gratitude."[16] Similarly, when at the height of the long LeSueur-Lindsey litigation George T. Denison described Mackenzie before the United Empire Loyalist Club of Toronto as "a cantankerous and quarrelsome little cad," the Toronto *Daily Star* replied not with a defense of Mackenzie's integrity but with a lesson in constitutional history, for the nature of which much could be forgiven:

> There is no mystery about Mackenzie. Such faults as he had, or were imputed to him, by the enemies of freedom, lay upon the surface. We all know that he led a rebellion. We all know that the grievances which led to the rebellion were real and such as to drive just men to extremities. . . . Most of us agree that the rising against Charles the First and the rising against James the Second were justifiable. . . .
>
> As to the principle for which William Lyon Mackenzie fought there is to-day hardly any doubt. Lord Durham would hardly be described as a quarrelsome little cad, nor Lord Elgin, nor Joseph Howe, nor Robert Baldwin. They were all for responsible government. Few Conservatives would now propose to go back to Family Compact or Downing Street rule.[17]

Such was the generally accepted, and acceptable, view of the significance of William Lyon Mackenzie in English-speaking Canada early in the twentieth century.

The "Makers of Canada," George N. Morang's series of twenty volumes detailing the course of Canadian history through the stories of its major figures, marked the convergence of the decidedly "whig" orientation of Anglo-Canadian historians and what Carl Berger has described as "the Victorian practice of biography."[18] The series marked, as well, the formal synthesis of an acceptable past by a generation of Canadian scholars. Taken as a whole, it not only drew upon more than thirty years of historical writing, but in so doing became an elaborate enunciation of Anglo-Canadian social and political mythology. The "Makers" series narrated (to use the words of Mircea Eliade on myth in general) "a sacred history." It told of how, through the active agency of individual character, far-sighted vision, political sagacity, and acts of heroism, was created a nation blessed with liberal institutions and a "responsible" form of government. Altogether, it was "a sacred story, and hence a 'true history'."[19] It spoke not of a past open to further interpretation but of a course of events which had somehow been foreordained by Canada's membership in a civilization which enjoyed irreversible moral and political progress.

No volume in the series was a more forcible example of this than the book which took the place of LeSueur's "Mackenzie." It was clear to George Morang that no account of Canada's "makers" could exclude Mackenzie, so immediately after (or perhaps even before)[20] his rejection of LeSueur's manuscript he asked George Lindsey to condense his father's two volume biography into one and to provide readers with a review of "Mackenzie's place in Canadian history" from a modern perspective.[21] The first chapter of the 1908 "Makers" edition of Charles Lindsey's *William Lyon Mackenzie*, was therefore written by his son George and constituted that review. Entitled "The Period and the Man," it, more than anything else in the series, revealed the extent to which Morang's achievement was, in effect, the first major chapter of what Donald Creighton was later to call the "Authorized Version" of Canadian history.[22]

Charles Lindsey's justification of William Lyon Mackenzie's erratic career as a political and social critic, and particularly of his part in fomenting rebellion, had been based upon the achievement of Responsible Government. "Much of the liberty Canada has enjoyed since 1840," he had declared in his 1862 preface, "and more of the wonderful progress she has made, are due to the changes which the insurrection was the chief agent in producing. Unless those changes had been made – unless a responsible government, especially, had been established – Canada would, ere now, either have been lost to the British Crown, or, ruled by the Sword, would have been stunted in her growth, her population poor, discontented, and ready to seek the protection of another power."[23] This, as has been seen, was the view held by most of the defenders of Mackenzie since the agitator's death. Accordingly, it was built upon by George Lindsey in his 1908 chapter on Mackenzie's contemporary significance. Quotations from newspapers and from learned historical tomes were marshalled in a steady testimony to Mackenzie's energy and to the blessings of Responsible Government. The *Globe* was quoted, stating in 1900 that "Few will deny to-day, in the light of history, that the cause of constitutional government in Canada was materially advanced by the action of William Lyon Mackenzie, and that results have justified the rising of 1837"; the *Star* was called upon to affirm that the Upper Canadian Rebellion "was one of a series of revulsions of popular feeling, recorded in British history, which has extended and broadened incalculably the British race and nation."[24]

Throughout the chapter, the achievement of Responsible Government was linked not simply to the broadly liberal institutions shared by all Canadians, but to the specific accomplishments of the political tradition that culminated in the formation and triumphs of the Liberal Party. Goldwin Smith and other authorities, including a biographer of Lord Durham, were called upon to draw the connection between Mackenzie and Responsible Government, but the quotation that constituted the crux of the Lindseys' argument was the one that declared:

> It may be that Mackenzie was impetuous and turbulent, but the rebellion of 1837 was at best a pitiful expression of the discontent which the greed and the oppression of the Family Compact had developed. Too much has been said of Mackenzie, and too little of the crying grievances which an insolent and autocratic executive would not redress, and of the privileges they were resolved to maintain. It is in such fashion that the decisive blow had been dealt to tyranny and privilege all down the splendid centuries of British history; and if in the story of Liberalism in all countries there are wild and sanguinary chapters, it is because only in that way could popular government be established and perpetuated.[25]

The extract was significant not because it came from a disinterested observer of the Canadian scene, for it had not, but because it was from a study of Sir Wilfrid Laurier and the Liberal Party.

III

It is necessary only to reflect upon the implications of the first paragraph of W. D. LeSueur's biography to appreciate the extent of his departure from the practice of history and biography in Canada. His story was to be that of "a personality and a period," but it was made clear in the sentences which followed that personality alone was not to be made the essential agency of social and political change. LeSueur's "Mackenzie" was intended to show that while its subject indeed precipitated the Upper Canadian Rebellion there were economic and political forces at work in England, America, and Upper Canada that, in his view, would "infallibly have given place to government of a democratic type." In short, the advent of Responsible Government was imminent by the 1830s; Mackenzie's rebellion merely prolonged its coming. "To say 'No Mackenzie, no Upper Canada rebellion,' " LeSueur wrote later in the book, "is to utter the most elementary historical truth. With many it has hitherto passed for a truth to say 'No rebellion, no responsible government'; but a careful and dispassionate reading of history is far from supporting such a view."

At the level of general interpretation, LeSueur took issue with the conventional view of Canadian history in virtually every important respect. He showed, for example, that social conditions were not increasingly intolerable in Upper Canada as the rebellion approached; that the colonial governors and the "Family Compact" each received a significant degree of genuine support from Canadian electors; that Mackenzie's rebellion could not have taken place without Mackenzie, but would not have occurred without the presence of Sir Francis Bond Head; that while Mackenzie laboured for the cause of Responsible Government prior to the rebellion, he little understood its implications for the practice of politics and in his declining years came in fact to regret its advent.

In his study of Canadian history LeSueur had come to realize that the established alliance between the reform tradition and the side of Virtue was not as clear-cut as previous historians had made out. No individual had helped create this fiction more than Mackenzie himself, and LeSueur took pains to suggest that a more balanced account was necessary:

No country in the world has yet enjoyed either a perfect government or perfect social conditions, and there were doubtless flaws in the state of Upper Canada when Mr. Mackenzie took its affairs in hand. What is difficult to understand is how it could have been very different from what it actually was, considering its origin and political constitution. Yet the whole period has come down to us laden with an odium largely the creation of the hostile criticism of a few men. If the present age should hereafter be judged by the criticisms of those who to-day take the least favourable view of its public life, what will its repute be? It is easier to create a tradition of evil than one of good. . . . To rejoice not in iniquity but to rejoice in *the truth* is one of the marks of a very superior grace. And so it has come about that historical criticism has found much more to do in the vindication, or partial vindication, of characters unduly blackened than in the darkening of characters too highly portrayed.

This was a passage of cardinal importance, for it pointed to one major reason why LeSueur's book met with such an antagonistic reception. Its essential heresy was not that it challenged the traditional justification for Mackenzie's career as agitator by attempting to dispel the myth of responsible government, but that it sought to rehabilitate those who had opposed the cause of constitutional reform, particularly the infamous "Family Compact." If there were elements of myth in the belief that the Canadian reform tradition was one of political good, no less was this the case for the idea that there was a tradition of evil which had given the cause of reform its moral *raison d'être*.

LeSueur's study of Mackenzie and his times sought therefore to strike an interpretative balance that would see historical justice done to the generally honest, if sometimes misguided, intentions of both reformers and their opponents. He clearly set out to deflate the reputation of Mackenzie, but did so for the purpose of asserting the integrity of the position held by his enemies, not for that of simple debunking. "Colonial secretaries, lieutenant-governors, judges, office-holders under the old system," he wrote to a friend in 1911, "have been ruthlessly robbed by me of those repulsive features under which an enlightened posterity has loved to

contemplate them . . . . Morang no doubt rolled up his
eyes to heaven and held up his hands in horror as he dictated
to his type-writer the words (addressed to me): 'You have
defended the Family Compact!' To take away a favourite
object of detestation is, I know, a worse offense against the
public than to impair an object of worship."[26]

The myth of a villainous Family Compact as well as that
of Mackenzie was thus exploded. "I will never ask you to
extend much admiration on the so-called 'family compact,' "
LeSueur had written to J. S. Willison shortly after receiving
word that his manuscript had been rejected by Morang, "but
don't you think it probable that, if a thing has been steadily
abused for a couple of generations, the condemnation [that]
might have cumulated becomes too strong[?] I suppose that,
theoretically, you might paint a fence till there was less fence
than paint."[27]

It must be noted that LeSueur's object as he chipped away
at the accumulated interpretative paint of a generation of
Canadian historians was not to lament the coming of a
popular democratic form of government to Canada. Nor did
he question the obvious fact that Canada experienced a
"responsible government" if defined in a procedural sense.
His, it must be recalled, was a moral perspective, and to him
the term "responsible" – once divorced from the procedures
of the Canadian governmental process – implied the notion
of moral obligation. What irked him about Canadian politicians, historical commentators, and the public at large was
that the two distinctly different conceptions of "responsibility"
had been construed as one even when abundant evidence
existed that the methods used in the practice of "responsible
government" mitigated against the exercise of moral responsibility. A politician's major obligation became that of
adherence to the platforms and needs of his party, not
necessarily to the public good. A party's main obligation was
to perpetuate itself in power, to use patronage and if need
be to subordinate principle to reach that end. For the
political party, the public interest had necessarily to be
equated with that of the party.

The heart of the myth of responsible government rested
in the fact that from its inception that mode of government
had been seen as *ipso facto* morally superior to that which
it replaced. As described in Canadian historical writing and
by politicians and journalists it had been given the air of

theoretical perfection. Yet, as LeSueur pointed out in numerous ways in his "Mackenzie," this could lead to self-delusion: "A consciousness of theoretical imperfection prompts to effort, sometimes to caution, sometimes to a wise moderation. It is the institution that is theoretically perfect that most needs watching, its very theoretical perfection creating a number of dangerous assumptions in its favour and throwing the public off their guard."

How, LeSueur asked, was party government morally more "responsible" than that which had emanated from "Downing Street"? Party, or Cabinet, government implied a shift of control over patronage from crown to party. The Crown's control over patronage had been part of Robert Baldwin's 1836 critique of British colonial rule; but, as LeSueur pointed out, "With quite as much point, or even more, Lord Glenelg might have asked him whether the grasping of the patronage was the chief or only object which the reformers of Upper Canada had in view in desiring responsible government. There are many today who would declare that the main significance of responsible government lies precisely there." However inadequate the rule of British North America had become before the 1840s, in an age that pointed toward democratic institutions and to a devolution of the British colonial empire, the fact was that from a moral point of view it was not necessarily "irresponsible." That "there was no government to defeat or save from defeat" meant that members of the colonial legislature could "better afford to vote according to their convictions" than could "the machine-elected and whip-disciplined successors of the twentieth century."

The author of "William Lyon Mackenzie" was above all an example of the historian as moral critic. His major criticism of the system of responsible government lay in the traditional but fallacious equation of "responsible" political practice with moral responsibility. Once Canadians were made aware that the two did not *necessarily* coincide he would have conceived his task to have been complete. For this reason, his seeming preference for the colonial system of government must not be construed as a desire on his part to have Canada return to "Downing Street" rule. The age of popular government had come to stay, he once said; there was no use lamenting that fact. His criticism of the partyism of the twentieth century was based not on a desire to depoliticize society but on a wish to make people aware that democratic politics too easily separated practice from conviction. That LeSueur posited no alternative political system simply indicates that he was a social critic, not a political theorist.

In the age of Mackenzie King, which had begun to dawn, LeSueur was vilified as a "Tory" who had no appreciation of the achievements of the liberal tradition or its founders in Canada. This was true only in the most limited sense. LeSueur was critical of the liberal tradition and had indeed come to admire the thought and career of Edmund Burke, but this was only because he wished to see the liberal's desire for individual freedom reconciled with the conservative's concern for order within the community, and to see moral conviction become the basis of political action. The difficulty of achieving this precarious balance in the twentieth century is suggested in the career of Arthur Meighen, the best exemplar of this aspect of LeSueur's view among Canadian politicians. Even with the association of LeSueur and Meighen, however, it is not possible to conclude that LeSueur offered a "tory" vision of Canada, a vision which denied the main currents of political thought in the nation. The author of "William Lyon Mackenzie" also believed that government should be in the hands of those who had the intellectual capacity, moral purpose, and expertise to formulate well-conceived policies. In this respect his thought foreshadowed in a general way the inclinations of those who gave rise to the League for Social Reconstruction in the 1930s. The mind of William Dawson LeSueur is one which defies easy compartmentalization within any of the conventional categories of political ideology.

IV

While the idea of Responsible Government was an important theme in LeSueur's study, its focus nevertheless remained on the enigmatic figure of William Lyon Mackenzie. He emerges from LeSueur's pages as a personality as complex as his body was energetic. He is painted neither as a hero nor a villain. It was LeSueur's conviction that the

full force of Mackenzie's character could not be revealed if
the man was described only in vague generalities. It was
necessary to let Mackenzie speak for himself. It was not
sufficient to note that his arguments were sometimes irrelevant; that his statements were too often inaccurate; that he
was frequently inconsistent in his positions. These, LeSueur
insisted, were "mere phrases" which provided an inadequate
account of the man. "To make the image vivid, to make
the man live, somebody must quote his own words: show
how frequently the same indefensible, sometimes shockingly
untrue, things were repeated, to what terrible excesses of
scurrility he did not hesitate to give way, how uniformly he
ascribed the worst of motives to his opponents; how little
he cared about misleading the ignorant as to the true condition of public affairs; how his hatred of opponents completely
dominated his interest in practical measures of reform; and
then show how, in spite of all this, there was a sound core
of humanity in the man; that he had a soul above mere
party politics; that, unscrupulous as he was as to means, he
had, in the largest sense, good ends in view; finally, that an
indomitable soul went to wreck through the tempestuousness
of its own passions."[28] Those, he concluded in his letter to
John Lewis, were the essential ingredients in the rebel's
character and actions. "Mackenzie," he added, "emerges
from my pages no ordinary man."

William Dawson LeSueur's "Mackenzie" was the first truly
critical biography to be written in Canada. It stood as a
direct repudiation of the memorializing tendency of virtually
all its predecessors, whether of individuals, such as *The
Hon. Alexander Mackenzie: His Life and Times* (1892),
or of groups, such as *Men of Canada: A Portrait Gallery*
(1901-2).[29] Critical, yet judicious (at one of the court cases
involving Lindsey and LeSueur a witness claimed that if
LeSueur were any more "upright" he would fall over back-
wards), it also declined to invoke the "Great Man" theory
of historical change made popular by Thomas Carlyle and
enshrined in the very title of the "Makers of Canada" series.

"We cannot look, however imperfectly, upon a great man,
without gaining something by him. He is the living light-
fountain, which it is good and pleasant to be near." So
Carlyle had written in his lecture on "Heroes."[30] This was not,
in itself, a statement to which LeSueur would have taken
exception, for he firmly believed in the social importance

of a moral exemplar. In that respect he inherited an element characteristic of the Victorian practice of biography. John Stuart Mill, Charlotte Yonge, J. A. Froude and others had seen the moral inspiration of the heroic individual as an antidote to the materialistic and commercial spirit of an industrial society in a rapid state of change.[31] Carlyle himself had suggested this, stating that the reverence given to Great Men constituted "the living rock amid all rushings down whatsoever; – the one fixed point in modern revolutionary history, otherwise as if bottomless and shoreless."[32]

This use of hero worship as a force resisting social disintegration was later to find expression in a number of works on the art of biography. James Baldwin Brown, for example, when writing *On the Uses of Biography* (1871), stated that by studying the "sterling great characters, such as England had, in times gone by," one might come to have less "to do than unfortunately we have with the . . . miserable huckstering spirit of the day."[33] In this context, it should be asked whether the spate of biographies written in Canada between 1890 and 1920 resulted, as Kenneth Windsor suggests, from the "heady nationalism" of the Laurier period, from an environment which "suggested opportunities not limitations,"[34] or from the anxieties common to Western industrial societies in which complex economic, social, and political forces seemed somehow to thwart the ability of the individual to shape his own destiny.[35]

W. D. LeSueur clearly felt such anxieties about the age in which he lived. His whole criticism of contemporary political practice was that the assertion of individual moral authority was thwarted by forces over which the single politician had no control. That he did not invoke a "Great Man" version of the Canadian past in his study of Mackenzie was partly due to his awareness as a historian that such social, political, and economic forces were important factors in the process of historical causation. Partly, too, LeSueur simply did not see Mackenzie as a positive moral example worthy of emulation; indeed, such moral force as did exist in Canada prior to the rebellions had come more from the camp of Mackenzie's opponents.

The general tone of LeSueur's "William Lyon Mackenzie" suggests strongly that its author was deeply saddened that certain elements in Mackenzie's character had prevented him from providing a constructive leadership for Canadians. "It is clear," he wrote, "that Mackenzie had an instinct to do justice. It was a misfortune that he so often allowed that instinct to be silenced by the blasts of passion." Elsewhere in his book LeSueur could note that "No one can read the early numbers of his paper and not feel that he had it much at heart to benefit the country; and yet it is equally clear that he was betaking himself to methods more adapted to promote strife and discord than constitutional progress." The biography tells a story that is suffused with a tragic dimension. It is this element, along with a critical spirit tempered with a sense of justice, that makes it more than a tract for its times, elevates it above the level of good historical biography, and gives it a unity that helps to fuse history and biography into art.

V

The text reprinted here is that of the original manuscript, written between 1907 and 1908, and of the preface to the revised edition of 1915. A typescript copy of this, the original and offending work, may be found in the Mackenzie-Lindsey collection in the Provincial Archives of Ontario. The revised version of the book, along with the 1915 preface, is on microfilm in the Rare Book Room of the University of Toronto Robarts Research Library; another copy is in the Public Archives of Canada in Ottawa. This version, however, has been so severely edited (with whole passages obliterated) that it is of little value, except for its superb preface.

It has been thought appropriate to leave the texts of both the biography and the preface without substantive change. Only necessary editorial corrections of inconsistency in punctuation and footnotes, and certain minor missing items of information, have been provided. The editor has, however, attempted to provide readers with explanatory notes where deemed necessary. These editorial notes have been incorporated into the author's own, following the text of the book, and appear within brackets. Some suggestions for further reading follow these notes. Finally, the subtitle of the book – "A Reinterpretation" – has been added by the editor. William Dawson LeSueur himself was aware that his book was "revisionist," though his primary aim was to tell the truth as he saw it. More than any Canadian historian of his generation, he was aware that "truth" in any absolute sense is the provenance only of the gods.

A. B. McKillop
University College
July, 1977

Notes to Editor's Introduction

1. See Charles Lindsey, *The Life and Times of William Lyon Mackenzie*, 2 vols. (Toronto: P. Randall, 1862); J. C. Dent, *The Story of the Upper Canadian Rebellion*, 2 vols. (Toronto: C. B. Robinson, 1885); Lillian F. Gates, "The Decided Policy of William Lyon Mackenzie," *Canadian Historical Review*, Vol. XL (September, 1959); J. E. Rea, "William Lyon Mackenzie – Jacksonian?", *Mid-America*, L (July, 1968) for some of these interpretations.

2. E. A. LeSueur to C. B. Sissons, 14 May, 1945. C. B. Sissons Papers, Vol. 3. Public Archives of Canada.

3. Maurice Mandelbaum, *History, Man and Reason; a Study in Nineteenth-Century Thought* (Baltimore: Johns Hopkins Press, 1974), p. 199.

4. W. L. Mackenzie King Diary, 1908-14, Wednesday, 27 December, 1911. Public Archives of Canada.

5. LeSueur to James Bain, 13 January, 1906. Henry Sproat Collection, Scrapbook, Vol. I, p. 107. University of Toronto Robarts Research Library, Rare Book Division.

6. *Ibid*.

7. R. C. Brown, "The Politics of Billingsgate," in Ramsay Cook and Carl Berger (eds.), *The West and the Nation* (Toronto: McClelland and Stewart, 1976), pp. 161-173. See also Carl Berger, *The Sense of Power* (Toronto: University of Toronto Press, 1970), pp. 199-207; S. E. D. Shortt, *The Search for an Ideal* (Toronto: University of Toronto Press, 1976), *passim*.

8. For discussion of "whig history" applied to the Canadian historical experience, see Kenneth N. Windsor, "Historical Writing in Canada to 1920," in Carl F. Klinck (ed.), *Literary History of Canada* (Toronto: University of Toronto Press, 1965), pp. 208-250. Windsor notes that ". . . most of the historians writing in the second half of the nineteenth century in Canada, whether serious or popular in their intentions, possessed that attitude to the historical process which is usually described as the Whig interpretation of history. For those of this sensibility, history is the contemplation of freedom broadening down from precedent to precedent towards an agreeable present. They believe in democracy and in social and economic progress. Their history is Protestant

in sympathy and secular in application. It divides individuals, institutions, and movements into those that are for and those that are against progress." (p. 215)

9. *Ibid.*, p. 220.

10. W. D. LeSueur, "Problems of Government in Canada," in A. B. McKillop (ed.), *A Critical Spirit: the Thought of William Dawson LeSueur* (Toronto: McClelland and Stewart, The Carleton Library # 104, 1977), pp. 214-223.

11. LeSueur to J. S. Willison, 19 December, 1905. J. S. Willison Papers, Vol. 25, folder 182. Public Archives of Canada.

12. Brown, *op. cit.*, p. 165.

13. A Radical, "Party Politics," *Canadian Monthly and National Review*, Vol. II (November, 1872), pp. 447-55.

14. LeSueur to Willison, 28 April, 1904. J. S. Willison Papers, *op. cit.*

15. LeSueur to G. N. Morang, 8 June, 1907. Lindsey Papers – Lindsey Section, Vol. v, "Lindsey *vs.* LeSueur: Evidence at Trial," Public Archives of Ontario.

16. *Canadian Methodist Magazine*, Vol. XXII (October, 1885), p. 381.

17. *Daily Star*, 7 June, 1912. See also "One Who Has Not Learned the Better Way," *Weekly Sun*, 22 May, 1912, for an account of Denison's speech. The "better way," by the standards of the *Sun*, was that which opposed "Downing Street" and pointed toward responsible government.

18. Carl Berger, *The Writing of Canadian History* (Toronto: Oxford University Press, 1976), p. 118.

19. Mircea Eliade, *Myth and Reality* (New York: Harper and Row, 1968), pp. 5-6.

20. This is conjecture only, based upon the fact that LeSueur's book was rejected by Morang in May, 1908, and George Lindsey's revision of his father's biography appeared very shortly thereafter. It appears likely that Mr. Lindsey was engaged in the difficult task of condensing his father's two volume study into one and writing the new first chapter before Morang penned his letter of rejection to LeSueur.

21. Charles Lindsey, *William Lyon Mackenzie*, Edited with Numerous Additions by G. G. S. Lindsey (Toronto: Morang, 1908), pp. x-xi.

22. Donald Creighton, *Towards the Discovery of Canada* (Toronto: Macmillan, 1972), p. 10. For an acerbic account by Creighton of the interpretative legacy of the "whig" version of Canadian history, see "Macdonald and Canadian Historians," *ibid.*, pp. 194-210, and "Macdonald and the Anglo-Canadian Alliance," *ibid.*, pp. 211-228.

23. Lindsey (1908), *op. cit.*, pp. xiv-xv.

24. *Ibid.*, p. 13.

25. J. S. Willison, *Sir Wilfrid Laurier and the Liberal Party* (1903), Vol. I, p. 2, quoted in *ibid.*, p. 14.

26. LeSueur to John Lewis, 26 December, 1911; cited in McKillop (ed.), *op. cit.*, p. 282.

27. LeSueur to Willison, 31 May, 1908. Willison Papers, *op. cit.*

28. LeSueur to Lewis, *op. cit.*, p. 281-82.

29. See Clara Thomas, "Biography," in Carl F. Klinck (ed.), *Literary History of Canada*, Vol. III (Toronto: University of Toronto Press, 1976), pp. 180-187.

30. In Fritz Stern (ed.), *Varieties of History*, 2nd ed. (New York: Random House, 1973), p. 104.

31. Walter E. Houghton, *The Victorian Frame of Mind* (New Haven: Yale University Press, 1967), pp. 316-24. See also A. O. J. Cockshut, *Truth to Life. The Art of Biography in the Nineteenth Century* (New York: Harcourt Brace Jovanovich, 1974), esp. pp. 64-86.

32. Stern (ed.), *op. cit.*, p. 104.

33. Quoted in Houghton, *op. cit.*, p. 325; see also p. 417.

34. Windsor, *op. cit.*, p. 229.

35. Donald Creighton's shift to biography later in the twentieth century may be considered in this light. See Berger, *The Writing of Canadian History*, pp. 220-221, *passim.*

ACKNOWLEDGMENTS

I would like to thank certain persons and agencies for aid in the preparation of this edition. Professor Lovell C. Clark of the University of Manitoba has been a constant source of encouragement and has given the entire manuscript his usual careful reading. A number of other members of the University of Manitoba History Department subjected an earlier version of the introductory essay to criticism at one of the department's colloquia, and I have endeavoured to strengthen the essay accordingly. Professor Ramsay Cook, of York University, was good enough to read the introduction as well, and pointed out several areas of weakness.

Canada Council research grants administered through the University of Manitoba Faculty of Graduate Studies and a travel grant from the J. S. Ewart Memorial Fund provided the funds necessary for archival work in Ottawa and Toronto and for the typing of the volume. Mrs. Carol Adam performed this last task with great care. Finally, thanks are due to Professor Carman Bickerton, History Editor of the Carleton Library, for encouraging the undertaking of the project from the outset.

A. B. McK.

PREFACE BY THE AUTHOR

The work which is here presented to the public was prepared for publication, substantially in its present form, just seven years ago. It had come into existence as a proposed volume in the historical series known as *The Makers of Canada*. I had undertaken it at the urgent request of the publisher of the series, but with some reluctance, the feeling arising partly from lack of attraction to the subject, which at the time I supposed had been sufficiently covered by the late Mr. Charles Lindsey's *Life and Times of William Lyon Mackenzie*, and partly from the fact that I had been called in to pronounce upon a manuscript life of Mackenzie by another writer to whom the task had in the first place been assigned. After an examination by the publisher himself and one of his editors, that manuscript had been adjudged not wholly satisfactory, and yet for certain reasons the publisher, as he told me, was rather desirous of using it. I read it carefully, with no shadow of personal interest in the matter one way or another, and sent my notes on it to the publisher with the result that he not only concluded not to publish it, but requested me to write a life of Mackenzie to take its place, so satisfactory did he consider my treatment of the subject and my general point of view.[1]

This proposal, when first made, I declined in decided terms. Application was then made in another quarter, and I was informed that a well-known historical scholar had consented to write the book.[2] Within a month, however, that consent was recalled; and I learnt later that the gentleman in question, who occupied a high academic position, had been dissuaded by friends from entering on a subject which he could hardly hope to treat quite independently without exciting partisan feeling and criticism, which might be hurtful to his influence as a teacher. In these circumstances the publisher renewed his appeal to me, and, as my relations with him had become close owing to my having accepted a position on his editorial board, to say nothing of the fact that a life of Count Frontenac, which I had contributed to his series, was on the point of publication, I allowed myself to step into the breach which no one else was offering to fill, and write a life of the rebel leader.

Had I been Socrates my daemon would probably have whispered to me "Don't!," unless possibly the sprite, or whatever it was, had happened to think that a lot of trouble would do me good. I heard no warning whisper, however, and took up the task in the fullest conviction that I was at liberty to treat my subject from my own point of view, and according to my own best interpretation of the facts. I had every reason to think this. The publisher knew me as a man of independent views, having himself at one time been connected with a publishing house in New York for which, during a considerable period, I had done literary work. Moreover it was precisely on account of my assumed freedom, as a retired public servant, from trammels of every kind, that he felt justified in begging me to undertake a task which a man of far wider historical knowledge than myself had felt obliged to decline just because he was not equally free. Then my notes on the first manuscript had made it perfectly clear that I was not prepared to accept any view because it happened to be the conventional one; that I hated anything like banality in the treatment of historical questions; and that I was not going to dance to anyone else's piping. Moreover, in a letter to the publisher, of which I regret not to have preserved a copy, dealing with certain objections with which he was being pestered as to my fitness to write the biography of Mackenzie, I made it very clear that I would write it in my own way and no other. I was then perfectly prepared to throw up the engagement had he said the word; but no, I was distinctly urged to proceed.

William Lyon Mackenzie was in his day a politician and a journalist. He expressed himself by word and action in the legislature of Upper Canada from 1828 to 1836, and in that of Canada under the Union from 1851 to 1858. But, above all, he expressed himself in writing in a series of newspapers which he both edited and published from 1824 to 1841, and again from 1853 to 1860. His most powerful work was done through the press. I naturally recognized from the outset that nothing would throw so much light on the character and aims of Mackenzie as a careful perusal of what he had given to the public in his papers; and purposed to consult them as far as they might be accessible to me. My first enquiries on the subject were discouraging: Mackenzie's newspapers were very scantily represented, so far as I could learn, in Canadian public libraries. Then something quite unexpected happened. In a letter to a friend in Toronto, enquiring whether, among the older families there, he knew of any who might possess papers bearing on the rebellion of 1837 – the central incident in Mackenzie's life – which I might be allowed to consult, I casually mentioned that I had been informed that Mackenzie's representatives possessed files of his newspapers and a considerable collection of documents bearing on his public life, but that these were very jealously guarded, and were practically inaccessible.[3] In making this observation I had not the most remote idea that my friend either would or could do anything in the matter, especially as I had told him in my letter that a prominent descendant of Mackenzie was violently objecting to me as biographer of his ancestor.[4] I was surprised, therefore, when my friend offered to communicate with another representative of the family, the one in whose keeping the papers were, and ascertain his views on the question of allowing them to be made available for historical purposes. I could see no objection to this, and authorized him to do as he had suggested. He met the gentleman accordingly and talked the matter over with him. In giving me an account of the interview he mentioned that, in reply to an enquiry on the point, he had stated that I was a "Tory." That statement was a bit gratuitous. I had been a public servant all my life till within a very few years of the time now referred to, and public servants of long standing are seldom partisans. Their standpoint is that of the public interest, and their sympathies are apt to move hither and thither as they see that being guarded or sacrificed, respected or trifled with. Some mistakes, however, are fortunate ones; and this particular one had the merit of putting the gentleman to whom the statement was made very fully on his guard in any communications he might later have with me. At least it should have had that effect. But there was more. My friend informed the gentleman referred to – though the probability is that he was previously aware of it – of the strong stand his kinsman was making against having the biography of their common ancestor entrusted to my hands; and if his reply was correctly reported to me he was quite disposed to judge of the matter for himself.

The result of these *pourparlers* was that I was invited to go to Toronto and discuss the question with the guardian of the documents. The gentleman who had brought about the meeting was a man of much influence and high social standing since deceased. We were good friends, and he may have praised me beyond my deserts. All I know is that, in spite of being a reputed "Tory," while the party of the other part was a strong "Liberal" – I think both terms deserve quotation marks as being mere names – I was very kindly met and hospitably entertained. A general conversation ensued in which reference was made to the kinsman's loudly and widely expressed opinion that I had a prejudice against the author of the Upper Canada rebellion which made it impossible for me to write a fair biography of him. I recall very few, if any, details of the conversation, now over nine years in the past; but I quite believe that I warmly deprecated that idea. How my life of Mackenzie would come out I could not tell, for I was then only on the outskirts of my enquiries, and had examined none but secondary authorities; but what I felt sure of was that the kinsman's suspicions of my literary integrity – if he really did entertain them, and was not simply having the truth brought to light – were unjust, and that I should have no difficulty in dealing fairly and candidly with the facts as I might find them.

The gentleman with whom I was then negotiating and who afterwards became my opponent in a lawsuit, stated in pleadings and in evidence given in court, that I then and there engaged to write a "fair and friendly" life of Mackenzie. I denied the statement on oath. A promise to be fair seems to me something most inane. One *promises* to do something that he is not obliged to do *unless* he promises; but every man is obliged to be fair, promise or no promise; he cannot be otherwise without dishonour; and the man who is prepared to be unfair will not be less so because he has promised to be fair. As to *promising* to write a friendly biography of anyone, it would be hard to imagine anything more absurd. What would be thought of a judge who promised to take a "friendly" view of a litigant's case? His lawyer may do that: he is paid for it by the litigant. The judge is paid for the higher duty of doing justly, and he is paid by the public. So, in the last resort, is the author: to the public he appeals, to the public his most faithful service is due. The man who writes history with a foregone conclusion not to be affected by evidence, or who pays for favours shown him, or facilities afforded to him, by withholding, or in any way perverting, the truth in the matter he is dealing with, deserves no less serious condemnation than the unjust judge.

That there was no agreement of the nature alleged is, I venture to say, almost conclusively proved by the facts which I now proceed to mention. After two years of labour my work was completed. The guardian of the Mackenzie papers reads it (with my full consent – he had *not stipulated* that he should do so) in manuscript, and is greatly dissatisfied with it, so much so that he writes to me withdrawing his consent to the use of the papers and demanding the return of any copies I had made of them. Was any reason alleged? None, save that the publisher of *The Makers of Canada* had decided not to publish my work in that series. Surely if there had been any breach of agreement on my part, this was the time to mention it. But no, the thing is not so much as hinted at. As I declined to accede to the demand for the return of the copies I had made, two letters followed at intervals reiterating it in gentle crescendo of insistency. In neither of them was breach of agreement, however distantly, referred to. These letters were all written in the year 1908. In 1911 came a fourth letter preparatory to legal proceedings for an injunction. This one was hostile and denunciatory in tone; but the main thing that was worth denouncing, if true, the violation of an agreement or understanding, is not mentioned. Had such an understanding existed there is only one hypothesis on which the complete absence of reference to it in this series of letters is to be explained, namely that the writer shrank from referring to it in writing. The simpler explanation is that no such agreement had ever been entered into.[5]

This view of the matter is distinctly supported by the wording of the second letter of the series referred to. I had written endeavouring to justify my position, and this was the reply I received:

> I beg of you to excuse my discussing with you the question raised by you in your letter, for I am anxious above everything not to express any opinion and to avoid all controversy. I have gone very fully into the history written and unwritten of this whole matter, and am convinced a great mistake has been made; a mistake which I am bound to avoid the consequences of so far as I can. My only statement then is that I cannot

sanction any book of yours on Mackenzie going to the
public (except in the Makers of Canada series) on the
strength of your having had unrestricted access to all
the Mackenzie papers and correspondence.

This is plain enough: "a great mistake" had been made, of
course by the writer himself, which he was anxious to repair;
and the way to do it was to restrict me to a mode of
publication which he knew to be closed to me. But why
charge himself with a "mistake," if he could have charged
me with a breach of agreement? The time to do that was
surely when the circumstances were comparatively fresh in
the recollection of both of us. Yet the charge was made
later; and it was mainly on the theory that there had been
a contract, and that I had not adhered to it, that an injunction
against my book was obtained.

A mistake, and a serious one, was certainly made if the
writer of the letter just quoted really expected, as he stated
in court that he did, that I would consult him before putting
anything into my book that was unfavourable to his ancestor.
Imagine a book constructed on that principle – an interested
relative holding a veto on the publication of anything
unfavourable to the person whose life was being written! He
expected me, he said, to act as I had done in the case of a
certain very private correspondence I had come across in
my examination of the Mackenzie papers.[6] The correspondence in question dealt with a public matter, but one which,
so far as I knew, had never been ventilated; and I therefore
thought it proper to leave it to the gentleman who was then
(1906) the legal owner of the papers – father of the gentleman into whose hands they passed about a year and a half
later – to decide whether use should be made of it or not.
This reply I received, transmitted through the *present* owner
of the papers, and produced by me in court, was a full and
frank permission to use it, the writer remarking of Mackenzie
and his correspondent that each was playing for his own
hand. This, as I considered, gave me a measure of the
freedom which both gentlemen were prepared to allow me
in the use of the collection generally; and I raised no further
questions of that kind, nothing that I afterwards saw suggesting any necessity for doing so. The reference I did make
was made entirely of my own motion, and not in consequence
of even the most shadowy understanding that directions were

to be sought by me as to what I should or should not use. And here I would remark that I should never have thought of raising any question regarding *printed* matter. What had once been given to the world through the press I felt myself at perfect liberty to reproduce, though that liberty has now been abridged, fortunately to no serious extent as things have turned out, by the courts.

Nor, as my work proceeded, did I conceal the fact that the record would have its dark spots. In the fall of the year 1907, the gentleman who had invited me to Toronto called on me at Ottawa to enquire how the work was progressing; and I then made a point of informing him of the shocking outburst of scurrility in Mackenzie's paper, the *Colonial Advocate*, which had provoked the attack on his printing office in the month of June, 1826, quoting one or two of the terms used. He seemed, as I thought, to receive the information with regret, but dropped no hint that such matter should be excluded from the book, and certainly made no claim to have a deciding voice as to whether it should go in or not. Yet what more favourable opportunity could there have been for doing so, if his position had then been what he afterwards declared it to be?

Let me now state a few facts in sequence. It was towards the end of the year 1905 that I engaged to write the volume on Mackenzie for the series already mentioned. It was in February 1906 that I went from Ottawa to Toronto, a reputed "Tory," to confer with the gentleman, a more than reputed "Liberal," who had the disposal of the Mackenzie papers. I have spoken of his kind reception of me; but I have now further to state that he was then proposing to vacate his house (in which the papers were) for several months, and that he very obligingly suggested that I should occupy it during the coming summer, and thus have the papers, for that length of time, under my hand. As it would have been practically impossible for me to have satisfactory access to them in any other way – unless indeed they had been presented to a public library – I thankfully accepted the offer, and from the 1st of May to the 30th of September made the best of my opportunities, though part of my time I found it profitable to devote to researches in the Toronto Public Library, where I received the kindest assistance from the late highly-esteemed Librarian, Dr. James Bain.

Returning from Toronto to Ottawa I pursued my studies

of the Mackenzie period, and also did no small amount of editorial work on the *Makers of Canada* series, work with which the publisher more than once expressed high satisfaction, and which is very kindly referred to by Dr. Parkin in the preface to the *Sir John A. Macdonald*. As my enquiries proceeded I saw clearly that, though the character of Mackenzie might gain in interest through the closer study I was giving to it, the man himself would hardly appear quite so constitutional a hero, nor quite so consistent a patriot as some had loved to represent him. I did not conceal from the publisher the impressions I was forming; and in the latter part of 1907 he began to be anxious as to the effect the character sketch I seemed likely to draw might produce in certain quarters.[7] The trouble dreaded by the historical scholar who had once thought of undertaking the work, was beginning. To appease the publisher's anxiety, or at least to give him independent means of judging what would be a reasonable estimate of the part Mackenzie had played in Upper Canada, I referred him to another historical scholar,[8] with whom I knew him to be in correspondence, and on whose judgment and knowledge he and others placed great reliance, suggesting that he should ask for his candid and unreserved opinion on the question. The answer he received met his enquiry very fully, and went so far beyond anything he feared would come from my pen that his mind was set quite at ease; and he wrote me saying that if certain parties made any trouble, he would know how to deal with them.

I had never meant to allow myself to be fettered in the expression of any views I might form, and this correspondence certainly justified me in believing that the publisher approved my attitude and would support me in maintaining it. He did not. Why? I do not know: he knows. I sent him the manuscript of my work in April, 1908. He read it and passed it over to the gentleman who had given me access to the Mackenzie papers. What consultation took place I know not, but after some delay, I received a letter from the publisher criticising my work with some severity as unfair to Mackenzie. I could only reply that I had endeavoured to be entirely fair; that I had omitted nothing creditable to him that I could find in the record, but had intentionally omitted certain accusations which former writers had brought against him; and on the whole had perhaps done more justice to the better points of his character than any previous writer, even of those most friendly to him, had done.

One great trouble with my book was that it was not conventional. It was not built on traditional assumptions. I had approached the subject with a desire to see things for myself, and I had seen things. The result was that the historical landscape I presented was not the old landscape. The landmarks had been shifted somehow, and the lights and shades were not familiar. The man who does that kind of thing runs risks, as I was soon to find out.

It was only after the mischief had been done that I read the delightful prelude to Anatole France's *Ile des Pingouins*. The author represents himself as having applied to a historian of high repute for some hints as to how he should write a book of his own, which was to be of an historical character. "I come, Sir," he said on entering the learned gentleman's library, "to get the benefit of your experience. I am struggling with a work of history, and am not making much headway." Shrugging his shoulders, the distinguished scholar replied: "My poor friend, why are you bothering yourself to *compose* a history, when all you have to do is to follow the general practice and copy the best known ones? If you have any new view or any original idea; if you present men and things in an unexpected light, you will take the reader by surprise, and readers do not like that. They only seek in history the stupid things they know already. Try to instruct your reader and you will only humiliate and vex him. Don't try to enlighten him: he will cry out that you are insulting his beliefs. Historians copy one another, and thus spare themselves toil and escape being thought conceited. Imitate them, and don't be original. An original historian is an object of universal distrust, scorn and disgust. Do you think," he added, "that I should have been considered and honoured as I am if I had put any novelties into my historical works? What are novelties? Impertinences!"

In my case, however, there was more in it than this. The portraiture of William Lyon Mackenzie in my book is as true as I could make it, but things were brought to light, writings long forgotten were reproduced, some of which were not altogether in his favour, but which helped greatly to complete the story of his life and make the whole more comprehensible. The reader of the following pages will judge of this for himself. How many lives are incomprehensible to us, or are read amiss, just on account of omitted chapters!

I was of course quite prepared to rectify any errors or omissions that might be pointed out in my book, and I offered to revise it carefully and see if, at any point, I had failed to do the justice to Mackenzie that I had certainly wished to do. This was not assented to. The manuscript I had sent was not typewritten, and it was a *sole copy*: that destroyed or withheld, and the book was gone. As mentioned above, I had been doing editorial work on the *Makers of Canada*, as well as writing Mackenzie's life, and was receiving a monthly remittance calculated to meet what was coming to me while the work lasted. Under this arrangement the payment I was to receive for my Mackenzie had been made by the time the manuscript had been handed in. As the latter had not been found satisfactory, and was not to be published, I asked to have it returned, sending a certified cheque for the full amount I had received on account of it. The cheque was sent back to me and my request for the return of the manuscript was refused, the publisher holding that the payment made to me closed the matter, and that he was free to do what he liked with the manuscript. His letter was closely followed by one from the owner of the Mackenzie papers, to the effect mentioned on an earlier page: my book had been ruled out of the *Makers of Canada* series, and I was prohibited from using in any other way, or publishing through any other channel, any information gathered from the Mackenzie papers; I was also to return any copies I had made from them.[9]

This was a pretty complete "shut-out" – my manuscript held up, and the right withdrawn to use the information which I had acquired at the cost of so much labour. I did not, however, acquiesce in these peremptory rulings, but, after demand duly made, entered action for the recovery of my manuscript, the money received for which I was willing, as before, to refund. The case came to trial in the High Court of Ontario, and was given decisively in my favour. It was finally tried before the Supreme Court of Canada, and a third time given in my favour, the general contention of the judges being that in a case where the inducement to the production of a book was in part a pecuniary one and in part the prospect of publication, the mere payment of the money consideration without publication could not convey a title to the possession of the work.

So I got my manuscript back after a delay of three years and a half and no little trouble and anxiety, not to speak of expense, from which legal proceedings, whatever their issue, are never free.

But worse was awaiting me. I have spoken of the assertion of the owner of the Mackenzie papers that I had entered into an agreement to write the life of Mackenzie in a "fair and friendly" way, that is to say with a friendly bias. That gentleman now entered action for an injunction against my using any of his materials, alleging breach of contract, and also urging that his permission to use those materials fell to the ground with the exclusion of my book from the series for which he understood it was being written. The case was tried in Toronto in November, 1912, before Mr. Justice Britton, who decided in favour of the plaintiff. I appealed and the Appeal Court confirmed his Lordship's judgment. I cannot myself think that justice was done in the premises. True, evidence was given that I had promised to write a "fair and friendly" life of Mackenzie, but that evidence, which was without a shadow of corroboration, I had unhesitatingly contradicted. His Lordship, however, made much of the statement, but nothing of the contradiction. He found it "inconceivable that the plaintiff would have permitted access to the papers had he supposed that such a manuscript would have resulted as the defendant produced." He had nothing to say as to the difficulty of believing that a self-respecting writer who had made – may I go so far as to say? – an honourable name for himself in his native country, who had filled for many years a not unimportant office under the Crown, who had been honoured by a Canadian university, and who, in the very year of the trial, was president of a society embracing many of the foremost representatives of Canadian literature and science, had bound himself, on the very threshold of an historical enquiry which was to occupy him two years, to conclude that enquiry in a certain prescribed sense, and give it a stamp of friendliness to a particular individual! What could possibly have moved me so to tie my hands and risk my character as a writer and a man? To discuss the matter for a moment on a low plane, there was no money in it. I did not want to write the book in the first place, and if I had persisted in my refusal to write it there was much else to which I could have turned my hand. His Lordship, however, saw no improbability in my having entered into an absurd and discreditable engagement for no assignable reason, so impressed was he with the idea that the owner of the papers would never have allowed anyone to use them for historical purposes save in the expectation that they would be used *ad majorem gloriam* of his ancestor.

If his Lordship's assumption was correct, we begin to see the force of some things we read in the magazine and papers. A couple of years ago, for example, Mr. Edmund Gosse expressed himself as follows: "The great danger of twentieth century biography is its unwillingness to accept any man's character save at the valuation of his most cautious relatives." The meaning to be gathered is plainly that the truth of biography is too frequently impaired by the pious caution of relatives. If policy is allied to pious caution, the effect is of course intensified. Mr. H. G. Wells, again, in an article in the *Fortnightly Review*, has pointedly declared that, speaking generally, biography is false with the worst of all falsehood, "the falsehood of omission." Judicious omission may make a wonderful difference sometimes in a story.

And now I wish to urge a point to which, so far as I am aware, no attention was given in the trial court, nor in the subsequent hearing in appeal. When I went to Toronto on the mission referred to I had only a superficial knowledge of the facts in Mackenzie's life. I had dipped into Kingsford's history, the portion of which dealing with Mackenzie is drawn almost wholly from Charles Lindsey's *Life and Times of William Lyon Mackenzie*; and I had also read the latter work in whole or in part. Owing to the dependence of Kingsford on Lindsey, the two were practically one, so far as Mackenzie was concerned. I had also read, but at an earlier date,[10] Sir F. B. Head's *Narrative*. I felt that all my work was before me, and that my definitive opinions were yet to be formed. I had no idea what I should find in the Mackenzie papers, if permitted to examine them; and neither, it may be added, had the gentleman who invited me to Toronto. By this I do not mean that there were any terrible mysteries in the papers, for so far as I examined them, there were not; but there were things – I refer now to matters which I was able to obtain from other sources, and have consequently published – which had an important, and not a favourable effect in forming my opinion of Mackenzie.

My book was shaped not by pre-formed opinion, but by post-discovered facts, post-discovered that is to say in relation to the date of my negotiation in Toronto. Yet the learned judge appears to have assumed that, when I had the interview in Toronto, I was already loaded up with all the opinions and impressions which I really derived from my subsequent enquiries and researches. If the reader, as he peruses the following pages, will kindly bear in mind that *every single quotation from Mackenzie's newspapers, save the very few I may have borrowed from Mr. Charles Lindsey's book, every reference to the Journals of the Legislature, or to a pamphlet of whatever name or kind, every quotation from a book, save those already mentioned as forming my preliminary preparation, every extract from correspondence between Mackenzie and anyone else, or from colonial office despatches*, came under my notice for the first time *after* the interview referred to, and during the long study I gave to my subject, he will feel how unjust that assumption was. Yet the book has been held up as showing what I thought, and how I felt, before anything of significance that it contains had come to my knowledge.

A remarkable point in the judgment is that his Lordship, who had apparently read the manuscript, pointedly declined to express any opinion as to whether I was right or wrong in my estimate of Mackenzie. Let me, however, quote his words:

> I deal with this matter simply as a matter of contract and good faith between the parties, *not expressing any opinion as to whether the defendant is right or wrong in his estimate of Mackenzie.* It does not, so far as it affects this case, make any difference whether Mackenzie was a man of high aims and unselfish purpose, contending against real wrongs permitted by bad laws, and perpetuated by unjust administration; or a mere adventurer, willing to point where he would not lead, a mere inciter to rebellion against laws that were just and administered by men able and honest.

That is to say, *Mackenzie might have been all that the latter part of the paragraph describes*; but if I had ventured to say so, or anything like it, no matter how the evidence might have been forced on me, I should have violated my contract with the owner of the papers. What kind of contract would that have been which bound a man to disregard evidence and give a false version of facts? It seems strange that his Lordship could have penned that sentence and not had a word to say against the immorality of manufacturing historical opinion by contract. As a matter of fact, my book, as anyone who peruses its pages will see, is very far from depicting Mackenzie as "a mere adventurer": no term could indeed be more inappropriate to the character in which he is presented. And as to "pointing where he would not lead," I have expressly credited him with readiness to lead, as well as to incite, and, so far, repelled the charge of cowardice which some have brought against him. Let the book, however, speak for itself.

To my mind there is a flat contradiction between the paragraph quoted and what his Lordship next proceeds to say, namely, that he quite recognizes "that the biographer should write truly of his subject," and also that he should be free "to draw such inferences as might please him." How could I be free if I was under a contract enforceable by law to produce such a book as would satisfy Mackenzie's relatives? Why did not his Lordship say: "I quite recognize that the biographer should write truly of his subject, but this particular biographer had parted with his liberty to do so, owing to the immoral contract that had been passed between himself and the owner of the Mackenzie papers. Whatever sacrifice of truth it might involve, he was bound to produce a book pleasing to that gentleman."

Passing over other points in the judgment which would call for comment in any complete analysis of it, I would finally remark on the support it gives to the plaintiff's contention that I had concealed from him my criticism of the manuscript life of Mackenzie submitted to me, as above stated, for examination. If there is anything in the world that must be *intentional*, it is concealment. It is a worm in the bud that feeds on damask cheeks and does other terrible things. In this matter, the worm was not troubling me. I do not believe that the thought of that slight piece of work ever passed through my mind on the occasion in question. Had it come into my mind, I should not have thought it had any bearing on anything we were discussing. In dealing with the manuscript, I had only one object, namely to solve the doubts of the publisher and his editor as to the worth of the work. It is worth repeating that it was on receiving my notes, and because of his satisfaction with them, that the publisher first proposed that I should write the life of Mackenzie.

His Lordship scents partizanship, however, in the notes. They showed "irritation on the part of the defendant when words of praise or commendation of Mackenzie were used." Any irritation I displayed was at the damnable iteration of the most banal kind of praise. I undertake to say that there is more praise of Mackenzie *that is worthwhile* in the book I have myself written than in the book I criticized, though the latter was especially devoted to doing him honour.

I must try, however, to draw to a close this long introduction, the element of egotism in which I recognize without seeing very well how to eliminate it and yet do justice to my own position. The five appearances of my book in court, three in connection with the first suit, and two in connection with the second, excited a certain amount of public interest; and I felt that, in finally bringing it out, it was due to the public, as well as to myself and my friends, to give my version of the whole difficulty. It is needless to dwell on the judgment rendered in the Appeal Division, which fully sustained that given in the trial court. The learned Chief Justice who delivered judgment had something to say as to my "moral duty" in the case. Ethics, if they fall under the head of science, are an uncommonly difficult branch of it, as Herbert Spencer found when he sought to crown his system of philosophy; and while the judgment of a court must be received with respectful submission, the *obiter dicta* of a judge on a point of morals do not necessarily or always inspire profound conviction. I have no sense of having wronged anyone in this matter. My whole conduct, I claim to have been sincere and straightforward. What was uppermost in my mind after the visit to Toronto above referred to was a sense of the confidence with which I had been treated, and of the liberty I was to enjoy in writing my book. Not only mentally, but in conversation with friends, I contrasted what seemed to me the largeness of mind of the owner of the papers with the narrow family views of the other gentleman, who had been moving heaven and earth to have the biography of Mackenzie taken out of my hands.[11] I could not help remembering of course that it was after being bluntly told that I was a "Tory," and with the full knowledge of his kinsman's objections to me, that he had suggested my going to Toronto to talk over matters with him. The obvious inference was that his point of view was a wider one, and that he was prepared to have the biography written by an honest pen without regard to family or party interests.

A word now as to the book itself. It is a new treatment of the life of Mackenzie from, as I venture to think, a fresh and independent standpoint. I had not been asked to import any originality into my work, and no doubt any moderately presentable pot-boiler would have met all the business requirements of the case. But, in spite of what Anatole France's (imaginary, we must believe) adviser told him, history is a thing that makes a very poor rehash; and my desire was, not to repeat what others had said, but to find out by research what I ought to say myself; and this I made a most honest attempt to do. These pages have not been written either to please or to displease anyone or to glorify or depreciate any individual or any political party or interest. My task was first of all to discover Mackenzie and then to describe him. As I proceeded with my enquiries I came to the conclusion that, if he had previously been discovered, he had certainly not been described. The whole man, the man in his complete individuality, was nowhere, so far as I could see. There was a great deal of information about him of one kind and another in the late Mr. Charles Lindsey's *Life and Times of William Lyon Mackenzie*; but the portrait of the man himself was conventional rather than convincing. That work, though it reveals the pen of a practised writer, was produced in some haste within a year after the death of Mackenzie; and I doubt much whether the author himself regarded it as the final verdict of history on the career he had sketched. It satisfied for the moment such public curiosity as was felt regarding a prominent man who had passed away; and it is not just after the tomb has closed that merits and frailties are very exactly weighed, especially when family affection holds the scales. . . .[12]

I have an idea that history in general is taken too seriously, or at least too solemnly. I do not mean that a writer can be too accurate in his statements or too careful in his deductions; but history is not housepainting, it is portrait-painting. It is the soul of things you want to get at, and if you want to catch the soul, you must lie in wait for it with your own. This implies a kind of freedom which continually verges on a sense of humour, and sometimes almost takes that form. "Give your soul a chance, let it flit about a bit," said the Aristophanic Socrates in a famous play. The advice is good for every one, and I would say almost particularly for the historian. The more freedom he gives himself to think in every direction, the more freedom he will bestow on his reader. Here is the book, however – long delayed, fiercely attacked, banned by the Bench, blessed by the Bar. *Lector benevole*, be kinder than the courts, give me a fair reading, and see if William Lyon Mackenzie is to be discovered in my pages. If so, *plaudite*, for I doubt whether you have seen the real man before.

W. D. LeSueur
Ottawa, April 23, 1915

Editor's Notes to Preface

1. The author of the rejected manuscript was James L. Hughes, an Inspector of Schools in Ontario. For the correspondence mentioned, see LeSueur to his publisher, G. N. Morang, 16 October, 1905. Lindsey Papers – Lindsey Section, Vol. Five, "Lindsey *vs.* LeSueur: Evidence at Trial," Public Archives of Ontario. Unless otherwise noted, all correspondence cited is from this source. That LeSueur was reticent to undertake the task of writing the biography is indicated in a letter to Morang, 20 October, 1905.

2. The well-known historian was Professor George M. Wrong, of the Department of History at the University of Toronto.

3. LeSueur's Toronto friend was T. C. Patteson, of the Toronto Post Office (LeSueur doubtless knew him because of his own career in the Ottawa Post Office). At this time the Mackenzie Papers were in the possession of Charles Lindsey, author of the *Life and Times* of Mackenzie to which reference has already been made. Upon Lindsey's death in 1908, provenance over them fell to his son, George Lindsey.

4. The "prominent descendant" was William Lyon Mackenzie King, Mackenzie's grandson and Assistant Deputy Minister of Labour in Laurier's ministry. In December, 1905, LeSueur had received a letter from Pelham Edgar, an editor of the "Makers" series, noting King's interference. Edgar to LeSueur, 29 December, 1905.

5. For the correspondence mentioned, see George Lindsey to LeSueur, 26 May, 1908; LeSueur to Lindsey, 31 May, 1908; Lindsey to LeSueur, 2 June, 1908, 17 June, 1908; LeSueur to Lindsey, 25 June, 1908; Lindsey to LeSueur, 27 October, 1911; LeSueur to Lindsey, 1 November, 1911.

6. The correspondence concerned was between Mackenzie and the reformer, John Rolph, when Rolph was in charge of the disposition of Crown Lands (1852). It concerned the possibility of dispensing patronage to Mackenzie. See Charles Lindsey to George Lindsey, ca. 19 August, 1906.

7. See Morang to LeSueur, 5 September, 1907.

8. The scholar was Adam Shortt, then Professor of Political Economy at Queen's University; the next year Shortt moved to Ottawa to accept the post of Civil Service Commissioner.

9. Morang to LeSueur, 11 May, 1908; Lindsey to LeSueur, 26 May, 1908.

10. LeSueur had devoted considerable attention to Sir Francis Bond Head's views in his lecture "The Problem of Popular Government," given at the University of Toronto in 1901. See *University of Toronto Monthly*, Vol. i (April, 1901), 229-241; Vol. i (May, 1901), pp. 257-263.

11. For the extent of King's interference, see LeSueur to Morang, 31 December, 1905; Morang to LeSueur, 2 January, 1906; Morang to LeSueur, 8 January, 1906.

12. Because of the injunction successfully brought upon LeSueur, he was forced to duplicate virtually all the research originally undertaken in the Lindsey home. The manuscript was re-written, with all material contained in the Lindsey collection and not available elsewhere excised. A paragraph in LeSueur's 1915 Preface noted this, but since the book published here is the original version, this paragraph has been omitted.

WILLIAM LYON MACKENZIE:
A Reinterpretation

CHAPTER ONE

THE BEGINNINGS OF UPPER CANADA

The story to be unfolded in the following pages is the story
of a personality and a period. The period was in itself a
critical one, and the personality was eminently adapted to
render it more so. Had William Lyon Mackenzie never come
to Canada, the old system of government would none the
less, through the action of general courses, infallibly have
given place to government of a more democratic type. Two
considerations alone suffice to place this beyond doubt.
Immediately to the south of Canada was a nation advancing
by rapid strides in population, wealth, and power, all [of]
whose institutions reflected the democratic ideal; while across
the sea was the Mother Country in which a great political
unrest prevailed – an unrest destined to be appeased for the
moment by the passage of the Reform Bill, but to manifest
itself anew not many years later in demands for a yet
broader representation of the people and yet more liberal
principles of legislation. It is not to be supposed, therefore,
that receiving continual accessions of population from the
mother land, and having ever before her eyes the spectacle
of the United States, Canada could long have remained
content with political institutions much less popular than
those existing in either country. The colonial status gave, in
the early days, a reasonable excuse for a certain restriction
of legislative power and a withholding of cabinet responsibility in the full sense; but we shall see, as our narrative
proceeds, how steady and unceasing was the pressure which
the people of Upper Canada exerted for larger powers of
self-government. But to understand the whole matter rightly
it will be necessary to make a rapid survey of the political
development of Upper Canada from the beginning.

From the date of the cession of Canada by France to
England down to the year 1792, the whole country was
governed as one province with its seat of government at

1

Quebec. When a loyalist population from the United States
during and after the Revolutionary war began to move into
the British provinces some surveys were undertaken with a
view to the allotment of land and what later became Upper
Canada was divided by Lord Dorchester into the four
judicial districts of Lunenburg, Macklenburg, Nassau, and
Hesse – names which were changed after the separate constitution of the province into Eastern, Midland, Home and
Western. The friction which had arisen between the French
and British elements of the population decided the British
Government to create two distinct provinces in one of which
the French might dominate and in the other the English,
and an imperial order in council of the twenty-fourth of
August, 1791, effected the separation, constitutions having
meanwhile been provided for the two provinces by the
statute commonly called the Constitutional Act, 31 George
III, chapter 31. That measure had not passed through
parliament without considerable discussion, participated in
by such giants of debate as Pitt, Fox and Burke.

Of these, Fox, as might be expected, showed most
sympathy with the commonly understood principles of
political liberty, but even he

> laid it down as a principle not to be departed from that
> every part of the British dominions ought to possess a
> government in the constitution of which monarchy,
> aristocracy and democracy were mutually blended and
> united; nor,

he added,

> could any government be a fit one for British subjects
> to live under that did not contain its due weight of
> aristocracy, because that he considered to be the proper
> poise of the constitution, the balance that equalized and
> . meliorated the powers of the two extreme branches, and
> gave stability and firmness to the whole.

He dwelt strongly at the same time, on the need for a check
upon the power of the Governor; and, for that special
purpose, desired to have a legislative council as independent
of him as possible, one elected by a special franchise quite
distinct from that created for the legislative assembly and
adapted to bring into political life the most responsible men

of the country. The one valid objection to this proposal of
Fox's was that the country did not at the time afford the
class of men he had in view; but it was not on this
ground alone, or chiefly, that his views were not accepted.
The legislative council was made nominative in order that it
might so far resemble more closely the Upper House of the
British Parliament. Burke on this occasion aired, as usual,
some very absolute views. "Monarchy," he said, "was the
basis of all good government, and the nearer to monarchy
any government approached, the more perfect it was, and
vice versa." Fox, with his stronger practical instinct, objected
to appropriating, as the Act proposed, one seventh of the
land to the support of "a Protestant clergy;" but Pitt
defended a provision the object of which he said was to
enable the government to endow and encourage "the Protestant clergy of the Established Church." Little did he foresee
the strife and heartburning to which this pious scheme, as he
and others – Fox was quite an exception – sincerely regarded
it, was destined to give birth.

The Act provided that there should be in each Province
a legislative council and an assembly, by and with the advice
and consent of which His Majesty should have power to
make laws for the peace, welfare, and good government of
those portions of his realm. The legislative council for Upper
Canada was to consist of not less than seven persons, to be
summoned thereto under the great seal of the province by
the governor, lieutenant-governor, or other person administering the government acting under the direction of his
Majesty; every person so summoned to hold his seat for the
term of his life, subject to certain provisions for vacating
the seat in case of necessity. Power was also given to his
Majesty by the Act to confer upon any subject of the Crown
by letters patent under the seal of either province "any
hereditary title of honour, rank or dignity of such province,"
and, "to annex thereto by the said letters patent, an hereditary right of being summoned to the legislative council of
such province." As first constituted the legislative council of
Upper Canada consisted of nine members of whom two
came out specially from England – William Osgoode and
Peter Russell. The first of these was made Chief Justice of
Upper Canada as well as Speaker of the Legislative Council.
Russell held a puisne judgeship, and after governor Simcoe's
retirement in 1796 became administrator of the government,

or as he was more commonly styled "President" of the province.

The legislative assembly was, by the Act, to consist of not less than sixteen members, to be chosen by constituencies to be marked out by the lieutenant governor. In the first assembly elected (1792) under the auspices of General Simcoe this number was not exceeded; but in 1800 three members were added to the house, and in 1808 the number was increased to twenty five. Then in 1820, under the administration of Sir Peregrine Maitland,[1] an Act was passed providing for an automatic regulation of the representation. One member was assigned to every county having a population of one thousand, and two members to every one with a population of four thousand; towns in which the quarter sessions were held, and which had a population of one thousand, to be also entitled to one member each; their population in that case to be deducted from that of the county in determining the representation of the latter. Counties having a population of less than one thousand were to be attached to the adjacent county of least population. The house elected under the provisions of this Act – the Seventh Parliament of Upper Canada – consisted of [40] members. Seven years later, when Mackenzie was elected, the number had increased to [48].[2]

The franchise established by the Act of 1791 was a sufficiently popular one considering the times. Any one was entitled to vote who, having been a resident for a period of twelve months preceding the elections, was possessed, in the counties of a freehold of the value of forty shillings a year, and in the towns of a house and lots of the yearly value of five pounds, or who had paid rent for one year previous to the election at the rate of not less than ten pounds a year. Full power was given, however, to the provincial legislature to alter these conditions.

The Province was thus supplied with the essential elements of the British Constitution – a Governor, representative of the Sovereign; a legislative council, doing duty for a House of Lords; and an elective assembly for the Commons. In proroguing his first Parliament in October 1792 Simcoe congratulated them on possessing "not a mutilated constitution, but a constitution which has stood the test of experience, and is the *very image and transcript of that of Great Britain*." He did not perhaps remember at the moment that, in his place in Parliament, when the question of a constitution for the Canadas was under discussion, after pronouncing a panegyric on the British constitution he had expressed a desire that it might be adopted as a model *as far as circumstances would admit.* Had he added this rider to his remarks on the later occasion he would, it is to be feared, have spoilt them for the controversial use to which they were put on many a subsequent occasion.

It was argued some years later by reformers that an exact transcript of the British Constitution must include a responsible executive council. There are in the Act four references in all to an executive council. Section VII says that certain examinations are to be conducted "before such executive council as shall have been appointed by his Majesty, his heirs or successors, within such Province, for the affairs thereof." Section XXXIV declares that

> The Governor or Lieutenant Governor, or person administering the government . . . together with such Executive Council as shall be appointed by His Majesty for the affairs of such Province, shall be a court of civil jurisdiction for hearing and determining appeals within the same.

Section XXXVIII gives the Governor or Lieutenant Governor power "with the advice of such Executive Council as shall have been appointed by his Majesty, his heirs or successors, within such Province, for the affairs thereof" to constitute and erect rectories "according to the establishment of the Church of England." Finally Section L empowers the Governor or Lieutenant Governor, "with the consent of the major part of such Executive Council as shall be appointed by his Majesty for the affairs of such Province," to make temporary laws for its good government pending the first summoning of the Legislature.

It is hardly necessary to remark that the phraseology used gives no indication of any purpose to render the executive council which his Majesty was to appoint responsible to the legislature in the modern sense.[3] Nor was there any constitutional necessity for the members of that body or any of them to hold seats in either branch of the legislature. The general feeling both in Upper and in Lower Canada, but particularly in Lower Canada, was against their holding seats in the Assembly.

The whole population of Upper Canada in the year 1792, when its first parliament met, did not much exceed twelve thousand, a very small number, considering the vast area over which they were scattered, with which to begin an experiment in parliamentary government. Moreover the British Reform bill was yet forty years in the future, and the tendency of the times in England was reactionary rather than progressive. It was a few years later than this that Wordsworth and Coleridge, as they took their country walks, immersed in high converse on congenial themes – the nature and function of the imagination, to wit, and whether poetry called for a special diction of its own, and what subjects were most suitable for poetic treatment – were stealthily followed by officers of the law as suspicious characters and possible hatchers of some deep conspiracy. It cannot be a matter of surprise if the nervous fears of the upholders of authority there were communicated to their representatives, administrative and judicial, here, with the result of causing the nascent institutions of the province to shape themselves rather on conservative, not to say tory, than on democratic lines. Simcoe was a fierce tory, though withal a most well-meaning man and devoted public servant. He was willing and eager to do all in his power for the people, but he was not anxious to see them assuming any large measure of political activity themselves.

The population of the province at this time, it must be remembered, consisted almost wholly of those American colonists who in the quarrel between King George the Third and his colonial subjects had espoused the royal cause. A certain proportion of them were persons of more or less social standing. They had been accustomed it is true to a liberal measure of local independence in their former homes, but having made the choice for monarchy as against republicanism, they were scarcely in a position to make an early protest, even had they been so disposed, against the actual conditions of British rule in Canada. They had come to a beautiful and a fertile country, but there was work to be done to create new homes for themselves in it, and the political system as yet could hardly be said to impede their efforts.[4] Another element in the population numerically small, but individually important, consisted of a few families of means who had come from the British Isles and of certain persons and a few prominent office-holders, likewise of

British origin. Circumstances therefore were favorable to the acquisition of influence by the propertied and official class and for the gradual formation of the type of society represented in later days by what was, without much rhyme or reason, but effectually for all that, called the "Family Compact."

Nor were the members of the class in question slow to perceive their advantage. Possessing education and worldly knowledge, some enjoying salaries fixed rather according to English practice and precedent than according to the narrower and more economical ideas of a new country, and others relatively large professional incomes while a few commanded the more important avenues of commerce, they really formed what Fox might have been content to regard as the nucleus of his proposed aristocracy. Then overshadowing all was the immeasurable power and prestige of the British Empire. The ill-success of England in her struggle with the revolted American colonies has perhaps, in this quarter of the world, tended in some degree to abate the sense of the greatness of the British power at that very time. But, seen in true historical perspective, that lack of success on the part of the nation which was shortly to meet and overthrow the colossal power of Napoleon, and whose army and navy were destined in a brief span of years to carry her to the very pinnacle of military glory, shrinks to very secondary proportions. As it was the colonies congratulated themselves with fear and trembling on an issue from their perils which, even when the power of France had been thrown on their side, was almost beyond hope.[5]

In the present status of Canada as a country counting her population by millions and her trade by hundreds of millions, possessing means of internal and external communication that challenge the attention of the world, rapidly growing in wealth and power, and exercising all but the most sovereign functions of nationhood, a little effort of imagination may be required to fully realize the preponderating influence of the mother country one hundred years ago or less. The theory at that time was that Great Britain was holding this vast domain in trust for the generations yet to be; she consequently could not hand it over absolutely to the few thousands who were actually occupying the soil. There was to be British liberty here in all essential respects – liberty of thought, of speech, of the press, and of action – but

not for the present at least, unlimited liberty of legislation,
lest British ideas and ideals should be departed from under
the influence of republican models.[6] Keeping these general
considerations in view, it is easy to discern the type of
society which was likely to be formed, and which in point
of fact was formed in the province of Upper Canada. That
there should be an aristocracy in the province was not looked
upon as an absurdity. Upon this point we need not appeal
to the "family compact" or its supporters, but may call as
witness a very prominent reformer, Dr. William Warren
Baldwin, the father of Robert Baldwin.

In a communication addressed to Lord Durham, dealing
comprehensively with the state of Upper Canada, the
gentleman whose name has been mentioned wrote as follows:

> The Constitutional Act contemplated a provincial
> aristocracy. Whether this idea originated with the
> framers of the Act from any conviction in their own
> minds of its necessity as a means of good government,
> resembling in a remote degree the aristocratic part of
> the English constitution, or as preserving to the divided
> province of Quebec a mode of affording to the inhabi-
> tants of the Upper portion a composition of the body
> politic similar to that of the Lower, it is now unneces-
> sary to discuss: it is plain that the French system of
> government in Quebec did afford such a foundation, and
> it seems quite consistent with wise legislation that the
> like foundation should be laid in Upper Canada.

The writer proceeds to express his regret that the plan which
Governor Simcoe initiated of making grants to responsible
persons of large tracts of land – from forty thousand to sixty
thousand acres – on condition that they should bring into
the country and settle a certain number of families propor-
tioned to the extent of the grant, had been discontinued. In
the case of the township of Markham, which had been so
granted, the whole area was about sixty thousand acres and
sixty families were to have been settled on farms of two
hundred acres each, the grantees advancing the money
required for settlement purposes, but expecting repayment
in the course of two or three years. As this arrangement
would still leave four-fifths of the land in the hands of the
grantee who would also receive back his advances it certainly
was well devised for the creation of lordly estates. "All

promised to work favorably," the writer continues, "for the new Province, while the township proprietors, answering in some measure to the seigniors of Lower Canada, would have laid the foundation of a rational and temperate aristocracy." Such an aristocracy "would have preserved in the peoples' minds an habitual sense of the nature of the government intended, and would have planted among them men of respectable condition of life to whom they would have looked for advice and example."

The policy afterwards adopted, Dr. Baldwin declares, had tended directly to encourage democracy. The township grants had been cancelled, but the settlers who had been brought in were confirmed in possession of their lands,

> the government becoming the factors of all the minute detail of settlement in every division of the Province. Large grants became unpopular; and thus were sown the seeds of an enduring democracy which must be the guiding spirit of the great mass of the people. In process of time the assembly, formed principally of small land-owners, soon adopted a species of hostility to the few individuals who happened to have acquired large tracts of land, on the ground that these private possessions greatly enhanced the misery occasioned by the government reserves of two sevenths.[7]

The writer makes strong complaint of the law passed in the year 1828 providing for the taxation of waste lands in the hands of private parties. He accuses the government of having introduced and pressed it "with the view of gaining a little shallow popularity." This tax, he states, "became a powerful obstacle in the formation of an aristocracy." Men who had large estates, which they wished to preserve for their families, found it so inconvenient that they were obliged to throw some of their lands on the market. And so, in this instance again, "the Government itself has worked largely in giving the spirit of democracy to the colonist."

It tends rather to upset the conventional idea of the respective roles of government and reform party in old Upper Canada days to find the former accused by so representative a reformer as Dr. Baldwin of trying to earn "a little shallow popularity" by imposing a small tax on waste lands unproductively held by private individuals in expectation of an advance in price. It is a little remarkable that it is precisely in connection with this measure that the government is accused in the celebrated Seventh Grievance Report of 1835 of having exercised undue pressure on two or three members of the legislative council in order to secure its passage.

Lieutenant Governor Simcoe returned to England in the fall of the year 1796. His correspondence with the Colonial Office shows that he received a caution from the Secretary, Henry Dundas, as to the inexpediency of forcing in any way the transfer of population from the United States to Canada. "I am of opinion" said the astute official,

> that in the very infancy of the Province under your government such emigration would not be productive of all the good consequences which your mind on the first impression may suggest to you. Population is often the effect, but never, I believe, the cause of the prosperity of any country. It is not (taken exclusively) found to be the true measure either of the strength, the riches, or the happiness of a country. . . . An ingrafted population (if I may so call it) to a great extent disregarding and outrunning (as it must do) all those regulations, laws, usages and customs which grow up and go hand in hand with a progressive and regular population, must be attended with a want of that regularity and stability which all, but particularly colonial, governments require. . . . It appears to me from what is stated in your letter that there is every appearance of settlers coming in from thence (the United States) in sufficient numbers, and of their own accord, without going out of your way to intice or allure them. In short my opinion is that, if care is taken to render the situation of settlers under your government comfortable and happy, the fame of their being so will undoubtedly spread and produce sufficiency of emigration from other states.

This dispatch was predicated upon a proclamation issued by Simcoe making tempting offers of land to any persons who would come to Upper Canada as settlers, a proclamation which he was specially anxious should become known in the United States. About ten years after the departure of Simcoe and very shortly after the arrival of lieutenant Governor Gore, it became evident that there was a troublesome and uncertain element in the population.[8] Gore himself, in an early despatch to the Colonial Office, divides the population into three classes, which he proceeds to describe. The first division consists of the U. E. Loyalists, the first settlers of the country, and of these he states that "in general they live comfortably, and some of them, comparatively speaking, are opulent." "It is from them," he adds, "that the Magistrates, Clerks of the Peace, and other civil officers in the respective districts of the Province are selected." The second division, consisting of "persons who have emigrated from Europe, chiefly from the northern parts of Scotland," are described as being "but indifferent farmers," but yet as having by dint of extreme frugality rendered themselves for the most part comfortable and independent. The last division, the more recent emigrants from the United States "have not all," he states,

> been represented to me in the same favourable point of view. Some indeed of that description, viz. Quakers, Dutch farmers from Pennsylvania, and many others have, it is said, proved peaceable and industrious settlers; but it is stated also that there are a considerable number from that country of a different description, who have come here adventurers, and have brought the very worst principles of their own Constitution along with them, and from what I have experienced, even during my very short residence here, endeavor to oppose and perplex his Majesty's government.

A couple of years earlier indeed, under lieutenant governor Peter Hunter,[9] so much nervousness existed on this subject that the legislature was induced to pass an Act "For the better securing this Province against all seditious attempts or designs to disturb the tranquility thereof," which gave to the government the power to banish from the country any person who had not been a resident for six months continuously, and who had not taken the oath of allegiance – a power which, in a case shortly to be referred to, was seriously abused.

There certainly were some political agitators in the country at the time, but the worst of them, as it happened, were of British, not American, growth. The most conspicuous of these was one Robert Thorpe, who was sent out in 1805 to fill the office of puisne judge, but who seems to have felt that he had a mission to reorganize more or less the affairs of the Province. As Mr. Gore had to ask the Home Government to recall him, his name has been duly entered on the martyr-roll of those who fell in the struggle for popular rights in the early days of Upper Canada; but a careful study of the documents bearing on his case will convince the dispassionate reader that the honours of martyrdom have, in this instance, been somewhat lightly, not to say ridiculously, bestowed.[10]

The war of 1812-1815, by the sharp contrast which it necessarily established between those who were prepared to give their best blood to preserve Canada for the British Crown and those who, secretly or openly, hankered after the flesh pots of the democracy they had left behind them, had the effect of causing a certain number of the latter to return whence they came. The sentiment of the country at large was certainly very strongly affirmed in favor of British connection and British institutions, and this naturally to the advantage and prestige of the class by whom this sentiment was *most* strongly affirmed. There can be little doubt that the war in this way did something to promote that semi-aristocratic constitution of society which characterized Upper Canada down at least to the period of the Union.

In a report made to the home government towards the close of the year 1815, Lieutenant Governor Gore, who had been absent from the province on leave for a period of nearly four years, stated that he had found it on his return, speaking generally, in by no means a depressed condition. In certain places there had been considerable destruction of property; but the circulation of money consequent on military expenditure had been beneficial both to the agricultural and the trading classes. On the sixth of February in the following year he met the legislature and found them in a highly amiable humour – so amiable that, out of their not overflowing treasury, they voted the very liberal sum of three thousand pounds to buy him a service of place. The reason for this beneficence towards a governor so long an absentee, and who had escaped all the burdens and anxieties of the war, is not very obvious. The humours however of a popular assembly uncontrolled by the Cossack whip of party are incalculable, and he who enjoys their golden moments should heed the poets' warning and beware the changing wind and darkening sky. The session of 1816 terminated on the first of April. During the recess a considerable amount of thinking must have been done on the state of public affairs, for when the legislature reassembled in February 1817 a strong disposition was shown to grapple with a number of important questions in a tolerably independent spirit. So unpleasing was the tone of their discussions to his excellency that on the seventh of April he put an abrupt stop to their proceedings by prorogation.

Gore left Upper Canada finally in June of this year, and in the very same month a man arrived in the province who was destined to leave a painful mark in its annals: the story of Robert Gourlay is one which no Canadian can read without regret. It forms the "curtain-raiser" so to speak, to Mr. Dent's *Story of the Upper Canada Rebellion*, where it is made to serve somewhat preposterously as an example of "Family Compact" tyranny, and consequently loses nothing in the telling.[11] What it chiefly illustrates is the nervous dread existing at the time on the part of the governing power of anything bearing the appearance of political disturbance. Gourlay was a man of good education and of strong and original views, and had been possessed of considerable property in England, which through various accidents and misfortunes he had lost. Having become possessed of some land in Upper Canada he came out to see the country and to decide whether perchance he might settle in it. The country impressed him very favorably, much more so than its form of government or the methods that were being taken to develop it. After residing in it for some months, studying its capabilities and generally diagnosing the situation, the idea occurred to him to issue circulars to local officers throughout the province requesting answers to certain questions, the last of which was as follows: "What in your opinion retards the improvement of your township in particular or the province in general?" Having obtained answers to his questions he proceeded to suggest that the several localities should select delegates to a convention to be held at Toronto (then York) to consider the state of the country and memorialize the British government thereon. The man's intentions, it may well be believed, were thoroughly good, but his methods were provocative to say the least.[12] "I beheld," says Sir Peregrine Maitland, Mr. Gore's successor in the lieutenant governorship, "in the character and address of the town meetings and convention the seeds of rebellion hastening to maturity."

The convention had met once during the temporary absence of Sir Peregrine in Lower Canada, where his father-in-law, the Duke of Richmond, was at this time governor general, and had adjourned without taking any very definite action; but it was to meet again. This his excellency determined it should not do, and hastily summoning the legislature he succeeded in persuading it to pass an act to render such gatherings illegal.[13] It was represented that the holding of conventions to deliberate upon the affairs of the province was a slur upon the constitutionally elected representatives of the people, as no such conventions could possibly be necessary if they did their full duty. Before the meeting of the legislature, which took place on the twelfth of October, Gourlay had been brought to trial at Kingston on a charge of libel, but, defending himself, was acquitted. A second trial at Brockville on a similar charge resulted in a second acquittal. Finally a great wrong was perpetrated. An affidavit was made before two justices of the peace that he was a seditious person who had not been six months in the country, and who had not taken the oath of allegiance, consequently that he might be summarily ordered to leave the country under the Act of 1804 previously referred to. True, he had not taken the oath of allegiance, but it was because he was a British subject, a Scotsman born in Forfarshire; while the only pretext for affirming that he had not been six months in the country was that during the summer of 1818 he had visited New York. In point of fact he had been in the country for a year and a half. Taking their stand on the affidavit the magistrates ordered him to leave the province within ten days, and when he refused to do so he was arrested and committed to the Niagara jail for trial at the next assizes. An application for release on a writ of *habeas corpus* having failed, he had to endure over seven months imprisonment before he was brought to trial. When the day arrived his mind had been so affected by his long confinement that he was in no condition to defend himself; and the sentence of the court re-affirmed that of the magistrates, except that, instead of allowing him ten days, it only allowed him twenty-four hours to leave the country. The sentence was a cruel as well as an unjust one, for Gourlay had considerable interests in the province and was earnestly desirous of becoming a permanent settler. There is no reason to doubt, however, that the chief agents in the prosecution sincerely believed that he was, politically, a dangerous man. And in point of fact he was really the kind of man whom most communities in all ages have accounted dangerous, for he had original ideas of his own and very small respect for common place opinions. Socrates in the free Athenian democracy was put to death, not for insulting the gods but, practically, for his ironical treatment of the opinions of the multitude; and if the "family compact," as such, had any hand in procuring the banishment of Gourlay, they might very safely have left him to a wider tribunal.

Broken in spirit and in estate, and deeply outraged in his sense of justice, Gourlay obeys the mandate of the court and, on the twenty first of August 1819, crosses at Niagara into the United States. Nine months pass, and another Scotsman in whose horoscope still more of strife and turbulence has been cast, steps blithely on our Canadian shore.

CHAPTER TWO

THE ADVENT OF MACKENZIE

It was on the twenty-eighth of May, 1820, that William Lyon Mackenzie, full of hope and ardour, in the flush of youthful manhood, confident of the future but stout of heart to meet whatever varied fortunes it might have in store, disembarked at Quebec from the ship that had borne him from his native Scotland. We can well believe that not without glowing anticipations he had passed up the broad and shining highway of the St. Lawrence, nor without a thrill that he gazed upon the high perched citadel of Quebec and all the grandeur and beauty of the surrounding scenery. And this too was British soil! and here and far beyond were the homes of a free people, inheritors of all that goes with the British name, of all that the British flag proudly floating on yon august height, symbolizes and protects! A less ardent nature than Mackenzie's might well have been moved to its depths by what was there presented to his eyes, and by the thought of the limitless possibilities of the land in which he was about to cast his lot. The land he had left was dear, but here was the land of expanding hope, the land where all things were possible to the resolute and the upright, a new fresh land in which old quarrels and hatreds and sorrows might be forgotten, and the future be written in fairer characters than the past. Surely it was the land for him.

It is not likely that much more will be learned of Mackenzie's ancestry or early years than is contained in the narrative published some forty-five years ago by his son-in-law Mr. Charles Lindsey.[1] He was born, as we are there informed, a double Mackenzie, his mother bearing the same surname as his father, on the twelfth of March, 1795, the same year which witnessed the birth of another Scot of objurgatory memory, Thomas Carlyle. His mother, who was a woman of strong character and great vitality – she lived to the age of ninety – was forty-five years old at the time of his

16

birth, her husband, Daniel Mackenzie, being only twenty-eight. The pair had been married on the 8th May 1794. Within a month after the birth of his child Daniel Mackenzie died from a cold contracted, we are told, at a dancing party. If the incident of the dancing party may be held to indicate a pleasure-loving disposition on the part of the father, the quality descended in full measure to the child, in whom it took the form, as he grew to manhood, of a strong vein of geniality and sociability, unhappily masked at times by certain less amiable characteristics. Fundamentally, Mackenzie, like Abou Ben Adhem, loved his fellow men.

In his mother's nature, as described to us, there is little of the pleasure-loving:

> She was so small in stature as to be considerably below the average size of her sex. In complexion she was a brunette; her hair was dark brown till whitened by age, and at ninety it was as abundant as ever and always long. Her dark eyes were sharp and piercing, though generally quiet; but when she was in anger, which did not often occur, they flashed out with such gleams of fire as might well appall any antagonist. The prominence of her cheek bones gave unmistakable indication of her Celtic origin. The small mouth and the thin compressed lips told of that unconquerable will which she transmitted to her son. The forehead was broad and high and the face seldom relaxed into perfect placidity; there were always on the surface indications of the working of the volcanic feelings within. The subduing influences of religion kept her strong nature under control and gave her features whatever degree of repose they ordinarily wore.[2]

Being herself an incessant reader of the scriptures and of such pious books as were current among the Scottish seceders, she tried hard to form on such diet the growing mind of her boy. No man can be wholly unliterary who has ever obtained, as Mackenzie did, a real grasp of the Bible. On the foundation thus laid he raised, as the years went on, an immense superstructure of miscellaneous knowledge; and in later life whenever he spoke or wrote, language and thought alike indicated that he was at home in the world of books, and particularly so in the field of history. Still, Bible and catechism and tractate were plied somewhat too

unsparingly in the domestic education of young William
Lyon, and some little trouble is said to have arisen in
consequence between him and his mother. The substantial
harmony of their relations was, however, never disturbed,
and there is evidence that he cherished her to the end with
affection and reverence.

The death of Daniel Mackenzie left his widow in great
poverty and painfully dependent upon the assistance of
relatives. She struggled bravely, however, and succeeded in
keeping a home for herself and her son, whom she sent to
school at Dundee. There he was generally at the head of
his class, arithmetic being the study in which he specially
excelled. He was not too studious, however, to give way
frequently to his strong sense of fun and humour; and even
in his school days his interest in the fairer half of creation
was very marked; he was always ready to help the girls
with their tasks, and particularly, we are told, the pretty
ones. Even in his boyhood he was an insatiable reader. His
mother would often express the fear that he would "read
himsel' out o' his judgment," a feat which, of course, is not
impossible. What is certain is that he entered on active life
with a well-stored, if not a very well-disciplined mind. The
facility with which he could bring appropriate quotations
and references to bear on subjects he was discussing reminds
one of a later Mackenzie, who, with less fire but more
balance, became an honored prime-minister of Canada.

What is further known of William Lyon Mackenzie's life
before he came to Canada may be told in few words. For
some years after leaving school he was employed in the
counting house of a Dundee wood merchant of the name of
Gray, of whom he spoke many years later as "an excellent
man and one of my earliest and best friends." It is conjectured that it was here that he acquired that thorough
knowledge of book-keeping which enabled him in later life,
as a member of the Upper Canada Legislature, to undertake
more than one difficult investigation calling for skill in
accounts. Leaving the employ of Mr. Gray he started in
business for himself, when still only nineteen years of age
or thereabouts, in the Village of Clyth some twenty miles
from Dundee. This did not prove successful, however, and
at the end of three years he determined to try his fortune
south of the border. This was in the year 1817. In 1818 he
was filling a position in the office of the Kennett and Avon

Canal Company. Later he was in London in search of
employment. He acknowledged in after years that his habits
about this time, or a little earlier, were not what they ought
to have been; but the lessons which his mother had implanted
in his mind came to his rescue and enabled him to effect a
sharp, decisive and, as his biographer assures us, final reform
in his mode of life. The idea of going out to Canada was
first suggested to him, Mr. Lindsey states, by Mr. Edward
Leslie of Dundee. The proposal was received with enthusiasm, and in the month of April 1820, the young Scotsman,
bidding farewell to his mother, who, however, followed him
two years later, took passage on the ship *Psyche* bound from
Dundee to Quebec.

The doctrine that "soul is form and doth the body make"
is older than the poet Spenser; it is natural to look for some
correspondence between the man within and the man without. The physical appearance of William Lyon Mackenzie is
thus described by the writer already quoted:

> He was of slight build and scarcely of medium height,
> being only five feet six inches in stature. His massive
> head, high and broad in the frontal region, and well
> rounded, looked too large for the slight wiry frame it
> surmounted. He was already bald from the effects of a
> fever. His keen, restless, piercing blue eyes . . . and the
> ceaseless, expressive activity of his fingers which
> unconsciously opened and closed, betrayed a tempera-
> ment that could not brook inaction. . . . The firm-set
> mouth indicated a will which, however it might be
> baffled and thwarted, could not be subdued. The lips
> firmly pressed together, constantly undulated in a mass,
> moving all that part of the face which lies below the
> nostrils; with this motion the twinkling of the eyes
> seemed to keep time, and gave an appearance of unrest
> to the whole countenance. . . . The deep-set eyes were
> over-arched by massive brows. . . . This assemblage of
> features,

adds the writer, "will at once be seen to have been striking
and characteristic."

The inference that must be drawn from this description is
that a constitutional restlessness was the master passion of
this new-comer to Canadian shores – a restlessness not caused
by outward circumstances, but springing from the very

structure of his own being, and finding its own possible appeasement in outward agitation. Had the whole psychology of the man been known to Sir Peregrine Maitland, well might he have exclaimed, "What boots it to have got rid of Gourlay if this man is to take his place?" It was not very long before Sir Peregrine must in truth have been indulging in some such uncomfortable reflection.

For the first four years after his arrival in Canada Mr. Mackenzie was engaged in mercantile occupations, with the exception of a very short period in the early part of the summer of 1820 when he was employed on a survey then being made of the Lachine Canal. During those four years he was in business in three distinct places, York, Dundas, and Queenston, a fact which may perhaps have some significance as an indication of temperament. The rolling stone, nevertheless, seems to have gathered some moss. The business at Dundas, which he carried on in partnership with Mr. John Lesslie of York, was decidedly profitable. A poster gives the style of the firm as "Mackenzie and Lesslie, Druggists, and dealers in Hardware, Cutlery, Jewellery, Toys, Carpenters' Tools, Nails, Groceries, Confections, Dye-stuffs, Paints, &c., at the Circulating Library, Dundas." This business was entirely under the local control of Mr. Mackenzie, his partner having a separate establishment of his own at York, in the book department of which Mackenzie had been employed before he went to Dundas. Early in 1823 the partnership between himself and Mr. Lesslie was dissolved, and after carrying on the business on his own account for a few months longer, he removed to Queenston, where he opened a store of a similar character. Before leaving Dundas, however, he had taken a very important step in a personal sense. In Scotland he had been acquainted with a Miss Isabel Baxter, a native of Dundee, who attended the same school as himself. He had not seen her for some years when they met at Quebec. Old associations reviving with augmented force in the new land, he asked her to be his wife, and they were married at Montreal on the 1st July 1822. The glimpses we now and then obtain of Mrs. Mackenzie in connection with the life of her husband, reveal a character of great excellence and attractiveness. Writing in 1862 Mr. Lindsey said: "Of this union the issue was thirteen children, three boys and ten girls; six of whom are now living; four daughters and two sons."[3]

It may safely be conjectured that before his removal to Queenston in the autumn of 1823, Mr. Mackenzie had begun to interest himself in Upper Canada politics. It is difficult, indeed, to see how apart from politics he could ever have satisfied that craving for agitation and contention that was so deeply implanted in his nature. Had he possessed a strong acquisitive instinct – a fairly well-developed passion for money-making – it is highly probable the Upper Canada rebellion would never have been heard. But Mackenzie cared little or nothing for money, though he seems to have possessed good business ability; and politics at this time must have presented a very tempting field to a man of his temperament. Selling out his business at Queenston he established at that place in the early summer of 1824 a paper, which during the whole term of its existence was an extraordinary reflex of himself. It was not published with extreme regularity, but its conductor was not much concerned over an occasional missing number. He thought people should only be too glad to hear the truth when he could give it to them; and that he was preaching a real political gospel he easily persuaded himself. The first number of the paper, which bore the excellent name of the *Colonial Advocate*, appeared on the eighteenth of May, 1824. What his point of view was at this time, and what the evils were which he set himself to redress, Mr. Mackenzie endeavoured to set forth in a letter written some twenty years afterwards, which his biographer, Mr. Lindsey, has published[4] with the comment that, though perhaps highly coloured, it contains only too much truth.

It is always well in a case of this kind to have a bill of particulars. Mr. Mackenzie's statements and complaints may be summarized in his own words as follows:

1. I had long seen the country in the hands of a few shrewd, crafty, covetous men, under whose management one of the most lovely and desirable sections of America remained a comparative desert.
2. The most obvious public improvements were stayed;
3. Dissension was created among all classes;
4. Citizens were banished and imprisoned in defiance of all law;
5. The people had been long forbidden under severe pains and penalties from meeting anywhere to petition for justice;

6. Large estates were wrested from their owners in utter contempt of even the forms of the Courts;

7. The Church of England, the adherents of which were few, monopolized as much of the lands of the colony as all the religious houses and dignitaries of the Roman Catholic Church had the control of in Scotland at the era of the Reformation;

8. Other sects were treated with contempt and scarcely tolerated;

9. A sordid band of land-jobbers grasped the soil as their patrimony, and with a few leading officials, who divided the public revenue among themselves, formed the family compact, and were the avowed enemies of common schools, of civil and religious liberty, of all legislative or other checks to their own will.

A country would certainly have been in a bad condition, of whom all this, or the half of it, could be truthfully said. It is only fair, therefore, to consider what a fair-minded commentator aware of the facts, might have said in rebuttal, or in moderation, of the several charges made, referring to them as numbered.

1. Mr. Mackenzie when he started his paper had not been quite four years in the country, so that he can scarcely be said to have "long seen" anything in it. The country was *not* "in the hands of a few shrewd, crafty, covetous men" though there may have been, and doubtless were, a few men of that character in it, as there have always been in every country. The country was in the hands of the Lieutenant-Governor and the legislature. The former was doing his utmost to check the schemes of crafty and covetous men, and the latter had it in its power to make good laws for the advancement of the general interest and did make not a few.

2. "The most obvious public improvements" were certainly not stayed by either the Legislative Council or the Governor. The Assembly was not very forward in voting money for public improvements. Money was scarce and taxation was most unpopular. Moreover the resources at the command of the legislature for fiscal purposes were very scanty.[5]

3. This is a very vague assertion. In small communities dissension is generally more rife than in populous ones.

4. This doubtless refers to the single case of Mr. Gourlay, a parallel to which could not be found in the annals of Upper Canada. Indefensible as the action taken against that individual was, it does not justify the assertion that "*citizens* were banished &c.*"

5. This refers to an Act òf the provincial legislature which was in force only a little over fifteen months, and was repealed before Mr. Mackenzie ever set foot in the country. Moreover, even by that Act, the people were not "forbidden from meeting anywhere to petition for justice," and Sir Peregrine Maitland in suggesting that an Act should be passed to prevent such political conventions as Mr. Gourlay had summoned expressly warned the legislature that they must be careful not to infringe in any way on "the sacred right of petition."[6]

6. This unsupported statement may be simply denied. It is probably founded like No. 4 upon a single case, that of Mr. Randall, a friend of Mr. Mackenzie's, who became involved in legal difficulties, and may have suffered, as others have done – as some have done in much more recent times – from legal chicanery.

7. True, a British statute, the Constitutional Act of 1791, set apart one-seventh of the land "for the support of a Protestant Clergy," and as another clause of the same statute authorized the constitution of rectories "according to the establishment of the Church of England," it had been inferred that by "a Protestant Clergy" was meant the Clergy of the Anglican Church. The Act, however, gave power to the Provincial legislature to vary or repeal the clauses relating to the allotment of land for church purposes. The question was, therefore, one for the competing interests in the Province to fight out or to compromise as they might judge best. To be on one side or the other in such a contest could hardly be in itself a stigma. Mr. Mackenzie himself, in his "Address to the Public," printed in the first number of the *Colonial Advocate*, said:

There is no doubt in our minds but that the English parliament, when it set apart these reserves for the use of a Protestant clergy, intended exclusively to establish the English Church and to endow it with the lands so reserved.

8. There was certainly a considerable assumption of

authority and superiority on the part of the "established" clergy, as they called themselves, and as they practically were in the early days, but this – a purely moral evil – was not inherent in the constitution of the country. It merely called for firm and dignified resistance.

9. It was the steady effort of the governors from the time of Mr. Gore onwards, to repress land jobbing. Sir Peregrine Maitland in his despatches to the Colonial office frequently deplores the extravagant land grants of a former period. The terms, however, in which the accusation under this head is made are too rhetorical for satisfactory examination.

Such might be the general tenor of an answer to Mr. Mackenzie's indictment. No country in the world has yet enjoyed either a perfect government or perfect social conditions, and there were certainly flaws in the state of Upper Canada when Mr. Mackenzie took its affairs in hand. What is difficult to understand is how it could have been very different from what it actually was, considering its origin and political constitution. Yet the whole period has come down to us laden with an odium largely the creation of the hostile criticisms of a few men. If the present age should hereafter be judged by the criticisms of those who to-day take the least favorable view of its public life, what will its repute be? It is easier to create a tradition of evil than one of good. A great poet has finely said that we live by admiration, and doubtless the higher life is so nourished; but if it were alleged that the spice of daily life, the average life of the common man, was depreciation, the dictum might be strongly defended. To rejoice not in iniquity, but to rejoice in *the truth* is one of the marks of a very superior grace. And so it comes about that historical criticism has found much more to do in the vindication, or partial vindication, of characters unduly blackened than in the darkening of characters too brightly portrayed.

The general elections for the ninth parliament of Upper Canada were to take place in the month of July, 1824, and the *Colonial Advocate* therefore came into the field in good time to exert an influence upon public opinion. The last assembly and the lieutenant-governor had parted on excellent terms. "I cannot," said his excellency,

> put an end to this session without assuring you how fully sensible I am of the judgment and temper which

have governed your counsels and given efficiency to
your various and extensive labours. . . . It will be no
less agreeable to your Sovereign than it must be satisfactory to the people of this province, to observe the
vigilant attention with which you have regarded every
question that can affect the welfare or security of your
country.

Mr. Mackenzie was not disposed to view this *entente cordiale*
with much satisfaction; entertaining a poor opinion, as he
did, of Sir Peregrine as an administrator he could not think
highly of a legislature upon which he would bestow such a
eulogium; it could not be very true to the people's interests.
The *Colonial Advocate* must see to it that the people are
awakened to sense of their rights and above all of their
wrongs, in order that they may elect men able to scorn the
blandishments and defy the threatenings of power. It was
no brief statement of his views that the conductor of the
Colonial Advocate laid before his readers in his first number,
but a well-nourished essay of hardly less than eleven
thousand words. It was worth reading, however, nor could
anyone read it without feeling that a new power had arisen
in the land. There was a rollicking air about it that bespoke
the high spirits and strong self-confidence of the man. If
there was to be a struggle who more fitted for it than he?
And wouldn't there be a good deal of fun in it any way?
And as he was going to be the champion of the people must
he not prevail in the end?

It was probably not long before a copy of the paper was
in the hands of Sir Peregrine Maitland, who had a delightful
cottage at Stamford about three miles from Queenston, at
which he spent the summer months. Before following him,
however, in his perusal of the lively sheet it may be well,
as he is a prominent figure for some years in our narrative,
to consider what manner of man the lieutenant-governor
really was. That his private character was estimable Mackenzie in this very number of his paper acknowledged. What
he says of him indeed seems to harmonize entirely with the
description given by the reverend Dr. Scadding in his *Toronto
of Old* (page 122). "To limit ourselves," says that agreeable
and useful writer,

to our own recollections, here at St. James' Church,
with great regularity was to be seen, passing to and

from the place of honour assigned to him, a tall grave
officer, always in military undress, his countenance ever
wearing a mingled expression of sadness and benevolence, like that which one may observe on the face of
the predecessor of Louis Philippe, Charles X, whose
current portrait recalls, not badly the whole head and
figure of this early governor of Upper Canada.

From his early boyhood Sir Peregrine had followed a
military career. As his service was incessant in a period of
active warfare his promotion was rapid, and in 1814 at the
age of thirty-seven he was made a major-general. At
Waterloo he commanded a brigade consisting of the 2nd
and 3rd battalions of the 1st Foot Guards, and for his
services on that memorable field he was created a Knight
Commander of the Bath.[7] Later in the same year he married,
somewhat against her father's will, Lady Sarah Lennox,
daughter of the Duke of Richmond. The latter, however,
quickly became reconciled to his son-in-law, and, when
appointed to the governor-generalship of Canada in the year
1818, managed to secure for Maitland the lieutenant-
governorship of Upper Canada. These were the days when
Liverpool, Eldon, and Castlereagh were swaying the policy
of Great Britain, and it would have been remarkable if they
had chosen to represent them in the colonies men distinguished for the breadth and liberality of their political views.
That Sir Peregrine Maitland was a high-minded, honourable
and conscientious man no one who reads his correspondence
can doubt; but it is also true that he took a timid and narrow
view of the duties of his position. He was genuinely desirous
that the country should prosper, yet feverishly anxious lest
the people should grasp too much power. He was not one
who would let the tares grow till harvest time; they must be
rooted out at once. It was thus that he rooted out Gourlay
and deprived the province of a man who might have been
of much use to it, and who might have proved a counterpoise
to Mackenzie. A dash of the easy-going temper of Sir Francis
Head, who would certainly have left Gourlay alone, would
have improved a character in which there were many fine
elements.

It is time, however, to let His Excellency read his copy
of that very diminutive sheet – the first two numbers were
printed in octavo form – the *Colonial Advocate*. He would

notice in the first place the motto chosen by the editor from his favorite poet Burns for his "Address to the Public" – a motto in which the wish is breathed

> That howe'er crowns and coronets be rent,
> A virtuous populace may rise the while,
> And stand a wall of fire around their much loved isle.

The rending of crowns and coronets is not a pleasant idea to a contemplative mind of decidedly conservative cast, and the virtuous populace may have struck his Excellency as a somewhat visionary and, in any case, not perfectly safe substitute for the established order of things in church and state. Truly a dangerous keynote for a Canadian publication! And what is this on the first page? "In this work it is intended to discuss the merits of public men and public measures with a freedom and plainness rather unusual in the greater part of our colonial publications." Nor does the writer lose much time in making good his promise; for on the second page, quoting a statement which some one had made that "this fine country has long languished in a state of comparative stupor and inactivity whilst our more enterprising neighbours are laughing us to scorn," he gives an explanation of the matter which comes directly home to the lieutenant-governor himself:

> We are blessed with a right valiant and most excellent military chieftain as our governor, Major General Sir Peregrine Maitland, to wit a Knight of noble birth and noble connexions, who after spending his earlier days amid the din of war and the turmoil of camps, has gained enough renown in Europe to enable him to enjoy himself, like the country he governs, in inactivity – whose migrations are by water from York to Queenston and from Queenston to York, like the Vicar of Wakefield from the brown bed to the blue, and from the blue bed to the brown – who knows of our wants as he gains a knowledge of the time of day by *report*; in the one case by the report of the Niagara gun; in the other by the *Gazette* published by, and not by,[8] authority and so forth.

But there is more: the Governor of Upper Canada is compared with the Governor of the State of New York.

> Look at De Witt Clinton: compare him with Sir
> Peregrine Maitland – the latter in the enjoyment of a
> princely salary; the former wasting the best years of his
> life in improving the resources of his country, without
> fee or reward other than the self-approbation of his
> own mind and the applause of millions of his fellow
> citizens.

And here, by one of those strange returns which Mackenzie
was always apt to make upon himself, he says that he will
not at present judge the question as between the two Governors absolutely – that he remembers the passage in Lord
Bacon's essays which says that "he that goeth about to
persuade a multitude that they are not so well governed as
they ought to be shall never want attentive and favorable
hearers;" or that other one which affirms that "it is not good
to try experiments in states, except the necessity be urgent
or the utility evident; and well to beware that it be the
reformation that draweth on the change and the desire of
change that pretendeth the reformation."

A reflection like this might probably relax the features of
his Excellency as he pored over his paper and some passages
a little further on might almost gain from him a smile of
approval:

> Sincerely attached to freedom, we yet think it not
> incompatible with a limited monarchy. We would never
> wish to see British America an appendage of the
> American Presidency: yet we would wish to see British
> America thrive and prosper full as well as does that
> Presidency. . . . We like American liberty well, but we
> much prefer British liberty. British subjects, born in
> Britain, we have sworn allegiance to a constitutional
> monarchy, and we will die before we will violate that
> oath.

That should have satisfied Sir Peregrine that no great danger
was to be apprehended from this man, unless perhaps he
happened to bethink himself of an eminent character who
made even stronger asseverations, who yielded in an hour
of temptation, and then – wept bitterly.

Some more sound doctrine from the Governor's point of
view was contained in the following passage: "In no part of
the constitution of Canada is the wisdom of the British
legislature more apparent than in setting apart a portion of

this country while it yet remained a wilderness for the support of religion." He would also entirely approve of a statement like the following: "There is no doubt in our minds but that the English parliament, when it set apart these reserves for the use of a Protestant clergy, intended exclusively to establish the English church;" but he would draw little comfort from it when he came in sight of the conclusion of the writer, that notwithstanding the intention of the British Parliament the proper thing for the provincial legislature to do – availing itself of the power given to it in the Act of 1791 of altering the disposition of the reserves – would be to make the provision applicable *to all sects indifferently* in proportion to their numbers. His estimate was that not one tenth of the population belonged to the Church of England, and only its proper portion would he assign to that or any other religious denomination. "This seventh," he says, "if given to support only one class of Christians, is equivalent to a system of temporal rewards and punishments; and if this is resorted to as the means of establishing religious opinions, it will make hypocrites enough." It does not seem to have occurred to the writer to enquire what the effect would be of making all denominations equally dependent on the state for support; but reflections on that subject came afterwards. There is an obvious reference to Dr. Strachan in the following passage:

We have known ministers connected with other churches, in coming into this province, change their religion and become episcopal clergyman. Christian charity induces us to believe that their motives were disinterested, but as some of them have grown very bigoted to their adopted faith, their sphere of usefulness is diminished, many attributing the change of principle to far less honourable motives than either conviction or conversion.

No fault can be found with the writer's ideas as to the kind of man needed in the public life of Canada:

We very much want men in Canada who have received a liberal education; men untainted by the enjoyment of power and place, who, if called on, would not hesitate to sacrifice their personal interests for the good of their country; and who, if elected to our House of Assembly would return to their homes at the end of a fourth or fifth session as free from the enthralment of patronage and place, of honours and pensions, as when they were first placed in the honourable situation of guardians of their country's rights.

This has undeniably the true ring; but has the popular assembly yet been found that sits in absolutely free impartial judgment upon the government of the day? Mackenzie lived to see that his ideal was at least as difficult of attainment under so called "responsible government" as under the system which he found so faulty.

The administration of justice was the next point touched upon. There was nothing here to create alarm – merely a hint that the proceedings of the Courts were a little leisurely, a trifle dignified, no suggestion of corruption, of partisanship on the bench or undue subserviency to the executive. "It occurred to us," the writer said,

> When we were in the Gore district at the last assizes that we wanted a Sir Matthew Hale in his miller's dress. It is not to be denied, however, but that Mr. Justice Boulton was very edifying in his way, and, we doubt not, decided with as profound professional wisdom as would have Sir Matthew; though perhaps it would have been as well if he had paid less attention to the town clerk of Ephesus's adage, 'Do nothing rashly.'

The writer proceeds to speak of the necessity there is for encouraging "competent professors of science and literature to emigrate hither," quoting the well-known lines of Pope about a little learning being a dangerous thing. He regrets the costliness of education, but says not a word to indicate his belief that there is in the province, as he later alleged when speaking of this very period, a class of persons who are "the avowed enemies of common schools." With all that is here said on the subject of education and its importance to the country, Sir Peregrine would entirely agree, as he himself had drawn the attention both of the legislature and of the Home Government to the urgent need of making better provision for the education of the people.

Some words of warm commendation are bestowed on Mr. John Willson of Saltfleet.

> He has done great good to this Province by advocating in his place in parliament and in his neighborhood the

cause of moral and religious instruction. . . . We greatly
esteem this gentleman. Many members of our legislature
get *less* useful the longer they are kept in parliament;
but his talents appear to us the more eminent and his
knowledge the more solid and extensive the longer he is
there.

This Mr. Willson was chosen Speaker of the Assembly then
about to be elected; but alas, like many others whom
Mackenzie at one time or another praised, he was destined
to suffer a serious fall in that gentleman's estimation. It is
interesting, however, to note that even in these aristocratic
times a plain Methodist farmer like Mr. Willson was able
not only to secure election to the legislature but to exercise
considerable influence in it.

Sir Peregrine would entirely sympathise with a eulogy of
agriculture which follows, but he would probably look
dubious over an observation like this: "We may yet flourish
without hastily severing the ties that bind us to the land of
intellectual grandeur – the country of our forefathers." "Why
talk of severing those ties at all?" he would say. "Why put
such an idea into the heads of the people?" Of course the
writer discards the idea; but to mention an idea and discard
it may be a very subtle way of introducing it. The spirit of
adventure was strong in Mackenzie: he adventured with
ideas, and we shall find this idea of separation flitting in and
out among his public utterances from a very early period.

It is remarkable how many questions of importance
relating to Upper Canada Mackenzie had already reflected
on to more or less purpose. We encounter a forcible plea
for greater freedom of trade, particularly with the United
States. Sir Peregrine could not have read the following
remarks with peculiar pleasure:

Our foreign commerce confined and shackled as it is, is
entirely in the hands of the British capitalists; our
lumber trade is merely encouraged to support British
worn-out shipping. We are inundated – glutted – with
British manufactures. . . . The whole together is a
system revolting to the feelings of every independent
thinking colonist. Our farmers are indebted to our
country merchants, our country merchants are deeply
bound down in the same manner, and by the same
causes, to the Montreal wholesale dealers. Few of these

> Montreal commission merchants are men of capital;
> they are generally merely the factors or agents of British
> houses, and thus a chain of debt, dependence and
> degradation is begun and kept up, the links of which
> are fast bound round the souls and bodies of our
> yeomanry, . . . while the tether stake is fast in British
> factories. Is it then to be wondered at that our houses
> of Assembly have successively been distinguished for
> their cringing submission to successive governors?

Then follow specific attacks on J. B. Robinson, Attorney
General, the member for York; [Christopher] Hagerman, the
member for Kingston; and L. P. Sherwood, Speaker of the
lately dissolved House, the member for Leeds.

Sir Peregrine's forte was not political economy, but he
could be pardoned for not seeing a very close connection
between the indebtedness of the farmer to the country storekeeper, of the country storekeeper to the Montreal merchant,
and of the Montreal merchant to the British manufacturer,
and any complaisance manifested towards himself by the
people's representatives. Truly *he* was in no position to
cause the British manufacturers to squeeze the Montreal
merchant, so that the latter might squeeze the Upper Canada
storekeeper, and the storekeeper the farmer, all to the end
of rendering the legislature submissive to his views. "Is this
kind of argument fair?" he would ask – "is it going to do the
country any good?"

The article concludes with an appeal to the farmers.

> On you alone, farmers, does Canada rely. You are the
> sole depositaries of civil and religious liberty. If you
> look to the provincial executives, they are foreigners,
> having an interest differing widely from yours, and are
> hardly able, even if we grant they have the will, to
> reconcile jarring interests arising from a crooked
> colonial policy. . . . Have the members of our legislative
> councils ever been other than the most obsequious,
> cringing worshippers of power? Have the honourables
> and reverends and right-reverends ever attempted ought
> towards consolidating your liberties? Have they not, on
> the other hand, done all that in them lay to abridge, to
> curtail, to crush them? . . . If you turn to the Bench to
> look for Holts and Hales will you find them? Will the
> judges guard your rights? Dare they do it? Will they

become the champion of your liberties? Remember Thorpe. . . . To yourselves, therefore, farmers, must you look for aid. The eyes of the whole colonies and of America are fixed on you. You are the only true nobility that this country can boast of. . . . If ye choose the wisest, the honestest, the most esteemed of your body; men who have long been known as tried patriots, in whose souls the voice of freedom is not yet extinct; who hold no offices under, or receive gifts from, the Crown; . . . if to such as these ye trust your liberties there is yet hope for your country. But if ye will, as heretofore, choose collectors and King's advocates, ambassadors, parasites and sycophants to manage your affairs, you will dearly rue it.

To all this what would his excellency find to say? He would admit that this man had the gift of eloquence, and that, though neither the nurseling of a university nor a classical scholar, he could shape his sentences aright. The question remained – what part was he destined to play in Upper Canada? A question difficult to answer. It would be impossible however not to notice that, with all his declamation there was the minimum of specification of actually existing evils. Liberty was said to be crushed, but how? The question was asked, would the judges dare to defend the right, but no instance was cited of their having shrunk from doing so. The only "shackles" referred to specifically were those upon commerce, due to a complicated and superannuated fiscal system; but this was hardly sufficient foundation for so passionate an appeal to the spirit of liberty. In the light of later events we can read what perhaps was holden from the eyes of his excellency, that the core, the vital nucleus of that appeal, lay in the words "parasites and sycophants" applied to members of the legislature who worked harmoniously with the executive. Here was the conviction that was destined to dominate, perhaps more than any other, Mackenzie's career, that sycophancy and support of the colonial executive were synonymous terms.

A negative point may be noticed: as yet there is no distinct formulation of the doctrine of "responsible government." The writer assumes that, as things are, an honest house could secure all that was necessary in the way of good government.

CHAPTER THREE

THE TIMES AND THE MAN

Mr. Mackenzie it is clear had not, during his four years' residence in Upper Canada, formed a very favorable opinion of the manner in which the government of the Province was conducted. It is possible he may have been a little helped in arriving at the opinions he had formed by the society in which he was thrown – which was decidedly of a "reform" cast. It cannot really be said that anything had happened during those four years of a nature to involve the government in any grave discredit; nor, indeed, did the criticisms bestowed on it in the first number of the _Colonial Advocate_ constitute, as these things go, a serious bill of indictment: placed side by side with his later version[1] of the conditions then prevailing, they are wonderfully mild. The fact is that things were improving, though slowly, and only needed some steady pressure from the representative body to make them hasten their pace. That the representative body was capable of being spurred into action had been demonstrated on more than one occasion. In the first session of 1818 the very assembly which, later in the year, put a ban on Mr. Gourlay's convention strenuously and successfully resisted the pretentions of the legislative country to alter its money bills, and entered on its journals for an everlasting remembrance the celebrated dictum of governor Simcoe with respect to the constitution which had been bestowed on Upper Canada. There can be no doubt that they were stirred up by Gourlay's proceedings to a livelier sense of their responsibilities for it was not satisfactory to find their constituents having recourse to an extra-constitutional agency for the representation of their wants or the redress of their grievances. The bill which they passed expressly safeguarded, as the lieutenant governor had advised, the right of petition; nevertheless they were uneasy in their minds as to what they had done and they repealed the act in March 1820, less than sixteen months after it was passed by a unanimous vote.[2]

34

The Act of 1820 providing for a substantial increase in the representation of the people was in itself a popular measure adapted to increase the weight of influence of the Legislative Assembly as a branch of the legislature. It is noticeable that Mr. Mackenzie does not, in his first article, make any specific charge against the eighth parliament; he hints that members are too easily influenced by the governing powers, but he gives no examples of their undue complaisance. He does not even say a word about the expulsion and disqualification of Mr. Barnabas Bidwell in the session of 1822, though this might have been plausibly used to give point to his general criticism. Bidwell had been elected in that year to fill a vacancy in the representation of the united counties of Lennox and Addington, greatly to the vexation of the ultra conservatives. He was an American by birth, had filled different offices in the United States including that of member of Congress, and, rightly or wrongly, was reputed to have brought some rather republican ideas over to Canada with him when he removed to this country in the year 1810. On these grounds alone he could not have been got rid of, but rumours had crossed the border, that, as treasurer of the county of Perkshire in Massachusetts, he had been short in his accounts and had fled the country to avoid prosecution. The rumour was not wholly without foundation, though Bidwell protested that he had never done anything really dishonest, and that the difficulties which, he acknowledged, had caused him to pass over to Canada had been woven for him by personal enemies. A motion for expulsion was founded on the facts as ascertained, and was carried by a vote of 17 to 16. That the division should have been so close under the circumstances does not speak ill for the independence of the assembly. Of the man himself it must in fairness be said that whatever cloud may have rested on a former period of his life, his record in Canada was not only irreproachable but in every way creditable. He was a lawyer by profession, a man of considerable ability, moderate and temperate in his views, and of a kindly disposition. He was an excellent speaker, and the probability is that he would have been extremely useful as a member of the House of Assembly.

Expulsion however, did not imply disqualification; to effect the latter object an Act was passed rendering ineligible any person who had held any important office in a foreign

country. This shut out Barnabas Bidwell, but the objection
did not apply to his son, Marshall Spring Bidwell, a young
man of twenty-three, also a lawyer with a rapidly rising
reputation, who at once came forward. At the close of the
poll the conservative candidate, a Mr. Clark, was declared
to be elected, but the election was set aside by the House
on the ground of corrupt practices. On the next occasion
the returning officer had received instructions not to receive
any votes for Mr. M. S. Bidwell, on the ground that he
was an alien. It was true that he had been born in the
United States, the son of a citizen of that country; that
neither he nor his father had ever obtained British naturalization; and that the Act of 1791 giving a constitution to
the Province had declared (section 22) that

> no person shall be capable of voting at any election of a
> member to serve in such assembly in either of the said
> Province, *or of being elected* at any such election, who
> shall not be . . . a natural born subject of his Majesty,
> or a subject of his Majesty naturalized by Act of the
> British parliament, or a subject of his Majesty having
> become such by the conquest and cession of the
> Province of Canada.

All this was true, but in point of fact the law had not for
years past been enforced, and many persons with no better
claims to legal British citizenship than Mr. Bidwell had been
elected to the House and had sat in it. The house took these
facts into consideration and refused to recognize the return
of Bidwell's opponent – this time a Mr. Ham. In the following session an Act was passed repealing certain parts of the
one under which Barnabas Bidwell had been disqualified.
Without removing the disability attaching to persons who
had held any important office in a foreign country, it
rendered generally eligible for a seat in the assembly any
one who had resided in the country for seven years previous
to an election, and who had taken the oath of allegiance.
This met the case of the younger Bidwell and enabled him
to be returned without question in the general election of
the following summer (1824). The impression he made on
the legislature may be judged from the fact that four years
later, at the age of twenty-nine, he was chosen speaker.

These proceedings on the part of the assembly, and the
concurrence of the Legislative Council in an Act intended

to render possible the election of a champion of liberal and progressive, if not radical, views of government, are far from indicating a hopeless or even an unpromising condition of things. There was evidently life in the institutions of the country, and if there was a "family compact" its influence on public affairs was certainly not unlimited.

In the session of 1821 the legislature had adopted resolutions declaring that no tithes should be exacted by the clergy of the established church, and an Act was passed founded thereon. This was not done in consequence of any attempt, or even proposal on the part of the clergy to exercise such a power but simply because certain expressions in the Act of 1791 were thought to leave an opening for a claim of this nature. The measure indeed was heartily concurred in by the church authorities who were very far from wishing to excite popular antagonism by putting forward such pretentions.

It was in the same session also that the first steps were taken by the legislature towards the construction of that great public work, the Welland Canal. A preliminary, but very insufficient, survey of the route had been made as early as 1818 by private parties who foresaw the immense importance to the development of the province of such a communication between Lakes Erie and Ontario. In 1821 a grant of public money was made for a more thorough survey, and in the session of 1824 an act was passed incorporating the Welland Canal Company, of which Mr. George Keefer was the first President, with a capital of £40,000. At this time a canal for small boats only was contemplated, and locks not more than seven feet wide were provided for. In the following year the views of the Company had greatly enlarged, and they obtained an Act increasing their capital to £200,000 so that they might adapt the canal to the passage of schooners.

The finances of the Province were at this time in a deplorable condition mainly owing to the fact that it was impossible to obtain from the legislature of Lower Canada any reasonable arrangement for the division of the duties there collected on over-sea imports, a large proportion of which was destined for, and consumed in, the Upper Province. An agreement had been reached in the year 1817 by which Upper Canada was to receive one fifth of the collections, but since that time its population had increased in far larger proportion than that of Lower Canada, and naturally it demanded an improved basis of division and a certain amount of arrearages. Delegates from the two provinces had met at Montreal and discussed the matter, but the Lower Canadians were unyielding, and no satisfactory conclusion was arrived at. The only recourse left was to appeal to the home government. A joint address was adopted by the two houses of the legislature, who also united in requesting the lieutenant governor to appoint Mr. Robinson, the attorney general, to carry it to England and support it by personal representation. His Excellency had intended to offer the mission to the somewhat aged Chief Justice Powell, but felt it his duty to comply with the unanimous nomination of the legislature. The Chief Justice unfortunately conceived grave offence at this, and three years later published an attack on the administration which not only seriously embarrassed his relations with Sir Peregrine Maitland, but drew forth the censure both of the executive council, of which he was himself president, and of the home government.

Leaving Canada in March 1822, Mr. Robinson reached England in April, and remained there till June of the following year. His mission was entirely successful, the British government intervening with the Canada Trade Act (3 George IV, chapter 119) which placed the financial relations between the two provinces on a fair and equitable footing, and provided that the actual amount which Upper Canada ought to receive should in future be adjusted by arbitration every four years. It may be added that the Upper Canada commissioner made so favorable an impression on the many public men of the highest standing with whom he was brought into contact, both by his professional knowledge and his general business, that the colonial secretary was led to tender him the lucrative as well as honourable office of Chief Justice of Mauritius at a salary of £3,500 sterling with an additional allowance for house rent. This flattering and advantageous offer Mr. Robinson declined, giving as a reason that attachments of a public as well as private nature led him to prefer his situation in Canada to one more lucrative in another colony, in which he would probably take less interest and might therefore be less useful.[3]

In many ways, some more and some less important, the eighth parliament of Upper Canada showed its sense of responsibility to the public and its desire to adopt progressive measures. It made close inquiry into the expenditure of the public revenue and called for a large amount of information from the lieutenant governor. A careful perusal of its journals will be found to afford little justification for the charge brought against it by Mr. Mackenzie of subserviency to the views of the executive. The mere fact that certain persons support an executive, or work in substantial harmony with it, does not prove their subservience to it though in those days, and even to the end of his career, Mr. Mackenzie seems to have thought so. Public opinion in the province was clearly beginning to assert itself, and all the more so because there was yet practically no party machinery to stifle opinion and concentrate attention simply on the question of party triumph or defeat.

A study of the early numbers of Mackenzie's paper serves both to reveal the man and to throw light on the actual condition of the country. Let us first discover the man. Mr. Canning at this time was foreign secretary in Lord Liverpool's cabinet and to him Mackenzie addressed two letters on the subject of the East India and China trade which he was desirous of seeing thrown open to Canada. In the first of these, published in his second number, he refers to a suggestion made somewhere – he does not say where – that Great Britain should sell Canada to the United States. "What!" he breaks forth,

sell Canada! Take the price of Wolfe's and Brock's blood! Set a value of her own children! The father in Britain sell his son and his son's rights to foreigners for a consideration! And what could that consideration be in heaven's name? – What sum could pay England for the blood of the brave men that has been spilt in gaining and defending Canada. Nothing less would pay her than the exalted satisfaction of knowing and seeing that she had made the Canadian free, contented and happy.

It is interesting to note that in the same letter he recommended a union of all the British North American provinces – an anticipation of the statesmanship of 1867, but a sufficiently obvious one, considering the conspicuous example of Canada's nearest neighbour, the United States.

One of the things Mackenzie had promised in his opening number was that he could use great freedom in the discussion

of political subjects and persons, nor was he long in redeem-
ing the pledge, as his second number contained an article
on Mr. Attorney General Robinson which certainly did not
err on the side of restraint or delicacy of phrasing. Amongst
the persons who attended Gourlay's convention were some
who had rendered service in the war of 1812, and had thus
become entitled to grants of land; and also some who held
commissions in the peace or other offices in the gift of the
government. Sir Peregrine had decided – very harshly, as it
must appear at this time of day – to withhold the land grants
in such cases, and to cancel the commissions of any who
were justices of the peace. Mr. George Hamilton, member
for Wentworth, was in the latter category, and the matter
being casually referred to in the assembly, the attorney
general defended the action of the governor, and said that
Mr. Hamilton had reaped "the reward of improper interference." This had happened in the previous session, but a
reference to it in a York paper roused all Mackenzie's
wrath. "Language would fail us," he said,

> to express in terms sufficiently strong our contempt and
> disesteem of that crown officer who, vested with
> ephemeral power could so far dishonour the floor of our
> senate as to make it the scene of his vulgar unfeeling
> sarcasms, and who, with the most consummate impru-
> dence could so unnecessarily add insult to injury. We
> are not yet done with Mr. Attorney General Robinson.
> We regard and fear his power as little as in our heart
> we esteem his conduct, and we will not sit down satisfied
> with barely terming him a burlesque on legislation. In
> the first schedule of the Canada Trade Act,[4] the first
> article mentioned as allowed to be imported is *Asses*.
> This was a measure of lawyer R's, and we have a
> curiosity to know at what he, who we are told, was the
> first of the braying species imported after the passing of
> the act, was valued. His abilities have been vastly over-
> rated. . . . We account him to be a vain, presuming,
> ignorant man, and *will bear the blame if we do not
> prove him such*.

Mackenzie did not reflect sufficiently on the effect which
such a reckless use of language would have on his own
standing in the community. Whatever a man's merits may
be otherwise, a certain "disesteem," to use his own word,

waits upon incontinence of speech. The tongue should not
wag the man.

The attack on Mr. Robinson was resumed in a more
formal manner in the third number of the paper. He was
accused of having shown a grasping disposition in the matter
of the charge made by him for his services and expenses
when acting for the province in England. Mackenzie was a
man who cared nothing for money himself, and who would
throw his last penny into any cause he had at heart. If
another man exhibited more worldly prudence he despised
him. He accused Mr. Robinson of "meanness of soul," and
of having exhibited himself "not as the disinterested patriot,
but as the mercenary hireling, the mere attorney." The
prediction is made that the object of his attack "will be
remembered, if remembered at all, not as one of the early
benefactors of Canada, not among her Chathams and Alfreds
and Pitts, but among her night birds, her bats, and her
owls." And yet we have only to glance forward a few weeks
to find in the same paper the following account of the
manner in which the attorney-general, from the writer's own
observation as he distinctly says, conducted himself in the
Niagara Assizes:

> As to the Attorney General his conduct was marked
> throughout with a degree of politeness to all who had
> to do with him, which, joined to his lenity as a public
> officer deserves commendation, and is a further proof
> that he who, as a legislator and as an adviser of the
> government, may recommend and approve of harsh,
> tyrannical and arbitrary measures, is frequently gentle,
> kind and agreeable as an individual and as a professional
> man.

It is clear that Mackenzie had an instinct to do justice. It
was a misfortune that he so often allowed that instinct to
be silenced by the blasts of passion.

As has already been hinted the early numbers of the
Colonial Advocate throw some interesting side lights on the
condition of Upper Canada in the year 1824, under so-called
"family compact" rule. Mr. Dent and others would have us
believe that that condition was shocking almost beyond
expression; but one could read through quite a number of
Advocates without finding anything to justify the picture
they draw. Many of the incidents mentioned, indeed, create

quite a different impression. There is an account in the second number of a funeral sermon preached by the Rev. Mr. Addison, an Anglican clergyman, on the death of a colonel Nichol of Stamford who had been killed by falling over the precipice near Queenston Heights. The preacher we are told

> spoke in glowing language of the martyrs, heroes and statesmen of Britain, of ancient and modern times, whose memories are held in grateful remembrance by their country; eulogized the memories of those patriots who, at the revolution (1688) supported the civil and religious liberties of their country even at the hazard of their lives; proved the great importance of character as descending from a father to his children.

This surely was not a bad or illiberal discourse for the times, coming, as it did from a member of the privileged church, and delivered, as it was in presence of the lieutenant governor and Lady Sarah Maitland.

Nor do we get an unfavorable impression of the appointees of the alleged "family compact." "Very lately," we read, "that fine old gentleman, Dr. Kerr, delivered up the broad seal (of the surrogate court) by a mandate from the King of Terrors." A successor to him was found "in the person of our much esteemed neighbour and magistrate and postmaster, Alexander Hamilton, Esq." It is not always, even in our own piping times of political progress, that one excellent official is succeeded by another equally so. A few months later the *Advocate* notices the death of the Hon. Thomas Dickson, member of the legislative council and collector of customs at Queenston, a man "universally beloved for his agreeable urbanity of manner, mildness of disposition and extensive benevolence." There is nothing whatever in the paper at this date to indicate or to suggest that the general atmosphere is one of oppression, corruption or restriction of popular rights.

In anticipation of the general election of the summer of 1824, the editor of the *Colonial Advocate* is glad to learn that "the people of Niagara intend to choose from among themselves a worthy and amiable young man as their representative." In these machine-ridden days it has a most refreshing effect to hear of "the people" actually intending to choose anybody; but clearly such things were possible in the days of our grandfathers and great grandfathers. "Mr. Edward McBride," the writer continues, "is allowed to be a well-informed gentleman, and no party has ever yet dared to question the manly independence of his principles." This is more good news, and it may be noted that no hint is dropped that the overwhelming influence of the family compact may be exerted against Mr. McBride, or that any attempt will be made to corrupt the electors. Mr. McBride was elected all right; the people wanted him and they got him. The only other constituencies particularly referred to in the *Advocate* are Oxford, Norfolk and Middlesex, and regarding these nothing is said of any possible or probable interference with freedom of election. In Middlesex, it is true, the writer dreads the influence which one of the candidates, Mr. Burwell, may be able to exercise through having a number of the farmers in his debt, and he takes the opportunity of giving a useful caution to the farmers against getting into debt. His apprehensions, however, were groundless, for the candidate on whose behalf he was concerned, Captain Matthews of jovial memory, gained his election.

Such are the glimpses we get of the way elections were carried on. How was it in regard to public works? There is an article in the paper about the proposed canal between Burlington Bay and Lake Ontario for which the legislature had made an appropriation. The work was to be done under the direction of commissioners the choice of whom rested with the lieutenant governor. "We are vastly well satisfied," says Mackenzie, "with the commissioners now appointed, and give Sir Peregrine Maitland the necessary credit for accuracy of judgment in this case." No suspicion is expressed, and clearly none was entertained, that this important public work will be converted into a feeder for the administration or prove the source of a corruption fund.

The instances cited would lack all significance if culled from a large number some of which pointed in an opposite direction. With one exception they are all taken from the second number of Mr. Mackenzie's paper, and constitute practically *all* the allusions to miscellaneous public affairs found in that issue. The third number, however, contains a statement of Mr. Mackenzie's *theory* as to how the business of the country was carried on. As this theory was fundamental with Mackenzie it is well to present it here. He never got away for an hour – one might safely say for a moment –

from that interpretation of things. "Arbitrary governments,"
he says,

> or such governments as have much in their gift, . . . for
> the sake of appearances, and indeed to preserve their
> influence, allow, not as a right, but by virtue of some
> gracious act, as it is called, a popular assembly or
> parliament. In this parliament *they place their managers*,
> whose first duty it is to take care that members who
> will not agree to act in all important matters as the
> executive pleases, but who stir up questions about
> abuses and misapplication of public moneys, and the
> like, may be bought over, to speak and vote entirely as
> their managers wish and direct. If the managers find a
> member possessed of vanity, he is invited to dinner by
> some great person and plied with wine and compliments
> on his abilities. If his taste inclines toward military
> rank, he is made a captain, colonel, or general; if he is
> covetous, some good government contract insures his
> silence at least; if he is engaged in some difficulty
> relating to law, or ship seizures, or irregular entries,
> depending on the will of the executive to smooth or not
> to smooth, additional difficulties are put in his way, his
> business is rendered peculiarly delicate and he too *must
> keep quiet*. . . . Thus the toils are drawn round this
> honest man; and his wife probably, and his friend in
> office, and his friend's friend; and many of his kindred,
> try, like Job's wife, to break his integrity: what strength
> of mind that patriot must possess who can withstand
> such forces! We apply these remarks *to no particular
> country under heaven*, but we think our readers will
> find little difficulty themselves in guessing our meaning.

But why, it may be asked, should so bold a tribune of
the people have left his readers to any guessing on such a
subject? If all this applied, and applied particularly, as is
plainly insinuated, to Upper Canada, why should not the
fact have been then and there openly asserted? And why
should not particulars have been given and names produced?
The hand that the week before had written down the future
chief justice of Upper Canada as "an ass" – "a vain, presuming, ignorant man" – and that on another page of this very
number of the *Advocate* was further to assail him as
"mercenary," "Mean of soul," and "the adversary of civil

and religious liberty," need not have hesitated to tell other men of their purchased silence, their base compliances, their corrupt compromises? Doubtless it was easier to frame a theory and leave the public to suppose that it was amply supported by facts. Where there is a predisposition to think evil, facts are really not required. One of the weaknesses of Mackenzie's character – imputed to him even by his best friends – was a proneness to suspicion. Add to this a disposition to judge both men and institutions by absolute rather than by practical, standards – not to speak of his natural love of agitation – and a key is found to much that destiny had in store for him and for the country through him.

The early numbers of the *Colonial Advocate* did not, as may be imagined, produce a favorable impression in all quarters, and a criticism of them by the editor of the official paper, the *Upper Canada Gazette*, drew forth a reply by Mr. Mackenzie, in which he went somewhat in detail into his personal and family history. He was particularly hurt by the accusation brought against him of "democracy and disloyalty." The doctrines he had advocated would bear, he declared, any inspection for they were of a truly British stamp. He had endeavoured to inculcate on all his readers "that godlike maxim of the illustrious British patriot, Charles James Fox," that "that government alone is strong that has the hearts of the people." Strange to say, Sir Francis Bond Head some thirteen years later, without quoting Charles James Fox or Mr. Mackenzie, uttered a sentiment very similar, but we shall come to that in good time. Continuing his defence Mackenzie says: "I have pointed out the neglect which successive governors, more or less ignorant of our wants, have been guilty of in regard to domestic improvements, and have delivered my opinion with the freedom of a Briton in Britain: is this treason?" He challenges his accuser to find any one who bears the name which from both his parents he had inherited, whether a relation of his or otherwise, whether of patrician or of plebeian birth, who had ever deserted, or proved disloyal to, his sovereign in the hour of danger. He proceeds to praise the people of Upper Canada:

It is a very great mistake to imagine that the farmers and country people in Upper Canada lack general knowledge. They are a thinking people, and I verily believe that not in an equal number of the people of any English county is there more general information diffused than in the Province of Upper Canada.

They are not to be "scoffed and mocked at by the satellites of government" with impunity. Going into family matters he tells how his paternal grandsire, Colin Mackenzie, had joined the Stuart standard in 1745 as a volunteer, while his maternal grandfather, also a Colin Mackenzie, "had the honour to bear a commission from the Prince, and served as an officer in the highland army. The article concludes with some details of his early life which have been given on an earlier page.

The editor of the *Colonial Advocate* was a busy man, but never too busy to take something else in hand if it had a tempting side to it. In the month of May 1824 the foundation was being prepared for a monument to General Brock on Queenston Heights, and the time had come to lay the foundation stone. So far as Mackenzie could learn no special arrangements had been made for this ceremony, and it seemed to him that he could not do better than attend to the matter himself. He accordingly drew up what he considered an appropriate record of the transaction, which he took and read to one of the commissioners for the erection of the monument. That gentleman, the Hon. Thomas Dickson, saw no objection to it, and Mackenzie did not think it necessary to consult the other one, the Hon. Thomas Clark. Originally there had been three commissioners, the third being the Colonel Nichol whose tragic death has been referred to. Another man might have been doubtful about proceeding without the sanction of the second commissioner, but Mackenzie was not a man for small hesitations. The place where others feared to tread had always an attraction for him. The next question, on which it does not appear that even Mr. Dickson was consulted, was as to what it would be proper to deposit with the record. The articles chosen were a copy of the first number of his own paper – that in which he had announced to the world his rather low estimate of the utility of Sir Peregrine Maitland as a governor – one copy each of the *Gazette* and the *Observer*, the first the official paper and the second favorable to the government, both published at York, and some coins. Then on the first of June, Mr. Mackenzie himself not being present, "brother

James Lapraik" laid the foundation stone with appropriate masonic ceremonies and duly sealed up therein Mackenzie's documents.

The Honourable Mr. Clark was not at all pleased with these proceedings and made some unpleasant remarks about Mackenzie and his paper. He pronounced the ceremonies "impertinent and officious," and referring to a statement in the published account to the effect that the documents had been placed in "wide-mouthed bottle," declared that the *Colonial Advocate* was "a wide-mouthed and scurrilous paper." And then, although some progress had been made with the stone work, the foundation stone, so well and duly laid by brother Lapraik was uncovered, the seal was broken, and the documents that were meant as a testimony to some distant posterity were not too respectfully removed.

An article which appeared in the *Colonial Advocate* of the eighth of July, 1824, written in view of the impending general election, affords a good illustration of Mackenzie's point of view and tone of thought:

> A perusal of the newspapers of these days as well as personal observation forces on me this conclusion that there is little dependence to be placed, as regards political principle, on those who are by way of distinction, styled gentlemen in this country; often inferior to the yeomanry in education, generally desirous of respect not for higher intellectual endowments, but on account of newly acquired wealth, a seat on the bench at quarter-sessions, or a commission in the militia or the like: this class are disliked by the farmers, and by them rarely trusted: they have no more resemblance to the English country gentleman of information and good breeding than a Canadian swamp has to a British city or Goose Creek to the Thames. Their manners are abrupt and often vulgar; their policy is to play the slave at York that, in their respective neighborhoods, they may the more safely act the tyrant.

The article concludes with the following appeal:

> Up, then, and be doing! Stir yourselves like men and strike at the roots of corruption in the persons of our late corrupt representatives. Send them to beg for the crumbs that fall from Sir Peregrine's table, but never

again trust your religion, your liberties, your peace of
mind, and indeed all you can and ought to love and
admire, to worthless beings who have no claim to your
favour, unless it be on account of their having made a
low bow, or given you a friendly shake of the hand
previous to an election day.

The excessive generality of these remarks can hardly fail to
strike the attentive reader, nor yet the fact that the appeal
is largely *ad invidiam*. There are some men who, not content
with scorning wealth and position for themselves, insist on
scorning all who do not share their scorn of these things.
Yet in every society there are individuals who while not
indifferent either to wealth or to position, yet made no
unworthy sacrifices to either. Mackenzie could not understand such persons, and could barely bring himself to believe
that they existed. He says as much indeed in this very
article: "How difficult it is for the mind to conceive the
existence of a person receiving profit and emolument, and
not being affected thereby." What he found difficult at this
time gradually became impossible to him; and, just as it did
so, the argument *ad invidiam* became more and more his
familiar and favorite mode of appeal to the public. That,
morally, it could not fail to be a hurtful one never seems to
have occurred to him.

No one can read the early numbers of his paper and not
feel that he had it much at heart to benefit the country; and
yet it is equally clear that he was betaking himself to
methods more adapted to promote strife and discord than
constitutional progress. Sometimes he is capable of a largeness of spirit that ill befits the extreme bitterness and
personality of his language on other occasions. The following
passage may be cited as an example:

When we were back amongst the poor people who were
suffering every hardship in the new townships from
poverty and bad roads, many of them desired us to be
as mild as possible in our comments upon the governor:
'That he was religious, humane, and peaceable, and if
his administration had hitherto produced little good to
the country, it may be it was not his fault, but the
fault of those about him who abused his confidence.'
Such an advice often repeated in such a quarter struck
us as singular, and we sighed to think that, if the

negative virtues can thus conciliate our population and rivet their affections, what such a power as is vested in our civil head might not achieve if he would study to promote the interests of mankind.

As yet we find no formulation in Mackenzie's writing of the principle of "responsible government."[5] On the contrary he throws the chief responsibility for the prosperity of the country on the shoulders of the lieutenant governor, not so much as hinting that a cabinet composed of members of the legislature could cope with that responsibility much better. He had the temperament which made it more natural for him to deal with individuals than with parties and with concrete facts than with abstract principles. It is a curious speculation what his career might have been if it had happened that the governor of the day had on the one hand gained his confidence and on the other treated him with confidence. What Mackenzie really wanted was *good* government, and he would much rather have had good government from a "civil head," to use his own term, than had, above all dishonest, government from the committee of a parliamentary majority. If we are to choose a father for "responsible government," or rather for the system which passes by that respectable designation, it must be, not William Lyon Mackenzie[6] but Robert Baldwin, a man anti-pathetic to Mackenzie in many ways.

This chapter may be advantageously brought to a close by a letter of Mackenzie's written about this time which came to light about three years ago. It is addressed to Mr. Charles Jones of Brockville, at that time a member of the assembly and later a member of the Legislative Council. It is written in a friendly tone in reply to some criticism by Mr. Jones of certain articles in the *Colonial Advocate*. These relations of friendship, or at least civility, between the two men were, unhappily of very brief continuance.

York, Decr. 1st, 1824

To Charles Jones Esq.,
Brockville

Sir,
I thank you for the plain manner in which you have pointed out what appear to you as the greatest defects

in the publication which I conduct. It accords so well
with my own view of propriety to speak what I think
that I derive pleasure from seeing others do likewise.
You seem to think I have formed an erroneous idea of
the Attorney General, and that acting on, or being
influenced by, that opinion, I do him injustice as a
public character. There is only one remark needed from
me in support of the opinion so freely given. The
Attorney General went to England as the accredited
agent of this Province, and he recommended, nay, I
am informed, he himself drew out a clause in the Union
Bill[7] making £500 value in property a necessary qualification in a member of the Assembly. For this one
action of his, even if I refrain from uniting to it his
advice to the English government to do away in part
with the dependence of the Executive or the colonial
House of Assembly in money matters, he deserves to
be pointed out as a dangerous person in that hour when
the interests of the people are required to be guarded
with peculiar and unceasing care gainst the encroach-
ment of rulers and crown officers, of which he is one.
. . . Such has been my view of the matter, and acting
thereon I have let my knowledge of Mr. Robinson's
humanity and forbearance as a crown officer when
going the circuit, his proverbial probity as a lawyer, his
high and unblemished character as a private gentleman,
lie in the shade, and have by argument advice and
satire, each in their turn, endeavoured to remind my
readers of Mr. Robinson when brought to the test, not
only in the last parliament, but in England as its (the
House's) organ. . . . You argue, if I aright understand
you, that I do not honour the judgment and penetration
of the members of the assembly by supposing him
capable of swaying their judgment to the loss of their
constituents. If you mean the last House I really cannot
bestow great praise upon them collectively. Able and
honest and independent members there were in that
House, but what could they achieve when overpowered
by the majorities amongst whom I so often counted
J.B.R. and that Hagerman whom, as some of the public
prints tell me, you once at least checked in warm but
not inappropriate language – language, Mr. Jones, that
endeared your name to many in Canada, language that

made not a few of those high spirits, whose approbation is worth thousands of grovelling souls, rejoice in your re-election to parliament. . . . Your idea and mine may be different on the scope of the word 'personalities.' If I meddle with none of Mr. Robinson's private affairs; if I do not disturb the sanctuary of his private friendships, his likings and dislikings, then I conceive I do him no injustice. Mr. Robinson as Attorney General, M.P., is fair game. Or if he is not you will have to show me my error in the £500 qualification that is with me the first test of his principles. . . .

This letter is written in a hurry and that hurry I cannot get the better of. The *Advocate* has still a great and unexampled circulation, but I am poorly paid; the agents in most places having little interest in the prompt payment of the accounts, and being often engaged in their own affairs to a degree sufficient to preclude much regard to mine, joined to the evils of an ill-regulated post-office, render my situation in a pecuniary point of view very irksome. I am not able to pay the necessary number of hands to get the paper out regularly. I often write half the paper, several dozen letters, read 100 newspapers, paste 900 directions on papers to their respective addresses and paste and tie up a hundred different mails to a hundred different agents in one week. If to this be added correcting the press, which I always had to do, making out and drawing accounts to those who owe me, you may suppose I repose not on a bed of roses. You have not, I hope, in reading thus far, got tired. I have done all this for a long time, and I shall do it for a still longer period if I can afford it. But never, never shall I, in public or in private, approve or laud for interest or private advantage conduct which I think not right. I have in the *Advocate* recommended religion; I have never, I think, admitted the usual immoral trash which fills newspapers to pollute its columns. It, the *Advocate*, is not to my mind. I would rather leave petty local politics, to go into the field of general and constitutional information at any time; but I am not an independent editor in every sense of the word; if I were, I would give you an *Advocate* every week regularly, as my time, now taken up in providing for the passing day, would be more my own, I would be better able to polish up those periods which you, and not you alone but many others, think a bar to the utility of the work as a colonial production. In conclusion I beg you will not be offended with my freedom. I believe you wish me success in my undertaking, or you would not have taken the pains you have done in writing to me. For this kindness be pleased again to accept my thanks, and believe me, Sir,

Yours obliged and very humble servant,
W. L. Mackenzie.

Mackenzie was at his best when he wrote this letter. No one can doubt the writer's sincerity. He means well. He is sincerely interested in the public welfare. He is outspoken and candid, yet withal moderate, in the utterance of his own opinions. *Si sic somper omnia*,[8] a happier career would have been his, and his name would never have been connected with an era of bloodshed, discord and hatred.

CHAPTER FOUR

THE CRITICISMS OF A JOURNALIST

If good intentions could have sufficed to make good government, Upper Canada could have been an uncommonly well governed country. Sir Peregrine Maitland was all that the people in the back country told Mackenzie and more, for he was a man of considerable perspicacity and judgment and of a strong sense of duty. Back of him was the Colonial office, brimful of good intentions: no one can read the despatches from that office without being convinced of the fact. It was fully recognized there that the policy pursued in the early days, particularly under President Russell and Lieutenant Governor Hunter, in the matter of land grants had been most injudicious, and it had been fully determined that such errors should not be repeated. Lands in future were only to be granted on condition of settlement and in proportion to the means possessed by the individual for bringing them under cultivation. "I am not sorry," writes Earl Bathurst on the twenty-fourth of July, 1821, with reference to a certain application,

> to have again an opportunity of distinctly expressing the opinion which I have always entertained that all grants of land at whatever period made ought to have been subjected to settlement duties, that the remission of these duties, whenever it has taken place, has been a violation of the spirit of His Majesty's instructions highly detrimental to the interests of the Province, and that whatever indulgence it might be proper in other respects to show to meritorious individuals receiving grants of land, it was essential that, on the point of settlement no relaxation whatever should take place.

The tone and spirit of this despatch are entirely characteristic of the general course of the correspondence emanating from the Colonial Office. Wrong views might prevail

there, contracted ideas, in some respects, as to the requirements of the country; but of indifference to the interests of
the colonists, or any desire to treat Upper Canada as a
field for selfish exploitation, it would be difficult for an
impartial investigator to discover a trace. Partisan writers
have made the name of "Downing Street" a by-word, but
Downing Street, whatever its failings might be, was a school
of honour and disinterestedness, and represented an influence which, while it lasted, tended to hold in check the
lower arts of political life. Undoubtedly it was a little slow
to see that the Canadian provinces would have to develop
to some extent on lines of their own, but it was not so
wedded to its own ideas as to be incapable of learning. On
the contrary it is easy to trace a steady enlargement of its
views keeping pace with the developing political life and
activity of the two provinces but particularly of Upper
Canada. An example of its impartiality as between parties
in the province is shown in a despatch of Bathurst's to
Maitland declining a request that the official gazette, part
of which was edited as a newspaper in the government
interest, should pass at a lower rate of postage than other
papers. Even were there no legal difficulties in the way, "I
am afraid," he said, "I should not be able to justify an
exemption of one newspaper for the purpose of promoting
its circulation in preference to any other." The colonial
secretary had no direct control of the post office, but, had
he approved of the request made, he might perhaps have
arranged the matter with the post master general.

The general election of July, 1824, was watched by
Mackenzie with exceeding interest[1] and his verdict – soon,
unfortunately, to be reversed – on the general result was
highly favorable. He described the new House, which met
on the eleventh of January, 1825, as being chiefly composed
of men who appeared to act from principle, and who were
indefatigable in the discharge of their duties.[2] This was high
praise, quite as high as any legislative body of our own
time is likely to merit, and yet the elections were held under
the auspices of a military governor of conservative leanings
aided by the terrible "compact." Owing to the growth of
population the new assembly contained forty-five members,
five more than the previous one. On the question of the
speakership there was no great manifestation of party feeling.
First Mr. Hamilton of Wentworth was proposed by his

colleague, Mr. Willson. Eighteen votes were given for him, but this not being a majority of the members present, Mr. Hamilton returned the compliment by proposing Mr. Willson, who receiving twenty-one votes was declared elected. Mackenzie in the *Colonial Advocate* was enthusiastic over the choice. "Instead," he said,

> of a lawyer, the first commoner in our land is a country farmer, and a member of a body of dissenting Christians whom the mitred priests of the *established* faith have looked down upon and discouraged from 1748 to this day. This day! 'tis a joyful day for Upper Canada, I had almost said for British America: the result of this election will gladden the heart and sweeten the cup of many a Canadian peasant in the midst of his toil; and the enlightened statesmen, as he silently watches the slow march of liberal principles, will hail the happy period when pure and undefiled religion shall be established on the ruins of priestcraft, when the sun of freedom shall arise and penetrate with his beams the darkest recesses of our endless forests.

The eloquence of these remarks is more conspicuous than their relevancy. A revised opinion of Mr. John Willson, whose election was to produce so splendid an illumination, will be forthcoming in due time.

Mr. Dent[3] comments on the incident as follows: "The reformers felt that they had achieved a triumph and were accordingly jubilant; but they soon found that the mere control of the assembly signified very little in the absence of executive responsibility." The reformers could not have been under any illusion in the matter as they were quite aware that the system referred to had never been introduced into either Upper or Lower Canada and that no request even for its introduction had ever been addressed either to the King or to the British parliament. What the reformers wanted was the leadership of some firm, clear-sighted man, well acquainted with public affairs and at once moderate and progressive in his views. For the lack of such a man, and perhaps of a spirit of union and discipline amongst themselves they wrangled with one another, as well as with the friends of the government, and did much less than they might have done to advance useful legislation.

Mackenzie published a paper after his own fashion and

greatly to please himself. What interested *him* most went into the paper first; what interested him less though it might reasonably have been supposed to interest the public more waited for a later turn, and often shared the fate of matter held over by not appearing at all. There is little use in searching the files of the *Colonial Advocate* for any connected account of the news of the day or for continuous comment thereon. The wind which swayed the keys of that organ blew as it listed, and no one could predict when it would swell in tempest, or when it would soothe the ear with a dying fall; though the readers of the paper were soon taught not to expect the latter mode too often. In November, 1824, Mackenzie removed the *Advocate* from Queenston to York, the number dated the 24th of that month being the first issued at the latter place. In a valedictory to the Queenston public he acknowledged that the paper had neither met his own expectations nor fulfilled the promises he had made in his first number. He speaks of the difficulties attending the publication of a newspaper in Upper Canada, and says that "there is not, as far as I can learn, one journal in the province, whether servile or independent in politics the proprietors of which can boast that it is a profitable concern in the mercantile sense of the word." The classification of all newspapers as either "servile" or "independent" is most characteristic, but why should any paper have put on the livery of servility, if it was not even pecuniarily profitable? One can imagine the enmity that would be created by the matter of course application of such a term to men who were playing the trade of journalism perhaps just as honestly as himself, but who had the misfortune not to share his political opinions.

As a kind of addendum to this article we have the following:

I think I shall be able to prove those men enemies to civil and religious liberty who cry out 'The people of Canada have enough to eat and to drink; what more can they desire?' The people of the Floridas had enough to eat and drink, yet they are now an integral part of the United States. The people of South America, as colonists of Spain, that weak and wicked government, had enough to eat and to drink, yet they are colonists no longer. The thirteen United States were not in a starving condition when they threw off their allegiance, yet they resisted what they believed to be oppression and resisted not in vain. Let it not therefore be supposed that, in Upper Canada, carelessness can long continue to pervade any department of the government without evil effects being produced. If liberty consists solely in abundance of animal food, then let the slaves in Virginia, that deceitful, because oppressed race, rejoice for they are free, . . . seeing that they have plenty to eat and drink, which in itself, by such doctrine, constitutes freedom!!!

It takes no less than three exclamation marks to express the writer's state of mind, but what does it all mean? It reads like an incitement to rebellion, and yet only three or four months before, he had been expatiating upon the absolute unthinkableness of a Mackenzie being guilty of rebellion. He did not know what was possible for *one* Mackenzie. We may infer from the passage that he was having some trouble in persuading the people of Upper Canada, who were enjoying a period of great prosperity, that their political condition was one of degradation. However he is only at the outset of his career of agitation and much can be done by perseverance.

The speech from the throne at the opening of the legislature (11th of January, 1825) adverted to the recent partial destruction by fire of the parliament buildings in which a quantity of important records had been destroyed; mentioned the fact that, since the legislature had last met, a considerable sum had been disbursed from the imperial treasury as aid to the sufferers in the late war; and conveyed the satisfactory information that, in accordance with the request of the late legislature, an amendment had been made in the charter of the East India company which would permit the importation of tea into Canada on more favorable terms; and further that the British import duty on Canadian wheat had been reduced. His excellency found it necessary to point out at the same time that the province was falling into debt and that measures ought to be adopted to restore the financial equilibrium. He stated that the King viewed with lively interest the efforts which the colony had directed to the improvement of its internal communications, and that "His Majesty's government was disposed to afford its co-operation in a manner that would materially facilitate the completion of those great works, projected by the commissioners for the improvement of our inland navigation." The speech concluded with the expression of a hope that there would be a continuance of unanimity in their proceedings and of mutual confidence between the government and the people.

Mackenzie could not have thought the speech of much importance as news or in any other point of view, for he did not find room for it in his issue of the thirteenth of the month; and when he published it a week later he gave, as an offset, three and a half columns of extracts from the message of governor De Witt Clinton to the legislature of the state of New York. Not till we come to the tenth of February is there anything like a review of what is going on in the legislature. So far he is entirely satisfied: There is, in fact, hardly a word of condemnation even for the writer's opponents. "We are nothing disappointed," he says, "in the high expectations we had formed of it (the new House) on knowing the names of its members; and it really gives us much pleasure to behold the ardour and constancy with which they discharge the sacred trust reposed in them by the people." A detail follows of a large amount of useful legislation in progress, and not the slightest hint is dropped that most, or even any of it, is likely to be blocked in the Legislative Council – a notable fact when we consider how constantly that chamber has been represented as the grave-yard of all progressive measures. Mackenzie must have been in a truly genial mood on that day for he continues: "There are several members in the House with whom we differ greatly in politics, yet to do them justice the greater part of them are indefatigable men of business, and what they do they seem to do from principle." "From principle," be it observed, not from "servility": if this tone could only have been preserved, if he could only have gone on believing in the possible integrity of political opponents, Upper Canada would have missed an exciting bit of history.

By this time, one regrets to notice, Mackenzie has fallen out with Mr. Charles Jones, M.P.P., his correspondent of the previous month of November. Mr. Jones had spoken of him, apparently in the House, as "impertinent" and "too contemptible to deserve notice." Mackenzie replies that when Mr. Jones's performances during the session come to be summed up they will probably be found "too contemptible to deserve notice." Looking back a number or two to see what can have been the cause of this sad estrangement, we see under date of 27th of January an article on the proceedings of the committee of the House charged with arranging for the reporting of the debates. In this article Mr. Jones, who was chairman of the committee, is spoken of as "dull Charlie Jones," and as a man "who talks nonsense by the hour." It is not impossible that Mr. Jones may have regarded these expressions as "impertinent." To be dull is not of course a crime, and in politics may sometimes be an advantage; and yet to be dubbed "dull Tom, Dick or Harry so and so" is apt to ruffle all but the most philosophic tempers. Henceforth there will be no civilities between Mr. Charles Jones and Mr. William Lyon Mackenzie.

The general election had brought forward and added to the House of Assembly some new men of considerable consequence. Marshall S. Bidwell has been already mentioned. Some years later Sir Francis Bond Head spoke of him as "an incurable American." Mackenzie himself would not have differed much with Sir Francis on this point, for at a later date he declared that Marshall Bidwell would at all times have preferred to see republican institutions established in Canada. However this may have been, the member for Lennox and Addington was destined to be a very useful member of the House of Assembly. His republicanism was a theory which he did not unnecessarily obtrude on the notice of his fellow-members; nor is there reason to believe that he would ever have approved of attempts to change the existing form of government otherwise than by constitutional means. No man in the House surpassed him in his grasp of legal and constitutional questions, and very few in this respect were his equals. His speeches were marked by keen argumentation and a certain quality of intellectual dignity. He was not a man adapted for popular leadership, for he had none of the arts or instincts of the demagogue; but he was a conscientious and capable legislator, and would have been an ornament to the bench of Upper Canada had he been raised to it as Lord Glenelg some years later desired. Peter Perry, Bidwell's colleague in the representation of Lennox and Addington, was a remarkable man in his way but one of quite different mould. Bidwell had been carefully educated and though as yet only in his twenty-sixth year, stood very high at the bar; Perry, a farmer and country store-keeper, had only received the scanty education obtainable at a country school. Bidwell was pre-eminently a student, a man of ideas; Perry a man of rude but powerful eloquence and strong common sense. Some years later a public writer very aptly called him "the unlettered Titan." That one constituency should have possessed two such men, and, possessing them, should have sent them to the legislature, does not speak badly for the times.

Another constituency, Middlesex, was also represented by two men who were in a manner complementary to one another, John Rolph and Captain John Matthews. The former is practically the hero of Mr. Dent's book *The Story of the Upper Canada Rebellion*, and naturally the author draws his character with some care. The following eulogy is perhaps not greatly over strained:

> Chief among his qualifications may be mentioned a comprehensive, subtle intellect, high scholastic and professional attainments, a style of eloquence which was at once ornate and logical, a noble and handsome countenance, a voice of silvery sweetness and great power or modulation, and an address at once impressive, dignified and ingratiating. His keenness of perception and his faculty for detecting the weak point in an argument were almost abnormal; while his power of subtle exposition had no rival among the Canadian public men of those times.[4]

We read further of "a dignity and even majesty in his presence that gave the world assurance of a strong man, while it at the same time effectually repelled unseemly familiarity." As we read we reflect. What is it to be "a strong man?" To have a vigorous and comprehensive intellect is to be strong – in intellect. To be tactful and watchful and calculating is to be strong – in the arts of defence, of self-protection; and yet all this does not quite come up to the idea which men in general have formed of a strong man. The poet Horace hit off that idea better in his "Justem et tenacem proposite virum,"[5] whose solid mind neither mob nor tyrant can shake. This was not John Rolph.

Mr. Dent himself tells us that there was a *per contra* to the eminent qualities he describes:

> Though he was a man of many friends, and was the repository of many familiar confidences, there was probably no human being – not even the wife of his bosom – who ever possessed John Rolph's entire confidence. There was about him no such thing as self-abandonment. This was not because he was devoid of natural passions or affections, or even of warm friendship; . . . but the quality of caution seems to have been preternaturally developed within his breast.

A man of that temper may approach the Rubicon, but he will not dare to cross it; or, to use a humble figure, he may look long and covetously over the hedge without bringing himself to steal the horse. He may play a dangerous game, but will always contrive that some one else shall take the greater risk. There is such a thing, we are told, as saving one's life – and losing it; and losing one's life – and saving it. The life that was supposed to be lost was only given, and given in return to the giver.

John Rolph was born in England in the year 1793, and was just two years older than Mackenzie, both having been born in the windy month of March. He came to Canada with his father Thomas Rolph shortly after the opening of the new century, and served as volunteer in the war of 1812. Returning to England he there pursued both legal and medical studies and qualified himself to practice both professions. Again he came out to Canada and settled in the county of Norfolk where in his double capacity of lawyer and doctor he found ample employment. Mackenzie was greatly impressed by his first speech in the legislature.

> We had anticipated much from him, and he surpassed our most sanguine expectations. . . . On this occasion the whole powers of his mind appeared as if suddenly called into action, and he burst upon his astonished and delighted auditory in all the graces of active eloquence. His impassioned energy of manner, and the modulated, well-marked cadences of his voice, gave double force to his periods, and justified the opinion which some of our most accomplished scholars had expressed, namely that his manner as a public speaker approaches nearer to the peculiar style of eloquence for which the English parliament is celebrated, than either to the oratory of the bar or that of the pulpit.[6]

A few words must be given to Rolph's colleague, John Matthews. This gentleman was a retired officer of the royal artillery, and had a pension founded on twenty-seven years service. The Captain was an Irishman by birth, and seems to have possessed in a marked degree the natural sociability of his countrymen. He was certainly "agin the government," but in this respect he differed from the great majority of his countrymen in Canada, whom some years hence, we shall find Mackenzie reproaching for their insensibility to the wrongs they were suffering, while governors commend them for their steady loyalty. He had none of the Zeus-like dignity which Mr. Dent ascribes to Rolph. He could be excessively familiar and gave himself away with a lavish hand. His radicalism was not always of the finest quality. "We liked," says Mackenzie,

> Captain Matthews' amendment to a police motion of Mr. Vankoughnett's very much. Instead of the courtly phrase in reply to the message 'we will give the earliest attention to your Excellency's gracious message,' the Captain moved that the House should substitute 'we will give due attention &c;' for, said he, 'we have many more important things to attend to at this time.'[7]

Captain Matthews had borne his Majesty's commission, and it hardly became him to place on the journals of the House a motion distinctly disrespectful to his Majesty's representative.

If Mackenzie had called his paper "the Kaleidoscope," the justification of the title would soon have become apparent. We have seen him praising the assembly in generous terms and not withholding words of appreciation even from political opponents. Six weeks later the skies have changed. He now doubts whether there are "three persons sitting in our House who would be allowed to detain even a thin House of the commons of England five minutes at a time." Not even three! And yet to go no further the House contained the attorney general, the mellifluous Rolph, and the logical Bidwell. There was surely no rampant Canadianism in this. A eulogy follows of the (still unreformed) British House of Commons, the writer holding that in it "all classes are in a manner represented by the ease with which wealth, and with wealth a seat in parliament, is obtained" – certainly an odd conceit for a radical reformer. Get wealth; with your wealth get a seat in parliament; and then you will make a good representative of the poor. But this is not all: we are told of the education which British members of parliament receive, partly from books, partly in the higher walks of business or the professions, and partly by travel. "Such men may be said to have seen something of the world. But what has the majority of our members seen? What do they know? Vastly little indeed." Such assertions would accord well with a plea for reducing the powers of the legislature, or, following Gourlay's idea, doing away with it altogether, but hardly with a demand for a great enlargement of its functions. Mackenzie did not care to ask himself what it accorded with: it was what he thought at the moment, and, it had to find utterance.

In the same article the legislative council is referred to derisively, but not a word is said about its obstructing the legislation of the assembly. In fact it would have been rather inconsistent, after representing the assembly in so poor a light, to complain that its measures were occasionally amended or even rejected. It is hard to say what the writer means exactly when he declares "I think that the parliament of this country will never do much good. If we receive liberal institutions it must be from England." This, be it remembered, was seven years before the Reform Bill. In any case, how could England endow the province with a more intelligent and better educated representative body? Even the gifted Mr. Rolph has by this time fallen several degrees in Mackenzie's opinion. "What light," he asks,

> has he thrown on the state of the province – what improvement has he proposed in the system of trial by jury – what has he done towards establishing the independence of the judges? He has sat on committees and combatted the attorney general noon and night, right or wrong. What does the province benefit by that?

And, strange to say, just as Rolph has declined in favor, Robinson has risen. The acknowledgment is very distinctly made:

> Mr. Robinson has risen in my estimation in regard to abilities from what I have seen of him during this session: indeed there are not a few of his remarks which I have listened to with pleasure; and some of the prop-

ositions he has made in parliament, the road bill
especially (with a few modifications) have my entire
approval.

So far then Robinson was ahead of Rolph who had done
little but wrangle. But there is more: "as a private gentleman,
as a lawyer, and as a law officer he stands as high in the
estimation of the country as any professional man in it."
Yet this is the very man who, only a few months before,
had been set down in the same paper as an ass, as flippant,
shallow, ignorant, covetous and self-seeking. The critic,
however, still distrusts Mr. Robinson's political principles
which, he says, "if not softened down, will forever unfit him
for a transatlantic popular assembly." He adds that Mr.
Robinson's career has been one of too unbroken prosperity
and that he needs the chastening hand of adversity to mellow
and humanize his character. There may have been a measure
of truth in the remark; in any case it was not unkindly
meant. His gracious mood extends to the lieutenant governor: "As to Sir Peregrine Maitland, when I fully consider
the difficulties of the crooked and perverse system with
which he, as a military man, has to contend, I really am
surprised that he is able to affect any good at all." Then
even he is doing *some* good in a very difficult position; and
as the attorney general is also doing some good, or trying to,
by introducing, and doing his best to carry, good measures;
and as Rolph is doing no good, but merely harassing the
attorney general, it is hard for a good reformer to know
what to think.

Mackenzie was well versed in the Scriptures and a golden
text occurred to him in this moment of perplexity:

I shall conclude these remarks with a quotation from
Scripture, which there are few senators and great men
who will repent having remembered when their mortal
pilgrimage draws towards a close: 'Be not weary in
well-doing, for in due time ye shall reap if ye faint not.'

Most truly did a certain wise young judge declare: "I can
easier teach twenty what were good to be done, than be
one of the twenty to follow mine own teachings." By no
possibility could Mackenzie have chosen a text which it was
more important that he himself – he of all men – should take
to heart. Could he have made it a principle not to be

departed from, the whole course of this narrative would have
been different.

Owing to financial difficulties the *Colonial Advocate* was
suspended from the sixteenth of June to the eighteenth of
December, 1825. The professed supporters of the paper were
treated by its proprietor to some home truths.

> People speak about the independence of some editors
> and the sycophancy of others. Now I will tell you a fact,
> my readers. It only wants a month of being a year
> since the *Colonial Advocate* commenced; thirty-four
> thousand full papers have been published in that time
> and there are five hundred persons who had the paper
> sent to them from the beginning, or from number four
> until now, who have not paid me one farthing, no *NOT
> ONE FARTHING*.

Does not such conduct, it is suggested, on the part of the
public explain the subserviency of other editors? Might they
not be almost forced, with "their families in want or an
execution hanging over their heads, to prostitute their talents
and their columns to the support of measures, however
insidious or unjust, which a venal or profligate magistracy
or legislature might desire to carry into effect?" Again mark
the extreme generality and purely hypothetical character of
the implied accusations. A few months before in reviewing
the session he had found nothing to call for specific approval
save certain measures introduced by, and certain sentiments
expressed by, the attorney general. If any "insidious or
unjust measures" were brought forward he drops no hint of
the fact; and yet, in the scheme of things which he had
formed in his own mind, and which he was doing, and will
continue to do his utmost to stamp on the consciousness of
the country – which he did in the end stamp on the consciousness of a portion of the country – there is a constant
strife in progress between the forces of Belial, represented
by the administration, and the forces of righteousness
represented mainly by himself.

Mackenzie does not talk cap in hand to his subscribers
whether paying or non-paying. "Some of my subscribers
complain of the irregularity of this journal." My uniform
answer of late has been: "If the principles of the paper and
its contents, when you get it, don't atone for its being sent
irregularly, please to withdraw your name from the list of

subscribers." A little later he writes: "Those who expect the
Advocate in future to assume the form of a regular newspaper had better send in their resignation immediately, as I
mean to continue it after the manner of the 'Sketch Book,'
that is at uncertain periods." Perhaps there may have been
in this a little of the courage of Juvenal's *vacuus viator*, for
Mackenzie was running very light at the time in the matter
of financial resources; but in the main no doubt it was pure
Mackenzie.

But more significant by far is the statement he makes
that his "sentiments on the science of government as applied
to Canada have gradually changed in many essential points."
What were these points? He does not say. Is it possible that
the hereditary instinct of personal loyalty, reinforced by a
growing respect for the persons actually charged with
carrying on the government in Upper Canada, was causing
him to doubt whether he had taken the right side in the
politics of the province? Certain it is that he makes the
approaching departure of Mr. Robinson for England the
occasion of some very friendly remarks. He thinks he was
shockingly used by the majority of the House – that is by
the reformers. There are his words:

> An apt illustration of the causes of Lord Castlereagh's
> last rash act might have been given in the treatment
> Mr. Robinson met with in the house of assembly. He
> was literally overwhelmed – his measures whether good
> or bad, whether the fruit of an enlightened mind or of
> an arbitrary and tyrannical disposition met one common
> fate.[8]

He describes one leading reformer, James Wilson of Prince
Edward county, as "a bull of Bashan bellowing and scream-
ing until he banished his antagonist argument and all from
the place." It is an accomplished bull that can both bellow
and scream, but Mr. Wilson appears to have been equal to
the double performance. "These honest patriots," he continues, "then contrived to drive dull care away on their way
home by a glass of port wine and an oyster supper – I know
where." One can understand Mr. Wilson's needing a little
lubrication for his throat after his severe vocal exercises, and
probably his comrades had more or less plausible reasons
for joining him.

Returning to Mr. Robinson Mackenzie says finally:

I would wish Mr. Robinson out of parliament or out of place. His former political career none condemned more boldly than I did. I have seen him this session without disguise. I have attentively watched his movements, his looks, his language and his actions, and I will confess it, I reproached myself with having used him at one time too harshly.

It is plain that the attorney general, the chief spokesman of the "family compact," if there was one, was the one man in the House who, closely studied, had made a distinctly good impression on the mind of this keen observer. There is a final good word too for the lieutenant governor who is said to have "noticed in very appropriate terms (in his prorogation speech) the want of attention which had been manifested to objects of importance to the public welfare." What an inversion of the legend that has come down to us – a military governor anxiously concerned for the public welfare, the popular chamber showing indifference to it! And it is William Lyon Mackenzie who puts things in that light. The mood did not last long, but it is not altogether an improbable conjecture that he was standing just then at the parting of the ways, and that a hand stretched out from the side that was ruling the province might have snatched him from a career of agitation and made of him a pillar of the state.

CHAPTER FIVE

SOME QUESTIONS OF THE DAY

It may possibly appear to some that an undue amount of attention has been bestowed on what, after all, are the mere preliminaries of William Lyon Mackenzie's career. It is, however, precisely at this period that his true original character can be studied to the best advantage. A year later he is committed beyond recall to a policy of unrelenting personal opposition to the Government of the Province; though a man of his mould will never wholly renounce his independence of opinion or action. In April 1825, as we have seen, he was sympathizing with Mr. Robinson and censuring the conduct of Mr. Rolph and his political associates. In May, 1826, he makes amends to Mr. Rolph: his harrying of the Attorney General was all right; he understood the gentleman better than he (Mackenzie) did. Robinson has shown "the cloven foot" – a favorite expression of Mackenzie's; in less picturesque language, he has continued to maintain tory principles. But even when Mackenzie was lauding him, his tory principles were expressly mentioned as a matter for regret, so why he should now be accused of showing the cloven foot is not easy to understand. A cloven foot is something one conceals when possible but Robinson gloried in his political principles.

It may be well here to pause in our narrative and glance at a few questions of the day which more or less agitated men's minds and of which large use was afterwards made by Mackenzie in his assaults upon the system of Government prevailing in Upper Canada.

The case of Robert Randal, though it scarcely rises to the dignity of a public question may, perhaps, be first mentioned, as it was one in which Mackenzie took a peculiar interest. We learn from Mr. Lindsey[1] that this gentleman was a Virginian by birth, settled at Chippewa on the Niagara river, whose acquaintance Mackenzie formed during his residence at Queenston. "Randal," Mr. Lindsey continues,

was a politician, and it is probable that his influence on Mackenzie first led him into politics. The proof is not clear; but Mrs. Mackenzie is of that opinion. Randal was a man who, with a keen eye to the future, selected land at different places where future towns are certain to spring up. He was entangled in law suits and in one way and another was cruelly victimized. His lawyers played him false, and the officers of the law conspired to defraud him. He became involved in pecuniary embarrassments, and was charged with perjury for swearing to a qualification which, based on a long list of properties, the ownership of some of which litigation had rendered doubtful, was declared to be bad. Mr. Mackenzie took his part and when Randal died he bequeathed a share of his property to the man who had been in some sort his protector. The connection produced its effect upon Mr. Mackenzie for life. Long before Randal's death, Mackenzie had embraced his quarrels and made them his own.

We are able to trace here a private influence which went to the framing of Mackenzie's opinions and the determining of his attitude to the Government of the Province. The statement that "the officers of the law conspired to defraud him" (Randal) is a very serious one, which perhaps hardly should have been made without a reference to names and sustaining facts. We certainly do not gather that impression from any specific statements made by Mr. Mackenzie himself in his own account of the matter given in the *Colonial Advocate*.[2] Randal, who originally possessed a valuable property on the Niagara River, including mills and water power, had sold or leased it to one Phelps. Prolonged litigation followed. Randal employed as his lawyer Mr. D'Arcy Boulton, then attorney general, upon whose elevation to the bench in 1824 the case passed into the hands of his son, John Henry Boulton, who had been made solicitor general, and who took as security for costs a mortgage on a property owned by Mr. Randal embracing a large portion of what is now the City of Ottawa, together with water power at the Chaudier Falls. The costs not being paid, Boulton foreclosed the mortgage and sold the property which only brought £300 over the amount of his bill. Randal complained that he had received no notice of the sale and that judgment had been prematurely rendered. On these grounds he brought action against Boulton, but without success. Mackenzie, in discussing the whole question, says that as to the merits of the original dispute with Phelps he would not hazard an opinion, and that he did not think any Court could get to the bottom of it unless specially constituted, *ad hoc*. As regards the case against Boulton, the trial of which he witnessed, he has less hesitation:

> It is very simple and although that gentleman defended his conduct with great spirit, and displayed a depth of research in the law of which we had thought him incapable, yet there was nothing in his address that impressed our mind in his favour, or in favour of the steps he had taken.[3]

With the manner in which the trial was concerned Mackenzie had no fault to find. "It must be allowed," he says, "that full scope was given both to the plaintiff's counsel (Mr. Rolph) and to the defendant to bring forward every pleading that would bear upon the matter at issue." The trial judges, Chief Justice Powell and Judge Campbell, impressed him most favorably. "The venerable appearance and hoary hairs added, in our estimation more dignity to the seat they occupied than would a throne of gold with a canopy of Tyrian purple." The chief justice seemed to understand the merits and demerits of the case perfectly. And as for Mr. Justice Campbell, were our life or our liberty in peril, we surely would not desire a more humane or upright judge. In all places, at all times, and by all parties we have heard his name mentioned with consideration respect and regard. Such is the reward a liberal soul desires in the decline of life to receive from a grateful country. Mr. Rolph, the plaintiff's counsel, is quoted as saying in the course of the trial: "Your lordships will always receive, and will always deserve, the commendation of all who come into your lordships' court." Mackenzie himself speaks of the chief justice as "the good old judge." Such were the men who sat upon the bench in what we are sometimes invited to regard as those tyrannous and benighted days.

The most burning issue of the time was that known as the Alien or Naturalization question. In the year 1824 the chief justice of England decided, in a case of inheritance that came before him, that no one who had continued to reside in the United States after the peace of 1783 could possess or transmit British citizenship, and that consequently no such person could inherit real estate in any part of the British Dominions. The unsettling effect of this judgment in Upper Canada, the population of which comprised so many persons who had left the United States after 1783 imagining that they carried British citizenship with them, and a large number of whom had acquired and bequeathed real property, may readily be conceived. Sir Peregrine Maitland saw at once the scope of the decision and lost no time in bringing the matter under the notice of the colonial secretary who replied by a despatch dated the twenty second of July, 1825, expressing the opinion that it would be desirable

> to confer by a legislative enactment the civil rights and privileges of British subjects upon such citizens of the United States as, being heretofore settled in Canada, are declared by the judgment of the courts of law in England and by the opinion of the law officers to be aliens.

The lieutenant governor was accordingly authorized to submit to the legislature of the province a bill for the relief of persons of that class who were then in the province, leaving the status of any who might afterwards arrive to be settled later. Any suitable bill which might be passed for that purpose might be assented to by the lieutenant governor in the King's name, notwithstanding the general instructions to reserve legislation of that character for the signification of his Majesty's pleasure.

The colonial secretary did not perceive, nor does any one at the moment appear to have perceived, that there were two sides to this matter – the strictly civil and the political – and that the legislation which might remedy one half of the difficulty was powerless to remedy the other half. In other words, while an act of the provincial legislature might confer property rights, it could not consistently with the terms of the Constitutional Act confer political rights. In the meantime, however, effect was given to Lord Bathurst's suggestion. An extract from his despatch was submitted to the legislature, and an act such as he had proposed was introduced into the legislative council and sent to the lower house.

Then trouble began. The majority of that house, the same majority which in the previous session had, according to Mackenzie, so needlessly, and almost wickedly,[4] baited the attorney general, burst into fury over what they regarded as the illiberal character of the council bill. The council had assumed, as it was obliged to do, the correctness of the decision given by the highest authority that the persons to whom their bill was to apply were not legally British subjects, and had proceeded to legislate them into that status on certain simple and easy conditions. The assembly, on the other hand, would have it that these persons *were* British subjects, and that any act passed should declare such to be the fact. They proposed therefore to amend the title of the bill and make it read "An Act to declare the law respecting the civil rights of certain inhabitants of this province." After the preamble in which reference was made to the doubts that had arisen respecting the status of these persons, they proposed to say:

> It is therefore expedient for the purpose of removing those doubts to declare the law upon the subject: be it therefore declared and enacted that . . . (definition of the class of persons) are and shall be considered to be and to have been to all intents and purposes and constructions whatsoever natural born British subjects, and to be, and to have been, entitled to all the rights and privileges and immunities of natural born British subjects.

The persons to whom the Act was to apply are described as follows:

> All persons who were born or whose fathers, or paternal grandfathers were born in the British Dominions, and who have since been resident in this province, notwithstanding that they resided in, or been citizens of, the said United States of America at or since the period when the independence of the United States was recognized and acknowledged by his Majesty's government.

This was sufficiently comprehensive, taking in as it did the latest new comer from the United States who could claim a grandfather born in colonial times, even though he himself, father and grandfather might all have fought for that country against Great Britain.

The bill amended in this slashing manner was sent back to the council. That dignified body looked at it with astonishment not unmixed with disdain. Still they so far repressed their feelings as to invite a conference with the assembly on the subject and meantime passed a resolution affirming that the intention of their bill was "to confer without reserve the rights, privileges and immunities of British citizens on all persons who have formerly been citizens of the United States and have never been naturalized by any act of the British parliament," and so "to carry into effect the gracious intentions of his Majesty." One of the chief objections made by the assembly to the council bill was that it did not, in terms, confer *political* rights. Strictly speaking the council could not properly have done this *in terms*, as civil rights alone were mentioned in Lord Bathurst's despatch, but their belief was that political rights would be included under civil rights, and the object of their resolution was to make this clear. A conference was held without any satisfactory result. A second was proposed and conferees were appointed by the assembly but, before anything was accomplished, the session was brought to a close on the thirtieth of January, 1826.

The assembly, foreseeing how things were likely to turn out, had, before the end of the session, memorialized the King describing the assumption on which the council bill was based as "a new and alarming construction of the law," and praying that measures might be adopted to prevent that construction from being enforced "to the prejudice, terror and disfranchisement of a large portion of the inhabitants of this province." Seeing that the British Government, its representative, the lieutenant-governor, and the legislative council were all doing their utmost to prevent the enforcement of the construction, this Macedonian cry for help has not a very genuine ring about it. The superior talents of Mr. Rolph, who again was dancing round the attorney general – but this time with Mackenzie's approval – were plainly at work in the business, as moreover the journals of the assembly show.

The legislature did not meet again till the fifth of December. Meantime attention had been called in England to the fact that the Constitutional Act strictly limited the franchise in Canada to three classes of persons, namely, (1) natural born subjects; (2) subjects naturalized by Act of the British

Parliament; and (3) persons who had become subjects by the cession of Canada to the British crown. If therefore the persons whose rights were in question were to be admitted legally to the franchise – *de facto* thousands of them had voted before, and had been doing so, and their fathers before them, for many years – one of two things had to be done: either the British Parliament must itself undertake the naturalization of these persons, or it must enlarge the powers of the provincial legislature. The latter was the course adopted. An Imperial Act was passed "to enable persons naturalized by any Act of the Assembly in Upper Canada to sit in either house of the provincial legislature and to vote for members of the Assembly." According to the instructions sent out from the colonial office any bill passed under the authority of this Act was to be reserved for his Majesty's approval, which it was stated would not be given to any Act purporting to be "declaratory to the general rule of law which appears to have been contended for." To place the view of the home government beyond doubt it was added that "subjects of the United States, whether born before or after the treaty of peace of 1783, are aliens and must in point of law be regarded in that character." The act must therefore provide for their taking the oath of allegiance. Those who had had their settled domicile in the country for seven years or more might then enter on their full privileges as citizens; those who had not been seven years in the province must complete that term before doing so.

Extracts from the despatch covering these points were laid before the legislature on the twelfth of December (1826), just one week after the opening of the session; but already, on the second day of the session, Rolph had moved for leave to bring in a bill to deal with the question. His bill proceeded to a second reading, but on the motion to go into committee an amendment was carried for its reference to a select committee. From this point onwards the attorney general seems to have had charge of the measure. A bill reported from the committee was read twice and referred to a committee of the whole house. On the following day progress was reported and the report was received by a vote of nineteen to one, the dissentient being the litigious Mr. Randal. A further report of progress was received by a vote of thirty-three to four; but when on the twenty-sixth of January the bill was reported, the division stood twenty to twenty, and Mr. Speaker Willson adding his vote to the nays the report was rejected. The committee resumed and amended their report but with no better result. A further amendment having been made in committee the report was at last received by a vote of twenty-one to nineteen; and by a vote of twenty-two to eighteen the bill was ordered to be engrossed and read a third time on the twenty-ninth of the month. The third reading was carried, but on the motion that "the bill do now pass" the vote again stood nineteen to nineteen when the casting vote of the Speaker threw it out.

Then an extraordinary thing happened. The party that had wrecked the bill suddenly repented of what they had done and Rolph, seconded by Bidwell, moved that it be again placed on the order of the day and that the rule of the house which forbade this be suspended for the purpose. The motion was entirely irregular and was opposed by those who were supporting the bill. It carried however. Having been recommitted the bill was reported without amendment and lost on the question of receiving the report. A second recommittal was followed by the same result, but on a third the report was received by a vote of nineteen to eighteen. On the fifth of February the third reading was carried by twenty-two to nineteen. The title of the bill as passed was "An Act to provide for the naturalization of such persons residing in this province at the time therein mentioned as may not now be entitled by law to be regarded as natural-born subjects of his Majesty." The legislative council passed it without amendment, and Sir Peregrine, in accordance with his later instructions, sent it home for his Majesty's approval. That approval, as we shall see, was not given – the end of the controversy was not yet.

The contention in the House of Assembly over this matter was in part but not wholly factitious; it represented in fact no small agitation of feeling existing throughout the country. Many of those to whom the remedial or relieving Act was intended to apply had been in the country, and taken a large part in its business and politics, during very many years without ever suspecting that their British citizenship could be called in question. Some had fought bravely in the war of 1812, and received direct from the crown grants of lands for their services. Some had filled various public offices; some had sat in the provincial legislature; some were

sitting in it at the very time; and many, in connection with
their public employments, had been called upon to take, and
had taken, the oath of allegiance. There was a widespread
though not universal feeling amongst those classes affected
that some larger and simpler means should be found of
removing whatever cloud technically might rest upon their
British citizenship than any that had yet been put forward.
It was consequently decided to petition the House of Commons asking for consideration of their case. This petition,
in which it was alleged that the Act passed did not truly
represent the views of the House of Assembly, was by the
advice of Mr. Mackenzie entrusted to Robert Randal, who
proceeded with it to England, and had more than one
interview with the colonial secretary. He came at an auspi-
cious moment. The too-short-lived administration of Mr.
Canning had just replaced the too long-lived one of Lord
Liverpool, and the formal and rigid Bathurst had made
room in the colonial office for the almost too sweetly
reasonable Goderich. After weighing carefully all the information within his reach the new secretary came to the
conclusion that, if things had gone wrong – and it seemed
to him that, to some extent, they had gone wrong – in Upper
Canada, the responsibility really rested with the Home
government. He recognized in the amplest manner that Sir
Peregrine Maitland had simply obeyed his instructions, and
that the bill which the legislature after much struggle had
passed, but which he had made up his mind not to recommend for approval, was precisely the kind of bill which
those instructions called for. In these circumstances he
simply took it upon himself to issue other instructions and
to invite legislation of a different character.

These instructions were contained in a despatch to Sir
Peregrine Maitland dated the tenth of July, 1827. "I cannot
too distinctly acknowledge," Lord Goderich says,

> that your Excellency and the Legislative Council and
> Assembly are not responsible for any misconception
> which may have been entertained on this subject. The
> bills which you have transmitted are in general framed
> in conformity with the instructions you have received,
> or deviate from those instructions only on the side of
> indulgence towards the parties whom it was proposed to
> relieve.

Proceeding to outline the bill which he now recommended should be passed, he said that it should provide for the immediate admission to the privilege of English birth "without any qualification or condition" of all such persons as had received grants of land from the provincial government, or who had held any public office in the Province, or who had at any time been admitted to take the oath of allegiance, or who had had their settled place of abode in the Province before 1820 and were still resident there. If any of these persons had not taken the oath of allegiance they should be required to do so. In regard to others who desired citizenship they should (1) complete seven years residence in the province, (2) take the oath of allegiance, and (3) register their names in some public office. The bill was not to embody any requirement for the renunciation of any allegiance or supposed allegiance to any foreign state; that matter was to be left to the law of nations. Lastly it was to be retrospective only, as the British Parliament would probably take up the question of the future arrangements for naturalization.

The provincial parliament met on Tuesday the fifteenth of January 1828, and great was the triumph of Rolph, Bidwell, Matthews and their associates in the Assembly when, on the twenty-third of that month, the lieutenant governor laid this despatch before the House. On the fourth of February they procured the passage after two amendments had been voted down of a resolution affirming "that the thanks to this House are due to his Majesty for so favourably regarding the interests of his people in this province upon their civil and political rights." The address to the King founded on this resolution, took a wider sweep, for it thanked his Majesty for having withheld his assent to the bills[5] "lately transmitted to your Majesty upon a subject deeply affecting the civil and political rights of your Canadian people." Motions were made objecting to this enlargement but without avail. The thanks to the King were meant of course as a censure on his Excellency, as well as a song of triumph over the attorney general, by whom, according to Mackenzie, they had been completely out-generalled in the preceding session.[6] It needed only a small part of the perspicacity of Sir Peregrine Maitland to see the point; but it required just a little more good temper than he possessed to conceal the fact. And so it was that when a deputation

from the house of assembly waited upon him to place the
address in his hands for transmission he testily observed:
"The instructions of which you now so warmly approve do
but suggest a measure which, in whatever form proposed,
was rejected by the House of Assembly in the second session
of this parliament in the desire to obtain a declaratory law."
How much better it would have been, seeing that his own
action in the matter had been so fully and precisely approved
by the home government, if he could have contented himself
with goodnaturedly congratulating the assembly on the
hopeful condition of a long debated question. As it was this
little outburst on his part simply gave an opportunity to
his enemies to pass further annoying resolutions – an opportunity of which they fully availed themselves. Not only so,
but they carried an address to the King, the terms of which
were far from agreeable to Sir Peregrine whose duty it was
to forward it. "Permit us," they said,

> most gracious sovereign, humbly to beg your Majesty
> to put the most favourable construction upon the con-
> duct of your faithful commons, and notwithstanding any
> misrepresentations which may be transmitted to the
> prejudice of the people in this province or of their
> representatives, we humbly beg leave to offer our
> assurance that we shall not cease to repose, as we have
> full reason to do, every confidence in the exalted justice
> of your Majesty and your Majesty's government.[7]

Sir Peregrine met this rude attack with becoming dignity.
"I have ever had," he said to the members who brought him
the document, "too much reason to repose with confidence
in the candour and good sense of the great mass of the
people to apprehend any injurious effect from the attempt
to excite a groundless suspicion that they are subject to be
misrepresented by me to their sovereign."

These bickerings did not, however, impede the settlement
of the main question. A bill was passed in the assembly and
sent to the council early in February. On the twenty-sixth
of the same month it was returned amended, accompanied
by the report of the special committee to which it had been
referred. That document the assembly ordered to be entered
in its journals, and no one reading it can fail to be favorably
impressed both by the temper and by the ability with which
the whole subject is discussed. The amendments were

accepted, and on the fourth of March his excellency came down to the House to receive the bill at the hands of the Speaker. Having been reserved in accordance with instructions for the consideration of his Majesty it was approved by the King in Council on the seventh of May following (1828), and became law by proclamation.

In the same session in which the Naturalization bill was so violently debated, the assembly adopted an address to the King praying that Chief Justice Campbell might not be allowed to sit as a member of the executive council. It was just about fifteen months since Sir Peregrine had sent to the House (in the opening of the second session) the colonial secretary's reply to a former request on the same subject. "I have received his Majesty's commands," wrote Lord Bathurst at that time,

> to acquaint you that it is highly expedient that the governor should have the advice and assistance of the first law authority of the province for his guidance in the administration of his government; that the greatest advantage has been derived throughout the colonies from this assistance, and that it does not appear that there is anything peculiar in the state of the province of Upper Canada which should make it advisable that this system should be changed.

Sir Peregrine of course acknowledges the address and promises to transmit it, but observes in his delicate fashion that he is "not yet enabled to explain what peculiarity in the present state of this province you allude to as inducing you to desire the change which you solicit." What the British government had in view was to surround the lieutenant-governor with competent and honourable advisers, and Chief Justice Campbell was the man upon whom Mr. Mackenzie had pronounced so high a eulogium. Still, in the following year the assembly had their way, for Mr. Campbell retired from the bench and his successor, Mr. J. B. Robinson was not called to the executive council though in accordance with a usage which had prevailed since the constitution of the province, he assumed, as chief justice, the position of Speaker of the legislative council.

Much time was occupied during the session of 1828 with the petition of one William Forsyth of Niagara Falls, who complained of having been violently dispossessed by order

of the lieutenant-governor of a certain piece of land which
he had occupied. There was little in the circumstances of
the case to excite sympathy for the complainant; on the
other hand they furnished passable material for political
agitation. Forsyth was an hotel-keeper at Niagara Falls, his
hotel being situated close to the cataract. Not being content
with the amount of business which so favorable a location
naturally brought him, he sought to render the public further
tributary to his prosperity by enclosing with his own property
a portion of the highway, so that any one who wished to
get the best view of the Falls had to get it from his premises.
The trespass on the public domain was so obvious and so
impudent that Sir Peregrine Maitland on being appealed to
did not think of advising an action at law, but gave instructions to Captain Philpotts[8] of the Royal Engineers to demand
the instant removal of the fence forming the enclosure, and
in case of non-compliance, to have it removed by his men.
Captain Philpotts carried out the order; called twice upon
Forsyth to remove the fence; and having received two
refusals set his men to work on the job which was very
quickly and neatly accomplished. The fence having again
been put up by Forsyth it was again removed in a similar
manner. This was the foundation of the complaint made to
the assembly and of certain actions brought against Captain
Philpotts and the Sheriff of the Niagara district. The actions
were quickly disposed of, as a counter suit for trespass
brought by the attorney general against Forsyth was
sustained.

Not so quickly disposed of, however, was the petition to
the assembly in which excellent possibilities of annoyance
for the administration were plainly discernible. Amongst the
witnesses whom the House wished to examine in reference
to the matter were Col. Nathaniel Coffin, adjutant general
of militia, and Col. James Givens, superintendent of Indian
affairs. Both were summoned and both refused to attend.
The Speaker's warrants for their arrest were placed in the
hands of Sergeant at Arms, David McNabb,[9] who reported:

In obedience to the warrants of the Honourable the
Speaker I proceeded to the house of Nathaniel Coffin,
Esq., for the purpose of taking him into custody. I
found his doors fastened, and was told by him and
James Givens, Esq., who was in the house with him,

that they would not be arrested unless the house was broken open and they were forcibly taken, and that if they were so arrested they would prosecute the Speaker and the Sergeant at Arms.

Later in the day, however, the officer announced that he had his prisoners at the bar, upon which the resolution of the House for their arrest was read to them and they were called upon for their defence. Givens stated that he had felt it necessary to ask permission of the major general commanding, and after some delay had received an answer refusing permission. Coffin had applied to the lieutenant-governor for leave to attend and had received from his Excellency's secretary an answer in these terms: "I am commanded to acquaint you that his Excellency cannot give the permission desired by you, not knowing what are the matters of which he (Forsyth) complains, or what are the facts in regard to which it is desired to interrogate you." On the motion of Rolph, seconded by Bidwell, the two gentlemen, notwithstanding the high authority on which each had relied, were committed to gaol on plain John Willson's warrant. As the House was prorogued three days later they did not languish long in confinement.

Sir Peregrine, it must be admitted, did not act in this matter with the best judgment, and his conduct was not approved by the colonial secretary, Sir George Murray, though he was not aware of the fact till after he had returned to England, the disapproval having been conveyed in a despatch to his successor Sir John Colborne. The house of assembly was wanting in courtesy to him in not informing him that they required to examine two officers in close official relation to himself and indicating the proposed scope of their enquiries. On the other hand he would have done well to overlook the omission and show an interest in supporting the authority of the popular branch of the legislature. A few coals of fire might have had a good effect. The session of 1828 in which the Naturalization bill was passed and the Forsyth case agitated was really very full of incident. An extremely interesting matter was taken up in the petition of Buckly Waters and 5696 others, who complained of a letter accompanied by an "ecclesiastical chart" which the Rev. Dr. Strachan had in the month of May 1827 addressed to Mr. Wilmot Horton, under secretary of state for the colonies. It was alleged that the energetic divine, not content with making the strongest possible case for his own church, and even stretching the facts a little with that laudable object, had unjustifiably disparaged other religious denominations carrying on religious work in the province. "The teachers of the different denominations," he had said,

> with the exception of the two ministers of the church of Scotland, four Congregationalists, and a respectable English missionary of a Wesleyan Methodist meeting at Kingston, are for the most part from the United States, where they gather their knowledge and form their sentiments. Indeed the Methodist teachers are subject to the orders of the conference of the United States of America; and it is manifest that the colonial government neither has, nor can have, any other control over them, or prevent them from gradually rendering a large portion of the population by their influence and instructions hostile to our institutions, both civil and religious, than by increasing the number of the established clergy.

Of the English church an encouraging picture is drawn:

> The people are coming forward in all directions offering to assist in building churches. . . . The tendency of the population is towards the Church of England, and nothing but the want of a moderate support prevents her from spreading over the whole province.

These were, to say the least, contentious statements, and a special committee of the House was entrusted with the duty of taking evidence with respect to them. Many witnesses were examined and the report of the committee throws an interesting light on the state of opinion and feeling in the province at the time. One passage is as follows:

> The insinuation in the letter against the Methodist clergymen the Committee have noticed with peculiar regret. To the disinterested and indefatigable exertions of these pious men the province owes much. At an early period of its history, when it was thinly settled, and its inhabitants were scattered through-out the wilderness and destitute of all other means of religious instruction, these ministers of the gospel, animated by Christian zeal

and benevolence, at the sacrifice of health and interest and comfort, carried among the people the blessings and consolations of our holy religion. Their influence and instruction, far from having (as is represented in the letter) a tendency hostile to our institutions, have been conducive in a degree that cannot easily be estimated to the reformation of their hearers from licentiousness and the diffusion of correct morals, the foundation of all true loyalty and social order.

The Rev. Dr. Strachan appeared himself before the committee. "Do you think," he was asked, "that the clerical labours of clergymen of your church would have a greater tendency to attach the people to our government than those of clergymen of other denominations equally devout and religious?" "I do," was the answer; but when asked on what grounds he thought that would be the case, all he would say was, "That is my opinion; I do not choose to give the grounds of it; they are various." Why the reverend doctor preferred to hide *in petto*[10] the reasons for his opinions upon a matter of much public interest, instead of seizing the opportunity to show of how solid and cogent a character they were, is a question in regard to which we are reduced to conjecture, and which some may answer by casting doubt upon the reasons.

Having received the report of its committee, the House adopted an address to his Majesty, the division on adoption standing twenty two to eight. "We have seen," they said,

> with equal surprise and regret a letter and ecclesiastical chart dated sixteenth May, 1827, addressed by the honourable and venerable Dr. Strachan archdeacon of York, a member of your Majesty's legislative and executive councils of this Province, to the Rt. Honourable R. J. Wilmot Horton at that time under secretary of state for the colonies, . . . as they are inaccurate in some important respects, and are calculated to lead your Majesty's government into serious error. We beg leave to inform your Majesty that of your Majesty's subjects in this province only a small proportion are members of the Church of England, that there is *not* any peculiar tendency to that church among the people, and that nothing could cause more alarm and grief in their minds than the apprehension that there was a design on

the part of your Majesty's government to establish, as a part of the state, one or more church or denomination of churches in this province with rights and endowments not granted to your Majesty's subjects in general of other denominations, who are equally conscientious and deserving, and equally loyal and attached to your Majesty's person and government. . . . We humbly beg leave to assure your Majesty that the insinuations in the letter against the Methodist preachers in this province do much injustice to a body of pious and deserving men who justly enjoy the confidence and are the spiritual instructors of a large portion of your Majesty's subjects in this province. We are convinced that the tendency of their influence and instruction is not hostile to our institutions, but on the contrary is eminently favourable to religion and morality, that their labours are calculated to make their people better men and better subjects, and have already produced in this province the happiest effects.

Another enquiry of much interest was that instituted upon the petition of Robert Addison and others, who complained of the operation of the wild lands assessment Acts. What clearly appears from the petition is that certain individuals were in possession of large tracts of unimproved lands that they could not do anything with, and that they greatly begrudged paying the assessment that was being levied under laws recently passed. One reason given for their not being able to sell their lands was that the Canada Company was offering lands on more favorable terms, or at least under more favorable conditions. In the same sentence of the petition the Canada Company is spoken of as "holding a vast monopoly of land," and the statement is made that for lack of purchasers the petitioners are entirely unable to sell their lands. It is a singular monopoly that leaves in the hands of others far larger quantities than they can possibly find a market for of the very commodity that the so-called monopoly holds. What the Canada Company had was capital, which enabled them not only to purchase land but to improve it, or by means of roads to render it accessible. The destruction of the poor has at all times been their poverty, and this was precisely a case in point. Some of these lands were free grants which the holders were vainly trying to turn into money; some were lands which had originally been free grant lands, but which had been bought for speculative purposes, with the effect in many cases of locking up most of what little capital the purchasers possessed. The problem with which many in Canada were grappling was how to turn an indefinite amount of wilderness into money in advance of such an increase of population as alone could give it value. Dr. W. W. Baldwin, as a very extensive land holder, was one of those who were most strongly opposed to assessment. Examined before the Committee he said that he had frequently seen excellent land put up at sheriff's sale, and not an offer made at all for it. "Land," he added,

> may be called unproductive when its owner derives no advantage whatever from it. It is so unproductive because it is uncultivated, and it is uncultivated because there is not sufficient population in the province to bring the uncultivated lands into requisition for occupancy; and this defect of population is occasioned first by reason of active obstacles thrown in the way of its increase by the mistaken measures of government (what these mistaken measures were the committee lost an excellent opportunity of enquiring); and, secondly and mainly, by the effects of the vast disproportion between the population, however prosperous we may view its increase, and the vast regions to be occupied and cultivated.

His conclusion was that "it is in vain that the government will attempt by the pressure of taxation to compel the owner of waste land to make it productive; time alone will effect the necessary proportion of things and we must await it."

In a supplementary answer this witness stated that he "did hope that the royal dissent would have stayed the measure." Dr. Baldwin, according to the opinion of Sir Francis B. Head, expressed a few years later, was a stronger radical than his son Robert, yet he was evidently prepared to believe that the home government might sometimes know better what was good for the country than its own legislature. The doctor gave some examples of land sales from the records of his own law office. One man had sold 200 acres in Douro for a cow. Another sold his location ticket for an equal amount of land in the same township for the casting of plough irons. A third offered in vain 1400 acres in Hungerford for $300, and so on. On the other hand it was testified that land in the best situation, near Kingston and York, was worth much over ten dollars an acre.

Almost the last act of the last session of the ninth parliament was to pass a resolution in connection with the case of Captain Matthews – a case in which the authorities, civil and military, of the time do not appear to any great advantage. The jovial captain, rather reckless in speech and not always discreet in action, has been mentioned before. Possibly had he not made for himself a certain reputation for these qualities what actually happened would not have happened – there is no knowing. Certain it is that a man is apt to be judged not so much by a single action – unless it be one of a very definite and critical character – as by his general course of conduct. However that may be the facts were as follows. There was revelry by night in Upper Canada's capital on the thirty-first of December 1825. A company of American players had been performing in town for a few evenings, with but indifferent success in a pecuniary point of view, and now the weather and roads were such that they could not get away. A few members of parliament and others bought tickets for a benefit to be given to them on that night. Party lines on this occasion seemed to be obliterated, or, to say the least, dimmed, for the subscribers were about half and half on either side of politics. Hilarity prevailed, not unassisted by the god under whose spell even the virtue of the severe Cato used to grow a bit warm. After the regular performance songs were called for. "God save the King" was sung and played with honours. Then Captain Matthews, always jocund and amiable – on this occasion particularly so – called for "Hail Columbia." The band, strange to say, could not play it. Then the Captain asked for "Yankee Doodle," which the band did play; and, as the first note was struck, he called out "Hats off!" His manner was festive; the whole audience was more or less festive, for there was not much of the year left to be happy in; but only malice could see any sinister significance in his action. Yet it was represented by some one to the military authorities that he had in a "riotous and outrageous" manner, called for foreign national airs, and demanded that hats should be removed while they were being rendered. He was summoned to Quebec to answer to the charge before the Earl of Dalhousie as commander of the forces, and from Quebec he was sent to England. His pension was stopped, but later was restored. Mr. Kingsford states that he never returned to Canada and that "by all accounts he did not long survive the event."[11] The records of the British army give the date of his death as the twentieth of August 1832. The proceedings taken against this harmless, if rather boisterous and indiscreet, gentleman produced a bad effect in Upper Canada. The committee of the legislature which investigated his case delivered their verdict in terms which perhaps betray a little of the rancour they attribute to the Captain's accusers. "There is no ground," they said, "for the charges which have been preferred against Captain Matthews, the malignity and falsity of which they believe to have derived their origin and support from political hostility towards him."

All the matters referred to in this chapter were at different times keenly taken up by Mackenzie, and for years afterwards furnished texts for attacks upon the administration and its supporters.

CHAPTER SIX

THE GERM OF THE REBELLION

After six months' suspension of animation the *Colonial Advocate* woke to life on the eighth of December, 1825. In the interval Mackenzie had had time to orient himself anew. The words of appreciation and sympathy which he had bestowed in the early part of the year on the Lieutenant Governor and the Attorney General had caused some of his friends to enquire whither he was drifting. He felt it necessary in resuming publication to set all such doubts at rest. "I owe it to myself," he declared,

> to say that from no part of my public or private conduct hitherto was there any just grounds for an inference that I had abandoned, or would desert, those glorious principles of whiggism which have animated millions of my fellow-creatures to prefer (as Lord Chatham expressed himself) poverty with liberty to gilded chains with slavery.

However suitably Lord Chatham may have used these words, they certainly had no application to Upper Canada at this or at any other time. There was no alternative there between poverty and slavery: the country was one in which the hand of the diligent in any well chosen industry made rich without regard to the political opinions which the owner of the land might hold or profess. Mackenzie, who had a real talent for journalism, might have made a fair profit out of his paper if he had not given away so many copies absolutely free, and above all if his liberty-loving subscribers had not defaulted to so shocking an extent in their subscriptions. The penalty sadly attaching to a great profession and appearance of disinterestedness is that people are apt to say "Oh, that man doesn't want money – he is heart and soul in the cause."

Political ideas were crude in those days: men had not had the training which responsible government bestows. Mackenzie gives us many an illustration of this. He says, for example, that he would like to have a share of the government advertisements in proportion to the circulation of his paper. In England, he points out, "advertising is done for the sake of giving general information and not as elsewhere for party purposes." His eye had not dipt into the future, otherwise he would have seen that two full generations after the death and burial of what he called "the family compact," the use of government advertising for party purposes was one of the most consecrated parts of the political system of the time, so much so that it had practically ceased to be regarded as an abuse in any sense. He lived, however, to have a foretaste of that system and to express his opinion of it.

The state of affairs in the province, Mackenzie proceeds to say, is essentially the same as when he last wrote: "The colonial system is triumphant; we have it in all its manifold beauties, in its meridian splendour – it is anything, everything, or nothing at all, changing from shade to shade like the chameleon – varying in hue and colour like the rainbow." He complains of vexatious changes, made by the home government in the customs regulations, and censures the provincial legislature for "voting away the contents of their country's coffers to clerks and officers for extra salaries even by ladlefuls." The legislative council is declared to be "rare and curious in its constitution beyond the power of man to describe." As to the lieutenant governor, he is "so very noble, just and magnanimous that we fervently hope his merits will be seen and valued at home, and that they will soon send for him back again." The phraseology is worth nothing. The legislative council is "rare and curious," but it is not at this time accused of being hostile to all sound and progressive legislation; and this is significant because Mackenzie was not a man to content himself with airy and decorative words if an important opinion was calling for expression. For Sir Peregrine Maitland it is plain that he entertained a feeling of personal respect, though he regarded him as unsuited to his position.

Many of the opinions expressed in the first number of the *Advocate* are re-stated. "The British Empire is the greatest and wisest the world has ever seen; but, as Canadians cannot be directly represented in it, they should have a larger amount of legislative freedom, particularly in commercial matters."

In this certainly there was sound sense. The editor is more strongly opposed than ever to a "political church establishment," which he spoke of as "that black and dark shadow to a free country." The union of all the British North American colonies is again recommended. Under the present system he sees "no end to the disputes which prevent the colonial legislature from giving that attention to local improvements which their importance demands." As things were it was impossible, he thought, that there should be mutual confidence between the assembly and the administration. But there had been such confidence in the very parliament that had preceded this one, and because there was confidence Mackenzie accused its members, bodily, of servility, sycophancy and corruption. Then when a house of a different complexion was elected he saw champions of reform like Rolph opposing all measures good or bad which the administration was supposed to favor. The plain inference would seem to be that the spirit of faction was what the province had most to dread.

Mackenzie however at this time had a great admiration for Rolph. He considered his "three hour speeches a great bore," but he came valiantly to his defence against an attack made upon him by Mr. Jonas Jones. That gentleman, who was not remarkable for the mildness either of his language or his manner, had said that Rolph had "a vile democratic heart and ought to be sent out of the country." Mackenzie affirmed on the contrary that Rolph was

> One of the most humane and amiable of Englishmen; a man who, to our certain knowledge, is loved and esteemed among his extensive circle of acquaintance beyond many; a man who employs three fourths of his valuable time in going about to heal the sick, clothe the poor, and speak comfort to the mind of the distressed; a man who would divide the last guinea he had with the first object of charity he met on the highway.[1]

The portrait of Mr. Jonas Jones is painted in less attractive colours. He is contrasted unfavorably with "the beasts of the field," for they fulfill the purposes of a beneficent Creator; likewise with "the birds of the air (which) sing the praises of Him who clothes them with a beautiful and varied plumage;" while Jones, by "giving the rein to his unruly and ungovernable passions, becomes, as it were, an unsightly blot in the midst of the fair volume of creation." A further criticism of Jones is that he has "a most forbidding countenance." He must have been a man of some facial versatility, for in the end of the article it is admitted that "when he pleases, he can assume a mild and amiable exterior."

The tendency of Mackenzie's mind was strongly didactic. He loved to give lessons alike to friends and foes, and he seized the opportunity of the approaching departure of Dr. Strachan for England to lecture him on the impropriety of deserting his flock. A portion of this lay sermon to a cleric may be quoted:

> Read Paul's epistles to Timothy and Titus, doctor, and then leave your congregation if you dare. Rest assured that the day will come when it will yield you infinitely more consolation if you are able to call to mind that you calmed with the words of everlasting truth the troubled conscience of some poor perishing sinner than that you was (*sic*) the favourite and prime minister of all the Lieutenant Governors on earth. . . . If you do go to London, and if you do attempt to bolster up a system of government more fit for Russians than Britons, you have good reason to fear that you will become the scoff and derision, the by-word and reproach of those for whom you shall have laid aside your gown and cassock, your Bible and Prayer Book, to become a dabbler in the impure and uncanonical mire of provincial party politics. . . . Like Cardinal Wolsey you may when too late, wish you had served your Heavenly King with the zeal with which you now obey the word of a colonial governor.

Those who knew the Archdeacon of York best knew how greatly Mackenzie misread his character in speaking of him as obedient to any one's word.

Not long after the prorogation of the Legislature on the thirtieth of January (1826) his Excellency bethought him of making a tour in the Midland and Eastern districts of the Province, his principal objective being the Irish settlement formed near Peterborough by Mr. Peter Robinson,[2] Commissioner of emigration. He found the colony in a thriving condition and received a very loyal address from the new

settlers. Addresses were also delivered at Port Hope,
Kingston, and one or two other places which his Excellency
visited. Whether any of these had been prepared beforehand
for political effect it is impossible to say; but certain it is
that the good people of Durham, in particular, did express
a poor opinion of the character of the legislative assembly
and of the value of its recent labours. They spoke of it "as
ruled by a band of factious demagogues whose acts per-
ceptibly tend to disorganize society, to subvert legitimate
authority and to alienate men's minds from the constitutional
government." This address, with others received by his
Excellency on his travels, was published in the official *Gazette*
together with the replies made. When the House next met
the reply to the Speech from the Throne contained the
following allusion to the subject.

> We should be wanting in candour towards your Excel-
> lency and justice to ourselves, were we not to express
> our sincere regret that your Excellency thought proper
> in some instances to receive and answer with compla-
> cency addresses which contained unwarrantable reflections
> upon a co-ordinate branch of the legislature.

Sir Peregrine, who in his day had borne with undaunted
front the thunders of Waterloo, was not crushed by this
remark. He had done his best, he said, to preserve good
relations between the different branches of the legislature,
but it was quite another matter to maintain a good understanding between members of the assembly and their constituents: that must depend on the estimate which the latter
placed on their faithfulness in the discharge of their duties;
and he really did not see how he could check the people in
the expression of their opinions. The gentle and pensive Sir
Peregrine scored this time: there was really no analogy
whatever between the ceremonious respect each branch of
the legislature owed to the others, and the attitude of the
electors towards their representatives. In which light indeed
would the Lieutenant Governor have appeared if, siding with
a temporary majority in the chamber, he had attempted to
stifle the voice of the people? Mackenzie sympathized, however, with the aggrieved commoners and hinted that the
contriving hand of Dr. Strachan was not altogether foreign
to the criticisms directed against them.

We come now to Mackenzie's definitive and irremediable quarrel with the reigning powers and the dominant class in the political system of Upper Canada. It did not spring from anything great; it was one of those conflagrations which a very little matter is able to kindle. In that little matter it is almost impossible not to recognize the germ of the Upper Canada rebellion.

The *Colonial Advocate* of the twenty-third of March, 1826, contained a characteristic paragraph which ran as follows:

> *Clerk of the Church* – a New Era! – Mr. Fenton, as it is said, having announced a forthcoming pamphlet upon the state of the York congregation, the Doctor (Strachan) made him new advances, and he has actually been re-instated as clerk of our episcopal church with an additional salary. 'Tis a good thing to be in the secret.

This was not a high kind of journalism. It attacked at once Mr. Fenton, a man in humble position, Dr. Strachan, a man in high position, and all who were interested in the credit of the church, Dr. Strachan had left for England and could not make his own reply to the insinuation that he had purchased the silence of his clerk with whom he had had some disagreement by increasing his salary. Mr. Fenton, however, lost no time in writing to the editor of the *Advocate* to say that there was no foundation for the statement he had made. That letter Mackenzie returned to him with a note saying that "as it could not be inserted without such a commentary as would be unpleasant to him, he had better not publish it." Why an unpleasant commentary should be appended to the letter of a man writing to correct a mis-statement regarding himself, is not apparent. Mr. Fenton was so little moved by fear of the unpleasant commentary that he straightway sent his letter to another paper, the *Observer*, by which it was duly published. This, however, involved delay, both papers being published weekly only; and one of the churchwardens who knew all the facts of the case, irritated by Mr. Fenton's failure, as he supposed, to contradict a statement damaging to the congregation which he knew to be incorrect, addressed a letter to the *Colonial Advocate* stating those facts without much regard to Fenton's feelings. That parson, he said, had lost his position owing to some trouble with Dr. Strachan, and had been

restored to his place without any increase of salary, at
his own earnest and pressing request and under a strong
appeal in writing to the benevolent feelings of Dr.
Strachan, in which he represented himself (with a family
to provide for) as feeble in health, indigent in circumstances, destitute of employment, and in short in every
respect an object claiming his charitable consideration.

The writer, who was no other than Mr. J. B. Macaulay,
afterwards Chief Justice of the Court of Commonpleas of
Upper Canada, added to his communication the following
words: "such fabrications cannot answer the ends you aim
at; they are only calculated to injure those you think to
serve, and provoke the just indignation of your readers."
Scarcely had this letter reached Mackenzie's hands when the
unfortunate Fenton's letter appeared in the *Observer*. Then
Mr. Macaulay repented of what he had done, and as a
couple of days would still elapse before the next issue of
the *Advocate*, he wrote a note to Mackenzie asking him not
to publish his letter, which had been written under a misapprehension. Mackenzie, however, was furiously angry at
this moment with Macaulay for his hint about "fabrications,"
and not too well pleased with Fenton for disregarding his
threat, and sending his contradiction of the *Advocate's*
statement to another paper. He therefore struck at both by
refusing Macaulay's request and publishing the letter. In this
way Fenton came in for his "unpleasant commentary," and
Macaulay had the pain of feeling that he had publicly
attacked a man who, so far as the matter in hand was
concerned, had fully done his duty. In fact mischief was
made all round. The following "Note by the Editor" was
appended to Macaulay's letter as published:

Had the Churchwarden confined his remarks to his
fellow-functionary, the clerk, we would most readily
have distributed the types of his letter of yesterday as
requested. But the tone he has seen fit to assume towards
ourselves is not to be borne. There was a time when
we looked upon *that Churchwarden* as one that would
become the most open, manly and independent of his
class, but it has gone by. We prized his talents, his
ability and judgment far too high. . . . The Churchwarden will find to-morrow that even to him we shall

not meanly truckle, nor shall we to any man, although
the blackest poverty should be on earth our reward.[3]

The use here made of the word "truckle" enables us to
understand what Mackenzie meant by it.

At this moment poverty was staring him in the face, but
a poverty which it is quite unnecessary to explain by his
unwillingness to "truckle." It was caused in the first place by
his abandonment of a steady and fairly profitable business
in order to betake himself to the notoriously precarious
professional of journalism; and in the second place by the
fact that, as a journalist, he conducted his paper to please
himself rather than with a direct view to business success.
At the same time anxiety was preying on his mind. If he
courted poverty, as he seems to have believed, by his
independence, he did not take his punishment well, for it
embittered his spirit. Any man who courts poverty should
be prepared to embrace her. "At all times during his life,"
says Mr. Lindsey, "Mr. Mackenzie was subject to great
elation at a brightening prospect and to a corresponding
depression in other circumstances." This is not the temper
required in one who, with his eyes open, is going to make a
martyr of himself in any great cause. The affair with
Macaulay and Fenton reflects one of Mackenzie's fits of
depression. But there was worse to follow.

Upon the publication of his letter in the *Advocate*
Macaulay wrote another letter to that paper which Mackenzie
refused to publish on account, as he states, of the abusive
terms in which it was couched. If there was nothing but
abuse in it Mackenzie would not have been injured by its
publication; possibly, therefore, there was more. The writer
finding himself shut out from the *Advocate* sent his letter to
the *Observer*. We know nothing of it save from some
extracts given in a later number of Mackenzie's paper, from
which we also learn that Macaulay had made use of a private
letter Mackenzie had written him in which the following
words occurred: "If I am enabled to maintain my old mother,
my wife and family, and keep out of the hands of the law
for debt, I care not for wealth and should as willingly leave
this earthly scene not worth a groat as if I were worth
thousands." The apropos and good taste of this declaration
to a man with whom he was not on good terms is questionable[4], but the use made of it by Macaulay was most

ungenerous and ungentlemanly. "Turn your attention," he said, "to subjects more acceptable to the public; and if you expect them, by buying your papers, to support you and your Mother and your wife and your children, pray try to deserve their charity a little better than you have done."[5]

A couple of weeks after the ventilation of this miserable matter in the columns of the *Colonial Advocate*, an article appeared pitched quite in the key of the memorable meditation of the usurer Alfins, for it contrasted the life of a farmer with that of a newspaper publisher greatly to the disadvantage of the latter. The farmer, *procul negotiis*,[6] had all the joys, the printer and editor all the sorrows. A hint was dropped of an intention to diminish the size of the paper and make it wholly non-political. This certainly was in the line of Macaulay's advice, though Mackenzie would hardly have liked to acknowledge any obligations to that gentleman. The size of the next two numbers was reduced, and in that of the fourth of May the following notice appeared: "To the Public. – The subscriber having determined to retire from the management of the *Colonial Advocate* at the conclusion of the next number, respectfully informs its numerous patrons that his successors will pay their respects to them in No. 75." Immediately below this appeared the following: "To Mr. J. B. Macaulay – Number 74 is engaged; but in the Advocate of the 18th instant the needful will be done in such of your affairs as have been entrusted to W. L. Mackenzie." Of the alleged withdrawal of Mackenzie from the editorship Mr. Lindsey says that "it appears to have been only an excusable device for keeping the personality of the editor out of view." The fact is that an orgy of slander and scurrility was in preparation and it seemed best, if only as a matter of momentary appearance, to let the responsibility for it rest on several individuals rather than on one.

The issue of the eighteenth of May more than made good its promise. Mr. Macaulay was in it, but there were others. The *pièce de résistance* of the number consisted of a long burlesque entitled "A faithful account of the proceedings of a general meeting of the contributors to the *Advocate*, held in Macdonell's parlour on the evening of Monday, May 1st, 1826." This, however, is preceded by an adaptation to the Attorney General of the words of scorn addressed by Constance in Shakespeare's "King John" (Act. 111.):

O Beverly! O Virginia![7] thou dost shame
That bloody spoil: thou slave, thou wretch,
    thou coward:
Thou little valiant, great in villainy!
Thou ever strong upon the stronger side

. . . .

Thou cold blooded slave etc.

This, as regards Mr. Robinson, was only a prelude; he was destined to figure largely in what followed. The contributors to the *Advocate*, to all of whom fictitious names are given, chose, we are told, as Chairman of their alleged meeting, "Dr. Andrew Tod." Mr. Caleb Hopkins was asked to open proceedings, which he did by launching into a most ruffianly and disgusting tirade against the Robinson family:[8] "The *Times* will tell you," he said,

that Mr. Canning was the son of Mother Hunn, the actress, but the delicacy of our York belles would be shocked if reminded that the present Attorney General is the hopeful progeny of Mother Beman[9] who kept the cake and beer shop in King Street; that the honourable Peter Robinson, whose pranks and Peterboroughs we hear so much of, with his learned brother, the Declaimer General against the Americans, were paupers of the lowest class for whom people now in York, taking pity on their forlorn condition, went about and begged handfuls of meal and York sixpences to keep them from actual starvation. The reputed father of these worthies was likewise an original in his way; and when he took his hopeful family into the boat with him for a very remarkable purpose, it would have been no loss to society if the heart of flint in the bosom of his son had then found a bed in the bottom of the deep, where the hardest pebble has a softer texture. This Virginian descended of Virginians has not forgotten the unshakable pride of his country; has he forgotten that it was long the Botany Bay of the British Kingdom the unhallowed receptacle of thieves, rogues, prostitutes and incorrigible vagabonds? Have the Robinsons anything to boast of in their Virginian descent. . . . Is it a secret in these parts that many, very many, such Virginian *nobles* as the Robinsons assume themselves, were descended from

mothers who came there to try their luck, and were
purchased by their sires with tobacco at prices according
to the quality and soundness of the article. And is it
from such a source that we are to expect the germ of
liberty? Nay, rather is it not from such a source that
we may look for the tyranny engendered, nursed, and
practised by those whose blood has been vitiated and
syphilized by the accursed slavery of centuries?

Turning next to Macaulay, Mr. Hopkins comments very
coarsely on his personal appearance, speaks of him as "that
pitiful mean-looking parasite," an "Upstart varlet," and "a
stink-pot of government." He is likewise charged, truly or
untruly, with the crime of having begun life as a barber's
apprentice. "Mr. Tom Moore" being called upon for a song
gives one the drift of which is that Macaulay is a coward.
This interesting line of criticism was continued in the two
succeeding numbers of the paper. Special attention is paid in
the issue of June the first to Mr. Henry J. Boulton who was
then offering himself as a candidate for the legislature, and
who had made bold to say "No man breathing has any
control over my conduct." Mackenzie takes up the statement
and proves to his own satisfaction that it cannot be true by
giving a list of the offices held by Mr. Boulton's friends and
relatives and laying stress of course on the fact that Boulton
was himself solicitor general. "*Dare* any man," he asks,
"whose relatives hold so many places under government say
he is master of his own actions in politics? It is an insult to
say so – he dares not." One would suppose from this that it
was a standing rule to furnish a man's friends for any
political derelictions of which he might be guilty; or that
it was a thing absolutely unknown for a man to prefer
principle to office. To go no further there was the recent
case of Fothergill; but to Mackenzie somehow it was inconceivable that the holder of even a petty office should have a
grain of independence. A postscript to the tirade against
Boulton warns the electors against committing their liberties
"to a man, who holding the off-1[10] position he does, has
allowed himself to be kicked in a public office without daring
to resent it."

One more number of the *Colonial Advocate* appeared, that
of the eighth of June, but before the sun set on that day the
printing office from which it was issued was wrecked by a

band of young men more or less connected with the families that have been assailed, who went there with that deliberate purpose.[11] The press was thrown down and broken and the type scattered promiscuously over the floor; some of it, it is stated, was thrown into the bay, which was not many yards distant. The probability is, that if that act of lawlessness had not been committed the issue of that day would have been the last. Mackenzie was in the deepest financial embarrassment, and when the affair occurred was over at Lewiston trying to settle some particularly pressing difficulty. He spoke afterwards of having been "rescued from utter ruin and destruction"[12] by the verdict which awarded him exemplary damages for the injury done to his property.

The conduct of the rioters as they are frequently called – though as they met with no opposition, and the whole thing was over in a few minutes, the word riot seems too strong a term to apply to the occurrence – is judged very severely by Mr. Lindsey and is condemned on general grounds by Mr. Kingsford[13] who, however, can hardly have been aware of the special provocation given in the columns of the *Advocate*, as he makes no reference to it whatever. The following passages from Mr. Lindsey's work throw light on the situation:

> Mr. Mackenzie's enemies were furious. He had stung them to the quick; but he had dealt with matters to which it would not be desirable to give further notoriety by making them subjects of prosecution. . . . There are unpleasant truths which though it be illegal to tell, cannot well be made a ground of action. Juries might be obstinate and refuse to convict a writer who, after unbearable provocation[14] had been stung into telling unpleasant facts, a little dressed up or exaggerated though they may have been to give effect to their narration. It was clear that Mackenzie could not be banished for sedition, . . . He had neither spoken nor published anything of a seditious nature. What then remained? The sole resource of violence; and violence was used.[15]

On the following page we read that Mr. Hagerman, counsel for the rioters, "did not venture to read the objectionable matter to the jury." Mr. Lindsey himself, very properly, did not venture to reproduce it in his work, published forty-six years ago: the consequence of this decent reticence on his part, and a lack of full acquaintance with the facts on the part of other writers, is that for the last two generations the wrecking of the office of the *Colonial Advocate* has been generally regarded simply as an attack by a haughty tory clique on the liberty of the press. Mr. Lindsey himself, however, in the passage above quoted, has given us clearly to understand that this was not the case. He speaks of "unpleasant facts, a little dressed up or exaggerated," which "though it be illegal to tell (them) cannot be made a ground of action." In such a case, he adds, nothing remains but "the resource of violence, and violence was used." One would almost suppose that the writer was putting in a plea for the rioters, but the context shows that such was not his intention.

The violence in his case was certainly most ill-advised – fatuous indeed to the last degree. How was the source of ribaldry to be dried up by doing a hundred dollars worth or so of damage to a printing office? An action was certain to lie against the perpetrators of such a deed, and there was manifest danger of exciting popular sympathy for the object of their attack. With a little money, the proceeds of a prosecution, the press could be re-established, and what would hinder it from again filling its columns with matter absolutely too offensive to be used in a prosecution for libel. "I and my companions," wrote Mr. S. J. Jarvis, one of the rioters, a couple of years later, "had the mortification to find that *no one* approved of an act, the impolicy of which (to say nothing of its bad tendency as an example) was too evident not to be seen by everybody, and by ourselves as well as others as soon as we reflected on it."[16] From a moral point of view the writer's mind was not troubled. "I call upon any man," he says,

> who may have preserved a file of the *Colonial Advocate* to turn to the number published on the 18th of May, 1826, as well as to those immediately preceeding and following it, and then to inform me, if he can, in what country, and at what time, the feelings of a whole society were ever so barbarously and cruelly outraged as they were by this man, whom no one had ever injured.

Still it would have been well if Mr. Jarvis and his friends could so far have restrained their feelings as not to have involved themselves in further mortification not to speak of pecuniary loss.

There were two remedies at law open to Mr. Mackenzie, a civil and a criminal, and by the advice of his friends he confined himself to the former. He employed as counsel in the suit which he brought, Mr. J. E. Small, Mr. M. S. Bidwell and a Mr. Stewart; while the defendants engaged the services of Mr. Macaulay and Mr. Hagerman. Mr. Macaulay stated the position of his clients in a letter to Mr. Small. After observing that they were quite aware, when they committed their act of aggression, of the responsibility they would incur, he proceeded to say:

> The real cause of the step is well known to all; it is not to be ascribed to any malice – political feeling – or private animosity; the personal calumnies of the latter *Advocates* point out sufficiently the true and only motives that prompted it; and I have now to offer to pay at once the full value of the damage to the press and types, to be determined by indifferent and competent judges selected for that purpose. Will you inform me how far your client is disposed to meet this proposal.

The letter concludes by speaking of the damage inflicted as merely pecuniary, "although provoked by repeated assaults upon private character and feeling not susceptible of any adequate redress." This proposal having been rejected on Mr. Mackenzie's behalf, Mr. Macaulay wrote again, on the 6th of July, stating that his friends were aware of, and could prove, the extent of damage done and were prepared to offer £200 as being amply sufficient to cover, not only Mr. Mackenzie's direct loss, but all contingencies; and that, if compensation was required beyond this they would add £100, making £300 in all, to close the case. This offer was also refused and the case went to trial before a special jury, the presiding judge being Chief Justice Campbell. There was no difficulty, of course, in proving the essential facts, or in establishing who were the parties concerned; all that the lawyers for the defence attempted to do was to prove that the *Advocate* had given great provocation; but, as they refrained from putting in evidence the passages which would most strongly have supported that contention, their argument was robbed of a great part of its force. That party spirit was not foreign to the deliberations of the jury may be inferred from the fact that it took them thirty-two hours of debate to arrive at a verdict. Nine of them had been taken

from the surrounding country where Mr. Mackenzie had
subsequently his chief support, and three only from the town
of York. Some wanted to give as much as £2000 damages,
while the lowest figures proposed is said to have been £150.
Finally a compromise was agreed upon and a verdict
rendered for £625, an amount three or four times greater
than the pecuniary loss inflicted. Mackenzie is quoted by
Mr. Lindsey as saying that the verdict "re-established the
Advocate· on a permanent footing." "Established" would
have been a more correct expression, as the *Advocate* was
so far from being on a permanent footing before that it was
on the very verge of financial collapse.

The press-wreckers were by this time able to gauge the
extent of their folly. They had in effect put their hands in
their pockets and the pockets of their friends – for a subscription was taken up on their behalf – to the amount of
£625 to equip the *Colonial Advocate* as it had never been
equipped before; and had, there is little doubt, rather
increased than impaired Mackenzie's popularity. The masses
are moved by simple ideas; and the idea that the freedom
of the press should not be interfered with is more level with
the general comprehension than the idea that the press
should abstain from odious personal insinuations and private
scandal. That the *Advocate* had indulged in scurrility at the
expense of a few individuals, whose favored position in
society naturally exposed them to more or less envy, would
not strike a large portion of the community at all a serious
offence; but that representatives of the favored class should
violently silence an organ of public opinion, and one aiming
specially at popularity, would be regarded almost as an
attack on the people themselves. From every practical point
of view, therefore, these young men, and most of them law
students, had simply, in their impetuosity, wounded the cause
they had at heart and given a substantial triumph where
certainly it was not deserved. If the die had not been cast
before, it was cast now. Not only had Mackenzie "stung his
enemies to the quick," as Mr. Lindsey says, but he had
shown the kind of thing he was prepared to do in order to
sting them. Henceforth he might strive to serve his country,
but a moral gulf, which there was no sounding or bridging,
had been fixed unalterably between himself and an influential,
and far from characterless, body in the state. When he wrote
as he did of the Robinsons, Boultons and Macaulays he did

not mean to leave any place for repentance or forgiveness; it was to be hatred and war between him and them to the end of the chapter. With regard therefore to his further aims all he could hope to do was to convert the mutual hostility between himself and these persons into a source of influence with the people. This he succeeded in doing to an unhappy extent.

CHAPTER SEVEN

ELECTED TO THE LEGISLATURE

Although William Lyon Mackenzie had triumphed in the law courts, subsequent utterances of his show that he was not wholly satisfied with the part he had himself played in the preceding stages of the business. *Nil fuit unquam sic unjar sibi.*[1] It was his fate to be continually doing and repenting, saying and unsaying, judging and reversing his judgment, and in this case he knew that he had done that which the verdict of no jury could make right.

The trial came off in October, and the amount of the verdict was paid over in November. On the seventh of December the *Colonial Advocate* again greeted its readers. It was not very good typographical form, for its proprietor had not had time since receiving the money awarded him to procure, as he proposed to do, a completely new equipment, and was therefore obliged to continue the use of the old. He promised the public, however, that they should have a first-class paper in the following spring. Another promise that he made was, "Patrick Swift," as an editor, should be no more. This turning down of "Patrick Swift," under whose pretended editorship in the previous month of May such hateful scurrility had disgraced the columns of the paper, must be regarded as a covert apology to decent public opinion for the orgy then indulged in. Unfortunately "Patrick Swift" and William Lyon Mackenzie were one and the same person, and it is not everyone who can effectually turn down himself. You may take your pitchfork, but if it is nature – your own nature particularly – you are trying to expel, never be sure you have seen the last of her. So at least thought Horace, and so too thought Pope, both wise men in their generation. Referring to the circumstances leading to the temporary discontinuance of the *Advocate*, Mackenzie says that he has "never written a line on the subject for the colonial press;" he hopes that when he does so he "will be able, calmly and

104

dispassionately to review the whole as becomes an impartial editor in a British colony under British law." This reticence on his part is significant, and so is his respectful reference to the British law in a British colony.

The fact is that Mackenzie knew in his heart that there was something vile in attacking political opponents with personal scurrility; and he sinned against the best instincts of his nature whenever he resorted to the practice. A much inferior man, Francis Collins, publisher of the *Freeman*, and a rabid opponent of the government, sided with him on the riot question, and expressed in his paper vast indignation at a remark made by Col. Fitzgibbons, that the attack on the *Advocate* office was the inevitable result of what had appeared in the paper. "Good and merciful heavens," exclaimed Collins, "Was there ever such a doctrine preached up by a British magistrate, that because a little scurrility is published in a newspaper, the inevitable result is that the house must be illegaly [sic] and forcibly entered and the property destroyed?"[2] This served Mackenzie's purpose and he transferred it to his own paper.[3] Yet a few months later, when Francis Collins was indulging in "a little scurrility" at his expense, he advances a very different doctrine. "If," he says,

the time shall ever arrive when no man shall feel sheltered in his personal feelings or private interests or social happiness from idle, wanton, interested, malicious or mistaken inuendoes, strictures, reproaches or calumnies, when such a time arrives the people will seek shelter from the tyranny of the press in the arms of a despotism strong enough to restrain, and in restraining to destroy, every vestige of its liberty.[4]

Francis Collins thought that a "little scurrility" was a very small matter indeed when weighed against damage to property, but Mackenzie was capable of seeing that it was the worst possible foe not only to social order but to political freedom. Is it possible that when he penned these remarks his thoughts did not revert to the scurrility in which he had himself indulged – with beneficial pecuniary results?

The *Colonial Advocate* of the eighteenth of January, 1827, bears, immediately under the title, the words, "Printed and published by W. L. Mackenzie, Printer to the honourable the legislative assembly of Upper Canada." A tender made by him for the printing of the journals of the House had been accepted. The engagement was not a very lucrative one, for the price was low, and the printer to the honourable the legislative assembly did not consider his contract bound him to any observance of political neutrality. On the first of March and later we find him advertising for sale a special edition of the journals printed from the same forms as the official edition, the whole to be well bound in boards and sold to subscribers for four dollars, or if bound in cloth for five dollars. "From the journals," he says,

the father of a family might teach his children, and himself learn, the acts, customs and usages of a free people as shown in the exercise of their constitutional civil rights. He who is in possession of the journals has got a political treasure, a key to the conduct and character of every man in parliament, and will be at no loss how to bestow his vote at the next general election.

There is no statement in the advertisement that the proposed distribution of a special edition has been sanctioned by the House. The thing would seem to Mackenzie essentially reasonable, and when a thing appeared reasonable to him he was not prone to ask advice about it.

It was in the spring of this year that Mr. Mackenzie addressed two letters to the Earl of Dalhousie, Governor General of Canada,[5] the main object of which was to recommend some form of representation for the North American provinces in the British parliament, but which, as was not unusual with the writer, contained some remarkable expressions of opinion on other points. He appears to be in favor of abolishing the provincial legislatures altogether for he writes:

I have long been satisfied that if the North American colonies were rid of these inferior and subordinate legislatures, which are and must be forever inefficient for the purposes for which they were intended, and allowed instead thereof a due weight in both branches of the British parliament, it would prove the foundation of their permanent and true happiness.

Representation in the House of Lords implied a Canadian peerage, but the writer in the expansiveness of his mood did not shrink from that. "A colonial peerage had been ridiculed, but my lord, Mr. Pitt, saw its usefulness, and if merit either on the bench or in the army and navy has deserved a Scottish or Irish current, it surely would not be less prized by a Canadian or Nova Scotian." He proceeds to express his opinion more fully as to the kind of legislatures Upper Canada has so far had.

> Of what elements are our houses of assembly composed? It is true we find here and there a man of genius and independence, of talents and integrity; but are not the great mass of our assemblymen either distinguished for their servile adherence to a governor's favourite, or for their pertinacious and obstinate opposition to every measure proposed by the administration of whatever nature. . . . Many of these legislators are qualified to sign their names, but as to the framing and carrying through a bill on any subject whatever, the half of them wisely never attempted such a herculean task.

Lest, however, Lord Dalhousie should think there was any intention on his correspondent's part to compare Upper Canada unfavorably with the United States, evidence is advanced to show that a much worse condition of things exists in the latter country. The New York *Commercial Advertiser* is quoted as saying, "We really begin to shudder at this growing and groundless disaffection to the present government." Another paper declares that "The halls of legislation, instead of being the sources of honour, of pride and of glory to the country, are converted into altars for the display of angry passions and vituperative personalities." The same authority continues, "Instead of elevated plans for the advancement of the commercial and political interests of the country, we have contemptible and low schemes for the promotion of party tools and the elevation of party favourites." In the opinion of a third the condition of things "presents a fearful commentary on free institutions themselves, and postpones to futurity the question whether man is so far a rational being as to be capable of self-government." There would have been abundant instruction in all this to any one who could have surveyed the facts with that single eye which brings light to the understanding. Side by side were two countries with political institutions materially different, but each labouring under its own political difficulties, one however, much more heavily, according to all accounts, than the other. In both cases the trouble appeared to be *with the people*, who for one reason or another – lack of knowledge, lack of intelligence, lack of interest or lack of the sense of public duty – did not seem capable of electing legislators at once capable and honest. The wider the basis of political action the more abundant seemed to be the abuses. The inference to be drawn, so far as Upper Canada was concerned, was that, not so much in change of political institutions was social and political progress to be sought as in a wise and faithful use of such means and instruments of progress as existing institutions afforded.

The doctrine of the natural equality of all men appeared to Mackenzie at this time very absurd. He concludes his first letter by expressing his entire assurance that Lord Dalhousie has at heart the good of the country, and trusts that his lordship will "long live to preside over this portion of the empire, and to sustain in these republican and levelling times the dignity of true nobility."

In his second letter he touches a question just then at issue between the governor general and the Lower Canada legislature, which was demanding that all the revenues of the Crown should be placed at its disposal. The colonial office was prepared to assent to this provided some permanent provision, or at least a provision extending over a reasonable term of years, was made for the support of civil government, so that the judges and the chief officers of the executive should not be in yearly terror of having their salaries stopped as the result of some disagreement between the assembly and the administration. This, however, was precisely the condition of affairs which the assembly wished to establish. Alluding to Lord Dalhousie's refusal to yield the point in dispute, Mackenzie says that it was generous on the part of his lordship "not willingly to prostrate the whole of the servants of his Majesty at the feet of the commons, at the mercy of their annual vote, contrary to the usage in England where the civil list is voted for the life of the King." He perfectly understood the objection to doing so; he saw that it would

oblige the officers of government to court popular favour for daily bread, and place the judges of the land in that slavish state of dependence on the populace which produced so much trouble in Massachusetts, and which in

New York has made cheap justice a byword, and the miserable pittance allowed the administrators of the law a reproach.

He did not foresee that within five years he would be insisting that the judges of Upper Canada should be held in precisely such a "slavish state of dependence." In the matter of opinions Mackenzie was always ready to let the morrow take thought for the things of itself. It is also to be remarked that while justifying Lord Dalhousie for refusing to yield to the assembly, he justified the assembly for refusing to yield to Lord Dalhousie. Were he a member of it, he said he would not vote one farthing of supplies so long as any portion of the revenue was not subject to its control.

Vast advantages, he was persuaded, would flow from the direct representation of the provinces in the parliament of Great Britain. The constituencies – through what regenerating power is not explained – would elect men "who would be able to watch over and protect the interests of these provinces in the general councils of our country;" and then we should have canals, great trunk roads, ocean packets, cheapened mail service and many other benefits, including "a judicious division of the counties of British America, with Lord Lieutenants, High Sheriffs of annual appointment, Deputy Lieutenants, etc. etc."

The letter reads like a palinode, for the writer towards the close admits – most unnecessarily so far as the Earl of Dalhousie was concerned – that he has been "too often led into useless arguments upon the local and personal disputes of individuals, upon the measures of the provincial government, and even more trivial subjects," instead of devoting his paper, as he should have done, to larger and more important topics. Still, "I can truly declare that I have ever desired the glory and prosperity of Britain." Significant also is the fact that in these two letters making together nine columns of print, there is not one word in condemnation of the administration of the government in Upper Canada; the only criticism the writer has to make falling upon the legislature and the electors, and as we have just seen, upon himself. It does not appear what response, if any, the Earl of Dalhousie made to these communications: doubtless he acknowledged them, but if so the fact does not appear to have been noted in the columns of the *Advocate*.

Amongst the measures of the administration which Mackenzie had opposed was one for the purchase by the province of stock to the amount of $200,000 in the Welland Canal. A statement which he made at this time may be put on record: "The farmers have as yet only *heard* of taxes; by and by they will feel them."[6] He predicted also that any member who voted for this assistance to a great public enterprise would seal his doom at the next general election. Prophecy had no terrors for the editor of the *Colonial Advocate*.

Reference has been made on an earlier page to the Canada Company. At a later date this company was denounced by Mackenzie as a monopoly, but at this time his disposition towards it appears to have been friendly. "We do sincerely hope," he says, "that their improvements may be attended with every reasonable advantage both to themselves and to the people of the country." Amongst the forgotten stories of the period is one in which Mackenzie is brought into relation with John Galt, the well known author, who for some years was manager in Canada of the company in question with headquarters in Guelph. In the month of March, 1825, Galt came out to Canada as one of the five commissioners appointed by the British government to take evidence as to the actual and prospective value of the lands which it was proposed that the company should take over. The arrival of the Commissioners at York was naturally regarded with much interest and Galt, who had already a considerable literary reputation, and who was perhaps still better known in Upper Canada through the part he had taken in endeavoring to forward a settlement of the claims for war losses in that province, was the object of special attention. Sir Peregrine, always hospitable, showed him every kindness, and Galt carried away with him the pleasantest recollections of evenings spent at government house. But this was not all. "I had great reason," he says,

> to be personally obliged to the editors of some of the newspapers for their publications. Among others I received a complete file of the *Colonial Advocate*. With the editor I was entirely unacquainted and as little aware of the character of his politics. . . . Before sending my letter of thanks, which was written soon after I received the file, I turned the papers over cursorily, and here and

there read a passage which apprised me of the character of their politics, particularly a series of letters addressed to the attorney general intended to resemble those of Junius; but I could not even acknowledge the present without noticing the coarseness, in such a manner, however, as to convey my opinion with some delicacy, and as the paper evinced superior local information, I ordered it sent to me.[8]

Not long after this Galt returned to England. In December of the following year (1826) he came out to Canada again. Meantime things had happened. Mackenzie, upon whom the delicacy of Galt's reproof had been wholly lost, had run amuck, as we have seen, in the preceding month of May. His office had been wrecked, the wreckers had been prosecuted, and without Galt's permission or knowledge his letter had been produced in the trial as a kind of certificate of the character of Mackenzie's paper. Galt had carried his delicacy too far; and to Sir Peregrine Maitland and the upper circles of York society it was no slight mortification to find that their guest of the year before had actually placed a weapon in the hands of their enemy. The letter is not printed in Galt's autobiography, and its preservation is due to the fact that the author, having obtained a copy of it from Mackenzie that he might see just what he had said, sent that copy to the *Official Gazette* for publication. As a memorial of the times it possesses sufficient interest to justify its republication here:

York, March 28th, 1825.

Sir,

I am very much flattered by your attention, and it gives me unaffected pleasure to receive the numbers which you have taken the trouble to preserve and to send me of your spirited paper. I do undoubtedly dissent from some of your sentiments, but I can appreciate the talent with which they are supported. Indeed I esteem an open opponent more than I do those sort of pluckless partisans who, like the cat in the adage let *I dare not* wait upon *I would.* [sic]

I have been too short a time in this country to form any opinion of its political temperament, and I have besides been the greatest part of the time confined to

my room by indisposition; but it is candid in you to
acknowledge that you have in some degree changed your
opinion of certain public characters.

Probably in colonies and places remote from the
supreme government, persons in public trust are apt to
consider themselves as part of that great abstraction
government; and to mistake attacks on their own
conduct as factious and seditious movements. On the
other hand, the motions and machinery of government,
being in a much smaller compass, are seen more in detail
than at home, and the workings of personal feeling are
apt, in consequence to excite more acute invidiousness.
To this I partly ascribe the tone of your letter to Mr.
Robinson, which displays very superior powers indeed
of sarcasm; but it must occur to yourself *now* that the
value of it would not have been lessened had some of
the points been *sheathed in softer language*.

But I ought to ask your parden for this criticism,
while I should be thanking you for flattering favour. You
can have no better task than the upholding of frank
courageous, spirit of independence among a remote
people. It is that which has made the great island of
our birth what she is; and when we compare her small
natural bounds and resources with the vastness of her
moral and political dominion, we may rest assured that,
with all the faults of her public men, her government
has hitherto been one of the greatest practical wisdom
that has yet withstood the test of time and the prostra-
tions of revolution and of war.

> I remain, Sir,
>   Your respectful and obliged servant,
>   John Galt.

Not a bad letter *per se*, on the contrary a good one, but
yet, like many other politenesses, not just the medicine the
case required. No worse service can be rendered to a man
than to gloss over his faults with fine phrases, or to apply
fine phrases as a healing balm, lest some little bit of honest
criticism may cause irritation. The letter was not calculated
to do Mackenzie good, and facts do not indicate that it did
him good. That letter had been produced in court just about
two months before Galt's second arrival at York. Knowing
nothing of what had taken place he was surprised and

mystified at the chill which he perceived in the social atmosphere which had been so genial and caressing, and particularly in the atmosphere of government house. The change was so marked that Galt sought an explanation and a correspondence of a somewhat painful character – at least he writes as if he felt it so[9] – ensued between him and Sir Peregrine Maitland. "When I heard," wrote Sir Peregrine,

> of the warm commendations of the talent displayed in attacks upon my government and of the intimation conveyed in your private letters as to the manner in which attacks upon public officers might be made with greater caution and equal effect, you will not be surprised that as governor of this colony I felt keener regret from the reflection that your residence here was alone owing to the circumstance of your being vested with the execution of a royal commission under the seal of this province, and that additional weight was afforded to your communications[10] by the very circumstance which I thought must have rendered them impossible.

Sir Peregrine's remarks in this letter concerning the *Colonial Advocate* and its proprietor were not flattering. The paper is spoken of as one "distinguished above all others by a scurrilous abuse of the government, and which was only saved from prosecution by the despicable character of its contents, and by the contempt of all persons of good feeling for its obscure and unprincipled conductor." It should be remembered, if we would understand matters aright, that it was only between Mackenzie individually and the government that these feelings existed. Baldwin, senior, Rolph, Bidwell and Perry, not to mention lesser men, were all active reformers, and Rolph in particular was, as we have seen, most pertinacious in his attacks upon Sir Peregrine's chief ally, the attorney general; yet was there never developed between these men and the upholders of the administration anything approaching the bitterness of personal hostility which marked the relations between Mackenzie and the same political party. Of this difference one explanation only can be given. It was not that Mackenzie's ideas were more advanced in a political sense than those of other reform leaders, because upon the whole they were less so, if by "advanced" we understand in harmony with the political methods and principles of later years. Nor was it that he was more intent than they on political reforms. It was purely and simply that he, in an unexampled degree, made *persons* the object of his attack. If a principle or a practice was unsound, then the person who upheld it must be odious: it was beyond Mackenzie's power to make any allowance for the point of view: that a man should have a wrong point of view, or what *he* considered such, was an offence in itself.

The sudden turns of opinion to which Mackenzie was subject find constant illustration in his writings. No fault had been found by the reform party, so far, with the Constitutional Act of 1791. On the contrary it was continually spoken of as the charter which secured the people of Upper Canada the full rights and privileges of British subjects. Now, however, Mackenzie discovers that

> The English Parliament some thirty or forty years ago passed an Act, without the consent of the people of Canada, by which these provinces are to be governed until it shall please the same wise body to pass another act (will we, will we) to alter, take away, or add to the rights of this conquered territory.

"This," he continues,

> is not a constitution, it is not freedom; it is a government which will be submitted to much upon the same principle upon which Ireland is managed, but it is not a constitution. . . . Were the people of Canada asked whether the mode of government set over them in 1791 was agreeable to their wishes, or did the more efficient argument of military force settle the question without a proper appeal?[11]

It is strange to think that the hand that wrote this singular attack on the wisdom and liberality of the British parliament was the same that eight or nine months before, had penned such effusive letters to the Earl of Dalhousie. So far were his fellow reformers of the period from sharing his views that eight years later they were insisting, and Mackenzie with them, in their controversy with Sir Francis Bond Head, that the Act of 1791, rightly interpreted, contained all the elements of British liberty and "responsible government." In lower Canada it was to that Act, and all which they held it to imply, that the French Canadian leaders continually appealed.

A couple of weeks before this, with what object it is not apparent, but hardly, one would say, for the strengthening of popular institutions, the *Advocate* had published a letter addressed by Robert Gourlay to the Upper Canada Assembly, in which that turbulent individual had said,

> Examine yourselves, and you will find that you are really little qualified for legislators though very good farmers, storekeepers and village lawyers. Examine circumstances in which you are placed and behold cases of imbecility. Examine records and confess that your whole statute book is a tissue of abominations. Your proceedings last session are beyond contempt.

This tallied pretty well with Mackenzie's own opinion of the legislature as expressed in his letters to Lord Dalhousie; but of what advantage was such depreciation of the kind of material available for the making of laws in Upper Canada? The trouble with Mackenzie, more than with Gourlay, was that he had to see his enemy before he could do any effective work; and his aim was far more distinctly the defeat and humiliation of the enemy than any constructive achievement.

Nevertheless he was gaining followers. In the home district especially his paper had given him a considerable measure of popularity, and early in 1828 he had determined to offer himself as a candidate for the county of York in the general election which was to take place in the summer of that year. At a political meeting held at Markham in the month of January he moved a series of not less than twenty-three resolutions embodying his views on the questions of the day. One of the grievances which he urged most strongly was the fact that the judges held their offices during pleasure, and not as in England in statutory independence of the Crown. It is not alleged in the resolutions that any abuses had grown out of this condition of things; nor is there any evidence in the annals of Upper Canada that the judges were in any way embarrassed in the discharge of their duties by not being on the same footing as their brethren in England. Mackenzie himself had much to do first and last with the tribunals of the country: in some cases he pays distinct tribute to their impartiality; in no case does he allege anything like partiality. His readiness at all times to appeal to them shows that they commanded his confidence.[12]

The *Colonial Advocate* of the fourteenth of February contains Mackenzie's address to the electors of York, a well-expressed document which shows how true a perception the writer had of the principles by which a public man should be guided. "I have no end in view," he says,

> but the well being of the people at large, no ambition to serve but that of contributing to the happiness and prosperity of our common country. The influence and authority with which you may invest me shall always be directed, according to the best of my judgment, for the common good; and it will be my care to uphold your rights to the utmost of my power with that firmness, moderation, and perseverance which becomes the representative of a free people.

Considering the legend which has so long prevailed as to the lack of popular liberty in the olden days of Upper Canada, it is worthy of note how continually the people are referred to as "a free people" – not a people who *ought to be free*, but as a people actually free.

The good people of York do not appear to have objected to Mackenzie's freedom of speech in the *Advocate*; at least he shows no fear of offending them by continuing to practise it. We find him, while working up influence in the county, describing Archdeacon Strachan as "the last and least of all abject partisans, enjoying, if he can be said to enjoy, all the comforts of wealth, affluence, and colonial splendour in a palace." In another number of the paper the same dignitary is spoken of as "the jackal of the lieutenant governor," and in a third as "a paltry, turncoat emigrant schoolmaster." Of the attorney and solicitor general it is said that "two meaner men are not to be found under the canoply [sic] of heaven." He also pays his respects to the Jones family:

> We have seen gentlemen from Brockville who inform us that the refuse and scum of society shall have a chance, once more to come to the top. The country will be both displeased and astonished to learn that it is chiefly through the Irish influence that these worthless and discreditable persons, the Jones, are likely to raise their hopes in a future parliament, and again to sell

and make merchandise of the privileges and rights of their constituents, and insult and disgrace the representative body.

The editors of the *Freeman* and the *Observer*, both at the time opposition papers, are "two of the most mercenary unprincipled hirelings in the country." The lieutenant governor referred to as "the old man" is accused of contributing "shameless vulgarities" to the official paper. Yet we turn a few pages and, in the conclusion of a speech of remarkable virulence against the admission of Francis Collins to the Constitutional Society, we find these words:

> Sir I would wish to live in peace with all men before God and the world. I envy no man, nor have I any revenge to gratify. The tomb will soon, very soon, cover these limbs of mine, and the dust of death will bury in oblivion the recollection of political triumphs or political reverses.

The speaker was at the lusty age of thirty-three, and if he was really moved to a tender melancholy by the thought of an early demise there was no suspicion of it in the terms he hurled at the head of Collins.

Collins at this time was one of the bitterest assailants of the government party. Some intemperate language he had indulged in against the attorney general led to his being indicted for libel, in retaliation for which proceedings he stirred up two criminal prosecutions against his opponents. He first laid a criminal information against seven of the persons who had been concerned in the attack on the *Advocate* office, notwithstanding the fact that Mackenzie himself had declined to do so; and afterwards laid a similar information against the seconds in an unfortunate duel which had taken place no less than eleven years before between Mr. S. P. Jarvis and Mr. George Ridout, in which the latter was killed. The surviving principal had been tried at the time for murder and acquitted; and that being the case it had not been thought necessary to prosecute the seconds. Mr. Collins, however, in his rage against the government brought the whole painful case – a case which drew tears from the eyes of Judge Willis by whom it was tried – once more before the public, to the great distress of a few individuals and with absolutely no advantage from any point of view. In the riot case the defendants were dismissed with nominal damages; in the duel case they were

acquitted altogether. Later in the year the libel charges against
Collins were brought to trial when he was sentenced to a fine
of fifty pounds and one year's imprisonment.

It was in the *Colonial Advocate* of May the twenty-ninth,
1828, that Mackenzie began the publication of his celebrated
"Black List," with the subtitle "Official Corruption and Hy-
pocrisy unmasked." Strange to say one of the first persons to
figure in it was Dr. W. W. Baldwin. He was the first of all
ridiculed for a proposition he had made to establish a kind of
feudal relation between the Indians on the Grand River and
their chiefs, and to give the latter – who might be called to the
legislative council – a certain jurisdiction over the tribesmen.
A few weeks later the Doctor was again in the list with a
quotation from the *Observer* to the effect that "Where self
was concerned, he (Baldwin) was always vigilant, always
active." The love that was lost between Mackenzie and the
Baldwins was a very minute quantity. Another person whom
we find there is John Willson, speaker of the late house of
assembly, on whom such warm encomiums had been lavished
on the occasion of his election to the speakership. He had
"shown the cloven foot," and made it clear "that he was
acting a deceitful and double part as a politician." The
attorney and solicitor general were of course in the list at an
early date, and, as time went on, it became a very comprehensive gallery in which passibly good company was to be
met. Fortunately for Upper Canada at that period there was
not much bad company to put into it.

One of Mackenzie's opponents in the York election was
Mr. J. E. Small, previously mentioned as being of his counsel
in the riot case. Mr. Small was a son of John Small, clerk of
the executive council, and on general principles ought to have
been an adherent and instrument of the "Family Compact."
Mr. Mackenzie, however, speaks of him as follows:

Mr. Small is held in much esteem by all who have the
pleasure of his acquaintance, and his personal character
has been deservedly high, even in the opinion of those
who are in opposition to the party with which he is supposed generally to act. We have had several dealings with
Mr. Small in the legal way, and his behaviour to us from
first to last convinced us, that, as a professional man he
is governed by the broad truths of honor and integrity.
To have said less under the circumstances would have

been doing injustice to himself as well as to his highly respectable family and connections.[13]

This was in reply to a correspondent who had asked for some information about the candidates. It shows Mackenzie in one of his best moods – taking pleasure in doing justice to a man who was his competitor for a coveted honour. At the same time he could not refrain, when printing Small's election address in his paper, from appending the words "Printed at the Government Office," in order to cast a slur on his independence.

Mackenzie ran his own election in the fullest sense. He had no committee to aid him. He did not wait for a requisition. He simply notified the electors some months in advance that he was going to offer himself as a candidate, and when the time came, he did. The county of York was at that time entitled to return two members, and it had its choice of four – William Lyon Mackenzie, James E. Small, Jesse Ketchum and William Roe. The two chosen were Ketchum, who headed the poll, and Mackenzie. Ketchum was a tanner by trade, a liberal in politics, and a man of much good sense, who enjoyed the confidence of the country for many years in succession. The election of Mackenzie opens a new chapter in his career. He is now a power to be reckoned with, for he has plainly caught the ear and won the confidence of a section of the people.

CHAPTER EIGHT

THE TENTH PARLIAMENT OF UPPER CANADA

Mackenzie was not a man under whose feet grass had much chance to grow. Within a few weeks after the general election which took place in July a petition was published in the *Colonial Advocate* setting forth the grievances under which the province was labouring. It had been extensively signed by the freeholders of York, and probably was the product of Mackenzie's active brain and ready hand. In any case it may safely be accepted as expressing his views on the political issues of the day. The principal grievances detailed were as follows:

The rejection by the legislative council of the most salutary measures passed by the Assembly.

The frequent want of a casting vote in the court of King's Bench owing to the absence of one or other of the judges.

The ill effect on the judicial function of the association therewith, in certain cases, of legislative and executive duties. The appropriation by the executive of a portion of the public revenue independently of the action of the assembly.

The extravagant augmentation of official salaries.

The appointing to, and retaining in, office of notoriously unsuitable persons.

The frequent absence of the lieutenant governor from the seat of government, and his lack of acquaintance with the people of the country, saving those whose official occupations placed them about his person.

The practice of charging with disloyalty those who questioned the policy of the administration "endangering that public feeling truly British and yet happily alive in this colony."

The undue influence exercised over electors in many ways.

The acceptance of office by members of the assembly without vacating their seats.

The pressure brought to bear on members of the legislative council to make them support the measures of the government.

Such were the evils existing in the body politic of Upper Canada in the year 1829, as seen and judged by Mackenzie and his friends. Not even yet, it will be observed, is there any distinct demand for "responsible government." So far as the more substantial of the grievances detailed are concerned, hardly a year passed after this that did not see one or more of them either removed entirely or considerably abated. True, the legislative council continued to exercise its constitutional power of revising and at times rejecting the measures of the assembly; but no careful student of the period can fail to be impressed by the soundness, moderation, and evident sense of responsibility which marked the proceedings of that much criticised body. It was indeed largely composed of persons holding offices of emolument under the government, but there was nothing to prevent these persons, on all ordinary occasions, from devoting their very best efforts, as legislators, to the public good. Their capacity in that character was increased by their official experience and the knowledge which it involved of public affairs, while the fact that their positions were permanent ones, both as legislative councillors and as office holders, exempted them from the necessity of courting a brief and flimsy popularity, and permitted them to consider public questions in a broad and impartial way. There remains the objection – theoretically unanswerable – that those members of the council who held offices of emolument at the pleasure of the government – there was no emolument attaching to a seat in the council – could not, if they happened to differ from the government on a question of policy, exercise their votes with perfect freedom.

Practically it may be doubted whether any public interest suffered materially from this cause. There was, as a rule, substantial harmony of view between the executive and the council and little occasion, therefore, for the exercise of pressure. Understanding by the executive the lieutenant governor, his views were those of the colonial office modified by his closer view of conditions existing in the province, and it is difficult to conceive a case in which he would desire to force views of his own upon the council. If such a case arose he would be extremely careful how he resorted to a line of action so indefensible. Certain of the "office-holders" were executive councillors whose pressure in a legislative body quite accords with British usage. One was chief justice Campbell, of whom Mackenzie had so high an opinion and who acted, *ex officio*, as Speaker. Another was the Hon. J. H. Dunn, receiver general, a man of known liberal views, who was taken some years later by Sir Francis Bond Head into his reconstituted council with Rolph and Baldwin as a colleague with whom they, as reformers, could harmoniously work.[1] Another was the Hon. Joseph Wells who was also in Sir F. B. Head's council and resigned on the issue raised by Rolph and Baldwin. There were five members, Thomas Clark, William Dickson, Neil McLean, George Crookshank and Angus McIntosh who held no office whatever. The whole body consisted at this time of eighteen members nominally, but of only sixteen practically, the bishop of Quebec who had a seat in it never attending, and Col. Thomas Talbot who had been called to it never having taken his seat. It may not have been an ideal legislative machine, but it may be doubted whether perfectly ideal things do the best work in this world. A consciousness of theoretical imperfection prompts sometimes to effort, sometimes to caution, sometimes to a wise moderation. It is the institution that is theoretically perfect that needs most watching, its very theoretic perfection creating a number of dangerous assumptions in its favor and throwing the public off their guard.[2]

The legislative council, it must be admitted, was slow to recognize the need for large reforms. In the matter of the clergy reserves, of the charter of the provincial university, the extension of municipal institutions, and generally in regard to proposals tending to alter the established political and social order its conservatism was extreme. At the same time it looked with a friendly eye upon, and gave its best assistance in shaping, all measures for the material improvement of the country by public works or otherwise; and its suggestions in matters involving points of law and the rights of individuals were always valuable. In bills involving much troublesome detail the assembly would have done ill without its assistance; as a rule it accepted its amendments with little demur, and sometimes with manifest appreciation of their utility. In conferences between the two Houses, the council always bore itself with dignity and credit. All this, though plainly recorded in the journals of both Houses, is practically forgotten, and the legislative council has come down to posterity as a body that by the very law of its being was a simple drag on useful legislation and on the prosperity of the province. Had such been the case Lord Durham, in his *Report*, could never have made such statements as the following:

> The course of the parliamentary contest in Upper Canada has not been marked by that singular neglect of the great duties of a legislative body which I have remarked in the proceedings of the parliament of Lower Canada – The Statute book of the Upper Province *abounds with useful and well-considered measures of reform.*

To get on the statute book they had to pass through the legislative council, and it was there that they got much of the careful consideration which, in its results, attracted his lordship's attention.

Within three or four years after the general election of 1828, several of the more substantial reforms demanded by Mackenzie and his friends of the County of York had been conceded. The Crown had handed over to the provincial legislature the complete control of the revenue collected under the imperial statute 14 George 111, chapter 83.[3] The statute of the judges had been altered in accordance with the wish of the Assembly. The chief justice no longer sat in the executive council, and no judge with the exception of the chief justice (as Speaker) sat in the legislative council. The drift of things was decidedly in the direction of a larger and more liberal system of government, and nothing was needed for the realization of other desirable reforms but steady persistence in demanding them and setting forth the arguments in their favor.

Sir Peregrine Maitland, who had had so many disagreements with the ninth parliament, and whose action in the Forsyth case was not, as we have seen, approved by the home authorities, was transferred towards the close of the year 1828 to the government of Nova Scotia. A number of addresses were presented to him expressing regret at his departure – a regret which, judging by what Mackenzie himself heard in the country districts,[4] may well have been sincere. Mackenzie, however, spoke of the addresses in his paper as "hole and corner productions, privately got up by the faction to be handed from door to door and submitted to those only from whom they expected to coax a signature."[5] It should not have been so difficult to admit that Sir Peregrine might have *some* friends and admirers in the country: the addresses did not compromise those who did not sign them, and the signers were entitled to express their opinions.

The date of Sir Peregrine's departure was the fourth of November; his successor had arrived the day before. This was another distinguished military officer and hero of Waterloo, Sir John Colborne. The new governor, there is good reason to believe, came out with a sincere desire to administer the government in a fair and liberal spirit. He had evidently been warned of the difficulties he might expect to encounter and put on his guard against falling under the influence of any political party. His attitude towards the official set was therefore at first one of considerable reserve. Replying to an address presented to him on his arrival and read by Dr. Baldwin, he spoke briefly but significantly as follows:

> Gentlemen, I receive your address with satisfaction, and I sincerely trust that, with your aid and exertions, we shall no longer hear of the political discussions to which you allude; fully aware that, whether they proceed from misconception or from the pertinacity and selfish views of a few individuals, the interests of the people will inevitably be sacrificed, the beneficent intentions of our government frustrated and its paternal care prove unavailing.[6]

This was somewhat Delphic. Who were the "few individuals" whose pertinacity and selfish views were a possible source of danger? The sermon might, as usually happens, be variously applied, and Mackenzie availed himself of his undoubted right to apply it to his opponents. In a current number of his paper he exclaims:

> He already leans on the people whom he has been sent to govern and . . . comes manfully forward and tells them that 'with their aid and coertions the political discensions of Canada will soon be set at rest'. This sort of language addressed by his excellency will assuredly give much satis-

faction, because it is the language of truth dictated by that best of senses, common sense.

For the moment the ardent reformer was hopeful.

The tenth parliament of Upper Canada met on the eighth of January, 1829. The result of the elections had not been favorable to the government party, and the new House affirmed its reform character by elevating Mr. M. S. Bidwell to the Speaker's chair by 24 votes against 21 cast for the former Speaker, Mr. John Willson. The speech from the Throne made on the whole a favorable impression, mainly owing to the fact that his excellency recommended the repeal of the Act (44 George III, chapter 1) under which Gourlay had been banished from the country, and which, though it had not again been brought into use, had ever since been regarded as a possible engine of oppression. The other chief subjects to which he directed attention were public education and the public roads. Good schools and good roads were two things in which Sir John Colborne very strongly believed.

The majority of the assembly thought it well to lose no time in defining their position, and they consequently incorporated in their reply to his excellency's speech a paragraph in which, claiming to be the "constitutional advisers of the Crown," they prayed his Excellency "against the imperious policy hitherto pursued by the provincial administration." "Although," the address continues,

they at present see his excellency surrounded by the same advisers as have so deeply wounded the feelings and injured the best interests of the country, yet in the interval of any necessary change this House entertains an anxious belief that, under the auspices of his Excellency, the administration of justice will rise above suspicion, the wishes and interests of the people be properly respected, the constitutional rights and independence of the legislature be held inviolable, the prerogative and patronage of his most gracious Majesty be exercised for the happiness of his people and the honour of his crown, and the revenues of the colony be hereafter sacredly devoted to the many and urgent objects of public improvement after making provision for the public service upon the basis of that economy which is suited to the exigencies of the country and the condition of its inhabitants.

His excellency, who had been taking his bearings during the two months he had been in the country, gave a brief and rather dry reply. "Gentlemen," he said,

I thank you for the congratulations and assurances contained in your address; but I must remark that it is less difficult to discover the traces of political dissensions and local jealousies in this colony than to efface them. With the conviction therefore that in many instances the most upright intentions have been discoloured by the medium through which they have been seen, I anticipate that the principles of the constitution, on being kept steadily in view, and the good sense of the people, will neutralize the efforts of any interested faction.

This second expression of his excellency's confidence in "the people" was not reassuring to gentlemen who themselves claimed to be "the people." A little rift was already beginning to show itself in the lute.

The ability of the junior member for the County of York was at once recognized by his fellow-legislators, who made him chairman of two committees, one on the Post Office and one on the Rights and Privileges of the House. As chairman of the former committee Mackenzie showed that faculty for grasping facts and marshalling facts which distinguished him through life, and was undeniably an eminent qualification for a career of parliamentary usefulness. The Post Office at this time was under imperial control and the fundamental idea which governed it was that people should have such mail facilities as they paid for and no more. The cost of conveying the mails depended on the state of the roads and bridges. A service once a week over bad roads cost as much as one twice or even thrice a week over good ones. The roads for the most part were in a wretched condition and the mail service was restricted accordingly. One of the recommendations of Mr. Mackenzie's committee was that the sum of seven thousand pounds should be "annually laid out upon the great road between Sandwich and Prescott in the most economical and prudent manner that can be devised, and that commissioners be appointed by the House in the acts granting the said sums." A further recommendation was "that the provincial legislature should assume the management of the post office department in Upper Canada, and that a law should be immediately passed to that effect." Some observations follow in which the adventurous spirit of Mackenzie may be plainly recognized. "They (the committee) cannot admit that any authority other than the provincial legislature has the power to impose a tax upon the correspondence of the inhabitants, or that any rate of postage or post regulation of the imperial parliament can have the force of law in Upper Canada." No action was taken on the report by the House and the imperial government continued to control the post office in Canada till the year 1851.

The other committee presided over by Mackenzie devoted its attention exclusively to two topics, the first being the question whether the lieutenant governor had the right to appoint the Clerk of the House; and the second the charges made by returning officers for election fees. The first enquiry was suggested by the late lieutenant governor's appointment of Col. James Fitzgibbon as Clerk of the Assembly, and the second by the bills rendered by sheriff Jarvis as returning officer to the candidates for the county of York in the last general election. No very clear light was obtained on the first point and Col. Fitzgibbon continued to hold his office. In regard to the question of fees the committee refrained from making any specific recommendation: "they content themselves for the present with laying before your honourable House such facts as came before them in evidence, trusting that the wisdom of the legislature will provide a remedy for any abuses that may be found to exist." If any abuses had been in sight the committee would have been only too happy to signalize them; meantime they could only hint that some might yet be discovered.[7]

The fires of enmity once started make fuel for themselves, as the events we have to narrate only too fully illustrate. Within a few days after his arrival Sir John Colborne had a petition presented to him praying him to mitigate the sentence passed on Francis Collins, then languishing in gaol – if a man could be said to be languishing who was continuing to edit his paper, and indulging in language which certainly showed no sign of languor. His excellency informed the petitioners that he did not see his way to interfering in the matter. Collins, however, had many friends among the advanced liberals, and the feeling was not confined to that party that he was suffering under a rather severe sentence. His case was accordingly taken up in the legislature and an address was adopted to his excellency by a vote of thirty-seven to three praying him "to

extend to Francis Collins the royal clemency by remitting his
sentence and restoring him to his family." His excellency,
after consulting Mr. Justice Sherwood by whom the sentence
was passed, replied that he regretted exceedingly that the
House should have made an application to him which the
obligation he was under to support the laws and his duty to
society forbade him to comply with. Manifestly it was not
desirable that the legislature, subject as it was to outside
pressure, should seek to interfere with the course of justice;
and Sir John Colborne doubtless thought it important not to
permit the establishment of a dangerous precedent. His action,
however, caused considerable irritation, and some of the good
people of the rising town of Hamilton gave vent to their feelings by hanging his excellency in effigy, giving him as a companion in that honour Mr. George Gurnett, the editor of a
local conservative paper. The members for the county of
Wentworth, scandalized at this proceeding, moved for an
enquiry. A committee was appointed and amongst the witnesses summoned were Mr. Allan N. MacNab, barrister of
Hamilton, and Mr. John Henry Boulton, solicitor general.
Upon appearing before the committee Mr. MacNab took the
ground that having been summoned to give evidence as to
what was called "the Hamilton outrage" he was not required
to testify on any other point whatever. Consequently, when
asked whether certain remarks made by Mr. Gurnett in his
paper were correct and whether there was a feeling of indignation in the neighborhood against Mr. Gurnett, he refused
to answer, though disclaiming all intention of being disrespectful to the committee. His conduct having been reported
by the committee, it was resolved, on motion of Dr. Baldwin,
that he had been guilty of a breach of the privileges of the
House, and on motion of Mr. Mackenzie that he be "committed to the gaol of York under the warrant of the Speaker
directed to the sergeant-at-arms, during the pleasure of the
House." On the latter motion the vote stood twenty-four to
sixteen. This was on the sixteenth of February, and Mr.
MacNab endured the regions of confinement until the third
of the following month when a letter which he addressed to
the Speaker – by no means a very penitent one – was accepted as a pretext for terminating his imprisonment by a
vote of twenty two to ten. Mr. Mackenzie's name does not
appear in the division list, but it is probable that had he been
present he would have voted with the majority as on the

twenty-fifth of February he had supported a motion, which was only lost by the casting vote of the Speaker, for the liberation of the captive. Among the ten stalwarts who voted for his continued confinement were Dr. Baldwin, Perry, and the two Rolphs.[8]

Solicitor general Boulton did not endure imprisonment, but he incurred the censure of the House in connection with the same matter. His trouble was an undue reliance on his own legal learning; so that when brought before the committee he told them that he would answer their questions if they insisted on it, but that, as a lawyer, he seriously doubted whether they had power to compel him to testify in regard to the Hamilton outrage, with which he had nothing to do. Like Mr. MacNab he professed great respect for them; he only wanted to place his legal opinion on record. This did not please the committee, and, instead of proceeding with the examination of the witness, they reported him to the House by whose order he received an admonition from the Speaker, whose language on the occasion was very dignified and appropriate. One observation which that able officer made seems to indicate that a certain old-fashioned toryism must have been lingering in the lap of his democracy. "It is," he said,

> to the spirit and firmness with which the House of Commons in England has upon all occasions asserted and maintained its privileges against the King and the House of Lords, and when necessary against popular prejudice, that our parent country owes her liberties and the best principles of her constitution.

The judicious politician of to-day does not speak of "popular prejudice" as something which the representative body ought to withstand. Like Pope's "soft dean" who "never mentioned hell to ears polite," the modern statesman is very careful how he speaks about popular prejudice.

Things, it will be seen, were not going altogether happily in Upper Canada just at this time. On the same day on which MacNab was committed to gaol Sir John Colborne wrote to the colonial secretary, Sir George Murray, that he had received several addresses from the house of assembly for detailed statements in connection with different branches of expenditure. "Most of these," he remarks, "were moved for by the editor of a York paper for the purpose of making his own comments on them and of keeping up a spirit of dis-

content in the province." Thus did his excellency recognize
Mr. Mackenzie's legislative activity. Better would it have
been if he had assumed that the information was wanted for
the most legitimate purposes and furnished it with all possible
cheerfulness. This was what he was instructed by the colonial
secretary to do. All the same, if Sir John thought that there
were some kinds of information that the Assembly would be
just as well without; if he was afraid that nothing but mischief would be made out of this little detail or that; was he
not anticipating the policy of much later administrations in
the happiest of political eras?

Sir John was not a man of illiberal ideas. He shows his
good sense by recommending a more liberal charter than that
which had been granted the previous year for King's College.
Both houses of the legislature, he informed the colonial office,
agreed that there should be no religious tests in connection
with the institution. If modifications in that direction were
not forthcoming "much dissatisfaction would be expressed
throughout the province." His views in regard to the legislative council – views fully shared by the council itself – were
also sound and progressive. "Composed," he said,

> as the legislative council is at present, the province has a
> right to complain of the great influence of the executive
> government in it. Out of the number generally present
> (fifteen) six are of the executive council and four hold
> offices under the government. It is exceedingly difficult,

he adds,

> to find persons qualified for it; but if about eight or ten
> more can be selected from different parts of the province,
> and the majority be considered independent, there can be
> no good reason for excluding the executive council.[9]

Sir John was quite correct in saying that it was difficult to
find suitable men to sit in the council. To have chosen additional members from the town of York would have given it
too local a character; and men were few throughout the
province who, having the requisite education and ability – and
these things were considered in those days –, were willing to
travel to York in the winter season, and give unremunerated
labour to the work of law-making or law-mending for two or
three months every year.

A further glimpse into Sir John Colborne's mind may be

obtained from a letter he wrote, before he had been quite four months in the country, to the Anglican bishop of Quebec whose jurisdiction then extended over both provinces, and who, it seems, had discountenanced a proposed visit of Dr. Strachan's to England. "I wish," writes Colborne,

> to treat him with the greatest respect and to prove that I am fully aware of his good intentions, his zeal for our church, and that the British government is grateful to him for his exertions; but I cannot blind myself so far as not to be convinced that the political part he has taken in Upper Canada destroys his clerical influence and injures to a very great degree the interests of the episcopal church and, I am afraid, of religion also. I think it a very fortunate circumstance that your lordship does not approve of his going to England. The alarm which a few sad fellows have raised against his assertions and statements is subsiding, and I am persuaded his departure now would be the signal for the cabalists to take advantage of his absence.

We must thank Sir John for that phrase, "a few sad fellows." There is an old world charm about it which disarms criticism. As to Strachan, the perfervid genius of the Scot was seen in him no less than in Gourlay and Mackenzie. Those three men could have fought a grand triangular battle. Each in his own way acted as a ferment in the country; each stirred public opinion in its depths; each was a motive of great force, though to Gourlay scant opportunity was given to show what he had it in him to accomplish.

As poor an opinion as Mackenzie had of Francis Collins, he makes frequent quotations from his paper about this time. In fact the severest things in relation to the administration that appear in the *Colonial Advocate* in the spring of 1829 are taken from the *Freeman*. Here is a specimen:

> His excellency has dropped down among a set of the greatest villains that ever disgraced the name of British government – a set of low-bred upstarts. He knows he has a terrible faction to deal with – a faction that has got the better of governors, judges and some of the most powerful individuals before now – a faction too strong even for the law of the land, a faction that can overturn any power in the colony save that of the people.

Yet Collins had none too good an opinion of the people after all, for a couple of weeks before he had said, as quoted by Mackenzie:

The first thing that sickens a European subject entering the province is the incessant hum of loyalty, loyalty, loyalty, both in whig and tory. For our own part we have been so disgusted with it that we often wished the term expunged from the English vocabulary. A fastidious and cringing dread of being viewed as radical or disloyal even by the meanest sycophants of office seems to pervade all classes of the Upper Canadian community.

He says expressly that he refers "both to the people and their representatives," when he asserts that

whenever they attempt an honest and independent thing some wily agent of corruption, knowing their weak point, shakes the batter in their faces, cries aloud 'radical,' 'democrat,' 'traitor,' and immediately they become petrified and shrink from their purpose.

Mackenzie himself, however, had something to say a couple of months later about the condition of the country. While on a visit to the United States[10] he addressed a letter to the *National Gazette* of Philadelphia which he reproduced in the *Colonial Advocate* of July the second. There we read:

Sycophancy and meanness bear a premium in the colonies, and persons who possess these qualifications are generally found fit for the magistracy and for filling the places of militia officers. The disgust and dissatisfaction excited among the people . . . by the high-handed arts of the minions who accept places in such a government is very great. Private individuals are persecuted and ruined for their opinions, spies and informers cherished and patronized, lands and tenements are a drug in the market, property does not afford one fifth of what its value is on the other side of the lake. . . . We are eaten up by monopolies; they are among the doubtful blessings of colonial government. A monopoly was lately granted by the British minister of millions of acres of the most fertile lands in the colony to a number of foreign mercantile adventurers called the Canada Company. . . . The colonists sometimes express their wishes by legislative bills and resolutions; but the bills seldom pass into laws, and the resolutions only serve to encumber the already loaded shelves of the lumber rooms in the colonial department, Downing Street. . . . The chief direction and superintendence of education has been entrusted to an emigrant priest, a convert from presbytery to the Church of England. Well and truly does Mr. Haliburton's remark made in the legislature of Nova Scotia apply to Upper Canada – 'the paw of the priest is on everything.'

It is not every writer who would care to hold his own country up to contempt in the columns of a foreign newspaper, however severely he might comment on its weaknesses at home. The charge of sycophancy is of course one of which Mackenzie will never tire. The Canada Company to which, not so long ago, he was wishing success, and to whose agent, Galt, he paid so much attention, is now a monopoly that is eating up the country. From the term "emigrant" applied to Dr. Strachan one might suppose that the writer was himself born in the colony; but the only difference between the two in this respect was that, whereas the editor had only been nine years in the country, the "priest" had been thirty – almost long enough, one would say, to wipe out the stain of his Scottish nativity. But this was not all. It would have been well if Mackenzie's communication had stopped here, but he had another arrow in his quiver and he let it fly:

The province of Upper Canada was ravaged during the last war, in which war, by the way, neither the people nor their interests were ever consulted. They fought bravely, however, like brave fellows, for British supremacy and against the prosperity, freedom and independence tendered them by this country (the United States). For the valor so opportunely displayed on behalf of the government of England they have met an ungrateful and thankless return.

This is painful reading from every point of view. The reader will perhaps recall Mackenzie's indignant outburst in an early number of his paper at the thought of England's selling Canada – "What, sell Canada! take the price of Wolfe's and Brock's blood!" Now it would seem that Brock's blood was spilt in aiding misguided Upper Canadians to repel the offer of "prosperity, freedom and independence." At that

time he could say, "we like American liberty well, but greatly
prefer British liberty. British subjects born in Britain, we have
sworn allegiance to a constitutional monarchy, and we will
die before we will violate that oath." Now the same writer
tells American readers, and repeats the statement in his own
paper, that Upper Canada was not a land of liberty at all –
that its people had fought not for liberty but for "British
supremacy," and against the liberty tendered to them by the
armies of the United States. The war, moreover, he asserts,
had been made without consulting the people or their
interests; yet it was not forgotten at the time either in Canada
or the United States that the war had been declared by the
United States, and had been forced on England in the very
crisis of her struggle with the power of Napoleon.

A very ineffectual session of the provincial parliament was
brought to a close on the twentieth of March. The motive power
for progressive legislation, it must be admitted, was in great part
lacking. The administration had practically no representation
in the assembly; all its members were in the legislative council.
Mr. Robinson, the attorney-general, was understood to be in
a certain sense its spokesman, but only as being in personal
sympathy with its policy, so far as it had one, without being
in any way responsible for it. Not only was there no constitutional necessity for his being in the house, but his position
there as a salaried officer of the government but not a
member of the executive council was a rather delicate one. It
was only in the legislative council that really official utterance
could be given to the views of the administration. The consequence of this was a great lack both of initiative and of
driving power in the matter of constructive legislation, particularly when a party hostile to the government was in command
of the popular chamber. The government would be slow to
bring forward measures to be torn to pieces whether good or
bad; and the dominant party would not be very zealous to
pass bills of large scope the execution of which would fall to
officials whom rightly or wrongly they detested. The most
fruitful sessions, therefore, were those in which the administration and the assembly were working in harmony.

It must be admitted that both in Upper and in Lower
Canada the administration represented rather the statical
aspect of the political problem than the dynamical. It seems
to have been assumed from the beginning that the provincial
legislatures would know what their respective provinces

wanted, and would initiate the necessary legislation: the executive government, more or less supported by the legislative council, was there to see that nothing was done to imperil the fundamental institutions of the country. It was hardly thought to be its business to tell the people what they wanted in the way of roads, bridges, schools, and other elements of comfort and prosperity. But legislation for these purposes involves taxation and people do not like imposing taxes on themselves. In Lower Canada the idea was absolutely hateful; in Upper Canada it was none too agreeable.[11] The government again not being liable to overthrow by a vote of the assembly was not under the necessity of consolidating its power by a judicious distribution of local expenditure, otherwise it might have made greater efforts to provide money for the purpose. It is obvious, therefore, that the conditions of the times were not favorable to heavy budgets or to rapid material development.

Sir John Colborne who, perhaps, in these circumstances expected too much from the assembled wisdom of the province expressed his disappointment at the meagre results of the session in what the journals of the House call

a most gracious speech. His gracious remarks were in part as follows: I cannot close this session without expressing my regret that the people will derive no immediate advantage from your deliberations on two subjects of primary importance, improvement of public schools and the measures that should be adopted to ensure good roads and safe bridges throughout the province. In allowing your roads to remain in their present state, the great stimulus to agricultural industry is lost.

In the midsummer of 1829 Mr. J. B. Robinson ascended the bench as Chief Justice of Upper Canada in succession to Chief Justice Campbell, who on retirement was knighted. Under the system then prevailing he was at once called to the executive and legislative councils, becoming president of the first and speaker of the second. Three years later he resigned the former position in deference to the views of the British government, while he retained the latter, also in accordance with their views, until the union of Upper and Lower Canada under the act of 1840.

Mr. Robinson had sat in the assembly as member for the town of York, and on his retirement Mr. Robert Baldwin came forward and was elected. His opponent was Mr. James E. Small, of whom we have heard before. To assist Mr. Baldwin's election Mr. Mackenzie published in the *Colonial Advocate* a statement made some time before by a Mr. Hogg of Milford Mills in County York that Mr. Small had, in some legal transaction, defrauded him of forty or fifty dollars. For having made this statement Hogg had been prosecuted for libel and the case had gone against him; but Mackenzie concluded that after what had taken place in Court the statement, as a statement, might be repeated with impunity to the disadvantage of Mr. Small's canvas. The election seems to have excited little interest for only one hundred and forty four votes were cast, ninety two of which were given to Baldwin, who was elected. Small now commenced an action for libel against Mackenzie who, though he engaged as counsel Messrs Baldwin and Sullivan, preferred after all to defend himself, which he did in a speech of four hours duration. A verdict was given in his favour, but with the costs of the suit against him. Of the conduct of the trial he speaks in his paper as follows: "The judge (Sherwood) summed up the evidence, and his charge to the jury was, in the opinion of every one with whom we have since conversed who heard it, as well as the jurors themselves as others, fair impartial and free from undue bias." He speaks of the "patriotic and intelligent jurors," and even the sheriff Mr. W. B. Jarvis comes in for praise: "The jury lists appeared to be accurately drawn up, and in striking the jury the sheriff conducted himself with the utmost fairness and impartiality."[12] Might not the "family compact" place this amongst its testimonials?

The legislature met for its second and, as it proved, its last session on the eighth of January 1830. The lieutenant governor in the speech from the throne referred in terms of congratulation to the agricultural progress of the country and expressed the hope that the legislature would afford proper encouragement to the individual labours of the people. He also announced that no vote would be required this year in aid of civil government or the administration of justice this year as the revenues collected for that purpose under 14 George 111, chapter 83, would be fully sufficient; there was moreover a surplus over from previous appropriations which would be available, as well as any money the assembly might vote, for public improvements, roads, education &c. It was of course a sign of the prosperity of the country that the very light duties levied under the statute referred to should have been so productive as not to call for any supplement from the liberality of the assembly, but none the less the situation was not pleasing to the reform majority for the less the government stood in need of their benevolence, the less pressures they could bring to bear on it. In the address in reply they indicated their point of view. "We cannot," they said,

> advert to the subject of the duties levied under the 14th George 111 and to the general resources of the country without respectfully repeating to your excellency our conviction that the unqualified recognition of our constitutional right over all moneys raised in, or to or for the uses of, this province can alone secure to us overdue weight in the constitution and enable us to realize the many and urgent objects of public improvement without unnecessarily increasing the burdens of the people.

The constitutional ground was here well taken, but the pretense that if placed in control of the revenue raised under the statute mentioned they could so readjust the appropriation of it as to have any surplus worth mentioning to apply to public improvements was absurd and hollow. They took the same opportunity of expressing to his excellency their regret at the continuance about him "of those advisers who, from the unhappy policy they pursued, have long deservedly lost the confidence of the country."

His excellency was not prepared to discuss with the assembly the question of his advisers, and as it would never do to discuss other points in their address and leave that out, he took refuge in a most laconic utterance, "Gentlemen I thank you for this address." Later in the session he found an opportunity of pointing out that so long as the Act 14 George 111, chapter 83, was the law of the land there was no use in finding fault with him for carrying out its provisions in accordance with the instructions he received from the British Treasury. This cause of disagreement however was on the point of disappearing, as a proposition for the repeal of the Act on very reasonable conditions was shortly to be made by the British government.

Mr. Mackenzie during this session displayed great activity and it is impossible to doubt the sincerity of his endeavours for the public good. He seems, however, to have been as keen over matters that were not of the highest moment as over those that were. He could "find quarrel in a straw" as readily as in some large constitutional principle. In matters of public expenditure he was always on the side of economy and had his zeal in this respect only been less allied with bitter and sleepless suspicion his influence in a most important department of public affairs would have been wholly, as in fact it was greatly, beneficial. The unclean thing which to-day stalks through the land, and passes by the name of "graft," was comparatively little known in the early days of Upper Canada. Early in the session Mackenzie moved for a committee to enquire into the management and expenditure of the Welland and Burlington Canals. Of this committee Mr. Ambrose Blacklock, one of the members for Grenville and a reformer, was made chairman. Dealing with the Welland canal the committee reported that charges of mismanagement had been made, and that on this account they had been "more strict and careful in their examination of the books and accounts of the company than they might otherwise have been." Having been thus strict in their enquiries they were able to state that

> although they met with occasional charges against the company perhaps not so moderate in amount as would have been willingly paid by a private individual; and although the transactions in the books embrace an expenditure of a million of dollars and upwards, they saw very little indeed to censure.

With regard to the Burlington canal they simply reported that a further appropriation of from four thousand to seven thousand dollars would be needed to complete it.

An important committee on which Mr. Mackenzie sat as chairman was one appointed on his own motion to consider the state of the currency which was then in great confusion owing to the variety of foreign coins circulating in the country and under a former statute recognized as legal tender at certain assigned values. The only outcome at this time of the committee's labours was the passing of a brief Act depriving all foreign coinage of the character of legal tender and also all English coins that had lost one twenty fifth of their weight. The committee, however, made close enquiry into the banking system and presented a large amount of information bearing on the general question.

The spirit in which Mackenzie was pursuing reforms was conspicuous in an address which the House adopted on his motion asking for detailed information on a vast number of topics all at once – the number of acres of land sold by the crown lands commissioner (Mr. Peter Robinson) since he had held that office, the gross sum received, amount still unpaid, prices charged, how money had been appropriated; amount of money received from the Canada Company and how appropriated, with the names and denominations of the clergymen, bishops and civil and military officers partaking thereof; amount of money in the hands of the commissioners of forfeited estates; an account of the receipts and expenditure of the casual and territorial revenues for the last five years; information for the past year in regard to revenues arising under 14 George 111, chapter 83; copies of correspondence etc., etc. The vast range of the information demanded suggested of course vast withholdings of information on the part of the government, and was so far favorable to the development of the spirit of complaint – the grievance spirit we may call it – throughout the country. It suggested also that there was now a man in the House who would not allow the family compact and its minions to repose on a bed of roses. Sir John, however, was a man of nerve and made a calm reply. Some of the information, he said, had been already given; part of it was in their own journals; some of it was always given as a matter of course, and would be this session as usual; some would be specially prepared and laid before the House as desired; certain statements, finally, could not be furnished without the consent of his Majesty's government.

As the session advanced the House seemed to lose to some extent its extreme partisan character. There was a change brewing in the country of which possibly members had received advice. Or it may have been that a little industrious application to public business – in which respect this session compared favorably with its predecessor – had promoted interchange of opinion and evidencing of view. It is certain that much more of individual independence[13] was shown in the voting than is possible in the present day. There was no government to defeat or save from defeat, and members could therefore better afford to vote according to their convictions than can the machine-elected and whip-disciplined successors of the twentieth century. They did not – theoretically – possess the power to turn out a government; their successors *do* possess that power – theoretically. But if that privilege was denied them, they could advance, and in a very measurable degree did advance, the interest of the country by useful legislation; they could watch over and check the expenditure of public money; they could at all times bring a strong moral pressure to bear on the executive; and the home government was ever ready to consider their petitions in matters which provincial legislation could not reach. Further they could not go. Plainly such a system of government, whatever its provisional merits may have been, could not last in a developing community. Its centre of gravity was too high. No government can justify itself merely by good works, still less by good intentions. It can only justify itself by *power*. The government of Upper Canada needed to be brought nearer to the source of power – the people.

CHAPTER NINE

A CONSERVATIVE REACTION

King George the Fourth died on the twenty-fifth of June 1830 and according to the law as it then stood his decease had to be followed by the dissolution six months later of any parliament called in his name. Sir John Colborne, however, did not wait for the ninth parliament to die by efflux of time, but dissolved it by proclamation dated the tenth of September. Writs for a new election were made returnable on the twenty-ninth of October, and the tenth parliament of Upper Canada was summoned for the seventh of the following month of January, about the usual date.

In all human affairs dependent in any way upon popular sentiment allowance must be made for the love of change. Two parliaments in succession had now been ruled by reform majorities, and party spirit had made as much as could reasonably be made – perhaps a little more – of the faults of government. Some of the addresses presented to Sir Peregrine Maitland before his departure from the country had pointed to a feeling in a portion of the community that fault-finding and accusation had been carried too far. Sir John Colborne in his earliest utterance after assuming that office had seemed to make his appeal from the wrangling of politicians to the good sense of the people. The election showed that, in point of fact, public sentiment had undergone a change, for a House was returned in which the conservatives had quite as decided a preponderance as the reformers had had in the last one. Robert Baldwin, Dr. Baldwin (his father), and John Rolph all lost their seats. Henry J. Boulton, who had been made attorney-general on the elevation of Mr. Robinson to the bench, was returned for Niagara, his brother George S. Boulton for Durham, and Mr. W. B. Robinson, a brother of the chief justice, for Simcoe. County York, however, was faithful to reform, returning (as before) Ketchum and Mackenzie, the former with 616, the latter with 570 votes;

while their unsuccessful competitors, Washburn and Thorne, received 425 and 243 respectively. Comparing the votes given for Ketchum with those given for Washburn it would seem that the county at this time was divided between the two parties in the proportion of ten to seven. When the legislature met there was manifestly no chance for the re-election of Mr. Bidwell as speaker. Mr. Archibald McLean of Stormont was proposed by Mr. William Morris of Lanark, seconded by H. C. Thomson of Frontenanc and elected without opposition.

During the recess Mr. Mackenzie had published a series of letters addressed to Sir John Colborne, of which his biographer states with great truth and moderation that "they are not free from remarks to which a general consent would not now be given."[1] A lively, if not painfully accurate, description of the government of Upper Canada may be quoted.

> The visible government of the province of which your Excellency is the head may, I think, be fairly described as an aristocracy of office holders, men nearly above all law with a monopoly of the paper currency, a monopoly of the places, offices, gifts, grants, territories, sinecures, crown lands, church lands, a monopoly of religion, law, legislation, indeed everything in their grasp. So it is, however, powers have been put into the hands of your excellency in conjunction with a very small number of other persons which make you as a body stronger than the rest of the community, consequently you may take from the community whatever you please – at least the restraint is but nominal.

The letter was addressed to Sir John Colborne, but was plainly aimed at the gallery. Certainly there was nothing in such sweeping and random assertions as these either to instruct or to influence Sir John. The summing up, however, is reasonably and forcibly expressed:

> The people of this province neither desire to break up their ancient connection with Great Britain, nor are they anxious to become members of the North American confederation; all they want is a cheap frugal, domestic government to be exercised for their benefit and controlled by their own fixed landmarks; they seek a system by which to insure justice, protect property, establish

domestic tranquillity and afford a reasonable prospect
that civil and religious liberty will be perpetuated and
the safety and happiness of society effected.

There is nothing to object to here save the implication that
these things were all more or less lacking in Upper Canada.
The people of the province were well content, as the writer
admits, with their connection with Great Britain; but surely,
as he wrote the words, he must have remembered how, not
so long before, he had accused them in an American paper –
afterwards copying the letter in his own – of having refused
liberty at the hands of the Americans in 1812. The province
had a cheap and frugal government with the sole exception
that the salaries of a few higher officials, especially the judges
of the superior court, were established rather on an imperial
than on a provincial footing. Other salaries were excessively
moderate. The executive councillors received for their services as such £100 currency each. All contingent expenses
were on an extremely modest scale. Mackenzie has himself
already been quoted as declaring that the people knew nothing practically of taxation – they had merely *heard* of it. As
regards the administration of justice he had had no fault to
find with it in his own experience. In the preceding session a
bill had been brought in by Dr. Baldwin for changing the
mode of impanelling. In explaining the measure that gentleman had said that "he would not assert that any wrong had
been practised heretofore in impanelling juries, but there had
been suspicion that impartial justice in this respect had not
been practised." The object of the bill was to remove *all*
ground for suspicion which might arise under the present
law. Discussing the same matter in committee the speaker,
Mr. Bidwell, had said that the selection of jurors should
never be lodged with any one who held his office during
pleasure. "It may be argued," he continued, "that no instance
has occurred in which this trust has been abused. He would
not say that it had, though he believed it had; but how can it
be proved even if it has been abused?" The careful and
guarded statements of these two eminent reformers certainly
do not imply any glaring or widely-recognized evils in the
judicial system.

It may be noticed that in his description of an ideal Upper
Canada, Mackenzie does not stipulate for the subjection of
the government to a majority of the popular House. All he

demands for the people is a government "controlled by their own fixed landmarks." What did that mean? Sir Francis Bond Head would have liked the phrase well, and had he unearthed it would certainly have been eager to quote it. Mackenzie however came nearer to the shining mark of "responsible government" in a sixteen column "Appeal to the People of Canada" which he published in the *Colonial Advocate* of the ninth of September, 1830. In this document he told the people: "You have far less reason to complain of the defects of the established constitution than of the corruption, ignorance, carelessness and subservience of successive assemblies." Still, the constitution wanted mending and this was his platform:

1. The entire control of the whole provincial revenues to be vested in the legislature, the territorial and hereditary revenues excepted.
2. The independence of the judges; or their removal to take place only upon a joint address of the two Houses, and their appointment from men who have not embarked in the political business of the province.
3. A reform in the legislative council which is now an assembly chiefly composed of persons wholly or partly dependent upon the executive government for their support.
4. An administration or executive government responsible to the province for its conduct.
5. Equal rights to each religious denomination and an exclusion of every sect from a participation in temporal power.

The first two of these reforms, as we shall see, were put in the way of being realized within a few months of the publication of this programme. The reform of the legislative council, though Sir John Colborne had personally recommended it, was destined to lag. Modern experience, indeed, shows that the current of reform in the matter of second chambers is apt to be lethargic. The fourth plank in his platform was the one in which Mackenzie demanded responsibility in the administration, and yet it will be observed that he speaks not of responsibility to the legislature, still less to a mere majority of it, but to the province. Of parliamentary majorities he thought but little, as was proved in the next parliament, and still more by his proceedings under the second conservative reaction of 1836. He looked beyond parties to the people, as Sir John Colborne professed to do. Had he been asked at this, or at any time, whether he was willing to commit absolute power to a mere parliamentary majority, it is questionable what his answer would have been. He only saw the truth that government ought to be responsible to the people in some very real and effective sense. If he failed to see in his mind's eye the plan of the machinery by which a real, and not a sham, responsibility could be secured, there are many in our own day who will attribute it to the difficulty of the problem rather than to the weakness of his thought.

Mackenzie's sojourn in the United States the year before had not been without effect upon his opinions. He states in his "Appeal" that by education and habit he had been "an admirer of aristocracy in which virtue, wealth, and ancient lineage were combined." His views, however, have changed and he does not see much future for aristocracy in Canada. He now believes in "rotation in office for clerks, postmasters, treasurers, collectors and others through whose hands the revenue passes." His faith in human nature is after all not very high, for he says few men can enjoy power – it is hardly a question of "power" with postmasters and clerks[2] – long and not become more or less corrupt; so that "more is lost by the long continuance of men in office than is gained by their experience." If there were any truth in this as regards men holding non-political offices it would be found that cases of malfeasance were numerous in direct proportion to length of service, which is notoriously not the case.

In November 1830 the Wellington ministry in England gave way to that of Earl Grey, Lord Goderich succeeding Sir George Murray in the colonial office. The latter though having the reputation of a military martinet had been by no means an illiberal administrator. An example of this was given when Sir John Colborne, disliking to ask the legislature for necessary supplement to the revenue collected under the imperial statute for, the maintenance of civil government, proffered to defer creating certain offices which it was thought advisable to create on public grounds. Sir George Murray did not approve of the idea at all. He thought on the contrary that it would be a good thing to have to appeal to the assembly as it would have, to use his own words, "the best means of forming an opinion as to the necessity of the offices and the proper amount of their contingent expenses." Not a bad sentiment for a tory of the unreformed parliament of Great Britain. Lord Goderich – later the Marquis of Ripon – who now assumed the direction of the colonial office was a man of extremely liberal and benevolent mind. It was he, it will be remembered, who, as colonial secretary in Mr. Canning's government, dealt with the Naturalization question in a manner so satisfactory to the reformers of Upper Canada. His return therefore to his former post gave promise of a large and progressive policy in all that related to the administration of the colonies.[3]

We find, accordingly, the new colonial secretary writing to Sir John Colborne in December 1830 to say that the imperial government means to place at the disposal of the legislature the revenues arising under the statute of 14 George 111 on the condition that an act shall be passed making a reasonable permanent provision for the salaries of the lieutenant governor and his secretary, the judges and a few leading officials. A later despatch (February 8th 1831) deals more fully with the matter, especially in relation to the salaries of the judges. As illustrating the disposition of the home government some portions of it may with advantage be quoted:

> In making this demand upon the liberality of his faithful Commons in Upper Canada his Majesty was desirous to secure to his subjects in that part of his dominions the full enjoyment of those advantages which have been so largely derived in this Kingdom from the independence of the judicial office. . . . The connection which happily subsists between the Canadas and this Kingdom suggests the propriety of transferring to those provinces every institution which the more ample experience of Great Britain recommends as calculated to promote at once the stability of government and the welfare of society at large. There is no branch of our civil polity which has been more fully proved to be conducive to these great ends than the establishment of judges independent at once of the royal authority and of the pleasure of the popular branch of the legislature. There was not, I apprehend, any legal or constitutional reason which would have prevented the King from granting the offices of the judges during their good behaviour; but to render that principle immutable it was necessary that

parliament should prescribe the form of commission to be used on such occasions. Accordingly the statutes passed in the thirteenth year of the reign of William III and in the first year of George III have deprived the Crown of all discretion on the subject.

The despatch went on to suggest that the legislature should pass an act "declaring that the commissions of all the judges of the supreme court shall be granted to endure during their good behaviour and not during the royal pleasure." It was added that no judge will in future be nominated as member either of the executive or the legislative council, with the sole exception of the Chief Justice of Upper Canada who will be a member of the legislative council "in order that they may have the benefit of his assistance in framing laws of a general and permanent character." Yet even in his case "his Majesty will not fail to recommend a cautious abstinence from all proceedings by which he might be in any political contentions of a party nature."

The legislature, we have seen, met on the seventh of January, 1831, and this despatch did not reach Sir John Colborne's hands in time to be communicated to it before prorogation. His excellency in his opening speech dwelt upon the progress the country had made in its commercial intercourse with the parent state, its increasing revenue and the accessions of population and wealth it was receiving through immigration which was then very active. The address in reply was of a conventional character; the constitution of the House forbade any unpleasant reflections on his advisers. Mackenzie, however, undeterred by the changed aspect of affairs, returned to a matter which he had brought in the preceding session and moved a resolution to the effect that "until this House shall decide where the power to appoint a chaplain lies, the services of a chaplain shall be dispensed with." This was lost by a vote of twenty-eight to thirteen. His speech on the occasion, as reported in the *Colonial Advocate*, was rich in historical illustration: the ancient Jews, Mahomet, the Crusaders, the massacre of St. Bartholemew, Tyre and Sidon, Carthage and Diana of the Ephesians were all brought into relation in one way or another with the topic of the hour.

The general question of a civil list was discussed in the House on the basis of the earlier despatch. What was specifically proposed by the home government was the revenue ac-

cruing under the Imperial Act, amounting at this time to
£11,500 a year, should be transferred to the control of the
province and that the legislature should in exchange permanently appropriate £8000 to the support of the civil
government, including the judiciary. Despite its conservative
complexion the House was not disposed to be too compliant.
The estimate for the lieutenant governor's salary was reduced
from £3000 to £2000, and an item of £2700 for pensions to
retired judges was struck out altogether, leaving the imperial
authorities to make up the shortage out of their only remaining resource – save the British treasury which had often
been drawn on in the past – the casual and territorial revenue.
One or two other reductions were made, and in the end the
amount of £6,500 was voted; but the Act of 1816, appropriating permanently £2,500 to the uses of civil government, was
at the same time repealed, so that the new vote amounted,
strictly speaking, only to £4,000. The bill passed by a vote
of twenty-six to sixteen, after Mackenzie had vainly endeavoured to "hoist" it to the first of April, a date, not perhaps chosen by accident, on which it was known the legislature would not be in session. "The Everlasting Salary Bill,"
as he promptly named it, now took its place amongst the
grievances of Upper Canada! Fifteen years later, under the
Union, a bill was passed making permanent appropriation for
the expenses of civil government to the amount of over
£70,000. The salaries provided for were as follows: Lieutenant Governor, £2000; Judges £3300; Attorney general
£300; Solicitor general £200; five executive councillors
£100 each, and the clerk of the executive council £200.

Notwithstanding the fact that his party was in a minority
Mackenzie was made chairman of a committee to which was
referred the report on the currency which his own committee
had made in the previous parliament. In due time he presented a report which a section of the House wished to have
laid on the table. A motion was made to that effect but it was
defeated by the decision vote of twenty-nine to eleven. A bill
was then reported from the committee, but it did not get
beyond its second reading. A motion made by Mackenzie for
a select committee to enquire into the state of the representation was carried by a vote of twenty-eight to eleven. Subsequent motions to choose the committee by ballot and to refer
the question to a committee of the whole House were defeated, and the committee was appointed just as Mackenzie

had proposed. Earlier in the session the House had adopted without a dissentient voice a resolution which he had moved asking for a

> full and particular account of all fees, salaries, payments, pensions and rewards for extra services, and all other income and emolument derived by all officers, clerks and servants during the years 1829 and 1830, with a statement as to whence the funds in each case were derived.

Two things are evident, first that the reformer wielded a considerable influence; and second that the House, however composed, stood in no relation to the government, which made it shrink from demanding the fullest information in regard to the expenditure of the public revenue.

In moving an enquiry into the state of the representation Mackenzie had referred to the Casual and Territorial revenue. "What," he asked, "does the hereditary, territorial and casual revenue mean? Mr. Speaker, in this colony? It means a secret job, Sir, of the ramification of which, I believe, neither the home government nor the people themselves are rightly informed." This mystery of iniquity was destined to be unveiled in the present session, for the lieutenant governor, having consulted the home authorities and obtained their permission, sent down to the House a full statement of the receipts and expenditure of the fund in question for the year 1830.[4] It cannot be said that the revelations were of a startling character. The average product of these revenues for some years previous had been something over £4,000, but in the year 1830 they had yielded £8,473. The heaviest receipts were for timber cut on crown lands, £3,420. Lands sold yielded £1,409; the use of the seal on land patents £826; seizures £777: all the other items were smaller, the lease of crown reserves only bringing in £276. Within the year the expenditures from the fund had amounted only to £4,087, out of which £1,000 stg. had gone to bring the lieutenant governor's salary up to £3,000, the remaining £2,000 being taken from customs dues levied under the imperial act. A salary of £1,000 was likewise paid to the Commissioner of Crown Lands, Mr. Peter Robinson. Dr. Strachan, in his capacity of superintendent of the provincial school board, received £270 stg. (£300 currency); and a few odd hundred were given to clergymen (anglican and presbyterian) and

school masters. All the payments from this fund were made
by the authority of the imperial treasury; and Mackenzie in
his manifesto of the previous September had approved of
its exemption from parliamentary control. But from the tenth
of September to the twenty-second of January was a period
of three months and several days to spare, ample for a change
of mind.[5]

The session had not advanced very far before it became
evident that trouble was brewing between Mackenzie and a
section of the assembly. Neither the attorney general nor the
solicitor general had any special reasons for being indulgent
towards him, nor were they the only ones to whom he had
given personal offence. The previous parliament, it has been
mentioned, had employed him to print their journals;[6] and,
during the recess, before delivery of the journals to the
House, Mackenzie had undertaken to distribute gratuitously
one hundred and sixty copies of them, *without the appendix*.
In his view of the matter the proceeding was wholly un-
objectionable, but others saw it in a different light. A committee was accordingly appointed "to enquire into the printing of the journals for the last session of 1830." Of this
committee Mr. Allan MacNab, now a member of the House,
was chairman. Possibly he had not forgotten the part taken
by Mackenzie in causing his incarceration; in any case, when
the matter came before the House, he moved,

> that W. L. Mackenzie, printer of this town, who was
> employed to print the said journals, had abused the trust
> reposed in him by publishing portions of the said journals
> and distributing the same for political purposes among
> individuals, not entitled to copies thereof – thereby com-
> mitting a breach of the privileges of this House.

Both the attorney general and the solicitor general gave it as
their legal opinion that there had been a breach of the privileges of the House, nevertheless the vote on the motion stood
only fifteen yeas to twenty nays, amongst those who opposed
it being sheriff Jarvis who had defeated Robert Baldwin in
the general election. Certain members of the committee did
not think that Mr. Mackenzie should be allowed to speak to
the motion, his conduct being in question, but the point was
decided in his favor by the speaker. In his speech he made
ample confession both of what he had done and of his notice.
"I did not," he said, "take the last contract with a view to

profit, but in order to be able to circulate the Journal freely among the people for political purposes."

The House was prorogued on the sixteenth of March and was summoned to meet again on the twenty-seventh of November following. The interval, though short, was long enough, Mr. Lindsey says, for Mackenzie "to arouse an agitation which shook Upper Canada through its whole extent." The agitation began before the session closed. Just a year before he had spoken of Sir John Colborne as "our most excellent lieutenant governor,"[7] now (*Colonial Advocate,* March 10th, 1831) he accuses him of interfering in elections and filling the Assembly with his creatures, and the legislative council with "his willing instruments, the lame, the blind, the halt, the deaf and dumb of the colony," and speaks of "the machiavelian and equivocal course of conduct he has all along adopted towards the people." "His whole history," he continues, "too clearly proves that he has joined with his councillors in their desperate designs to reduce Upper Canada to the death-like silence of a military depotism."

But this was only part of the indictment.

> The immense revenues he (Sir John Colborne) now receives out of the taxes here, in all $15,000 a year . . . over and above his military pay out of the taxes in England, enable him to save a great amount annually besides keeping up an extravagant and costly table to which assembly men have often been invited by *twos and threes,* and tampered with, and efforts made to influence their votes on important questions by his relatives and families *as we are well prepared to prove.*

The statement follows that the reason Sir John wants a permanent civil list is that he may be able "to Willis or Thorpe any other judge or officer who might feel a spark of honest independence arising in his mind at the high handed acts of a gloomy military government." The fact was, as we have seen, that the granting of the civil list – an extremely slender one – was to be made the occasion of placing the judges on the same footing as in England. "With juries selected by such men as sheriff Jarvis, at the dictation of the executive council who would dare to open his lips while the dungeon was yawning for its victim?" This is a singular statement considering how widely and freely Mr. Mackenzie was opening his own mouth at this moment, and also the fact that he had twice had personal experience of sheriff Jarvis's conduct in connection with jury trials and had commended his impartiality on both occasions.

There was something at the same time in Mackenzie which impelled him when he saw or heard of any distinctly good action on the part of an opponent, to give him due credit for it. Thus in a number of his paper published about this time he commends the charges delivered by Judge Sherwood at Brockville and Judge Macaulay at Kingston. "They were far more liberal and tolerant," he says, "than some of the events of late years have taught us to expect." What specific words or acts had taught him to expect illiberality or intolerance on the part of these judges he might have found some difficulty in saying. It holds true, as a rule, that Mackenzie is specific in his commendations, but in his accusations and denunciations runs into generalities.

The *Colonial Advocate* was quite unable to keep up with the publication of the debates, and consequently we have in its columns echoes of them long after the session had closed. Nor was the editor at all afraid to publish the speeches of his opponents. At heart Mackenzie was an honest man, though in his rages he would indulge in flings and insinuations that were far from just. He reports the solicitor general (Hagerman) as saying in the debate on the civil list: "I ask any honourable member what is it that an honest man would wish to do if he were in a state of nature which he cannot do under the protection of the just and equal laws of this free and happy country." Mr. Speaker McLean speaking on the same subject said:

It was popular to say that the government was corrupt, but was this House to be misled by such misrepresentations? He knew they would not be. If there was any dissatisfaction in the country it was altogether caused by the increasing exertions of factious and disaffected persons who wanted to bring about a revolution. . . . Notwithstanding all that had been said about the feeling that would be excited if a permanent grant were to be made out of the revenue raised under the 14th George 111, chapter 83, he verily believed that in the part of the country he had the honour to represent (Stormont) nine tenths of the people did not know that there was any such act, or that any revenue was raised under it.

Mackenzie's comment on this was that he could well believe in the ignorance of any constituency that could return such a man as Mr. McLean. Yet he himself had said, not so long before, that the people knew practically nothing of taxation.

Plain John Willson, farmer and Methodist, whose election to the speakership in 1825 had given Mackenzie so much encouragement, had also something to say on this question. Bidwell had expressed the opinion that they should consult their constituents before passing the bill. "What," said the member for Wentworth,

> do the plain, honest farmers know about salaries to governors and the incomes of the judges and law officers? They send us here because they suppose we know better about these matters. Did the honourable member expect him to go home and travel over the country asking such questions as 'Well, Tom, how much do you say the governor ought to have?' 'Dick, leave your teaming, and tell us your opinion concerning the amount of salary to be paid to the chief justice: What shall we give him a year?' – 'Harry, what do you say?' The honourable and learned member could not be serious in requiring us to consult the plain, honest worthy people of Upper Canada upon matters which he (Mr. Bidwell) knew we were far better able to decide than they. We ought not to ask them. They don't expect us to delay legislation for such a purpose, although members who are angling for popularity have the people in their mouths on all occasions.

This outbreak on John Willson's part drew forth the accusation from Mackenzie that he had insulted his constituents by calling them "Tom, Dick and Harry." It must be confessed that the spirit of democracy could not yet have been fully awake in Upper Canada, or John would have contented himself, as modern statesmen do, with thinking those things and not uttering.

Mackenzie's view of the civil list issue was characteristic. The bill had been brought forward at this time because it was supposed that there was not a House "corrupt enough to sanction anything proposed by authority." Yet we knew that that very House had just cut down the provision requested by the home authorities from £8000 to £4000. "Were they," he said, "to pass this bill the other colonies, this whole continent, would despise their pusillanimity, and the very name of legislator of Upper Canada would become synonymous with that of fawning sycophant." It was hard for men, some of whom at least must have been as conscientious as Mr. Mackenzie, to be told that if they voted as their judgment prompted them to vote they would be "fawning sycophants." In private life a man would repel to the utmost of his power such an attack on his liberty of opinion; and it is not surprising that a fierce resentment arose in the House of Assembly against a member who, claiming freedom for himself, so little respected the rights of his fellow-members.

A few weeks after the prorogation of the legislature Mr. Mackenzie set out on a journey to Quebec with the object, Mr. Lindsey states, of conferring with some of the leading politicians there. It was an unfortunate circumstance that conditions existing in Lower Canada, presenting but slight analogy to those prevailing in Upper Canada, should have produced an embittered state of feeling which had the effect of stimulating and intensifying whatever dissatisfaction had been generated in the sister province. The first thing that struck Lord Durham when he arrived in Canada and was brought face to face with the facts was that the cases of the two provinces were fundamentally dissimilar. In each case, however, the legislature was quarrelling with the executive, and, when two persons are quarrelling with a third, they are not apt to criticize too closely the grounds of one another's grievances, but rather to unite if possible for joint action; even if they have to quarrel afterwards, themselves, over the differences which, for the moment, they ignore or hold in abeyance.[8]

There is no published record of what took place between Mackenzie and the gentlemen whom he went to see. We are indebted, however, to his trip to Quebec for a very lively description, such as flowed naturally from his pen, of an exciting incident which happened by the way, the crushing in the ice a few miles above Quebec of the steamer 'Waterloo' on which he had taken passage. This was first published in the *Colonial Advocate* and afterwards transferred to his *Sketches of Canada and the United States* (London 1833). It is also given at full length in Mr. Lindsey's work and may perhaps be abridged here.

The steamer had left Montreal on Saturday, the fifteenth of April, remained all night at William Henry (now Sorel),

reached Three Rivers before noon and pushed on to Des-
chambault about forty miles above Quebec. The possibility
of reaching Quebec depended on whether or not the ice-
bridge formed as usual at Cap Rouge had given way, as it
was daily expected to do. A man now came on board and
said he had positive information that the ice had given way;
meanwhile large blocks were floating down the river. Upon
the information so given the captain decided to proceed, but
had not gone much more than half the remaining distance
when he found all further progress barred by ice: the
"bridge" at Cap Rouge had *not* given way. Turning back
some distance he anchored in clear water in what he thought
was a safe place; and though there was naturally some
anxiety among the passengers, one after another they all went
to their beds. Mackenzie who had an interesting book to read
did not turn in till after one. He fell fast asleep, but was
awakened at two by a Mr. Lyman of Montreal, who told him
they were in danger; that a field of ice had come down, and
was driving the boat on the ice still fast above Cap Rouge.
"The ice," says Mackenzie,

> made a dreadful din, but I confess I apprehended noth-
> ing so went to sleep again, and was again awakened. We
> had dragged one anchor and lost the other, and had
> drifted into the midst of the ice. The vessel had become
> unmanageable. The efforts of the crew to back her out
> were useless the cables being in the ice. Several passen-
> gers declared their conviction that we should all go to
> the bottom; but I lay still in my berth and listened to
> their arguments *pro* and *con* until half past five. In a
> moment, as it were, some vast mass of ice came down
> upon her with tremendous force; the engine instantly
> stopped, and in less than a minute she filled. I jumped
> up in my shirt, caught hold of my trousers and over-
> shoes, and was soon on a large cake of ice on which
> they had hauled the ship's boat and a bark canoe. . . .
> After helping to haul the boat a little further on the ice
> I went close to the steamer, observed that the water
> ceased to make as at first, and returning to Captain
> Perry took his advice as to the chance I had of going
> down if I returned for my clothes and baggage. He
> thought I might venture and in a moment I was on
> board; got my watch and my pocket book from under

my pillow, seized hold of my saddle bags, valise, great
coat, and other clothes, and without hat or boots made
for the land.

The other passengers were ahead of him by this time, but he
overtook two, Mr. Lyman and a poor woman "who had
almost given in and was weeping bitterly." He kept company
with these, until, as he says, "by the good providence of God
and the wonderful bridge of ice He had that morning provided for us his humble creatures, we all got safely to land at
the village of St. Nicholas about sixteen miles above the city."

One can well believe that he was "hoarse with cold and
very much fatigued," laden as he was with baggage, when he
finally reached a place of safety. The other passengers, who
had left their baggage behind, now "offered rewards to the
Canadian peasants" to bring it ashore. Mention is made of
the assistance given by Mr. Sutton, "a most hospitable and
friendly man who resides in the seigniorial house of St.
Nicholas;" also by the parish priest, Mr. Dufresne, "who took
an active and lively interest in behalf of the wrecked;" while
the captain, his officers and crew are highly praised for their
courage and faithfulness in the hour of danger. The following
tribute to the French Canadians deserves to be quoted:

> I must not omit to state that the sterling honesty of the
> Canadians in humble life never appeared to me in a
> fairer light than in their transactions of the morning of
> the shipwreck. Not one pen's value of property did the
> humblest of their peasants,[9] or peasants' boys, attempt
> to secrete or lay claim to. No! It was delightful to see
> the little fellows, one by one, come up to Mr. Sutton's
> with their loads, and lay them down among the baggage
> without even claiming praise for their exertions. Had
> some of our legislators who made individious compari-
> sons between the Upper and Lower Canadians last winter
> in the Assembly, been with me to see the benevolent
> creatures exert themselves on our behalf, they would
> certainly have felt ashamed of their censures.

It may be added that this narrative as printed in Mackenzie's
Sketches bears as an epigraph the following quotation from
McGregor's *British America*:[10] "If we look for a more
correct or moral people than the Canadian *habitants,* we may
search in vain."

CHAPTER TEN

MACKENZIE EXPELLED FROM THE LEGISLATURE

It would be interesting to know exactly what passed between Mackenzie and the leaders of the opposition in Lower Canada; but that advantage is denied us. From the fact that Mackenzie, who was naturally far from reticent, has said nothing on the subject, it may be inferred that any divulging of the negotiations would have defeated the object in view. Certain it is that on his return to Upper Canada he resumed with more vigour than ever his self-appointed task of agitation. If he had any boats left to burn he burnt them now. He recommended sending agents to London to represent the views of the people, and professed confidence that his Majesty King William, who had just ascended the throne, would prove to be their friend, and that his government would "exert its utmost powers to fulfil their just and reasonable requests." His advice was adopted in many places, county York, as might be expected, taking the lead. "Mr. Mackenzie," Mr. Lindsey writes,

> was personally present at many of these meetings, and even in such places as Brockville and Cornwall he carried everything as he wished. Each petition adopted at those meetings was an echo of the other; and many appear to have been exact copies of one another. To produce a certified copy of the proceedings of the York meeting was sure to obtain ascent to what it had done.[1]

This was no doubt an expeditious way of getting signatures to a previously prepared manifesto, but a little more local discussion would have given stronger evidence of independent and intelligent conviction. Still, probably the method pursued did not differ very greatly from that subsequently followed in getting up counter petitions. What the petitions now being circulated asked for was, in the first place, that the King would

> cause the same constitutional principle which has called your present ministers to office to be fully and uniformly acted upon in Upper Canada; so that we may see only those who possess the confidence of the people composing the executive council of your Majesty's representative.

Other demands were that the legislative assembly should have the control of all the revenue raised in the province – a request which ignored the arrangement just sanctioned by an act of the legislature; that the clergy reserves should be secularized; that local assessments would be levied by municipal councils elected by the people; that all exclusive privileges of an ecclesiastical kind should be abolished; that provision should be made for impeaching public servants who betrayed their trust; that judges and ministers of the gospel should be excluded both from the legislature and from the executive council; and that the law of the primogeniture should be abolished.

Considering that the executive at the very time these petitions were drawn up enjoyed the confidence of the representative body; that there was so little unanimity of sentiment and opinion in the province on the subject of the secularization of the clergy reserves that their secularization was only brought about twenty-three years later by the vigorous, uncompromising championship of George Brown; that the home government had already manifested a disposition to exclude all judges from the legislative council, it need hardly be said that many matters of great actual importance were being pressed upon the attention of his Majesty. The question of the extension of municipal institutions was, however, decidedly of this character. That progress in this particular direction had been retarded by the undue conservatism of the legislative council is beyond question; yet progress was being made, and the session of the legislature then impending was to witness – without any intervention whatever of the home authorities – the passing of an Act which one of the best authorities on the history of the period speaks of as "marking a new departure in the municipal government of Upper Canada,"[2] one namely, incorporating of the Town of Brockville with a charter providing for local control in matters of assessment and expenditure. This measure was followed within two years by the granting of similar, or more enlarged, charters to Hamilton, Belleville, Cornwall, Port Hope and Prescott. It was therefore precisely at the moment when Upper Canada was learning how to help herself in municipal matters, and when antiquated prejudices in favour of the British quarter-sessions system were being overcome that the interference of the home government was called for. It must be admitted at the same time that the sending of such petitions was calculated to awaken the provincial executive to a keener sense of the necessity for adopting progressive measures. No governor cared to have petitions going home complaining that, under his administration, the interests of the country were being neglected. Even ill-founded complaints have at times their uses.

The legislature was summoned for Thursday, the seventeenth of November, 1831. The speech from the throne mentioned the intention of his Majesty to change the tenure of office of the judges from "during pleasure" to "during good behaviour," and invited the legislature to pass an act to that effect. This instalment of reform did not suggest to Mackenzie any abatement of his efforts. On the very next day he gave notice that he would on the following day move for leave to bring in a bill to repeal the law providing a salary for the chaplain of the house of assembly. He introduced the bill accordingly, and by a vote of twenty-eight to four it was referred to a committee of the whole. The bill was finally carried by twenty-nine to four. The salary it may be mentioned was provided for by a provincial act 41 George 111, chapter 6; and the bill now passed was entitled "An Act to repeal so much of the law now in force as authorizes the payment of a salary to a chaplain of the House of Assembly." This did away with the salary, but did it do away with the chaplain were he to tender his services gratuitously? To guard against the moral risk of official prayers, Mackenzie moved, and carried by the casting vote of Mr. Speaker McLean, a resolution affirming "that this House will henceforth dispense with the services of a chaplain, and that the fourth rule of this house be, and the same is, hereby repealed." Exit the Rev. Dr. Phillips, and now two hundred good dollars per annum are liberated for the more substantial uses of the province. The action taken by the House was not pleasing to Sir John Colborne, a very devout churchman, or to the church party, and yet the House which passed the bill on

Mackenzie's initiative, was shortly to see and hear itself
denounced by him as slavish and sycophantic to the executive government.

Having achieved these triumphs before the address in reply
to the speech from the throne had been adopted, Mackenzie
availed himself of the discussion on the address to move an
amendment recommending the passage by the imperial
parliament of

> a law constantly admitting wheat and flour, the produce
> and manufacture of the North American colonies into
> the United Kingdom either free of duty or at a fixed
> rate of duty so much under the scale of duties that may
> be levied on wheat and flour, the produce and manu-
> facture of the United States or of any foreign country as
> may afford an adequate permanent protection to these
> staple articles of Canadian produce in the market of the
> United Kingdom.

The motion was defeated, the vote standing yeas thirteen,
nays eighteen; but it shows Mackenzie as an early advocate
of preferential trade within the empire. Trade relations with
the colonies did in fact at the time rest on a certain preferential basis, and a couple of years before this the house of
assembly had expressed, in replying to the speech from the
throne, a strong sense of the beneficial character of the trade
arrangements then recently made. Mackenzie's idea was to
render systematic and permanent that which had been granted
by special acts of legislation, and which might resting on such
a basis be some day – as in fact they were – withdrawn.

Very early in the session petitions began to pour into the
legislature on the same general lines, but going more into
detail than those prepared for transmission to the King. One
of these – from the township of Vaughan in his own county –
Mackenzie moved should be entered on the journals of the
House. The motion was not opposed, but when he proceeded
to move that it should be referred to a select committee of his
own naming consisting entirely of reformers – Perry, Buell,
Ketchum, and Shaver, with of course himself as chairman –
it was moved in amendment and carried that it should be
referred instead to a select committee to be chosen by ballot
the following day. The committee as chosen consisted of
Ketchum, Perczy, Elliott, Duncombe, Thomson, A. Fraser
and Samson. Ketchum, Mackenzie's colleague, was a sound

and sane liberal, and most of the others were, or had been, of liberal tendencies. Samson had only a few days before moved two resolutions, one on the subject of the clergy reserves, and the other with reference to the charter of King's College, in both of which the right of the Church of England to any position of privilege in the country was strongly challenged. The report made by the committee, printed in the appendix to the journals of the session, was comprehensive and moderate. The petition had demanded that the Crown and clergy reserves should be abolished and that "the sale and disposal of all lands and other public property be regulated for the future only by law." Upon this the committee remark that

The Crown Reserves as well as the waste lands of the crown in this province cannot be considered as belonging exclusively to Upper Canada; they were acquired by the blood and treasure of the parent state, and are now vested in his Majesty for the benefit of the British empire. His Majesty has therefore the indubitable right to reserve or dispose of those lands as he may deem most advantageous to his subjects generally; but should the manner of reservation or disposal at any time interfere with the settlement or prosperity of the province, a respectful representation of his Majesty will, your committee are convinced, procure redress.

The petition had also asked "that the public debt of this province may not be augmented for any purpose whatever, unless the project shall have been first submitted to the people for their approbation." Upon this point the committee observe that

they are not aware of any mode by which the approbation of the people of Upper Canada can be obtained for augmenting or decreasing the debt of the province except through their representatives in the Assembly. No addition can be made to the public debt without the consent of this House, and a discretion in this, as well as in all other respects, must necessarily be reposed by the constituent in his representative.

Mackenzie, who had inspired this petition and a score of similar ones, was well content with a house of assembly that he could sway; but, whenever the legislature was so composed that this was impossible, he tried to get directly at the people.

It has before been remarked that there was far greater freedom of voting at this period than there has been in later times. Many illustrations of this were afforded during the present session, of which perhaps one may be cited. Howard of Leeds, a strong liberal, seconded by Shaver of Dundas, an equally strong one, moved that a statement in detail should be laid before the House, showing what moneys had been paid in to the treasurers of the eleven districts of the province during the last three years; also of the appropriation of such moneys within that time; by what authority such appropriations were made and the amount of the unappropriated balance in each district treasury. A discussion ensuing, Mr. Willson of Wentworth, who was getting quite reckless in displaying his "cloven foot," moved, seconded by the attorney general, the adjournment of the debate, which was lost by a vote of twenty-two to ten; and the motion was carried by the same division. In this case conservatives like Berczy, Jarvis, Lewis and Werden voted with Mackenzie and his usual associates against the recognized conservative leaders, including the attorney general and the solicitor general. At the same time after the motion for an address had carried, when the attorney general (who had some good ideas of his own in business matters) suggested a recasting of the second paragraph, the suggestion was adopted without division. It was not very unusual to find the attorney general and the solicitor general voting on opposite sides of the house, and in general a man's vote might be taken as an index of his individual opinion.

The *Colonial Advocate* meanwhile, as may well be imagined, was not inactive. On the twenty-fourth of November an article had appeared under the title of "The State of the Colony" in which the action of the House of Assembly in the matter of the Vaughan petition was severely censured. "The people of this province," it said, "will probably be able to form a tolerably fair estimate of the manner in which their petitions on public affairs are likely to be treated in the representative branch of the legislature when they learn the manner in which the first of the series has been disposed of." He then tells how instead of being referred to its friends it had been referred to a committee chosen by "a species of vote in which the constituents of members could not learn how they had acted." Those who were "opposed to the rights of the people" of course supported this proceeding. Just a week later appeared an article entitled "Excellent Example of Lower Canada," in which stronger expressions were used. "The contrast," said the writer,

> between their executive and ours, betwixt the material of our assembly and theirs, and between the use they make of an invaluable constitution and our abuse of it is anything but satisfactory to the friends of freedom and social order in Upper Canada. Our representative body has degenerated into a sycophantic office for registering the decrees of as mean and mercenary an executive as was ever given as a punishment for the sins of any part of North America in the nineteenth century. We boast of our superior intelligence, of our love of liberty; but where are the fruits? Has not the subservience of our legislature to a worthless executive become a byword and a reproach throughout the colonies? . . . In our estimation and judging the tree by its fruits, the Lower Canadians are by far the most deserving population of the constitution they enjoy, for they show themselves aware of its value. Judging the people here by the representatives they return, it might be reasonably inferred that the constituents of the McLeans, VanNoughnets, Jarvises, Robinsons, Burwells, Willsons, Boultons, Mc-Nabs, McMartins, Frasers, Chisholms, Crooks, Elliotts, Browns, Joneses, Macons, Samsons and Hagermans had immigrated from Grand Tartary, Russia or Algiers the week preceding the last general election; for although in the turgid veins of their members there may be British blood, there certainly is not the appearance of much British feeling.

This language was meant to sting and it stung. The chamber which the people had elected was nothing but "a sycophantic office for registering the decrees of a mean and mercenary executive." O for a Cromwell to appear upon the scene, order away "that bauble," and turn the whole pack out of doors! There were some moody mutterings in the purlieus of the chamber; in twos and threes the "sycophants" took counsel; and on the sixth of December it was evident that a plan of action had been formed. For on that day Mr. Willson of Wentworth, he of "the cloven foot," rose in his place and moved a resolution to the effect that

> the privileges of parliament were established for the support and maintenance of the independent and fearless discharge of its high functions, and that it is to the uncompromising assertion and maintenance of these privileges in the earlier periods of English history that we are chiefly indebted for the free institutions which have been transmitted to us by our ancestors.

To this resolution the drift of which was well understood Mr. Bidwell moved two amendments, both of which were lost. The second, on which the vote stood sixteen yeas to twenty-four nays, was that, after the words "English history" in the original motion, the words, "and a free press in more modern and enlightened times, nothwithstanding many different attempts to destroy its liberty," should be inserted. An amendment was next moved by Samson (Hastings) and seconded by Thomson (Frontenac) to strike out all after the word "that" and substitute a declaration that two articles published in the *Colonial Advocate* (those above referred to) of which the text is cited,

> are gross, scandalous and malicious libels, intended and calculated to bring this House and the government of this province into contempt, and to excite groundless suspicion and distrust in the minds of the inhabitants of this province as to the proceedings and motives of their representatives, and is therefore a breach of the privileges of this House; and that W. L. Mackenzie, Esq., a member of this House having avowed himself the author of the said articles be now called upon for his defence.

The debate could not be concluded on that day and it was adjourned to the next and the next. In the course of it Mr. R. D. Fraser (Grenville) said to Mr. Mackenzie that if he had addressed such remarks to him personally as were contained in his article he would have horsewhipped him for it, which emphatic words were ordered to be taken down by the clerk.

Rising at length to speak in his own defence, Mr. Mackenzie began by impugning the tribunal before which he was being tried. "If," he said,

the *Colonial Advocate* contains paragraphs which
honourable members do not like, or which according to their notions of libel ought to be punished,
let the House address the lieutenant governor and require
the conductors of the paper to be brought to trial before
the ordinary tribunals of the country. . . . You, the
House, are unfit judges for the cause is your own; the
paragraphs complained of ascribe sycophancy to some of
you, nay to the majority of you; if it is fit that the writer
to be tried should be tried for giving an unfavourable
opinion of you, let it be before a jury of the country.
Their verdict in your favour would heal the wound in
your reputation; but your own vote that you are not
sycophants would not hinder the country from judging
you by your conduct and thinking unfavourably of you
like the editor in question, if that conduct is such as they
cannot approve.

As an *obiter dictum* he remarked that "four fifths of the
twenty-five journals published in this colony are in raptures
with the lieutenant governor, the councils, and the house
of assembly." One can judge from this what an up-hill task
it must have been to create discontent in a "colony" so
disposed, for the press must have afforded *some* indication
of the state of popular feeling.

The speaker's second point was that the proceedings against
him were an attack on the freedom of the press.

Censure of a government causes enquiry, produces discontent among the people, and this discontent is indeed
the only means known to me of removing the defects of
a vicious government and inducing the rulers to remedy
abuses. . . . The more the country know of your acts"

– he was not called in question however, for divulging an *acts*
of the House [sic] –

the more severely editors animadvert upon your public
conduct, the more will that conduct become a matter of
enquiry and discussion, and the country will look into
your actions and weigh your characters thereby.

"Would you wish," continued the speaker,

all check from the press put a stop to? Assuredly there is
no medium between allowing all opinions to be publish-

ed and of prohibiting all . . . If the legislature shall (as these proceedings indicate in my case) assume the power of judging censures on their own public conduct, and also assume the power to punish, they will be striking a blow at the interests of the people and the wholesome liberty of the press. Where bad judges, hypocritical governors, wicked magistrates, sycophantic representatives can, by the doctrine of contempts, exercise at will a censorship over the press, and punish the journalist who strives to promote the public interest by a fearless discharge of an unpleasant duty, misrule and injustice will be the inevitable consequence.

But there was another aspect of the matter: Had the House always been as jealous of its dignity and influence, as sensitive as to its honour, as it was showing itself on this occasion? Entering on this enquiry Mr. Mackenzie quoted from a paper, the *Gore Mercury*, lately established at Hamilton, and owned, as he said, by Mr. McNab, a member of the House, some ribald verses by "Sammy Switch" on the subject of the defunct ninth parliament in which the reformers had so large a majority. A single verse may suffice to show the quality of the stuff.

For months this ribald conclave
   Retailed their vulgar prate,
And charged two dollars each per day
   For spouting billingsgate.

It is questionable whether the tenth parliament was called upon to undertake the duty of avenging a gibe at its predecessor, but its failure to do so hardly stopped it from vindicating its own honour. Burlesque verse, moreover, is not equal as a vehicle of insult to plain prose; and had Mackenzie confined himself to that medium, it is hardly likely he would have been called upon to answer for the indiscretions of his muse.

Other instances however, were cited. The same paper had editorially accused him personally of "wickedly exciting the people of Upper Canada to discord, dissension and rebellion" and of having practised "fraud, falsehood and sheer humbug" in connection with his township meetings. The Kingston *Herald*, published by Mr. Hugh C. Thomson, M.P.P., had brought a similar accusation of "sycophancy" brought by him against the majority of the people's representatives – an accusation implying the betrayal by them for base personal ends and in a spirit of miserable servility of the interests not only of their own constituents, but, of the country at large.

As to withdrawing or apologizing for anything he had said Mackenzie absolutely refused to do so. "Not one word," he exclaimed,

> not one syllable do I retract: I offer no apology; for what you call libel I believe to be solemn truth, fit to be published from one end of the country to the other. I certainly should not have availed myself of my privilege, or made use of the language complained of on this floor; but since I am called to avow or disavow that language as an independent public journalist, I declare I think it mild and gentle.

On the conclusion of his speech Mr. Mackenzie retired from the House, when Mr. Morris (Lanark) moved, seconded by Samson, that the debate be adjourned till tomorrow and that it be the first item on the order of the day. The morrow having arrived Mr. Perry moved that the order of the day be discharged. Lost, yeas fifteen, nays twenty-seven. The debate was not concluded on that date, which was a Saturday. On the following Monday the minutes having been read, Samson, seconded by MacNab, moved that

> William Lyon Mackenzie, Esq., a member of this House, having avowed himself the author of the articles published in the newspaper called the *Colonial Advocate* mentioned in the resolution of this House of Saturday last, which articles are grossly false, scandalous and defamatory, and having been heard in his place in defence of the same, has by the whole tenor of such defence, flagrantly aggravated the charge brought against him, and is therefore guilty of a high breach of the privileges of this House.

The drama was hastening to its conclusion. Perry, seconded by Lyons (Northumberland), moved in amendment

> That as this House has allowed many other publications to pass without punishment or censure, reflecting on the character and motives of its members for many years past, and as addresses to the Head of the Provincial

Government for the time being have been published in
the Official Gazette containing such reflections with
answers of his Excellency expressing his thanks for the
same, and as this House by its resolution of Saturday
last has asserted its privileges, and shown its determination hereafter to take notice of such offensive publications, it is not expedient to take any further notice of
the said libel published in the *Colonial Advocate*.

Had the government party been wise they would have been
satisfied with this motion of Perry's. It accepted the resolution of the House declaring that Mackenzie's articles were a
breach of the privileges of the House and spoke of them as
"offensive publications," such as would not hereafter be
allowed to pass without censure or punishment. Coming from
Mackenzie's own side of the House this might certainly have
been regarded as triumph enough. It was voted down, however, by twenty-six to fourteen. An amendment dealing with
a minor point was moved by the attorney general and carried.
Then came the final resolution moved by Samson and
seconded by Werden "that William Lyon Mackenzie, Esq.,
be expelled [from] this House." Perry moved in amendment
that a committee of privilege should be appointed "to inquire
and report to this House what other, if any, libels have been
published against the proceedings of this House or any of its
members since the commencement of the present session."
Lost, yeas fourteen, nays twenty-four. Duncombe of Oxford,
who had hitherto voted with the majority, now moved "that
William Lyon Mackenzie, Esq. be called to the Bar of the
House and that he be reprimanded by the Speaker." This
motion only obtained seven votes, but amongst them were
those of Bidwell, Perry, Ketchum and Randal, the weightiest
men in the House on the reform side. The main motion was
then put to the vote and carried twenty-four to fifteen,[3]
whereupon a new writ for the county of York was ordered.

The most dangerous prestige that can be given to any man
whose influence is dreaded is the prestige of persecution; and
that, not for the first time, were Mackenzie's opponents now
bestowing on him. The first occasion was when his printing
office was wrecked, and he obtained, together with his first
degree in martyrdom, a substantial sum wherewith to repair
all losses and support future campaigns. And now he was
receiving his second degree, and being sent back to York, a

county utterly intractable to conservative influence, with the far flashing aureole of "Expulsion" round his brow. If he was popular before he was an idol now. In three weeks he was back in his seat, graced with a very handsome and valuable gold medal and chain which his constituents had presented to him "as a token of their approbation of his political career." On the obverse the rose, shamrock, and thistle were entwined, surrounded by the legend, "His Majesty King William, the People's Friend." In the interval between the issue of the writ and the day fixed for the election there was considerable excitement in the town as well as in the county. Mackenzie was carried round the town on the shoulders of his admirers in most tumultuous fashion. A petition had been presented to the lieutenant governor calling on him to dissolve the legislature on account of the way in which they were wasting their time and "neglecting interests of the most vital importance to the welfare of this populous and flourishing portion of the British empire." It is true the province was in a flourishing condition and gaining population rapidly, but whether this was the psychological moment for referring to these gratifying facts may be a question. To the deputation which waited on him with the petition his excellency returned a reply which was certainly brief, and which the parties interested thought was unsympathetic. It was these words: "Gentlemen, I have received the petition of the inhabitants." So unsatisfactory indeed was it considered that a meeting was at once held at which resolutions were passed declaring the reply "insulting to the feelings and opinions of a body of freemen," and recommending the holding of meetings to consider "the expediency and propriety of praying that his Majesty would be pleased to remove our present lieutenant governor, and in future appoint civil instead of military men to the head of the government in this province." It was at the same meeting that it was decided to present Mr. Mackenzie with a medal.

It ought to be possible at this date to take a dispassionate view of these occurrences. "No Power," says May,[4]

exercised by the Commons is more undoubted than that of expelling a member from the House as a punishment for grave offences. . . . Expulsion is generally reserved for offences which render members unfit to sit in Parliament and which, if not so punished would bring discredit upon Parliament itself.

A list follows of the various offences which have been so
visited concluding with "libels and various other offences
committed against the House itself." "When members," the
writer continues, "have been legally convicted of any such
offence, it has been customary to require the record of conviction to be laid before the House. In other cases the proceedings have been founded on reports of commissioners, or
committees of the House, or other sufficient evidence."[5] The
House therefore was clearly within its legal rights in expelling
Mr. Mackenzie without bringing the matter before the
ordinary courts. The question then arises, was there justification? Or was arbitrary power exercised to crush a political
opponent? If it was not a libel upon the representative body
to say that it had "degenerated into a sycophantic office for
registering the decrees of a mean and mercenary executive,"
it is hard to say what would constitute a libel. Grant that this
was Mackenzie's honest opinion, it was none the less an
insult of a very gross kind. That it was sufficiently offensive
to call for a reprimand from the Speaker was affirmed by the
vote of seven of his strongest political friends; that it was a
libel such as, if repeated, might properly call for punishment
was affirmed by practically the entire reform wing of the
House. If those who were not touched by Mackenzie's
criticism viewed it in that light, is it very surprising that
those upon whom the full force of the insult fell should have
regarded it as justifying his expulsion?

It might be said and was said that the House should not
attempt to dictate to the county of York whom they should
choose to represent them, and that if Mr. Mackenzie was
good enough for his constituents that was all that was
necessary. On the other hand it was contended that the
House had an organic union and life of its own; that it was
not a mere aggregation of disconnected units; that it was
governed by laws written and unwritten which must be upheld; and that no particular constituency could claim to
maintain within it a representative whose attitude and conduct
towards a majority of his fellow members was such as to
destroy all confidence and respect between him and them.
The proceeding nevertheless was from a political point of
view highly inexpedient. No really astute political leader
would have countenanced it; and it is probable, as a recent
writer[6] has hinted, that the House was feeling the want of
the balanced mind and cautious temper of the Chief Justice,

who, as attorney-general, had been for eight years, its leading spirit. The *Advocate* would not be silenced – Mackenzie had challenged the House to prosecute him as a publisher; and it might surely have been foreseen that Mackenzie's own popularity in his county would be increased. He had now found his public – a public prepared to follow him very far, and for whom in the meantime no language of denunciation or contempt applied to the dominant class could possibly be too strong. The House was now going to find itself involved in a bitter and hopeless conflict, not only with Mackenzie as an individual, but with the powerful county which he represented.

During Mackenzie's brief absence from the House a question was raised by Bidwell as to the late date, as he regarded it, fixed for holding the new election. The returning officer's advertisement was dated the seventeenth of December, and yet the polling was deferred to January the second. When the representation of the town of York had become vacant by the resignation of Mr. Robinson much greater expedition had been used. "He brought this matter before the House," he said,

> on general grounds and thought it was hardly compatible with freedom of election to allow the executive to use a discretionary power as to the time of holding the elections. . . . He thought it was a duty they owed to themselves and to their constituents to enquire why the present election had been put off to so distant a day.

He moved, seconded by Perry, for an address to the lieutenant governor to enquire "by whose advice it was that the election for the county of York had been fixed for so distant a date." Constitutional consciences were tender in those days – singularly tender, indeed, for an age of tyranny. Mr. Bidwell hardly foresaw that the time would come under the political system he was desirous of introducing, when, to suit the convenience of an administration, a constituency would be kept open, instead of three weeks, seventy-five weeks, or, to be very exact, one year, five months and one week.[7] A general debate arose but the motion secured only seven votes. Jesse Ketchum, Mackenzie's colleague in the county, both spoke and voted against it.

He might think the time too long, but he would not censure another for thinking differently – he required to be fully satisfied a person deserved blame before he would censure him; until he was satisfied there was something wrong on the part of the executive government, he would not vote for anything that implied a censure.

Manifestly Mr. Ketchum was not cut out for an agitator.

When election day came Mackenzie had something in store for the freeholders – nothing less than a formal "Impeachment," as he called it, of the lieutenant governor and his advisers, amongst whom were included not only the executive council but the legislative council and the legislative assembly. The document, like most of the author's productions, was of vast length – by measurement very nearly, if not quite, nine thousand words; in no fewer could the iniquities of the different branches of the state be told, the lieutenant governor's alone extending to fifty-nine heads, not to speak of the general arraignment of his character with which the "Impeachment" closes. It is impossible to speak of the document as an honest one. Of the lieutenant governor it says:

He believes that you were made to be governed – to be ruled – to be taxed – to labour – and to laugh or weep, sigh or be merry, as directed by vice regal authority. . . . He wishes to keep you ignorant in order that you may be obedient in order that you may be enslaved. . . . He believes that the liberty of the press is the invention of Beelzebub, and that newspapers and newspaper editors are the scourge of mankind. . . . He has been bred to believe the people only of importance as pigs and sheep are of importance in order to furnish Governors, Generals, Colonels, Captains and Legislative Councillors with subsistence, and he treats them accordingly.

These principles he is said to hold "in common with Archdeacon Strachan, Chief Justice Robinson and those venerable bodies the executive and legislative councils all of whom are horror-struck at the very name of political responsibility to the people."

A document conceived in this spirit cannot be expected to deal dispassionately with the details of the subject, and nothing could be less dispassionate, or more one-sided, than the writer's presentation of the various matters he brings forward. He took the opportunity of repeating the charge which had caused his expulsion: "I have charged the present house of assembly with sycophancy in my capacity as a public journalist; I here before you and in the face of the world reiterate that charge as applied to the majority of its members." He speaks of "the good old days of Sir Peregrine Maitland" – which perhaps would surprise Sir Peregrine – and says that

> The country cannot be restored [sic] to a state of tranquillity, confidence and quiet, but when his excellency Sir John Colborne shall have been recalled from his government, and his administration changed by the removal of the persons composing the present executive council; when places of Henry John Boulton and Christopher Alexander Hagerman, the present attorney and solicitor general shall be filled by other persons and the people of the province allowed to amend their late choice of a representation.

Mackenzie's re-election was practically unopposed, one vote only having been cast for a certain Mr. Street who ventured to oppose him. After the declaration of the poll a procession of the electors escorted their hero to town. Mounted on a sleigh was a printing press, and banners displayed such mottoes as "Liberty of the Press," "Bidwell and the Glorious Minority," "A Free Press the Terror of Sycophants." The *Colonial Advocate*, giving an account of the proceeding, says: "The people carried their member into his own house on their shoulders, and next morning assembled in such numbers at the Parliament House as to cause much terror and anxiety to many of the members."

Wearing the medal and chain bestowed upon him by his constituents Mackenzie was introduced to the House by Messrs. Ketchum and Perry as "member for the county of York in the place of W. L. Mackenzie, Esq., expelled [from] this House." On this there was an outburst of applause from a crowd that had gathered at the bar. A young man named Barnabas Cotton, noticed as having been particularly noisy, was brought to the bar. Now Barnabas was a reformer, and the solicitor without further ado moved that he should be committed to the common gaol during the pleasure of the House. Perry and Bidwell, however, thought that the young man should first be heard in his own defence; and the former seconded by the latter made a motion to that effect. Here was danger. There was no knowing what a high-spirited youth who had evidently sat, politically, at the feet of Mackenzie might be loaded with; yet the motion came very near being carried: all the liberals voted for it and some of the conservatives. It was lost, however, by just one vote; and Perry finding that he could not get a speech from Mr. Cotton moved that it was inexpedient to take any further notice of the matter, and that he be discharged. This was carried by twenty-eight to thirteen.

The next day the horizon darkened. Mackenzie's "Impeachment," as read to the electors of York county, had been published in the *Colonial Advocate* of the day before. The solicitor general (Hagerman) now rose in his place in the House to a question of privilege, and after reading the document in question, and also an article that had appeared in another part of the paper entitled "To the People of Canada," charged "William Lyon Mackenzie Esq., a member of this House with the publication of the same, as false, scandalous and malicious libels upon this House in contempt of its privileges." Having been asked by the Speaker whether he acknowledged the authorship of the writings complained of, Mackenzie said that he did, and requested the inulgence of the House for half an hour while he retired and prepared his defence.

After about that lapse of time he returned and drawing forth the medal and chain, which he had put off after his introduction to the House, he again put them on, and stated that he would wear them while he held his seat, if only for an hour. He tried to read the address he had received from his constituents with the medal but this was declared out of order. " 'Let the House remember," he cried,

that they are trying the people of the county of York, not me, and if they turn me out, the people will feel it their duty to come to the bar to defend their rights.' They had declared him to be a libeller; if so the whole county of York were libellers. . . . He could tell the House that this disgraceful attempt to put him down had made friends for him in the country that he never otherwise would have had, and the steps they were now taking would have a similar effect. . . . If they persisted

in their present course they would shortly have to send
for the Highlanders in the garrison to protect them.

A question of order having been raised, Mr. Mackenzie
appealed to the House against the decision of the Speaker,
and a large majority having supported the chair, he exclaimed
that it was all a farce. "Yes, it was all a farce and a mockery
for him to make a defence before such a tribunal – he would
disdain it. He would never again attempt to make a defence
before this House; he had got all he wanted out of them, and
would now appeal to the country." The report, made by
Collins and copied into the *Colonial Advocate* with a note to
the effect that it was "fair and without prejudice," goes on to
say: "Here Mr. Mackenzie bundled up his papers, after
giving them a kick or two to put them in order, and walked
out of the House amidst loud cries of order! order! order!
from all sides."

It seems never to have occurred to Mackenzie that the true
and proper defence of what he had spoken and written was
to take his numerous propositions one by one and *prove them
true*. This might have taken an enormous time, but as he had
been called upon for his defence, he was entitled to all the
time he required. It was not enough to say that the county
of York agreed with him – that they fully endorsed his
alleged libels – for the county of York, or at least his supporters in the county, like any other aggregation of men,
might be led away by party spirit. To say that they would
come to the bar of the House to defend their rights was
simply to threaten that to which in the end he resorted –
insurrection.

Mackenzie was in the midst of his defence when a message
was received from the legislative council drawing attention
to his article of impeachment as a breach of *their* privileges.
The issue of the matter was, however, close at hand. On
Mackenzie's retirement from the chamber, the solicitor
general moved his expulsion on the ground that he had, "not
only reasserted the gross, scandalous and malicious libel" for
which he had been previously expelled, but had "in the said
articles endeavoured by false, scandalous and malicious representations, to cause his Majesty's subjects in this province to
believe that the majority of their representatives should be
held in abhorrence by posterity as enemies to the liberties of
the people they represent. Wherefore," the motion continued,

"it is resolved that the said William Lyon Mackenzie be
expelled [from] this House, and declared unfit and unworthy
to hold a seat therein."¹On motion of Mr. McNab the words
"during the present parliament" were added to the resolution.
The debate was adjourned to the following day, when the
motion as amended was carried by a vote of twenty-seven
to nineteen.

Mr. Mackenzie did not re-appear in the House during this
session. He was again enthusiastically returned, but not till
after parliament had been prorogued. The *Colonial Advocate*
gives a varied selection of the opinions expressed by the press
of the country on his expulsion. Most of these opinions were
decidedly unfavorable to himself, but he was never afraid to
publish the censures of opponents; he seems to have counted
on their increasing his popularity. Thus the *Kingston Herald*
is quoted as calling him a "spiteful, unbridled, and indis-
criminate scoffer." The *Montreal Courant* said: "It is much
to be regretted that the Assembly of the sister province has
taken up this affair. Mr. Mackenzie is a demagogue who has
raised himself to ephemeral popularity which after a little
effervescence would have become vapid." The *Montreal
Herald* on the other hand was glad to see "the determination
shown by the house of assembly to vindicate their own
honour and respectability by the expulsion of Mr. Mackenzie.
This gentleman," it added, "may be anything in private life –
with what we have nothing to do, but in his political character
he has long been a frantic disturber of the business of that
House and of the general peace of the province." The
Hamilton *Free Press*, on the other hand, declared that the
county of York and the province "had been deprived of the
services of as useful a member as holds a seat in that House."
The *Christian Guardian* and the *Brockville Recorder* both
disapproved of the action of the Assembly, though the former
stated that it did not "pretend to justify these offensive paragraphs, nor advocate the general policy of the author."

In the debate on the second expulsion Bidwell bore warm
testimony to the value of his fellow-reformer's services.
"Another objection," he said, "to the proceeding is found in
the acknowledged talents, research, industry and usefulness
of Mr. Mackenzie in the House – qualities which would in-
finitely over-balance all his defects." Perry spoke up and said
that "the member for York received more abuse in this House
than he gave out of it." Mackenzie did not set up, so far as

appears, that defence for himself; but in any case the majority blundered sadly in the line they took. Mackenzie was a far less dangerous man in the House than out of it. He never could have dragged the reform section of the House at his heels as he did the County of York, and on pain, therefore, of isolating himself by his own actions, he would have been compelled, as a member of the Assembly, to keep within such bounds as the reform party in general approved. As it was, he was isolated by the action of the majority, set free from party ties and restrictions and flung, so far as it was in their power to do it, into the arms of the people. If their desire had been to double his qualifications as an agitator their action would not have been better directed than it was.

The part normally taken by the legislative council – henceforth one of the chief objects of Mr. Mackenzie's attacks – in the legislation of the province is well illustrated in the records of this session. On the thirteenth of January that chamber returned, with a long list of amendments, an assembly bill entitled "An Act to incorporate a joint stock company to improve the navigation of the Grand River." These amendments, evidently the fruit of close and laborious attention as well as of superior business and legal knowledge, were all accepted by the Assembly by a vote of twenty-nine to nine. Again, on the twentieth of January, the Council submitted to the Assembly a lucid and well reasoned statement of its reasons for *not* accepting certain amendments made by that body to a Council bill on the subject of the confirmation of the titles to estates derived through aliens. On consideration of these reasons the Assembly, without division, "receded from its amendments." Many cases substantially similar could be culled from the Assembly's journals; and it is only fair that such facts should be remembered to the credit of the Council when so much in the way of obstruction is laid to its charge.

CHAPTER ELEVEN

MACKENZIE IN ENGLAND

Mackenzie's third election to the tenth parliament of Upper Canada took place on the thirtieth of January, 1832. On this occasion he had two competitors, – Mr. Jas. E. Small, who stated that he did not wish to be considered as opposing Mr. Mackenzie, of whose expulsion he did not approve, and only ran because there was some reason to believe that the resolution of the House had disqualified that gentleman as a candidate; and a Mr. Washburn, a straight supporter of the action of the Assembly. To Mr. Washburn twenty-three votes were given; to Mr. Small ninety-six; to Mr. Mackenzie six hundred and twenty-eight. There was no mistaking the mind of the county of York.

Mention had been made of the petitions that were being circulated and signed setting forth the grievances of the province on the lines suggested by Mr. Mackenzie in his paper and in his public addresses. A counter movement of considerable dimensions was at the same time in progress; addresses to the King were being signed expressing satisfaction with the government of the province and the general condition of things. An extract from one of these "loyal" addresses as they were called is given in the *Cobourg Star* of February 29th, 1832. "Although," the memorialists say,

we are not ignorant of the imperfections of all human institutions, and admit the possibility of abuses in the most perfect system of organized government, we are yet persuaded of the pre-eminent excellence of the British Constitution; and we humbly beg leave to inform Your Majesty that we enjoy in this province its impartial protection and paramount advantages; that we have no real complaint against the administration of justice; that no oppressive taxes are imposed; and that the civil and religious liberties of the people are not endangered by the system of government now exercised in this province.

Unhappily the serpent had entered paradise as the address goes on to state:

It is our painful duty to confess the existence of insidious and crafty politicians within the province, who are aiming at the subversion of every British principle and feeling . . . We beg respectfully to state to your Majesty that the petitions to the imperial government which have been clandestinely circulated and promoted by designing individuals in this province for the purpose of mere self aggrandizement, are wholly deprecated by us as containing no reasonable nor well-grounded cause of complaint, but as tending to the destruction of harmony and mutual confidence amongst the people of this province. . . . We feel ourselves called upon by our duty to our Sovereign, to our country, to ourselves and posterity to counteract these malevolent and mischievous designs by representations of the truth at the foot of the throne.

The two sets of petitions arrived in England about the same time to the no slight perplexity of the colonial office. Looking first on this picture and then on that, it was difficult to believe that both professed to represent the same original.

Considering the excited state of public feeling and the many personal enmities that had been aroused it would not have been surprising if here and there outbreaks of violence had occurred. On the whole there seems to have been little of this; but Mr. Mackenzie himself was the victim of a particularly dastardly attack in the town of Hamilton, on the night of the nineteenth of March. An open political meeting had been held on that day at which the two parties had contended for the nomination of the chairman. One W. J. Kerr, superintendent of the Burlington Canal, was determined that the sheriff of the Gore district should take the chair, while the reformers wanted a Mr. Sheldon. Kerr had his way and the reformers returned and held a meeting of their own elsewhere with the chairman of their choice. Of what was said or done at either meeting there does not appear to be any record. Mr. Mackenzie spoke of course,

and probably in his usual strain. It may reasonably be
conjectured that what followed sprang in some way out of
the events and utterances of the day. In the evening Mr.
Mackenzie had retired to the house of a Mr. Bailey, and
was occupied in writing, when the same Mr. Kerr who had
been so active at the meeting entered the house unbidden.
Going into the room in which Mr. Mackenzie was and
seeing how he was engaged he asked him in a kind of joking
fashion whether he had yet settled all the grievances of
Upper Canada, after which he beckoned him to the door,
making it appear that he had something to say to him
outside. Mackenzie followed, and scarcely had he stepped
outside the house when two men fell upon him and beat and
kicked him severely. How far they would have proceeded if
Mr. Mackenzie's cries of "Murder" had not quickly brought
help, it is hard to say. As soon as steps were heard approaching they took to their heels. Kerr, however, remained on
the spot, hypocritically pretending to have been trying to
protect Mr. Mackenzie. He was prosecuted, nevertheless, at
the ensuing assizes for his complicity in the matter, the
Solicitor General, Mr. Hagerman, appearing as Crown
Prosecutor and Mackenzie's old antagonist Judge Macaulay
conducting the trial. The outcome was that Kerr was fined
one hundred dollars, a most inadequate punishment even
allowing for the greater value of money in those days, for
so detestable a crime.[1] Mr. Mackenzie, though he received
some ugly cuts on the head and face, was not seriously
injured, as he was able to return home next day, and four
days later to take a very active part in an open air meeting
in that town.

The meeting in question seems to have been on the same
plan as the Hamilton one. It was organized by the reformers,
but the public generally were invited to attend. As at
Hamilton there was some contention as to the Chairmanship.
In the end one Thomas Carfrae, Jr., was appointed. The
conservatives, being in a majority, quickly dominated the
meeting whereupon the reformers receded from the meeting
and started one of their own with Mr. Jesse Ketchum as
chairman. Ketchum and Mackenzie and one or two other
leading reformers were standing together in cart ready to
address the multitude when, according to the account given
in the *York Courier*, a paper not friendly to the reform
cause,

> Some twenty or thirty Irish lads, who entertained no
> very favourable sentiments towards these patriots, ever
> since their gross and impudent attack upon the vener-
> able Catholic Bishop dashed into the middle of the
> Yonge St. mob, seized the waggon and galloped off with
> it, patriots and all, to the utter consternation of the
> Yonge streeters and to the infinite amusement of the
> multitude. The waggon orators finding themselves thus
> unexpectedly in the hands of the Philistines and aban-
> doned by their own mob quickly scattered themselves
> out of the waggon, some by jumping and some by
> tumbling out, amid abundant salutes of rotten eggs, etc.

The attempt at [being] humourous is apparent and no doubt
the day had its humours; but it does not appear that the
problems of the time were brought much nearer to a settlement. When two rival mobs take to discussing politics the
rules of Aristotle or bold, calm, Socratic dialogues do not
follow. In this case the mob which particularly represented
the finer traditions of the British constitution marched to
the office of the *Colonial Advocate* and broke the windows.
Mackenzie was afraid his house would be attacked, and
ordered Col. Fitzgibbon who, as a magistrate, was on the
ground doing his very best to preserve or restore peace, to
call out the troops. The Colonel refused to do so, but
assured Mr. Mackenzie that he would protect his house
against which, in point of fact, no demonstration was made.

It was now decided by the reformers of the Home district
to commission Mr. Mackenzie to go to England as the
personal advocate of the views and requests they were
putting forward in their petitions to the home government.
It was remembered that Mr. Randal had achieved a measure
of success when he undertook a somewhat similar mission
in connection with the Naturalization question in 1827, and
this gave ground for hope that their later delegate might
also secure a favorable hearing. Mackenzie was not a man
to shirk the proffered duty, so gathering his papers together,
all that he might require for his anticipated discussions with
the colonial office, and taking a number of petitions in his
own charge he transferred the management of his paper to
Mr. Randal Wickson, and, about the middle of April, 1832,
left for New York, whence he was to sail for England. From
Albany and New York he wrote some interesting letters to

the *Advocate* which were reproduced together with a number of other contributions of his to that paper, in a book which he brought out the following year in England under the title of *Sketches of Canada and the United States*. Mackenzie wisely excluded from that volume the more violent of his political writings, though his political stand point is sufficiently indicated. The general impression which the book leaves upon the reader is that Upper Canada in those days was rather a happy country to live in – one in which taxes were so low as to be practically unfelt; in which justice was well administered; in which land was very cheap, while soil and climate were of the best; and which only needed a little touching up in a few constitutional points to be all that heart could wish. The writer's style is natural and lively with a decided stamp of geniality and bonhomie. And *that was the man* when he was not under the influence of that evil genius of envy and suspicion of which something has been, and unhappily more remains to be, said.[2] It would be interesting did space permit to quote in full a letter written by Mackenzie on board the packet "Ontario" at sea. He seems for the time being to have dismissed all thought of the political dissensions in which only a few weeks earlier had been taken so active a part. He describes with great gusto the liberal and varied bill of fare provided on board the good ship, and speaks of the excellent appetite he is able to bring to it. Total abstinence habits did not much prevail in those days, and Mackenzie finds no fault with the port, madeira, claret, champagne, and other liquors served freely to the cabin passengers. He seems indeed to be in excellent spirits and temper. Possibly when his thoughts reverted to the questions he had been debating with so much heat in the little community of York, and in the township meetings throughout his country, they may not have loomed so large seen between sea and sky on the vast bosom of the Atlantic. Or perhaps the sifting breezes of the ocean may have blown away some of the chaff of personal bitterness which made no small portion of their bulk. In any case Mackenzie was a happy man on ship board, and if he could have taken a voyage round the world it would have been better for him and everybody; certainly few men would have picked up more useful information in such an odyssey than he. The cabin library supplied him with a good assortment of reading. "Except *Lawrie Todd*,"[3] he writes,

I do not remember having allowed myself leisure to read a novel for years, until within these last three weeks, when I have perused Irving's *Tales of a Traveller;* Bulwer's *Pelham*, Devereux, Eugene Aram, Paul Clifford and *The Disowned*; Disraeli's *Young Duke*; Col. Hamilton's *Cyril Thornton*; Sir Walter Scott's *Anne of Geirstein*; James Hogg's *Shepherd's Calendar*; Cooper's *Water Witch*; Marryatt's *Naval Officer*; and *The Tale of Crockford's.*

With good air, good eating and drinking, good reading and doubtless good sleeping, the time must have passed very pleasantly.

One thing which greatly helped the general sense of *bien être* that Mackenzie enjoyed on this voyage was the fact that being temporarily relieved from pecuniary anxiety, and having the respectable status of member-elect for an important Upper Canada constituency, not to speak of his dignity and responsibility as delegate to England, he was on a footing of equality with the best on board the ship. At heart there was much of the tory in him; and had the tories of Upper Canada been wise he would never have given them the trouble he did; possibly also no one would have written his biography. It may be noticed in passing that he sympathised with the steerage passengers whose lot on board ship was far from being strewn with comforts. "It is perhaps necessary," he says, "that one should have felt the misery of a steerage passage, in order to judge of the comparative comforts of a packet's cabin. It is better to begin life in the steerage of society and finish it in the cabin than to have to walk forward in old age or late in life."

On the twenty-ninth of May, about noon, Mackenzie stepped on English soil at Portsmouth, and he recalls the fact that it was exactly twelve years before almost to the minute that he arrived at Quebec – "twelve years spent in hard, fatiguing, arduous, and (as I trust) useful service – a service that I do not by any means regret, for my humble exertions have been well and amply rewarded and that too in the way and manner calculated to afford me the most enduring satisfaction."

Sir John Colborne did not put quite the same estimate upon his "humble exertions" for on the eighteenth of June he writes to Lord Goderich as follows:

Mr. Mackenzie has now laboured for more than seven years, I believe, with activity and perseverance to create discontent and disaffection in the province. He possesses in a peculiar degree that cunning and effrontery which it is probable will generally attract the attention of some part of the population, and ensure the partial success of any demagogue. He has had recourse to every species of calumny, falsehood and deception which would promote his views and get his journal and almanac into circulation . . . ; and by addressing his statements particularly to the natives of the United States settled in Upper Canada . . . and by taking advantage of every temporary excitement and of the injudicious acts of several of his opponents, he has enjoyed a popularity in this district for a longer period than persons of his character usually retain their mischievous influence.

Referring to the attack that had been made on Mr. Mackenzie at Hamilton which he understands Mr. Kerr, a magistrate, is accused of having countenanced, if not encouraged, Sir John goes on to say: "There are many magistrates, I have no doubt, unfit for their situation in a province located as this has been; but it is unreasonable to expect that a magistrate be removed on an *ex parte* statement." At this time Kerr was under indictment but had not yet been tried. Moreover, Sir John was a little astray in describing him as a magistrate: his name had been published as in the commission of the peace, but he had never accepted the office – had not taken the qualifying oath, and had never exercised magisterial functions.

On arriving in London, Mr. Mackenzie took up his quarters first at 16 Great Smith Street, and afterwards at 19 Wakefield St., Brunswick Square. He had the good fortune to be present in the House of Lords on the fourth of June (1832) when the Reform Bill, after six days' consideration in committee, was read a third time and passed. Had he been present a few days earlier he might have heard language exchanged between their lordships almost strong enough for the meridian of Little York. On this occasion things were fairly peaceable, and he was much struck by the noble and dignified appearance of the Prime Minister, Earl Grey. "Well does Earl Grey," he writes to his paper,

merit the high station and distinguished rank to which
he has been called; truth and sincerity are stamped on
his open, manly, English countenance; intelligence and
uprightness inscribed on all his actions. . . . His lordship
had need neither of the peerage nor the post he fills to
point him out as one of the first among men; he was –
he is – one of that aristocracy of nature which, in any
free country, are found among the pillars of its liberties,
and in any despotism among the foremost to break the
tyrants yoke, or perish in attempting it.

The petitions to the House of Commons of which he was
the bearer Mr. Mackenzie entrusted to the hands of that
extraordinary industrious person, Mr. Joseph Hume,[4] who,
engaged already in reform of every kind of abuse discoverable in the United Kingdom, was rejoiced to extend his
activity to the British colonies. Of Mr. Hume's general
benevolence and humanity and the soundness of many of
his views there can be no reasonable doubt; but it may well
be doubted whether on the whole his influence on the progress of events in either of the Canadas was beneficial. Two
other persons of importance with whom Mr. Mackenzie
became acquainted at this time were Daniel O'Connell and
William Cobbett.[5] His description of Cobbett is interesting
and *suggestive*:

He is evidently a man of an ardent temperament, of
strong and powerful passions, and I believe his object
is to increase the comforts and lessen the miseries of the
people; but it is evident that he is not very scrupulous
as to the means of bringing about this great good. Mr.
Noah of New York in his *Advocate* and Mr. Cobbett
in his *Register* appear to me to have adopted the maxim
that 'all's fair in politics.' They both put forth in a
powerful strain of sarcasm or invective against 'political
opponents, statements not always so correct as they
might be.'

If Cobbett with a full knowledge of the facts could have
drawn Mr. Mackenzie's portrait there might have been a
striking likeness between the two pictures.
On the thirteenth of June Mr. Mackenzie opened correspondence with Lord Goderich by informing him that he
had been

deputed by many thousands of the people of Upper
Canada to bring over to England addresses to his
Majesty and petitions to the House of Commons; to
support the prayers of the same by evidence, when
required, and to use every possible lawful effort to bring
the condition of the province, its wants and wishes
under the early consideration of the British nation and
government.

He proceeded to mention the different committees and
localities whose views he represented, and stated that he,
Mr. Hume, Mr. Viger, agent for the Legislative Assembly
of Lower Canada, and Mr. George Ryerson, who had been
deputed by the Methodist body to make certain representations in their behalf, were ready to wait upon his Lordship
at such a time as he might appoint. To this communication
he received a reply of a very disappointing character. The
under Secretary for the colonies, Viscount Howick, son of
the Prime Minister, wrote to say that while Lord Goderich
was ready to hear any observations he might have to offer
upon the affairs of Upper Canada "as an individual interested
in the welfare of that province and as a member of the
Assembly," he could not recognize him "as being deputed
to act for any other persons, nor can he," the letter continues, "enter upon any discussion with you upon the
measures which his Majesty's government may think it right
to pursue." These, Lord Howick observed, "can only be
made known to the people of Upper Canada through the
medium of the Governor of the legislature; it is to one or
the other of these authorities that any complaints which
individuals may have occasion to make should properly be
addressed."

This letter came as a great surprise to Mr. Mackenzie. In
replying he spoke of it as shutting the door of the colonial
office "upon all that vast mass of facts which I have offered
to submit as deputed on behalf of the unrepresented landowners and inhabitants of Upper Canada in support of the
allegations of their petitions." He referred to the precedent
of the recognition of Mr. Randal. This argument was not
met at the time – it required perhaps a good deal of consideration; but Mr. Mackenzie having brought up the point
again several months later, Lord Howick dealt with it in a

letter which it may be well to quote here. "With respect," writes his Lordship,

> to your remark that when Mr. Randal came to England to complain of injustice [to] Lord Goderich I not only discussed the question with him but also gave him an official letter pledging his Majesty's government to do certain things . . . I am directed to remark that the two cases are wholly dissimilar. Mr. Randal repaired to England to remonstrate against the final enactment of a provincial statute there awaiting his Majesty's decision, which deeply affected the interests of the body by whom he was deputed to act. Lord Goderich discussed that specific grievance with him, as he would have discussed with any other individual or body of persons any other specific measure in which they had a peculiar interest. You on the other hand invite a discussion of every measure connected with the administration of the provincial government – of every principle by which it is guided. That demand is made in the language of open and undisguised hostility, not .with the view of affording the secretary of state such information and such suggestions for the public good as your experience might enable you to supply (in which light your communications would have been thankfully received) but in furtherance of a direct accusation against the legislature, the lieutenant governor, the judges, and the public officers of Canada collectively. Under such circumstances to engage with you in the wide range of enquiries on which you seek to enter, would be to divert the official correspondence of this department from its proper channel, and would place the legislative, judicial and executive authorities of Upper Canada in a position of which they would have the best reason to complain and in which they could not continue to conduct the public service.

This letter is instructive as showing the impression Mr. Mackenzie had made on the colonial office after several months spent in the prosecution of the objects for which he had come to England. It is necessary now to return to the correspondence of 1832. Lord Howick, replying to the letter in which Mr. Mackenzie had expressed his surprise and disappointment at the position taken by Lord Goderich, denied that there was any shutting of the door upon "the mass of facts" referred to. He repeated that the Colonial Secretary was quite ready to hear what Mr. Mackenzie had to say, and added: "He only declines, as you have no authority from any recognized body, to enter into any official discussion with you upon the public affairs of the colony, or to admit that you are the organ of those whom you term the unrepresented landowners and inhabitants of Upper Canada." It is interesting to remember that the writer of these letters was subsequently the Lord Grey who filled the office of Colonial Secretary in Lord John Russell's Ministry (1846-1852), whose "Letters on Colonial Policy"[6] contain so much that is wise and liberal, and who did, to no small extent, aid in the development of "responsible government" in the colonies.

Mr. Mackenzie's first and second interview with Lord Goderich which took place on the second of July and the third of August respectively did much to dissipate the unfavorable impression produced in his mind by Lord Howick's official communications. On the first occasion he was accompanied by the gentlemen he had named in his letter, and on the second by the same with the exception of Mr. George Ryerson. He found his Lordship very conciliatory in manner and most attentive to everything that was said. He could not understand so much amiability apart from a large measure of conversion to his own views. He left the colonial office after the second interview "well satisfied that measures are about to be taken that will go a great way towards neutralizing the existing discontents." A couple of months later his hopes were not running so high, for in a letter addressed to the people of the county of Hastings we find him saying:

Lord Goderich spoke so friendly to me and acknowledged the existence of the wrongs of the people of Upper Canada complained of with so good a grace, that I really was of opinion he intended to dissolve the Tory Assembly at York and give the people another choice. Never was any one farther from the reality – he and the other noblemen and gentlemen of the cabinet keep their places not for the sake of reform, but in order to satisfy the public with as little reform as pos-

sible and keep real reformers out of office. To Upper
Canada I perceive that Whig and Tory are all the same.
General Maitland, Baron Aylmer, Governor Colborne
and Dr. Strachan are uncompromising tories. Does that
make them one whit less suitable for their places in the
eye of a reforming aristocratic cabinet two years in
office? *No indeed* but the contrary. . . . The colonial
department feel on the subject of reform in Canada
precisely as the persons in office with you and the
placemen of the Assembly feel – *they hate it, but they
fear an united people.*

Mackenzie expressed his dissatisfaction in a letter to Lord
Goderich in which he said: "I regret that as yet the people
of the colony appear to have been unable to find one solitary
act for the general good in regard to existing grievances done
or ordered in Upper Canada by the reform ministry during
the two years nearly of its existence." This statement could
not have struck Lord Goderich as a particularly fair one
considering what had been done by the reform government
in the matter of transferring to provincial control the
revenues raised under imperial statute, and also in the matter
of rendering the judges independent of the crown. Mackenzie
was aware that he was not contributing to the happiness of
the colonial office, for he wrote to his paper: "I am sure
that Lords Goderich and Howick do not thank the violence
of the local government for having been the means of
sending me here." It is not certain that the noblemen in
question attributed his presence in London to "the violence
of the local government," but whatever their theory may
have been as to the cause of his coming, Mackenzie was
probably correct in conjecturing that the fact of his having
come did not inspire them with thankfulness.

Mr. Mackenzie's supreme talent for agitation has been
strongly asserted by his biographer, Mr. Lindsey. But he
had other qualities which under favoring circumstances
would have fitted him for a far different role. Some of the
talents which he made subservient to the work of agitation
would have stood him in good stead as a minister of the
crown. He was methodical, prompt, keen, amazingly industrious, and incorruptible. He would have expected people
around him to work, and he might at first have been somewhat hasty and summary in his judgments. But he would

have appreciated and rewarded faithful service, and experience would gradually have tempered any tendency to precipitateness of thought or action. He would have been keenly intent on serving the public. His difficulty would have been in confining himself to his own department, particularly when he had once got it into good order. He would have envied other ministers any "abuses" with which they might appear to be grappling. Power, responsibility, and the necessity of co-operating with others would have tamed his excessive individuality and given him a totally different outlook upon the world. He would have seen that a man might be an office-holder and yet not a sycophant, – that he might receive a salary and yet in the performance of his duties aim most disinterestedly at the public good and give more than value for his stipend. He would have learned to make a certain allowance for inertia in a world in which all men were not as mercurial as himself. It was his misfortune from first to last to be in a position to criticise, never in a position to construct; until criticism, censure, invective and suspicion – suspicion above all – became the master habits and passions of his soul.

In the letters which he addressed to his paper from London Mr. Mackenzie did not omit to nurse the agitation to which he had given so fair a start before leaving the province. Thus on the twenty-fifth of October he writes:

England obliges us to buy in the dearest markets many articles we want, and conjures the money out of the farmer's and mechanic's pocket by placing over us an unsocial military government. . . . The whole authority is not in the people for whose benefit authority is professedly upheld, it is in the hand that guides the bayonets of the military. . . . Instead of being allowed to buy at the cheapest market and sell at the dearest, we are compelled to buy tea and innumerable other articles at the worst markets[7] in virtue of laws we never consented to. . . . If the West India or East India proprietors stand in need of bills and bayonets to protect their tottering monopolies of black slaves and green tea leaves, that is no reason why the Yonge Street farmer should work harder in order to keep the lash going, or that the girls should have to knit two pairs of stockings in place of one, to purchase therewith inferior tea, bought cheaper than common in India for the especial use of their grandmothers. Our freedom would be England's wealth.

Then follow some noteworthy remarks upon the Scottish people. "A more gallant race," he says, "never was, nor never will be," but their government like that of Canada has been in the hands of an autocracy.

These Scotch aristocrats, bankers, entailed lairds and else are, as a body, the meanest and most worthless of God's creatures – they have oppressed their countrymen for centuries, and condescended to acts of sycophancy, servility, aye and tyranny to retain their power, the very recollection of some of which makes me shudder. It is to them and their spawn in Montreal & Quebec that Scotland owes the character, often unjustly given her of being sycophantic and servile. A nation of such men as Andrew Fairservice and the generality of the Scotch sent to the Assembly in Upper Canada have not done much to wipe out the stain.

He finds an illustration of the servility he speaks of in a "Doctor Somebody who lived sometime in Scarborough and wrote under the signature of Guy Pollock."

There was, indeed, a certain Robert Douglas Hamilton, M.D., living at this very time at Scarborough, and writing occasionally under the name of "Guy Pollock." He had been in the country about three years and was hardened "syco-phant" enough to say that during that time there had not been any attack on the freedom of the press to his knowl-edge. He could not see what greater freedom any paper could ask than the *Colonial Advocate* was constantly exercising. All any paper could do more would be "to publish open manifestos of rebellion." He also uttered the following sentiments which sufficiently stamp his character:

With respect to liberty, the most sacred of all principles, the definition of it is easy: every man who personally or through a representative of his own choosing, has a voice in the making of the laws which he has to obey is in possession of liberty. With this privilege, if he complains of tyranny, the tyranny is his own, and his complaints prove neither more nor less than that he has abused his privilege and consequently is unworthy of them. In other words if the free electors of Upper Canada have returned bad members to the House of Assembly, it is their own fault, and proves that, like the inhabitants of South America they are in possession of more liberty than they can either appreciate or rightly exercise.[8]

"Guy Pollock" wrote much in this strain. Perhaps he was not conscious of the "servility" of his utterances.

Of no man was it ever more true than of Mackenzie that a change of sky does not involve a change of mind. What he was in Canada that to all intents and purposes he was in London. He writes:

I intend to complain of the meeting of the Upper Canada legislature[9] under the present circumstances. Considering the reasons that were urged and the favourable manner in which ministers received those reasons, and promised to give them a careful and immediate consideration, the allowing Sir John Colborne to remain another week in the colony, and the calling again the present legislature, and acts calculated to weaken public confidence in his Lordship and his colleagues, and I confess that my confidence is weakened greatly – but there is a noble remedy at hand.

The "noble remedy" he believed to lie in the new House of Commons to be elected that year under the provisions of the Reform Act; but could anything more strikingly illustrate the sanguine and overweening temperament of the man than his allowing himself to believe that, on the strength of his representations, even backed by the petitions he had brought over, the British government would summarily recall the lieutenant governor and order the dissolution of the Upper Canada Assembly? However courteous and conciliatory Lord Goderich may have been in personal intercourse, these were precisely matters such as he had informed Mr. Mackenzie at the outset he could not undertake to discuss with him. In a letter dated December 29th, 1832, Lord Howick was finally instructed to say:

Lord Goderich does not consider it consistent with the duties of his office to enter into any explanation with yourself or with any other private persons of the views which his Majesty's government may entertain respecting the propriety of dissolving the present Assembly of the province of Upper Canada.

In the main the views which Mr. Mackenzie was deputed to urge upon the attention of the colonial minister were reasonable views. Had he confined himself to stating general principles and supplying illustrative and uncontrovertible facts he would have accomplished all that he did and more. What he had to do was to show that Upper Canada should be allowed a larger measure of self-government; that the legislative council should be rendered more independent of the executive; that municipal institutions should be extended; that non-sectarian education should be more liberally provided for; that a larger measure of commercial liberty should be conferred upon the province; and finally that to try to fasten a state church upon it was in the highest degree unadvisable. All these propositions with the exception possibly of the last would more or less have commended themselves to Lord Goderich, a man of truly liberal mind. We have seen, however, what impression Mackenzie's attitude and temper made upon that minister, who was compelled to see in him not a temperate critic of evils and grievances but a partisan full of angry impatience to have everything changed in the direction of his wishes.

Had Mackenzie's letters to his paper fallen under the Minister's eye the impression referred to would certainly not have been weakened. Writing under date the seventeenth of December, 1832, he says:

> The longer I remain here the more clearly I see that Whigs and Tories are neither more nor less than two parties of factions of wealthy and influential men who have conspired to plunder the great body of the people time about – the whigs taking the helm when the tories become too detestable to be endured, and going below whenever toryism has got a refreshed character by a few years pretended opposition to misrule. . . . I vainly hoped redress from Lord Goderich's sense of justice – but it is evident that he will keep up just as much of the oppressive system as he can.

The Minister would also have gathered from the same source that the writer's quarrel was, not only with the constituted authorities in Upper Canada, but to a large extent with the people themselves. Thus on the sixth of November he writes:

> I have some curiosity about the result of the election for Oxford and Haldimand. Haldimand showed rottenness at the beginning and Oxford exhibited an utter indifference to the public welfare at the last election which gave me much pain. . . . I hope a free press will do something in Upper Canada – I trust it will instil a sense of duty and obligation into those large constituencies of farmers whose cruel and ungenerous behaviour at the last general election has inflicted so many evils upon their country.

As usual Mackenzie had judged the Colonial office, and the British Government as a whole, rashly, and all that he had said to their disadvantage had to be unsaid, and was unsaid, when, early in March, 1833, news reached him from Canada of what Lord Goderich had actually done – of the despatch he had sent to Sir John Colborne under date of the eighth of November. Writing to the London *Morning Chronicle* on the subject he expressed himself as follows:

> In short although there are some passages in this remarkable document in which I do not fully concur, it will doubtless be considered by the country, as a whole, the most satisfactory and conciliatory answer ever given to memorials from beyond the Atlantic. . . . It has rarely fallen to my lot, as a representative of the Canadian people, to be able to speak in commendation of the measures of his Majesty's government towards Upper Canada. I can, however, in the present instance, and most heartily do thank them for having shown that they are disposed to do all that can be constitutionally done to promote to the utmost extent the civil and religious liberties of my country.

Mackenzie had still some unfinished business with the colonial office, where early in the year Lord Goderich was replaced by Mr. E. G. Stanley (afterwards Earl Derby); and as some other questions shortly arose which he thought it necessary to discuss in the same quarter, it was not till the twenty-fifth of June that he was able to turn his face homewards. Taking passage in a ship called the "Jordeson" he arrived at Quebec on Sunday, the eighteenth of August, spent a couple of days there and at Montreal, and reached York on Monday the twenty-sixth.[10] Both at Quebec and at Montreal he received marked attention from the leaders of the loyal Lower Canada Opposition. At each place a public dinner was tendered to him which, alleging pressure of private business, he declined. At Quebec he gave as a further reason that he did not think he had been sufficiently successful to warrant anything in the way of a public demonstration. The course of events in Upper Canada where, even in Mackenzie's absence, perfect peace had not been reigning, must now engage our attention.

CHAPTER TWELVE

A FACTION-RENT PROVINCE

The second session of the eleventh parliament of Upper Canada had been prorogued on the twenty-eighth of January, 1832, just two days before Mackenzie's return for the county of York after his second expulsion. The third session was summoned for the thirty first of October. Mackenzie was in England grappling with the colonial office and was not likely to return before the session was over. Still, in the eyes of his opponents to have allowed his name to remain on the roll-call of the House would have seemed to stultify the resolution they had been at the pains of passing that he was "unfit and unworthy to hold a seat in the House during the present parliament." There was a very scant attendance of members to hear the lieutenant governor's opening speech on the thirty-first of October. There was no quorum in fact for the despatch of business on that day or the next. On the following one there was little more than a bare quorum, but MacNab, anxious that there should be no delay in the matter, moved, seconded by George S. Boulton, the reading of those portions of the journals of the House relating to the previous expulsions of Mr. Mackenzie. This having been carried by a vote of fifteen to eight, McNab moved, with the same seconder, that inasmuch as Mr. Mackenzie had been declared "unfit and unworthy etc." he could not sit or vote in this House as a member thereof. This was carried on the same division after an unsuccessful attempt on the part of Mackenzie's friends to adjourn the debate. On the following Tuesday – there having been no quorum on either Saturday or Monday – MacNab moved for the issue of a new writ, which was carried by nineteen to ten.

Thus for the third time was Mackenzie expelled. The response of his county was to elect him once more on the twenty-sixth of the month. At this time of course he was in England, and nothing was done in the House regarding his seat for over two months. The reformers thought that perhaps the tories were tired of the contest or thought it inexpedient to pursue it further: they did not know what was coming. On the ninth of February, just four days before the legislature was prorogued, MacNab, seconded this time by W. B. Robinson, brought forward another motion for expulsion, expressed in nearly the same terms as the last. A motion for the adjournment of the debate, another for the postponement of action till the next session, and a third proposing the previous question, were successively lost. The main motion was then carried, but by a majority of one only – eighteen to seventeen – showing that in the opinion of the more reasonable conservatives the matter was being carried too far. In this last debate the friends of Mackenzie displayed intense and not unjustifiable indignation. The action of the majority was a flagrant abuse of power and it is difficult to understand how two lawyers so competent as Boulton and Hagerman could have persuaded themselves that the course which they urged the House to take was a legal one. The first expulsion (December 12th, 1831) was prompted by an article, published in Mackenzie's paper, of which he acknowledged himself the author; and the second on a most deliberate repetition of the offence. For the third and fourth the only reason alleged was the *opinion* which the House by a party vote had expressed as to his unfitness and unworthiness to occupy a seat in it. The House had no power constitutionally to create, by resolution, a disqualification of this nature, and it could not have created it by bill, for a bill would have required the concurrence of the other two branches of the legislature which, assuredly a bill to this effect would not have received. The debates on the first two expulsions were far from revealing the same burning sense of injustice that was manifested in connection with the third and fourth, but particularly the fourth, the postponement of which almost to the last day of the session gave it a look of calculated vindictiveness.

His motion having been carried, MacNab endeavoured to complete the business by getting the House to order a new writ. Here his precarious majority failed him, the vote standing, yeas sixteen, nays nineteen. Mackenzie's friends stoutly maintained that the terms of the motion for expulsion did not properly vacate the seat, and some of the conservatives agreeing with them the motion failed. The matter of the new writ was thus left to be fought out in the next session, when it assumed a new aspect.

The session was rendered further memorable by the proceedings taken in both Houses on that despatch of the colonial secretary's which had been mentioned as having caused Mackenzie to sing palinodes when he received news of it in England in his advices from Canada. Lord Goderich was eminently a man of good intentions; but the better a man's intentions are the more necessary is it that he should have therewith a strong dose of every day common sense – the kind of common sense which enables a man to know his mind, to see things plainly, and to be definite in his judgments regarding them. It was one of the wisest of men who said "Qui fait l'ange fait la bête," which some one has rendered alliteratively "Ape the angel, achieve the ass." It would be unmannerly to apply the English version to so estimable and intelligent a nobleman as Lord Goderich, but really the French original meets the case: there was too much of the angel in his despatch of the eighth of November 1832 and consequently too much that was "bête." He wanted to be *so* just, *so* considerate, *so* impartial, *so* benevolent towards all parties that he just overdid it; and like the actors in a certain well-known fable into which an ass enters, ended by pleasing nobody in particular.

That Goderich had been influenced to some extent by Mackenzie cannot be doubted. At the same time he had formed his own opinion of the man and of his method, as we have already seen and are further to see. He could not wholly trust his statements, for there was information enough in the files of the colonial office to show that some were inaccurate or exaggerated and that others were irrelevant. Yet it was evident that the man was in earnest, and that he had already a considerable following in Upper Canada, which his remarkable talent for agitation might greatly increase. These were the days of the "great agitator" (O'Connell) and of many lesser ones and a large part of the effort of the government of the day was expended in trying to keep agitation within bounds. Prudential considerations then, if no others, made it necessary that Mackenzie's views and statements should be brought publicly to the notice of the Upper Canada executive; how best to do it remained the practical question.[1] His lordship was extremely anxious to show an example of exalted justice and perfect openness of mind, but there was no remedying the radical weakness of his position in expounding views most of which he repudiated and repeating statements for the correctness or in some cases even the good faith of which he found it impossible to vouch. His despatch bore evidence of its deferential, semi-apologetic tone of the conflicting sentiments that went to its composition – fear of giving just offence to the provincial authorities on the one hand and of dealing adequately with the "grievances" exposed by Mr. Mackenzie on the other.

"During several months past," the despatch begins, "I have been in occasional communication with Mr. William Mackenzie upon the subject of the grievances said to exist in Upper Canada, and for redress of which various petitions have been addressed to his Majesty." Mr. Mackenzie, his lordship explains, had been the bearer of some of these petitions; and he had gladly availed himself of the opportunity of obtaining from him such information as it was in his power to give respecting the wishes and opinions of those by whom he had been deputed to act, while adhering to "the general rule of declining to explain the views of his Majesty's government on questions of Canadian policy to any person except the governor of the province." He was now, "from the voluminous mass of that gentleman's correspondence," selecting those documents which professed to embody the substance of his case, and copies of these he was enclosing to the lieutenant governor; his intention being "to follow Mr. Mackenzie through those parts . . . which appear essential to the consideration of the practical questions which he had undertaken to agitate." In doing so he would "pass over in silence some details which have been introduced with no perceptible tendency to elucidate the subjects in discussion and much invective and sarcasm which would have been much more conveniently spared."

We seem to discover a little verbiage here, but the colonial secretary, like King Agag of unhappy memory, was treading delicately. The essential facts, however, could not be concealed first that his lordship had been giving a patient ear to an individual who even in papers meant to be of record, could not refrain from sarcasm and invective of no illuminating value, and second that the constitutional authorities of Upper Canada were to be called upon to answer this person's charges.

"It is with no intention [of] disrespect," continues his lordship,

> to Mr. Mackenzie, that I remark that he had adopted a style and method of composition singularly ill-adapted to bring questions of so much intricacy and importance to a definite issue. . . . Mr. Mackenzie would have himself understood as speaking the sentiments of the entire population of Upper Canada excepting only a few public functionaries whose interests are opposed to those of the people at large. It is not necessary, however, to have a very large experience of public controversies of this nature to be aware of the levity with which such pretensions are continually advanced upon the slightest and most inadequate ground.

In regard to the number of persons for whom Mr. Mackenzie would properly claim to speak his lordship, when he wrote this despatch, was under a serious misapprehension which he afterwards fully acknowledged. The signatures to the Grievance petitions had been carelessly counted in his office, and reported to him as twelve thousand and seventy-five. A second and more careful count made the number twenty-four thousand five hundred. On the other hand the signatures to the so-called loyal addresses numbered twenty-six thousand eight hundred and fifty-four, so that, even on the basis of the actual facts, there was no foundation for the claim that Mr. Mackenzie represented practically the whole country.

Touching on the paper entitled by Mr. Mackenzie "Observations on the state of the representation of the people of Upper Canada in the legislature of that Province," his lordship, visibly preoccupied with his own exculpation, says that he "must decline to pursue the discussion into those redundant and misplaced details with which Mr. Mackenzie has encumbered it. . . . If it were fit," he adds

> to review the past history of the province it would be impracticable to assume Mr. Mackenzie's paper as the basis of such an enquiry since it is drawn up in an utter disregard of method, and in such a manner as to render the difficulty of distinguishing between assertion and proof, deliberate statements and the exaggerations permitted to an advocate almost insuperable.

All this was clearly meant to gild the pill, but it quite failed of its purpose; in fact the more reason the colonial secretary showed for not taking Mr. Mackenzie very seriously, the less justification did there appear to be for his asking the government of Upper Canada in its different branches to occupy themselves with pleadings and denunciations which, both in their substance and in their quality, were already so familiar to them.

A long examination follows of "the great object of Mr. Mackenzie's censure – the election law passed by the lieutenant governor, council and assembly of Upper Canada in the year 1820." Here his lordship remarks that the deficiencies in Mr. Mackenzie's documents were not less regrettable than their redundancies: in a most protracted discussion of that law, for example, far from attempting to refute, he had not so much as noticed the arguments by which it was usually vindicated. These his lordship proceeds to set forth at length, but for whose benefit it is hard to say, for the whole subject must have been quite as well understood in Upper Canada as in the colonial office. At the same time it must be acknowledged that his Lordship's summing up of the matter is able and instructive.

Mr. Mackenzie had included in his widely drawn indictment certain measures to which he objected which, though brought forward, had never become law, upon which Lord Goderich observes that he "will not pause to investigate the propriety of measures which were never carried beyond an ineffectual attempt."

Under another point his Lordship frankly declared himself of Mr. Mackenzie's opinion, – as to the expediency, namely, of not excluding any class of persons from the franchise whose religious convictions made it impossible for them to take an oath. The Society of Friends or Quakers had already been granted relief in this matter, and Mr. Mackenzie had pleaded the cause of the Tunkers and one or two other small sects. Sir John Colborne was instructed to call upon the law officers of the province to report on the subject; and as the matter involved Imperial legislation the colonial secretary professed himself ready to introduce a bill into the British parliament to effect the object in view.

He was not ready, however, to enter on the enquiry "whether at a comparatively remote period prosecution against editors of newspapers were improperly instituted or not." It was "needless to look beyond Mr. Mackenzie's journal to be convinced that there is no latitude which the most ardent lover of free discussion ever claimed for such writers which is not enjoyed with perfect impunity in Upper Canada." Endeavouring to heap the Pelian of grievances past and gone upon the Ossa of those still in being, Mr. Mackenzie had dragged in the law prohibiting political conventions passed in Gourlay's time (1818) and repealed, as we have seen, sixteen months later: upon which Lord Goderich remarks, "To what end such complaints are preferred I am wholly at a loss to surmise." *Sancta simplicitas!*[2] Did his lordship really think that Mr. Mackenzie's statements were prepared for his instruction alone? Did he forget that their destination was Upper Canada and that "the people" might not scan them with the same cold, critical eye as the colonial office?

And so it was that he gave Lord Goderich a repetition of the Alien question although he acknowledged that the settlement arrived at in 1827 under instructions from Lord Goderich himself was "just and equitable," and had "removed one grand cause of discontent." For purpose of agitation a dead grievance is sometimes nearly as good as a living one.

Mr. Mackenzie had complained of the use of undue influence by officeholders in elections. The colonial secretary does not know whether to believe the charge or not. He says that "as a writer habitually engaged in political controversies Mr. Mackenzie may not be fully alive to the injustice of advancing charges against the servants of the public unsupported by distinct evidence of their truth." He feels it his duty "to refuse credit to such imputations unless clearly substantiated by evidence;" and yet he gives a caution to Sir John Colborne on the supposition that they *might* be true:

> In the absence of more definite statements I can only instruct you that his Majesty expects and requires of you neither to practice, nor to allow on the part of those who are officially subordinate to you, any interference with the right of his subjects to the free and unbiased choice of their representatives.

That this passage should have stung Sir John Colborne and his sympathisers in both Houses of the legislature is not surprising. In the acknowledged absence of evidence that he had done or permitted a certain improper thing, he is cautioned not to do or permit.

Mr. Mackenzie had charged that

> information as to the objects to which the people's money is applied is annually refused, in respect to a great part of the funds of the colony, by the colonial governors, to unanimous addresses of successive assemblies – the royal instructions being the plea of such refusals.

Lord Glenelg cannot understand to what facts the writer refers, but he takes occasion of observing that,

> if the royal instructions are supposed to forbid the most unreserved communication to the house of assembly of the manner in which the public money of the province, from whatever source derived, is expended, such a construction is foreign to his Majesty's design.

"There is no portion," he adds, "of the royal revenue, whether the proceeds of crown lands, or from whatever other source derived, of the employment of which the house of assembly should not have the most ample and particular information which they may at any time think proper to call for." If his Lordship had stopped here, the admonition, considering the facts of the case, discoverable in the journals of the legislature, would have been irritating enough, but he thought it well to add the general reflection that "Nothing is to be gained by concealment upon questions of this nature, and a degree of suspicion and prejudice is not rarely excited which, however ill-founded, often appears in the result to be incurable."

Another complaint made by Mackenzie was that certain ecclesiastics were "accommodated with seats in the political councils of the state." He referred, of course, to the fact that the Anglican bishop of Quebec, whose diocese at that time embraced Upper Canada, the Roman Catholic bishop of Regiopolis (Kingston), and archdeacon Strachan were members of the legislative council. Here his Lordship made a great slip and one really not very excusable in a colonial secretary: he spoke of the legislative council as a "board," deeply wounding thereby the dignity of that co-ordinate

branch of the legislature. It was understood, he said, that
the ecclesiastical gentlemen who had seats "on that board"
did not take part in any of the secular matters agitated
there; still he was not sure that their presence was desirable,
and he would be glad to have Sir John Colborne's opinion
on the subject. Of course they held their positions for life,
and there could be no thought of removing them; but
perhaps if they would voluntarily resign "they would best
consult their own personal comfort and the success of their
designs for the spiritual good of the people." One can
imagine the feelings with which John Strachan would receive
an invitation from Mr. Mackenzie, kindly conveyed through
the colonial secretary, to resign his seat in the legislative
council for the reasons so kindly suggested!

The remainder of the despatch, which was an extremely
long one, can only be very cursorily noticed. In paragraph
after paragraph the amiable writer, while not accepting, or
at least vouching for, Mr. Mackenzie's statements, which he
rarely finds substantiated in a satisfactory manner, makes
them the text now of suggestions, now of hypothetical
admonitions to the lieutenant governor. *If* so and so is true,
or *if* there is any foundation for it whatever, then it would
be well to do or to abstain from doing so and so. Such is
the burden of the document, and a burden, it need hardly
be said, quite calculated to [be] wearying to those who were
exercised thereby. A slightly different note is struck now
and then. In the matter of Mr. Mackenzie's demand for a
disapproval of the action of the assembly, in regard to the
representation of the people, his lordship wonders "in what
language such an interference by government would be
denounced by that gentleman himself on any occasion on
which he concurred with a majority of the House." With
reference to his prediction of bloodshed and civil war and
the separation of Upper Canada from Great Britain in case
the demands of the reformers were not granted, the remark
is made that "against gloomy predictions of this nature every
man conversant with public business must learn to fortify
his mind." The arguments adduced in support of the demand
for a dissolution of the legislature and a new election seemed
to his Lordship not only inadequate but in some cases to a
point in the opposite direction. One was the angry and
excited state of the public mind, which appeared rather to
be a reason for not holding an election just then. In con-

clusion Lord Goderich informs Sir John Colborne that he had written this despatch "with a view to publicity," and given him authority to make it public in whatever manner he may think most convenient.

This memorable document probably arrived at York about the end of December or beginning of January. Having been instructed to publish it Sir John Colborne devoted no small amount of reflection to the question how best to do it. He felt sure that if he sent it, with all the companying matter in the shape of Mr. Mackenzie's letters and memoirs, to the Houses of the Legislature, it would provoke angry debate, and at one time he was tempted to defer publication till after prorogation. What finally determined him, as he states in a private letter to Goderich, not to withhold it from the legislature was that it seemed to him to furnish an able refutation of many of Mackenzie's allegations. He had noticed that Mackenzie's friends had assumed a very subdued tone as if aware that his mission had not been a great success; and he thought that the publication of the despatch would help their discomfiture.[3] It might perhaps have done so if Mackenzie's enemies had been a little wiser – if they had made the most of the despatch as it was, pulled it over to their own side, and taken what little there was in it of (mainly) hypothetical admonition for themselves in not too haughty a spirit. Instead of this, however, they would have none of the colonial secretary's reproofs for themselves; they wanted them all concentrated on Mackenzie. By this unreasonable course of conduct they almost forced the secretary of state into a camp in which certainly he had no desire to be, and created the impression throughout the country that his agreement with Mr. Mackenzie was vastly greater than it really was. In a word they helped to give body to grievances which the colonial minister had plainly intimated he regarded as mainly fictitious and unsubstantial. We have now to follow the document in to both Houses of the legislature, to which it was referred by message on the nineteenth of January, 1833. Five days later a motion was made by Samson (Hastings) in the Assembly that one thousand copies of the despatch and of such parts of the documents as had not already been published should be printed for the use of its members. To this an amendment was moved by William Morris (Lanark) embodying three resolutions, the first declaring that the documents related exclusively to matters contained in petitions from certain inhabitants of the province forwarded to his Majesty's government by Mr. Mackenzie; the second, that the House had no desire to become the organ of communication between his Majesty's government and the petitioners or their agents, and this not from the slightest feeling of disrespect to his Majesty or his Majesty's government, but because they deemed it incompatible to the people generally "to receive and enter on their journals documents and papers intended to bring the House and its proceedings into contempt." The allegation here made was so far correct that, as we have seen, Lord Goderich himself spoke of the documents as displaying "sarcasm and invective" which would well have been spared. The third resolution thanked his excellency for communicating the documents to the House, but stated that, for the reasons mentioned, the House was unwilling to place them on its [records], and begged to be allowed to return them together with the despatch of Lord Goderich to his excellency.

The stalwarts on the government side, including the attorney and solicitor general, supported this motion, but other conservatives such as Jarvis, Vankoughnett, Lewis and Samson found it too strong, and it was defeated by a small majority. In amendment then to the main motion (Samson's) Perry moved the printing of the papers in their entirety. This, as an amendment, was carried by twenty-six to fourteen, but when put as the main motion was carried only by twenty-two to nineteen. The matter was allowed to lie for several days, and then on the ninth of February, Perry seconded by Bidwell moved an address to the King thanking him for the attention he had given to the representations and petitions, not only of his faithful commons, but of his faithful and loyal people in the province, and detailing the reforms recommended in the colonial secretary's despatch. The mover and seconder, particularly no doubt the seconder who was a man of acute mind as well as of superior legal training, must have exerted all their skill in drawing up this list which reads as if, in regard to each of the matters touched upon by the colonial secretary, it had been fully recognized that the province was labouring under some burden or some wrong. Perry knew that his motion would be voted [down], but that that would not hurt it as a campaign document.

In amendment the solicitor general moved an address to the lieutenant governor thanking him for his message, acknowledging that "the noble secretary of state was actuated by the best motives in framing it," but expressing regret that his Lordship had not sufficiently considered how little worthy of credit was the person to whose statements he was drawing attention, because, if he had he "would have considered it utterly unnecessary to enter into so elaborate an examination or refutation of anything advanced by him." The address goes on to say that "the remedy for any ills alleged to exist is placed in the hands, and is within the constitutional powers of the legislature of the colony;" and expresses confidence that the people of Upper Canada

> will take care to exercise their rights as freemen and British subjects in such a manner as will ensure the election of representatives who will maintain our excellent constitution, guard our rights, and, with the concurrence of the other branches of the legislature, adopt such measures as may appear necessary for removing any just grounds of complaint.

This address was carried by a vote of eighteen to ten, after which it was moved and carried that "the documents accompanying the despatch of the honourable the secretary of state for the colonies be not entered on the journals."

It was immediately after the despatch of this business that the vote was passed declaring Mr. Mackenzie incapable of sitting or voting in the House, as mentioned in our last chapter.

In the legislative council the step which the majority of the Assembly had shrunk from taking was taken: the despatch and accompanying documents were returned to his excellency with an elaborate address, the product of the chaste and vigorous pen of the Speaker, Chief Justice Robinson. Credit is given to Lord Goderich for his good intentions:

> They (the Council) do[4] not entertain the thought that a minister of the crown can ever apply himself to the affairs of this colony with any other wish or intention than to do good, and they recognize in the voluminous despatch which had been placed before them the most anxious desire to place in their true point of view some

question to which the attention of his Majesty's government had been called, not merely, as the Council is
aware, by an individual, but by the petitions of a
number of his Majesty's subjects in this province. For
the desire thus shown, the legislative council cannot be
otherwise than thankful.

Proceeding to Mr. Mackenzie's statements the address says:
"Enough appears in the tenor of his lordship's observations
to make it manifest that they have been made with a very
unusual disregard of truth and in spirit of wanton and
intemperate hostility to the legislative and executive authorities in this province." It is admitted that possibly there are
some persons in the province who will derive satisfaction
from observing "the condescending and respectful manner
in which representations of so peculiar a character have been
received and replied to, notwithstanding it was evident they
were outrageously insulting to all the constituted authorities
of this colony, and scarcely less to the people at large." As
to the legislative council, or "any portion of the people
having the truth under their view, it is not in the nature of
things that they can view such statements as compose Mr.
Mackenzie's voluminous correspondence in any other manner
than with the most unqualified contempt." There is the ring
of sincere indignation in the following passages:

> It has been painful to the legislative council to see that,
> in a discussion founded upon these documents, the
> office of the lieutenant governor of this province and
> the names of some of the most responsible of the King's
> servants are, even hypothetically connected with imputa-
> tions which no one can easily tolerate to find connected
> with his name. . . . Upon several of the questions which
> in this despatch are most elaborately discussed, no
> dissatisfaction or difficulty prevails or ever has pre-
> vailed; no person living here ever heard or imagined
> that they were seriously talked of or thought of as
> grievances; and the minds of the people are so far from
> being disquieted by them, that it is probable not a word
> would be heard upon them in travelling from one
> extremity of the province to the other.

The Council makes a firm stand upon their own rights
and privileges as a co-ordinate branch of the legislature, and

not a mere "board" as his lordship has styled them. They protest against the assumed right of influencing the conduct or controlling the attendance of individual members;

and strictly speaking any suggestion as to what the ecclesiastical members of the House should or should not do in their capacity as legislators were as much out of place as though they had referred to the functions to be exercised by the Archbishop of Canterbury or York in the House of Lords. As a matter of fact the practice of these members had accorded with the views of the colonial secretary, but it may be necessary, it is hinted to assert their independence by a different line of action.

As to the alleged obstructiveness of the council the address affirms that the relations of the Council and the Assembly had been almost invariably harmonious and marked by mutual helpfulness.

It is the very intention of our constitution that the several branches of the legislature should act as mutual checks upon each other in order to prevent the too hasty adoption of measures of doubtful expediency; but when this check is interposed it is not unlikely to happen that persons of impatient and impetuous tempers look with an unfavourable eye upon the barrier which obstructs the fulfilment of their wishes, and exert unscrupulously every effort to undermine or overturn it.

A few weeks after the prorogation of the legislature the startling announcement was made that the attorney and solicitor general had both been summarily dismissed by the home government; and when it was further learnt that this was on account of the part they had taken in promoting the expulsion of Mr. Mackenzie in the previous session, the exultation of Mackenzie's friends and the chagrin and disgust of the government party can be imagined. It appeared that the colonial secretary had some months before expressed to the lieutenant governor his regret at the course the legislature had taken in this matter, which seemed to him open to constitutional objection. When therefore news of the third expulsion (November 6th, 1832) reached England, he wrote to Sir John Colborne instructing him to inform the two law officers (to whom he correctly assumed that his views had been communicated) that his Majesty "could no longer avail himself of their services." Boulton at once went to England to plead his own cause. The colonial office had at this time just passed from the hands of Lord Goderich to those of Mr. E. G. Stanley (afterwards Lord Derby). Mr. Mackenzie, who was in London at the time, pleaded strenuously with the new secretary against any reversal of his predecessor's decision. After weighing the matter, however, Mr. Stanley concluded to restore Mr. Hagerman to the solicitor generalship; to transfer Mr. Boulton to Newfoundland as chief justice; and to send Mr. Robert S. Jameson to Upper Canada as attorney general.

These arrangements, of course, caused vast disappointment to those reformers who had hailed the dismissal of Boulton and Hagerman as a signal act of imperial justice. But meantime some of the representatives of the government party had been behaving themselves very badly. One or two newspaper scribes indulged in language quite comparable to the most violent of Mackenzie's utterances, and like him had predicted revolution and bloodshed if their views were thwarted. Conspicuous for extravagance and brutality was an article published in the *Upper Canada Courier* of the first of May. Lord Goderich is spoken of as a "political imbecile;" and the English government is warned that "the minds of all the well-affected people of the province begin to be unhinged" – the writer's own mind was momentarily unhinged beyond a doubt –

and, instead of dwelling with delight and confidence upon their affections are already more than half alienated from that country; and, in the apprehension that the same degrading and insulting course of conduct is likely to be continued, they begin to cast about in their mind's eye for some new state of political existence, which shall effectually put the colony beyond the reach of injury and insult from any and every ignoramus whom the political lottery may chance to elevate to the chair of the colonial office.[5]

It is not recorded that these fatuous sentiments found any echo throughout the province, totally at variance, as they were, with those expressed both by the Council and the Assembly in their replies on the subject of the colonial secretary's despatch.[6]

CHAPTER THIRTEEN

THE COMBAT DEEPENS—MACKENZIE FIRST MAYOR OF TORONTO

In spite of the brave showing made by the reform leaders in the house of assembly of the triumphs won by Mackenzie in England as testified by Lord Goderich's despatch, there is clear evidence that the achiever of these triumphs returned to Canada in a rather despondent frame of mind. Before leaving England he had had several interviews with the new colonial secretary, Mr. Stanley. One matter which he urged upon his attention with great vigour, and, as he thought, with no little success was the expediency of advising his Majesty to disallow certain bank acts passed by the Upper Canada legislature in 1831, and assented to by the lieutenant governor in the king's name. So persuaded was he that he had carried his point that he wrote to his paper to say that the thing had been done. The sequel will be told later.

The minister was, however, not at all responsive to his general arraignment of the colonial government or his plea for an elective legislative council. "Mr. Stanley," he writes,

> made many observations, but I cannot say that they amounted to an admission that he was favourable to a change of system. . . . Perceiving that he expressed no opinion favourable to an elective council . . . I reminded him of his oft repeated sentiments and added with great plainness of language that, if I had not formed a wrong estimate of the sense and intelligence of the people of Upper Canada, they would not long endure a system which was considered an insult to the age and continent in which they lived; and that if obstacles to reform were made by the new whig government, the population would perhaps proceed summarily to remove all difficulties in the way of their attainment of a pure representative government in which their wishes and

wants would be attended to in a different manner from
which they were at present.

This was the kind of language which Lord Goderich had
said statesmen had to fortify their minds against, and as
Mr. Stanley is not reported to have been greatly impressed
by it, the inference may be drawn that his mind was fortified.
It was on this occasion that, as Mr. Lindsey mentions, an
archbishop was kept waiting in the ante-room for half an
hour. Mr. Mackenzie supplies the additional information
that it was an Irish archbishop.

The despondency which Mr. Mackenzie exhibited on
returning to his field of labour in Upper Canada was not
due solely to the slowness of colonial ministers to throw
themselves into the work of reform as he had outlined it;
it arose also in no small measure from the lack of zeal and
devotion shown by not a few of his followers in the province.
One strong note of his character was disinterestedness. He
was absolutely above paltry, and too much above prudential
considerations. The information afforded in his paper as to
the financing of his mission to England brings out this
characteristic in a clear light. A central committee had been
formed to receive subscriptions for that object. There was
also a special committee for the county of York. The
following contributions were received.

Members of the County Committee	£ 78
Inhabitants of Town of York	80
ˮ Counties York and Simcoe	93
Niagara District	13 ˮ 7
Kingston	18
Leeds	10
Other counties a little under	35
	———
	£327 ˮ 7

Of the amount collected, which some minor subscriptions
made up to 330, 180 was spent by the central committee in
the province – how is not stated; perhaps in paying for the
services of Mr. Randall Wixon who replaced Mr. Mackenzie
in the editorial chair of the *Colonial Advocate*. Mackenzie
received the balance, £150. His expenses, however, came to
£676. To meet them the committee borrowed £380 on their
personal responsibility, and Mackenzie himself borrowed in

London another sum of £146, to meet which, he remarks, no funds have as yet been provided by the country. "If," he continues,

> the reformers of the country hang back, as they did in the case of Mr. Randall, who was most disgracefully and dishonourably, treated by those whom his mission had greatly benefited, I shall assume and pay the whole sum for which the committee are in arrears, even if the sacrifice of part of my real property should be required in addition to the proceeds of my printing establishment, which I imagine will be the case.[1]

In reply to a letter from the committee of the Home and adjoining districts expressing their satisfaction with his conduct while in England we find Mackenzie writing –

> I regret to say that the information I have received from one section of the province is rather less satisfactory than that which has reached the committee. In some places there is a strong feeling of dissatisfaction because I remained so long abroad and accomplished so little. . . . It is to be regretted that the friends of good government and equal rights are so easily elated and easily depressed.

Someone had said that a man's philosophy is the supplement of his character. It looks like it when we find Mackenzie preaching that people should not be too easily elated or depressed.

Other passages of the letter are worth quoting as throwing light on the writer's state of mind at this time.

> The friends of freedom in Upper Canada will yet have many difficulties to encounter, and perhaps by injudicious conduct their troubles may be multiplied; there are, however, strong grounds for hope. Time which does almost everything is on our side; population is rapidly increasing; and political education can no longer be arrested. I once thought that if we had the British constitution in practical operation in this country, it would ensure good government by checking the abuses I have seen committed by persons in authority; but I have since lived long enough to see that I was in error.

The British constitution cannot be enjoyed by any distant, dependent province; and, even were it otherwise, a cheap elective representative government appears to be the most suitable to supply the wants and wishes of the people. . . . When the question of the comparative advantages of an intelligent elective chief magistrate from among ourselves, and a half-pay officer, a stranger to our customs and whose interest will often be the opposite of ours, comes to be discussed in Upper Canada, I feel satisfied that our fellow citizens will also[2] insist on choosing their own governors.

The writer at this time practically agreed with the view of the Home government as to the inapplicability of the system of "responsible government" to Upper Canada. The difference was that the former expected that Upper Canada would grow into fitness for that system, while Mackenzie regarded the colonial relation as fundamentally incompatible therewith. The authorities were for retaining the colonial relation and letting the colony gather strength and local independence with years; Mackenzie was for dissolving it and falling back on purely elective, or democratic institutions.

Shortly after returning from England Mr. Mackenzie announced his intention of not continuing the *Colonial Advocate* after the election of the next legislature which would probably take place in the summer or autumn of 1834. The issue of that paper, however, of the twenty-eighth of October contained a notice of a different tenor. "A sudden and unforeseen domestic calamity, operating with other causes" had changed his intention of continuing for another year in charge of the business and induced him to "seek relief from a very anxious and fatiguing duty in retirement." The present issue of the paper was to be its last one. The paper, nevertheless, continued in existence and under Mackenzie's charge, but with the name changed from *The Colonial Advocate* to *The Advocate* till the fourth of November, 1834, though the publication was somewhat irregular.

The domestic calamity alluded to was the death of an infant son whom in honour of the English reformer he had named "Joseph Hume." Mr. Mackenzie was a man of strong domestic affection, and such a loss would affect him deeply. As already hinted, discouragement, springing from various causes, was at this time creeping over him. About a month later we find him saying:

> When I published the first number of the *Colonial Advocate*, I did so with pleasure and satisfaction – when seven years ago this day, I recommenced the series after the destruction of the press, I was as free and willing a recruit as ever entered the service. It is not so now. I engage in the management of this journal, and agree to conduct it solely from my own resources until the meeting of the next House of Assembly, from a conviction that I cannot honourably retire at this moment, but with a reluctance to continue that I cannot conceal. I have no distrust of my own sincerity in the cause of the people, but I begin to distrust the people themselves: I much fear that they will be found to fail in that disinterested love of country in the absence of which all efforts to serve them effectually will be in vain.

In another part of the same paper he says:

> The events of the last eighteen months have made some editors more democratic. . . . I have watched the progress of aristocracy and democracy in America, and my belief is that under the former neither life nor property is secure,[3] while under the latter people live in peace and safety, enjoying with contentment all the happiness of which in this life the bulk of mankind appear to be susceptible.

We read on and come to the following outburst:

> It is not with us as in the United States where the taxes and public moneys return among the people to enrich them. Here the vast sums drawn from us for Canada Company's land, Crown and Clergy sales, and large portions of the taxes, drain the country of a safe circulating medium, leaving it at the mercy of a heartless grovelling crew of land speculators, sycophantic shopkeepers and interested circulators of baseless bank rags,[4] who being joined to a sensual hireling priesthood, exercise a most unhappy influence over public affairs and prepare the country for much misery hereafter.

In this selfsame year, 1833, William Lyon Mackenzie had published a book – already noticed – on many pages of which the happy state of Upper Canada was described, and in which the statement was made that the taxation therein was extremely light, and that there was no better country under the sun, if as good, for the industrious emigrant, and this notwithstanding all the author had also to say about priesthoods and oligarchies and military government. Yet now it was a country in which neither life nor property was secure, and altogether inferior to the United States.

The fourth and last session of the eleventh parliament had been summoned for the nineteenth of November. Assuming himself to be a member of the Assembly, no new writ having been issued since his election in November of the previous year, Mackenzie presented himself before the clerk of the House to take the usual oath. The clerk, Col. Fitzgibbon, declined to administer it without instructions from the Speaker, which that officer was not prepared to give, considering that the vote of the ninth of February re-affirming Mr. Mackenzie's unfitness and unworthiness to sit in the House as equivalent to a vote of expulsion. On the following day Bidwell moved a resolution to the effect that

W. L. Mackenzie, Esq. had been duly elected and returned to represent the county of York, and being under no legal disqualification is by the law and constitution a member of this House, and upon taking the oath required by law, (which it is hereby declared to be the duty of the Commissioner appointed for that purpose to administer) will have a right to sit and vote in this House.

The motion was lost, the vote standing seven to eighteen. Six days later Ketchum in a very sensible and temperate speech moved that "all proceedings had by the House last session relating to William Lyon Mackenzie, returned to serve as knight, representative of the county of York be expunged from the journals of the House." "You have got Mr. Mackenzie very low down," he said,

take care you do not end your proceedings by raising him higher and higher in the esteem of the province. The Canadians are a generous and friendly people, they do not like to see a man persecuted. They think and I

think your conduct towards him unfair and unlawful.
. . . Our persecution of him may end in placing him,
Mr. Speaker, in the chair you now fill. (Great laughter)
You may make him governor before the game is over.
(Increased laughter) . . . I repeat it, the individual you
want to disgrace, you will make a man of great consequence, whether he will or not. He makes some very
great blunders, but you cover them up by making still
greater. . . . You go on denying or undervaluing public
opinion – see that in the end it do not prove too
powerful for you.

The warning was wisely given by a man of substance,
character and recognized benevolence,[5] but it fell on deaf
ears. At the bar of the House there was an ear that was
far from deaf, that of Mackenzie himself, and it is an
interesting surmise whether, as his colleague, amid the
laughter of the House, exclaimed, "You may make him
governor before the game is over," he did not with a tremor
of excitement, recall the prophecy delivered to another,
"Thou shalt be king hereafter."

To Ketchum's motion Perry moved in amendment "that
W. L. Mackenzie had been duly elected and returned to
represent the county of York at the last election." One point
he put well in asking, "How can we find fault with the other
branches of the legislature, if they presume to set their
opinions above the law, if this House sets the example?"
His amendment was carried (as against Ketchum's motion)
by fifteen to nine, but the motion as amended was lost by
one vote. On the same day Mackenzie himself addressed a
strong and, on the whole, moderately worded protest to the
lieutenant governor. "The people of the county," he said,

> are desirous that I should continue to take charge of
> the petitions and bills, watch over their dearest interests,
> plead the cause of the poorest of their number, and
> object or assent in their name to money bills, loans,
> municipal regulations etc. . . . Knowing my principles,
> intimately acquainted with my conduct, they have given
> your excellency and the late lieutenant governor the
> most unequivocal proofs of their concurrence in my
> proceedings.

He asks his excellency either to dissolve the House; to
recommend them to review their vote of the twentieth of

November; or to inform them as governor Gore did in a former case that he did not consider the representation of the country complete, and could not assent to any more bills till the county of York was fully represented. He ends by declaring that the people "have only to consult the constitutional annals of our nation to learn that resistance to oppression becomes a solemn and sacred duty, when through high-handed measures, they find themselves deprived of their rights."

In the previous session an act had been passed dividing the county of York into four ridings and assigning a member to each, thus doubling its representation in the Assembly. The measure as it passed the Assembly gave the county six members, showing that the dominant party was not opposed to a very great augmentation of the county's voting power; but the legislative council had thought so large an increase at the time to be inexpedient and had reduced the number to four,[6] an amendment which the Assembly had accepted. This change in the basis of the representation had been put forward as a reason why a writ should not be issued. Mackenzie having mentioned the alleged difficulty in his letter, the question was referred to the new attorney general, Mr. Jameson, who promptly reported that as the new act was not to come into force until the next general election everything should in the meantime be governed by the old law. In replying to Mr. Mackenzie his excellency slyly remarked that if a new writ had not been issued in the last session it was due to the opposition of his own friends who, with a few conservatives, had voted bodily against it. He denied that it was any part of his duty to interfere between Mr. Mackenzie and the Assembly, and according to modern ideas his position was a sound one. To Mackenzie, however, any interference by anybody with anything was justified provided only it met his views or advanced his purposes.

The battle, however, had not been fought out in the House of Assembly. On the second of December Perry moved a long resolution dwelling on the sacredness of the elective franchise and protesting against the assumption by any branch of the legislature to pass any vote that should have the effect either of disfranchising any voter or of disqualifying any person to be a candidate, or to take his seat when elected. Such a stretch of power, the resolution declared, "must be viewed with horror and disgust, and execrated by all lovers of freedom, good order, and constitutional liberty." He also took his excellency to task for his remark to Mr. Mackenzie on the way his friends had voted on the question of a new writ, and concluded by asking for papers in the matter of the dismissal of Boulton and Hagerman, and for a copy of the despatch expressing disapproval of the expulsion of Mackenzie. This motion only secured twelve votes, seventeen being recorded against it. Finally a motion by Samson stating that Mr. Mackenzie having been expelled from the House, and declared unfit and unworthy to sit therein, the House, convinced of the propriety of such expulsion and declaration, would not allow him to take a seat or vote, was carried by eighteen to fifteen. A motion by MacNab for the issue of a new writ followed, and was carried by a vote of sixteen to fifteen. The debate lasted from ten A.M. to ten P.M., and was marked by extreme bitterness of language on both sides.

Thus was Mackenzie thrown back once more on the electors, and once more they returned him by acclamation, exactly two weeks after the ordering of the new writ. His election address was, as usual, of portentious length, and in the multitude of his words there lacked not considerable exaggeration. For example we read that "Judge Thorpe, your representative, was basely slandered, beggared and banished to the deadly climate of Sierra Leone by the very same faction who are now persecuting me." We have heard of Judge Thorpe before: for his troublesome meddling in politics he was recalled from Canada and offered a judgeship in Sierra Leone, which he accepted. That was his banishment by the "Family Compact" to Sierra Leone. Considering how the province was teeming with abuses at the moment – at least as Mackenzie viewed it – it was singular that he should have had to stir up the pure minds of the electors of York by a rehearsal and misrepresentation of a case that had occurred a full generation before. "To take part with the people," he says, "has been the signal for proscription." But there was no proscription for Rolph, for Bidwell, for Perry or for Ketchum; and Mr. Mackenzie would not have served the people less, but more and better, if he had refrained from the language which, in 1826, brought about the destruction of his press, and in 1831 his expulsion from the legislature. He also states that he will shortly go through the country and consult with them "privately" respecting the general welfare. He repeats this statement later in the address, italicizing the word "private." "I was not born," he exclaims,

> to be a slave. I never will barter my freedom for any earthly good. . . . If the government of Upper Canada or its officers in the house of assembly shall much longer trifle with that right, it will be for the electors to decide whether they will continue to obey constitutional enactments.

Then follows a remarkable attempt to instil suspicion into the minds of the people. He tells them that the lieutenant governor had in 1829 informed the legislature that the King's government would willingly supply the whole militia with arms provided the men would take care of them. "For what purpose," he asks, "were they to be thus armed? Was it that the militia of one county might be called out to reduce the population of another to a state of ignoble servitude?" It would be difficult to imagine more mischievous language. One thing is certain – that the government which freely offers to arm the whole militia of a country cannot have any apprehensions of disaffection on the part of the people; cannot be conscious of any wrong-doing towards them; must on the contrary be very conscious of deserving their support.

That the electors were to a considerable extent imbibing the sentiments of their representative is shown by certain resolutions that were passed after the declaration of the poll, one of which was to the effect that all laws that had been passed, or which may be assented to, "since this county was unjustly deprived of its share of the representation, have been enacted unconstitutionally without our consent, and are therefore not binding on us: taxation without representation is tyranny."

A couple of hours later a strange scene is taking place in the hall of the legislative assembly. Mackenzie, with his indenture of election in his pocket, and attended by a considerable number of his faithful electors, though not quite the cream of them according to all accounts, has come to the House to claim his seat. He is standing outside the bar with a group of his friends while the rest of them have found seats in the gallery. MacNab is speaking on the question of receiving a certain petition from the county of

York, when some of the visitors in the gallery hiss. The house is cleared and Mackenzie is ordered to leave with the rest. He refuses, stating that he has his indenture, and that the writ had been returned to the clerk of the crown in chancery who was then present in the House. The sergeant-at-arms, instead of seeking instructions from the Speaker, takes Mackenzie by the collar in order to force him to the door. A stout highlander in turn seizes the sergeant-at-arms and holds him off; at the same moment the door having been opened to afford exit to Mr. Mackenzie, a number of his excluded friends rush in again. Finally the House is cleared of all but Mr. Mackenzie, who, as the sergeant-at-arms informs the Speaker, claims to remain as a member. Discussion ensues. Mr. MacNab expresses very unfavorable opinion of the sample they had seen of Mr. Mackenzie's supporters: he had looked in vain to see if there was a single respectable person of the county amongst them. The Speaker decides that Mr. Mackenzie must retire and he obeys.[7] On the following day Mr. Mackenzie wrote a brief letter to the lieutenant governor complaining that the clerk of the crown in chancery had refused to administer the oath to him as a member of the House, and asking that he might be allowed to take the oath before his excellency. The latter, having consulted the attorney general, replied that he had authorized the clerk of the executive council to administer the oath, if there should be any further difficulty in getting it done by one or other of the regular commissioners, to wit the clerk of the Assembly and the clerk of the crown in chancery. On enquiry it did not appear that either of these officers had been to blame in the matter. One had not been applied to at all. The other had been applied to at a moment when it was not possible for him – the House being engaged on a question of order – to inform the Speaker of Mr. Mackenzie's re-election, and not subsequently. Mackenzie availed himself of the arrangement suggested by the lieutenant governor and took the oath before the clerk of the executive council.

Before he had done so, however, in fact on the very day following the scene above described, proceedings were taken in the House to prevent his taking his seat. Morris moved a resolution, which after a recital of facts, went on to say that, "as the said W. L. Mackenzie has never made reparation to this House for the gross injuries which he has attempted to inflict on its character and proceedings, there is no reason to depart from the resolution of 1832." MacNab moved to add words distinctly carrying expulsion; and after two ineffectual attempts had been made to adjourn the debate, the motion so amended was carried. A few days later the kindly Ketchum tried to get the proceedings expunged from the journals but in vain. Nor was any new writ issued. Mr. Mackenzie chose, therefore, to consider himself still a member, and on the tenth of February walked in and took his seat. As soon as he was observed the sergeant-at-arms took him by the arm and said he must retire. Mr. Mackenzie protested that he was a member of the House, and had been sworn by a commissioner appointed by the lieutenant governor, adding that he would not retire except by compulsion. The official then with gentle force led him to the door. He shortly returned and was again removed. A few minutes later he entered the House a third time, and as he made some resistance to expulsion, the sergeant arrested him and informed the Speaker that he was at the bar. A discussion ensued. Perry moved that he had a right to sit; Bidwell that the resolution (of expulsion) of the seventeenth of December should be expunged from the journals: both motions were lost. A motion by Berczy, that he should be admonished by the Speaker and discharged, was then carried. Mackenzie, in the *Advocate* of the thirteenth of February, says that the Speaker invited him to confess that his remarks in the *Advocate* concerning the House had been improper, but that he refused to do so. Had those remarks, he goes on to say, been made in the House, and had the House declared them improper, he would have bowed to its decision; but that he would have felt he was sacrificing the liberty of the press "by admitting that editors have not the power to censure public men, subject only to such consequences as may result from a civil and criminal suit before the usual tribunals." The "usual tribunal" in this case would have been, as Mackenzie knew, a jury selected from the county of York, the majority of whom would probably not have been very sensitive as to the reputation of the legislature.

It happened that just about two years before this, the popular party in the Lower Canada legislature had expelled from the Assembly the member for Gaspé, Mr. Robert Christie, and, upon his re-election by his constituency, had expelled him again and again, the expulsions, as in Mackenzie's case, numbering five in all. The charge against Mr. Christie was that as Chairman of Quarter Sessions he had made reports to the government damaging to certain members of the Assembly. Of these proceedings Mackenzie entirely approved though they had the effect of *completely* depriving the county of Gaspé of representation, whereas the county of York still had an efficient representative in Mr. Ketchum. It was contended by Mr. Neilson, one of the liberal leaders in Lower Canada, that a constituency *could not possess the right to send to the House any person notoriously objectionable to it*. This was also the ground taken, if not distinctly avowed, by the MacNabs, Morrises and Boltons, who voted for Mackenzie's expulsion.

Before dismissing the eleventh parliament it is necessary to consider the attitude which it took on the question of the Bank Acts, which Mr. Mackenzie, when in England, had exerted himself so strongly to get disallowed. Whether in consequence of his representation or not, the secretary to the Treasury wrote to the Colonial office pointing out certain amendments which, in the opinion of the Lords of the Treasury, ought to be made in the bills. The bills themselves had not been disallowed; but the question of disallowance had evidently been under consideration. The lieutenant governor on the sixth of January laid before the House a copy of the communication which he had received on the subject, and, in accordance with his instructions, invited their attention to the matter. In an instant almost the House forgot its quarrels over the representation of York and the injuries done to Mr. Mackenzie, and joined in a unanimous – save for one vote, that of Mr. Ketchum – protest against what they regarded as an unjustifiable interference with the right of the Canadian legislature to regulate the purely domestic interests of the province. Strange to say Mackenzie rejoiced in the outburst – rejoiced that the House had repudiated the very interference on the part of the Home authorities which he had invoked.

Bidwell took a leading part in the proceedings. The House was considering an address to the King on the subject, when he moved an amendment, which was at once accepted, and which made the address practically his own; only two short paragraphs of the original draft being left standing. In the first paragraph the House expressed its

extreme apprehension and regret that your Majesty had
been advised to entertain the intention of disallowing
two acts of the legislature of this colony, which were
passed more than two years ago;[8] the one for increasing
the capital stock of the Bank of Upper Canada, and the
other for incorporating a second banking association in
this province under the name of the Commercial Bank
of the Midland District.

The third paragraph in which Bidwell's hand appears
acknowledges the power conferred on his Majesty by the
Act of 1791 in regard to provincial legislation, but declares
that the disallowance of these Acts is "contrary to the spirit
and meaning of the constitution and to the principles of
good government." That Act was never intended "to give a
power of interference with our internal affairs." "It is
manifest," the address continues,

that if your Majesty's ministers, at a distance of more
than four thousand miles, and not at all controlable
by, or accountable to, your Majesty's subjects here,[9] . . .
can dictate a different course in relation to measures
affecting ourselves only, from that which the people by
their representatives, and with the concurrence of the
other branches of the provincial legislature have chosen,
we are reduced to a state of mere dependence upon
the will and pleasure of a ministry irresponsible to us
and beyond the reach and operation of the public
opinion of the province.

It is granted that power must be conceded to the head of
the empire to prevent the operation of colonial laws that
are incompatible with treaties or with the just rights of other
parts of the empire, but, with these exceptions, it is submitted
"that no laws ought to be, or rightfully can be, dictated to
or imposed upon the people of this province, to which they
do not freely give their consent through the constitutional
medium of representatives chosen by and accountable to
themselves."

There is an explanation of everything in this world if it
can only be got at; and the practicably unanimous support
given to this address is a phenomenon which will bear a
little explanation. The side of the House which was chiefly
annoyed at the criticism by the House authorities of the

Bank Acts was the conservative side; while the side which most felt the interference of those authorities in a purely provincial matter was the reform side. Thus two somewhat differing indignations joined to make a formidable demonstration. Each party was glad on this occasion to have the other's support; and no doubt Bidwell and his fellow reformers were particularly glad to be enabled with the help of the whole conservative side, to put on record so firm a declaration of provincial independence in home matters. In a colony in which such sentiments as these asserted themselves there was not much danger of liberty being trampled under foot.

On the sixth of March, 1834, the legislature was prorogued; and on the same date the town of York became, under a new charter, the city of Toronto. His excellency in his closing speech, referred to many valuable measures in which the two Houses had concurred; and it is true that, in spite of the wrangling over the Mackenzie case, the session had not been unfruitful in useful legislation. He regretted that they had not adopted "some practical mode of applying the funds set apart for the purposes of education," which had been placed under their control. On the other hand again, he commended the attention they had devoted to the improvement of the communications of the province, whereby industry had been stimulated in every district. The population of the province, he stated, had doubled in eight years,[10] while the imports by the St. Lawrence were increasing at the rate of one-third annually.

The reformers of Toronto had not been favorable to its incorporation as a city, professing to dread the increased burden of taxation likely to be entailed. They nevertheless brought forward candidates in all the wards (five) into which the new city was divided; and in the elections which took place on the twenty-seventh of March, gained a majority of the city council. Each ward returned four representatives, two aldermen and two common councilmen. Mr. Mackenzie presented himself for alderman in St. David's ward, and was returned at the head of the poll with 143 votes.[11] According to the charter the mayor was to be chosen by the city council; and a meeting at which nineteen members were present was held for that purpose on the third of April, when Mr. Mackenzie, the rejected of the legislature, was **elected by ten votes to eight, he himself abstaining from** voting. A few years later when publishing a paper in the United States, he attributed his election to "the votes of some native-born Americans in the Common Council," and probably his recollection of the matter was correct.[12] Having been elected he applied himself with vigour and earnestness, as might have been expected, to the discharge of his official duties. Unfortunately he was far from receiving the undivided support of the citizens; and a great outcry was raised over a rate which it was found necessary to levy of three pence in the pound. A meeting called by the mayor for the twenty-ninth of July, in order that he might make certain necessary explanations to the tax-payers, ended tumultuously, and was adjourned to the next day. The place of meeting was directly over the meat market, and some violent stamping on the part of the audience brought the floor down with ghastly results, a number of persons being caught on the butchers' hooks below, while others were seriously, some fatally, injured by the fall. It is stated that seven or eight died of their injuries while others were maimed for life.

An incident of much importance in the year 1834 was the publication by Mr. Mackenzie in the *Advocate* of the twenty-second of May of a letter addressed to him by the tireless reformer, Joseph Hume, which has become famous in Canadian history as the "baneful domination" letter. The first part of it referred to the proceedings against Mr. Mackenzie in the previous session.

> Your triumphant election on the sixteenth of December and ejection from the Assembly on the seventeenth must hasten that crisis which is fast approaching in the affairs of the Canadas, and which will terminate in independence and freedom from the baneful domination of the Mother Country, and the tyranical conduct of a small and despicable faction in the colony. I regret to think that the proceedings of Mr. Stanley . . . encourage your enemies to persevere in the course they have taken. But I confidently trust that the high-minded people of Canada will not be overawed, or cheated of their rights and liberties, by such men. *Your* cause is *their* cause, – your defeat would be their subjugation. Go on therefore, I beseech you, and success – glorious success – must inevitably crown your joint efforts. . . . The proceedings between 1772 and 1782 in America

ought not to be forgotten; and to the honour of the Americans, and for the interest of the civilized world let their conduct and the result be ever in view.

Mr. Mackenzie could certainly claim in later years that, if he raised the standard of revolt in Canada against "the baneful domination of the Mother Country," he had the warrant and encouragement of an English member of Parliament for the metropolitan county of Middlesex.

The latter part of the letter was devoted to a most vicious attack on the Rev. Egerton Ryerson, who had lately been expressing some disapproval of Mr. Hume's proceedings. A few years earlier there had been more or less political sympathy between Mackenzie and Ryerson, owing chiefly to the vigorous manner in which the latter had controverted certain pretensions and statements put forth by Dr. Strachan in his celebrated "Letter and Ecclesiastical chart." For some time past, however, things had been on a different footing, and Mackenzie had bitterly denounced Ryerson for his complaisance towards the government. To enforce his observations he had said, working over a now favorite theme:

> The father of the editor of the *Guardian* lifted his sword against the throats of his own countrymen, struggling for freedom against established churches, stamp acts, military domination, Scotch governors and Irish government; and his brother George figured on the frontier in 1812, and got wounded and pensioned for fighting to preserve crown and clergy reserves and all the other strongholds of corruption in the hands of the locusts who disturb and infest the province.

In September, 1833, the *Colonial Advocate* republished from the Cobourg *Reformer* an article entitled "Clerical Bribery" which commenced as follows:

> The secret is out. Three separate sects have been bought by the government – the Wesleyan missionaries (English), the Synod, and the Canadian Wesleyans; these have fixed the value at which their honour, honesty and independence is held: the first is bought at £900, the second for £800, and the last for £600. The public revenue has been prostituted by the purchase, and the receivers are branded with lasting and deserved infamy.

The cause of this strong language was that the British
government, having no power to divide the clergy reserves
between the different Christian denominations, had decided,
as a temporary measure, to assist the Presbyterians and the
two branches of the Methodists in their missionary work
in Canada, an arrangement in which Mr. Ryerson had
acquiesced.

In publishing Mr. Hume's communication the *Advocate*
said: "The indignant feeling of the honest old reformer
when he became acquainted with the heartless slanders of
the unprincipled renegade, Ryerson, may be easily conceived
from the tone of his letter." The tone, certainly, was
remarkable. "I candidly acknowledge," says the honest old
reformer,

> that of all the renegades and apostates from public
> principle and private honour which, during a long
> course of public life, I have known (and with regret I
> say I have known many) I never knew a more worth-
> less hypocrite, or so base a man as Mr. Ryerson has
> proved himself to be.

Indignation, however, does not totally exclude pity, for the
writer dreads that "the pangs of a guilty and self-condemning
conscience must make his venal and corrupt breast a second
Hell, and ere long render his existence truly miserable."
Even the pity, it will be observed, is somewhat savagely
expressed, and it seems to have vanished entirely when the
writer proceeds to say that Mr. Ryerson "deserves to be an
outcast from every honest society." Mr. Ryerson was a
fighter from the beginning, as well as a man of long views
and excellent memory. He made a very telling reply to
Mr. Hume at the time, and held himself in reserve for a
certain Philippi which was not very far in the future.

Why Mr. Mackenzie chose to print a letter obviously not
meant for the city and the world, and one sure to create
contention and mischief which, as mayor, he might have
been supposed anxious to avoid, is a question of moral
psychology into which we need not very deeply enter. There
are people here and there who search for trouble as for
hidden treasure, and it seems as if Mackenzie belonged to
that class. He did love to drink delight of battle with the
Upper Canada peers and their benchmen, and here was an
unrivalled opportunity. Hardly had the letter been published

before there was an outburst of indignation from the whole conservative press of the province, while not a few of the leading reform papers expressed surprise at Mr. Mackenzie's lack of judgment in printing it, and hastened to disclaim sympathy with the sentiments expressed. A wild excitement reigned in Toronto, where, in the space of six hours, an address to his Majesty denouncing the letter was signed by upwards of twelve hundred citizens.

The matter was also taken up, as might have been expected, in the city council at a special meeting held on the ninth of June, when Mr. Alderman Gurnett, publisher of the *Courier*, moved a resolution condemnatory to the letter, and declaring that whatever difference might exist in the province, no people could be more ardently attached to their sovereign and to the institutions of the Mother Country than the people of Upper Canada; and that none would resist more firmly any attempt to separate them from the British Empire. Unfortunately it was Mr. Gurnett's own paper the *Courier* which, a little over a year before, had hinted at "casting about for some new state of political existence." If he had forgotten the fact, the friends of Mr. Mackenzie in the council did not fail to remind him of it. An amendment to Mr. Gurnett's motion was moved by Mr. T. D. Morrison, declaring that a wrong construction had been put on Mr. Hume's letter, and that, properly understood, it was entirely justified. This was carried by a vote of twelve to seven. It is reasonable to suppose that the "native-born Americans" were among the twelve.

CHAPTER FOURTEEN

THE TWELFTH PARLIAMENT —
A WAVE OF REFORM

The government party in their proceedings against Mackenzie had overshot the mark; they had not carried the country with them, as the general election, which was held in the month of October, made very plain. It must be remembered that Mackenzie had not all this time been pleading his cause alone. One of the reasons he made for discontinuing his own paper was that it could be spared, as there were now a number of other papers championing the cause of reform. These were all with him in his quarrel with the Assembly, and some had struck a note not very dissimilar to his own in regard to the governing class. It cannot be doubted that hostility to that class was now a rising force in the province. A leading French Canadian politician, a few years before this, was asked to draw up for Sir James Kempt, newly arrived as governor-general, a memorandum on this state of the province (Lower Canada) and the cause of its troubles. In fulfilment of this task he pointed out some of the errors into which the government had fallen, but the chief influence which he saw at work was that of the demagogue. "The natural independence of the human mind," he wrote,

> will ever lead the multitude easily to credit the assertion that those who rule them, wrong them; therefore he who will loudly denounce the abuses practised by superior authority, unfold a string of grievances, and hold himself forth to the people as the assertor of their rights, will soon find a ready path to popularity. It is not the individual who fascinates the eyes of the people; it is the doctrine that flatters their ear.[1]

Much flattering doctrine of this kind has been disseminated in Upper Canada also, and not without result.

The probability indeed is that, had it not been for the ill-judged and untimely publication of the "baneful domination" letter, the victory of the reformers would have been even more decisive than it was. They gained complete control, however, of the house of assembly. In Toronto J. E. Small, a moderate reformer, defeated sheriff Jarvis. He had the support on this occasion of Mr. Mackenzie, who drew up a tremendous bill of indictment against his opponent – a more tremendous one by far than Mr. Small, in his election speeches, seemed disposed to endorse. The county of York, now divided into four ridings, returned a solid reform delegation; David Gibson for the first riding, W. L. Mackenzie for the second, T. D. Morrison for the third and John McIntosh (a brother-in-law of Mackenzie's) for the fourth.[2] The county of Wentworth, which had been conservative, went over to the reform side, as did the counties of Halton, Frontenac and some others. Mr. Allan MacNab found a seat in the newly formed constituency of Hamilton. In a House which now numbered sixty one members the reformers were generally able to count on a majority of not less than twelve or thirteen.

The "baneful domination" letter had undoubtedly created a certain counter current. It convinced a considerable number of persons that Mackenzie's ulterior aims were of a dangerous nature; and the insulting expressions which it contained with reference to the Rev. Mr. Ryerson deeply offended the Methodists. The conference of that body, which met at Kingston in the month of June, passed a resolution expressing their

> unqualified disapprobation of the letter from Joseph Hume, Esq., M.P., to W. L. Mackenzie, Esq., and of the slanderous attack made therein upon the character of our beloved brother, the Rev. Egerton Ryerson, in whose integrity and honourable principles we are happy to express our unshaken confidence.

Many stories which must be taken for what they are worth, or judged according to the reader's standard of probability, were current at this time, tending to show the distrust that was felt in many quarters as to Mr. Mackenzie's judgment and stability of character. One was to the effect that Bidwell was in court at Kingston when the news of Mackenzie's election as mayor of Toronto was received, and he at once exclaimed, "Mackenzie has reached his climax; he will now go down faster than he has risen." Another related that Ketchum had said, "Mackenzie is never at home when prudence makes a call on him." "A Lover of Canada," writing to the *Patriot,* said: "Mr. Ketchum, who carried him into parliament on his shoulders, has often told me that he was a dangerous man; that he had some information, and was an industrious, restless, snarling, petulant, testy, rash little fellow, void of good sense and prudence." This certainly was making free with Mr. Ketchum's name, and called for denial if it was a misrepresentation of that gentleman's opinion. The author of a pamphlet entitled "The celebrated letter of Joseph Hume, Esq., M.P. to W. L. Mackenzie, Esq. Mayor of Toronto," wrote:

> Messrs. Bidwell and Perry have said that they will have nothing more to do with him . . . ; that if they are elected to parliament they are determined to cast him off at once; that they opposed his expulsions on principle, and not on his account, but on account of the electors and the elective franchise; but he has taken advantage of this and disgraced them. These things the publisher has the best authority for stating, and he defies Mr. Mackenzie to produce a declaration from either of the above gentlemen to the contrary.

The "Lover of Canada" above quoted, who wrote as being in general sympathy with the movement for reform, also said: "True reformers in this country are aware that our grievances are few and may all be speedily removed by the application of proper remedies."

One or two other significant expressions of opinion may be quoted. Mr. Charles Fothergill, the man who had lost his office of King's Printer some years before on account of his criticism of certain acts of the government, when representing Durham in the Assembly, offered himself as a candidate for the third riding of York. In his address to the electors, he speaks of having come out "in opposition to those who are avowedly disaffected towards the best and most sacred institutions of our country. That treason," he adds, "which has so long lurked in obscurity and darkness amongst a few designing men . . . has of late (presuming on the support of traitors at home) ventured to stalk abroad at noon day." Addressing a community mainly of farmers, to whom it would have been idle to attempt to misrepresent their own condition, he said further: "In this highly favoured country blessed by the bounties of Providence in an eminent degree, and in the possession of a free representative government, we have the broad basis of future greatness, happiness and prosperity." More remarkable still was the speech delivered by Dr. Rolph, who had now been for some years out of politics, at a dinner given to sheriff Jarvis after his defeat:

Did the farmers of this favoured and flourishing province receive the visits of the tax gatherer, the proctor, or the parish overseer? Was not their industry totally untaxed? . . . Gentlemen, I believe there is too much virtue, moderation and good sense in the members elected to the house of assembly to render them aiders or abettors of Mr. Mackenzie's covert, but no less sanguinary and wicked, devices. I have conversed with many whom he has classed as thorough good reformers, who abhor both him and his treason to an extent he little dreams of, and which he will find, notwithstanding all his intrigues, will occasion his political destruction.[3]

Mackenzie himself, just before the general election, in an address to the reformers of Upper Canada, had shown, for him, surprising signs of deference to the dominant sentiment of "loyalty." "Under the protection of Great Britain," we read,

this province may arrive at a very great height of prosperity. It is an advantage to have our imports and exports clogged with as few duties as possible at Quebec, and to be under the wing of an old, a rich, and powerful nation, able and willing to encourage our trade and agriculture. We cannot be independent. Three hundred thousand settlers, thinly scattered over a vast extent of territory, and far distant from the sea, could not possibly set up for themselves. . . . Who would protect their foreign trade? Who would guard their immense frontiers? How could they secure the free navigation of the St. Lawrence?

"The chief cause," he stated in the same address, "of the grievances which retard the progress of this colony is the power given to successive secretaries for the colonies to exercise an undue influence on our domestic affairs." He did not remind the public that, just a year before, he had been urging "successive secretaries" to exert a greater amount of interference than they themselves thought proper or constitutional. The legislature was summoned for the fifteenth of January, and the reformers had great pleasure in using their majority to restore Mr. Bidwell to his former position as Speaker. The speech from the throne dwelt on the prosperity the country was enjoying, and urged the legislature to do all in its power to "encourage the present ardour for improvement." There was no mention of the "baneful domination" letter, but certain sensitive spirits thought they detected significance in the satisfaction his excellency expressed at the numerous loyal addresses he had received for transmission to the King, affirming the strong attachment of the people to the parent state. Consequently when the reply was being framed under the auspices of the acute Bidwell the following neat paragraph was introduced.

> These fresh demonstrations, welcomed as they are by his Majesty, will serve to correct any interested misrepresentations intended to impress his Majesty with the belief that those who desire to reform many public abuses in the province are not well-affected to his Majesty's person and government. . . . We deprecate the spirit with which these differences (of opinion) have been applied by some in office to impeach the loyalty, integrity and patriotism of those who conscientiously dissent from them on questions of public policy and expenditure.

Sir John Colborne had to make some reply to these pretty remarks, and this is what he thought of, which on the whole was not so bad:

> Your discountenance of the unworthy efforts to which you advert will promote that moderation, temper and allowance for conscientious difference of opinion so requisite in political controversy, and tend to discover persons of political integrity who will labour zealously to correct abuses without impeding public improvements, whose counsels will be serviceable to the public, while they watch over our excellent constitution, the law of the land, the prerogative of the crown, and the inherent rights of the people.

There may possibly have been here a reference to Mr. Mackenzie as a person whose counsels were not, in his excellency's opinion particularly "serviceable to the public," and who, while fervent in the denunciation of abuses, had shown himself opposed to such improvements as the extension of the banking facilities in the province.

A passage in the address which deserves special attention was one in which the House took a position in favor of a purely non-political distribution of patronage.

> Were . . . the favours and patronage of his Majesty indiscriminately bestowed on persons of worth and talent, who enjoy the confidence of the people, without regard to their political or religious opinions . . . the connection between this province and the parent state would long continue to exist and be a blessing mutually advantageous to both.

An interesting point here is that, as late as 1835, an Assembly in which the reformers had a marked preponderance, expressed, by implication, perfect satisfaction with the exercise of patronage by the Crown, through the local executive (the only way in which it could be exercised), simply asking that it should not be governed by narrow principles of political exclusiveness. Sir Charles Metcalfe a few years later tried to realize this idea, but Messrs. Lafontaine and Baldwin would [have] none of it; and from that day to this, no party, broadly speaking, has regarded patronage in any other light than as an adjunct of power and a means for its perpetuation.

In the debate on the address an amendment was moved by ex-Speaker McLean designed to put on record a reference to the "baneful domination" letter. It was defeated by a vote of twenty-five to sixteen; but two or three prominent reformers took the opportunity of defining their position with regard to that discord-breeding document. "If," said Mr. Duncombe, who later supported Mackenzie's insurrectionary movement,

> Mr. Hume had shown us that the British government was ruling us with a rod of iron, that our addresses were neglected and our wishes disregarded, there might be some excuse for his conduct. But that is not the

case, for I will appeal to the journals of this House, that when we passed addresses last session on various subjects connected with the welfare of this country, whether they have not been attended to with the most favourable disposition on the part of his Majesty's government to our wishes. And I do not recollect any occasion when this House addressed his Majesty's government and their address was unattended to.

Perry on the same occasion declared that if Mr. Hume wrote that letter he must have been "misinformed to think that the people of Upper Canada desired any change, for he would stake his existence that, where one would be found for it, twenty would be found against it."[4]

On the same day on which the address was passed, Mackenzie moved the appointment of a Grievance committee, to consist of himself, Dr. Duncombe, Dr. Morrison, David Gibson and Charles Waters. Dr. Duncombe does not appear to have acted on the committee; at least the report is not signed by him. The other members were three representatives of the county of York, the hotbed of the grievance spirit, and the members for the county of Prescott. Mackenzie had, no doubt, his own views in choosing the committee; but it seems singular that the formulation of the grievances of the province should have been left to three new and untried members of the House, Gibson, Morrison, and Waters – men of no political mark whatever – and one man representative of all that was most extreme in political opinion and attitude. It looks as if the more judicious members of the House found it easier to let Mackenzie have his way than to contend with him. Of course they reserved the power to judge the report when presented; but, as it happened, the report was only presented at the very close of the session, when there was no time to judge it. The House then ordered a thousand copies to be printed – by which means it was put into circulation – but no motion for its adoption was carried or even proposed. The document formed a volume of something less than five hundred pages and certainly is a monument of Mackenzie's industry and driving power. The description given of it by Sir Richard Bonnycastle comes very near to a fair appraisal of its value. "We must acknowledge," says that interesting and fair-minded writer, in the exercise of the candour we profess, that amidst the mass of its garbled and confused statements, mixed as they are with private history uninteresting to the public, it contains some statistical and useful information, extracted, it is true, by the paste and scissors mode, but yet requiring labour and application. . . . Had this work been accomplished by the able and real leader of the radical party it would, from his legal knowledge and other requirements, have conveyed to the government much that it was befitting it to know, and which, divested of that atmosphere of misstatement which disfigured its contents, would have enabled that government to have arrived at once at conclusions equally clear and satisfactory.[5]

On the sixteenth of February, 1835, Mackenzie moved, seconded by McIntosh, that the resolution of the second of November, 1832, by which he had been expelled from the House, and declared unworthy and unfit to hold a seat therein during the then existing parliament, should be expunged from the journals. This having been carried by twenty-seven to fourteen, a further resolution was carried by an equal majority for the expunging of all declarations and affirming that *because* the House had thus pronounced him unworthy and unfit to hold a seat he was therefore disqualified from taking his seat. The latter vote should have been made unanimous. The session was brought to a close on the sixteenth day of April with a rather tame speech from his excellency, who must have felt that the popular chamber, at least, was governed by ideas very different from his own. On the day preceding the prorogation, Messrs. Thorburn (third riding of Lincoln), Duncombe (Oxford), and Mackenzie were, by resolution, appointed directors of the Welland Canal as representing the government of the province which had taken stock in it to the amount of $200,000. On the same day an address to the King was adopted in committee, reported, passed through all its stages and adopted by the House, complaining of the obstructive action of the legislative council, and charging it with having rendered unavailing the exertions made during a most laborious session to pass a number of measures of the utmost importance to the country. Had the council wished to make any reply to this manifesto, or as it might almost be called, declaration of war, they could not have done so during the few hours of the session that elapsed after its passage, particularly occupied as they were with bills and messages which that House kept sending to them up to the last moment. They did reply, however, in the following session, the lieutenant governor, then Sir Francis Head, having communicated to them a despatch from the colonial office in which the complaint of the Assembly was referred to. Their statement of the case is well worth reading as a document of the period, and a few words may properly be devoted to it here.

The Assembly in their complaint had judged nine measures, amongst those rejected, as worthy of special mention. As regards four of these the council frankly acknowledge that they had rejected them on principle, and refer to the reports of committee in their journals as proving the careful attention the several subjects had received. Being constituted as an independent and co-ordinate branch of the legislature they felt that their duty to the community required that "after they shall have enabled themselves to judge of the merits of the bills in which they are asked to concur, they should exercise their judgment honestly and firmly, neither sanctioning by their vote what they do not approve, nor rejecting what they believe to be just and expedient." Amongst the other five bills was one the main object of which was to impose high protecting duties on flour and other articles of food imported from the United States, whether for consumption or export. Their reason for rejecting the bill was that the consumers in the province consisted, in great proportion, of emigrants, who had come to the country with little means, and who were under the necessity of purchasing provisions for their families while clearing their lands. To increase the price of living to persons so situated in order to give a higher price for their produce to agriculturists who surely ought to be able, with an extremely fertile soil, to hold their own home market did not seem just or reasonable. Moreover ever since the bill had been rejected Canada had been *exporting* flour to the United States, so that the bill would have been wholly imperative if passed. The principle of the bill, furthermore, had always been opposed by the Assembly till 1835; and then it had once been voted down, and at another stage only carried by a casting vote. Yet the rejection of a measure so dubiously supported, even in the House in which it originated, was a *selected* instance of the Council's obstructiveness. Perfect wisdom, perhaps perfect disinterestedness, does not reside in any individual or aggregation of individuals; but a close view of the facts will lead the impartial student to believe that the legislative council discharged its functions, as a rule, with superior intelligence and an earnest desire to safeguard and promote what it considered the best interests of the province.

The *Advocate* passed out of existence as a separate journal on the fourth of November, 1834, when it was amalgamated with Dr. O'Grady's paper, the *Correspondent*, which henceforth became the *Correspondent and Advocate*. The two papers had hitherto been conducted in a very similar spirit of bitter antagonism to the administration; and, now that they formed one, Mackenzie was under no restraint in regard to the expression of his sentiments. On the whole, indeed, he wrote with more violence in its columns than he had done in his own paper. He had conceived an altogether peculiar enmity to the banking institutions of the country – an enmity which extended to all persons connected with the banks whom he saw flourishing financially. It was under the inspiration of this unhappy feeling that he wrote as follows in the *Correspondent and Advocate* of the twenty-seventh of August, 1835: "I do not look for a change in the system of granting bank charters until the good people of Toronto and Hamilton[6] are prepared to pull down the splendid mansions and make a bonfire of the gorgeous furniture of half-a-dozen broken bank directors to appease the indignation of the ten thousand labourers and tradesmen whom their tricks have ruined. I say 'prepared,' for it is well known that no such scenes as have taken place at Baltimore[7] can possibly occur at Toronto. No, thanks to your good fortune we have British bayonets and British troops ready to protect the rogues and maintain order in such a case. . . . As to the common folk, the farmers and tradesmen, neither the law nor the bayonets were intended for their protection." There was nothing of which Mr. Mackenzie was more strongly persuaded, than that he was a friend of the people, but did he really believe that he was rendering them a service in propagating ideas of this kind? A year had not elapsed since in an address to the Reformers of Upper Canada he had expressed himself as follows:

In appealing to the people of Upper Canada I might
fairly venture to compare the advantages they enjoy
with the evils of which they complain, and readily admit
that their lot, even as contrasted with that of their most
favoured neighbours, it not that of misfortune or which
justifies discontent. But the blessings enjoyed by the
inhabitants of this fine country should not be adduced
as a reason why they should be satisfied with real
grievances which can and ought to be removed.

One would hardly suppose that the same hand had penned
the sane and moderate statement of October, 1834,[8] and
the inflammatory discord-breeding tirade of August, 1835.
Shakespeare says that "one man in his time plays many
parts." This "one man" certainly did.

Mention has been made of Mackenzie's appointment in
the session of 1835 as director of the Welland canal. He
had long been convinced that there had been serious mismanagement, not unmixed with fraud, in connection with
the carrying out of this great public work. In the very last
issue of his *Advocate* (November 4th, 1834) he had spoken
of "the rapacious junto around the governor, aided by such
knavish jobbers as Merritt and his co-workers in public
undertakings, where the expenditure was always four times
larger than the estimate." He now had an opportunity of
enquiring fully and closely into the canal accounts, as well
as into the condition of the work. The better to do this he
spent the greater part of the summer of 1835 at or near
St. Catharines. The result of his labours was the discovery
of many irregularities including a number of transactions of
very questionable aspect. With his usual impatience to appeal
to the public he printed and circulated at his own expense
a temporary journal called *The Welland Canal*, in which
he gave an account of his findings in advance of their
submission to the house of assembly.[9] This was not a very
correct mode of proceeding, but Mackenzie was never greatly
enamoured of mere correctness. *The Welland Canal*, however, was far from being a mere record of facts; opinions
were freely dealt in, and the numbers, as they successively
appeared, partook largely of the character of campaign
documents. Much as Mackenzie desired to serve the public,
still more strongly did he desire to crush and humiliate
opponents – those whom he was pleased to regard as enemies

of the people. His great error – that which in the end blasted his career – consisted in hating too bitterly, condemning too utterly, despising too recklessly those whom he placed in that category. There is a profound truth in the saying that he who hateth his brother walketh in darkness, and knoweth not whither he goeth; nor is the man who hates saved from this disability, because in another direction, his dispositions are benevolent.

On the third of February, 1836, the legislature being in session, Mr. Mackenzie made his report to the Canal committee. His charges against the management embraced no less than thirty distinct heads. The first and most comprehensive was that the accounts were kept irregularly, with intent, as he believed, to defraud the public. He commenced giving his own evidence before the committee on the ninth of February, and then examined other witnesses at great length, only closing his proceedings on the twenty-sixth of March. Mr. Merritt, president of the canal company, whose conduct was so seriously impeached, began examining witnesses on the twenty-eighth of March and closed three days later. Finally the committee made their report. The books and accounts of the company had, they stated, been kept in a very irregular and improper manner, but they could not say "that any intentional fraud against the public or the canal proprietors had been brought home to any individual officer of the company, or that the misconduct complained of in this respect was calculated to benefit the individuals connected with the management of the canal." It appeared also that there was a total shortage of $7,000 in the funds, and that – as charged by Mr. Mackenzie – incorrect returns had been sworn to by the secretary; but the committee had no hesitation in exonerating that officer from any criminal intention, as the error was not one involving any fraud. They discussed the charge made against the officers of the company of tampering with the press, the only proof of which was the discovery of a letter from the editor of the *Patriot* enquiring whether the company could give his paper any printing or advertising. It was an age of wild villainies.

The report as a whole, though made by a committee drawn almost entirely from the reform side of the House, was not particularly sympathetic towards Mackenzie. He had gone too far in his suspicions and accusations; had seen things in a worse light than there was any necessity for, so that even his political friends could not sustain the position he had taken. At the same time much of his work was undeniably useful and did not a little to place the management of the canal on a better basis for the future. Were he alive to-day – well, he might still find some work of the same kind to do.

Sir John Colborne's term of office in Upper Canada was now drawing to a close. The Grievance Report of the previous session, accompanied by various addresses of the house of assembly, couched in the language of complaint, had influenced in some degree the mind of the colonial secretary, at this time Lord Glenelg. The correspondence that ensued between the minister and the lieutenant governor was of such a nature that the latter was led to tender his resignation. His recall had however been already decided on; and a question of no small difficulty was how and where to find a man able to grapple successfully with the administration of a province in which discontent seemed to be growing apace. How felicitously the problem was solved we shall presently see.

Meantime Sir John had once more to meet the parliament of Upper Canada. The session, destined to be a stormy one, opened the fourteenth of January, 1836. His excellency had the misfortune to arouse in his opening speech a very lightly-sleeping dog. "The peculiar position," he said, "of Lower Canada, and the similar constitution under which the institutions of both colonies are secured, do not allow the dissensions in that province to be regarded by you with indifference, nor indeed without deep regret, anxiety and apprehension. Already," he added, "these dissensions have tended apparently to discourage emigration and the transfer of capital to this country, and have acted disadvantageously in respect to the terms on which the large loan authorized by the legislature was negotiated in England." At this moment official commissioners appointed by the British government, Lord Gosford, Sir George Gibbs and Sir Charles Grey, were in Lower Canada enquiring into the troubles there. Referring to this fact Sir John, with an accent probably that revealed the veteran commander, the man of nerve and resolution in the hour of trial, uttered these words: "But whatever measures may be adopted in consequence of the recommendations of the commissioners or whatever alterations may be proposed to remedy the evils to which I have adverted, you may rest assured that the constitution of these provinces will be firmly upheld."

As it happened, just two months before this Mr. Mackenzie, accompanied by Dr. O'Grady, had gone on a kind of fraternal mission to the Lower Canada liberal leaders. "They went," says Mr. Lindsey, "as a deputation from leading men and influential reformers in Upper Canada, to bring about a closer alliance between the reformers in the two provinces."[10] Their reception, we learn from the same source, was most cordial, all the liberal members of the assembly crowding round them "to testify the sincere interest they took in the progress of good government in Upper Canada, and to tender them their hearty co-operation."[11] It is not to be wondered at, therefore, that the reformers were roused by Sir John's clarion tones. "We deeply regret," said the address in reply,

> that your excellency has been advised to animadvert upon the affairs of the sister province, which has been engaged in a long and arduous struggle for an indespensable amelioration of their institutions and the manner of their administration. We respectfully but firmly express our respect for their patriotic exertions, and we do acquit them of being the cause of any of the dissensions and embarrassments existing in the country.

Sir John with mild and quiet dignity replied: "Gentlemen – It is with great concern that I have attended to some portions of this address." These, so far as appears, were his last spoken words to the legislature. On the twenty-first of January he informed the Assembly by message that his Majesty's answer to its complaints would be communicated to it during the then current month. Four days later the Speaker informed the House that Sir Francis Bond Head had taken the oaths of office as lieutenant governor.

Many were the expressions of regret at Sir John's departure from the province. His friends loved him; his opponents could not hate him. Mackenzie, though he denounced him at times with extraordinary bitterness, had moments of sympathy with him. A sketch of his character and administration which appeared about this time in the Toronto *Courier*, a conservative paper, is so judicious and impartial that it merits republication:

Notwithstanding our admiration of Sir John Colborne's administration viewed as a whole, there have been parts of it open to exception, and which it would not be just to pass over on this occasion. . . . Abuses existed, and still do exist, in the public offices of which he could not be ignorant, and yet till very lately he took no strenuous measures for suppressing them. In the distribution of his patronage he frequently disregarded the claims of those whose long residence in the country entitled them to the first consideration and bestowed offices and places of emolument upon men in many instances incompetent, who had but recently arrived in the country, and whose main recommendation was the prefix of Captain or Lieutenant to his name. Although not entirely responsible for the appointment of the magistracy, and compelled by necessity to act upon the recommendation of others, he yet knowingly entrusted the commission of the peace to persons whose ignorance, youth and inexperience rendered them totally unfit to discharge the duties of a magistrate. Again it was not unusual for his excellency to reward his enemies and neglect his friends. A desire to trim, to hold the balance between conflicting parties, and to win over the opponents of his administration by offering them a sop, frequently led him to strengthen their hands by investing them with authority and emolument, which they converted into weapons against the giver. A certain yielding facility of temper contrasting strangely with his military promptitude and energy of decision, betrayed him into these errors. . . . Could he but get the needful supplies from the Assembly he seemed comparatively careless how the minor matters – the mint and cummin – were disposed of by our Perrys, Roblins and Mackenzies.

If we contemplate him as the first gentleman of the colony, as the guardian of morality and religion, and if we follow him into his privacy and inspect his social and domestic character, we are bound to say that his personal character has exercised as beneficial an influence on the morals, as his administration on the prosperity, of the province. . . . His happiness lay in the bosom of his family, and when seated at church among them, he looked, with his tall patriarchal figure, so placid, yet so dignified; he reflected internal peace so brightly, yet so mildly, in his benignant aspect, that man must be bad and bigoted indeed who could look upon him without admiration and respect.

And now a new chapter opens in the history of Upper Canada.

CHAPTER FIFTEEN

SIR FRANCIS BOND HEAD AND THE QUESTION OF RESPONSIBLE GOVERNMENT

A few days before the arrival of Sir Francis Head Mr. Mackenzie had received a letter from Joseph Hume which read in part as follows:

> You will learn with as much pleasure as surprise of the recall of your present lieutenant governor, and of the appointment of Sir Francis Head to succeed him. Of the causes which have produced this very fortunate change I will not now dilate, but congratulate you and the people of the province on the choice made of Sir Francis.

What could this possibly mean but that Sir Francis was a man after Joseph Hume's own heart, a thorough-going reformer? Naturally Mr. Mackenzie spread the good news abroad; and when the new governor reached Toronto on Saturday the twenty-third of January, 1836, he was startled to find the walls of that burg placarded with the words: "*Sir Francis Head, A Tried Reformer.*" Startled – because he was not aware of the fact himself. Up to this time he had never, he tells us, "joined any political party, attended any political discussion, or even voted at an election." Still, as he had come to a province understood to be in crying need of reforms, with instructions to effect them if possible, and with every disposition to carry out those instructions, he probably thought the name might pass for the present.

But how had this particular gentleman come to be chosen by the British government? The story, so far as there is a story, must be briefly told. Sir Francis was in many respects a typical Englishman of the upper class, well-educated, of good family, self-confident, resourceful, prompt in action and ready to take risks if he thought the principle on which

246

he was working was right. For a man who had never taken any part in politics he certainly developed a wonderful faculty for handling political arguments. He had been in the army and had retired on half-pay as major of engineers. He had travelled extensively in Europe and South America, had endured great fatigues and some perils, and learned pretty well how to take care of himself. He was known in the world of letters as the author of some lively books of travel. In his own county, Kent, he had been appointed an assistant poor law commissioner under the act lately passed, and had applied himself with great zeal and energy to his work. "His conduct and principles," wrote Hume to Mackenzie in the letter above referred to, "have been much approved of." Mackenzie lost sight of this commendation by his fellow-reformer when, not long afterwards, he accused Head of having starved and oppressed the paupers of Kent.

Still, how had he come to be chosen for the lieutenant governorship of Upper Canada? It would appear that, in the scarcity of candidates of required eligibility, some one had recommended him to the colonial secretary. Even this is not certain for a legend is current to the effect that it was his younger kinsman, Sir Edmund Walker Head – later governor general of Canada – who was designated for the office, and that the appointment of Sir Francis was a simple blunder. However that may be Sir Francis was a greatly astonished man when, one night in November, 1835, he was awakened from his slumbers at a place near Romney Marsh in Kent, where he was carrying on his official labors, by a king's messenger who had brought him a letter from the colonial secretary tendering him this appointment – one of which he had never dreamed and wholly foreign to his previous occupations and interests. Still, there was the letter, unmistakable in its tenor, and requesting him to see the colonial secretary in Downing Street at half past eight in the morning. There was nothing to do but to dress and to drive into town with the king's messenger. Arriving at his own house at about six, he had a consultation with his family, and then hurried to his appointment. His mind was made up to decline the office and he did so. The minister, however, begged him not to decide the matter so summarily; and Sir Francis so far yielded as to consent to discuss it with the under secretary of state, Mr. James Stephen, sometimes called, from the great intellectual influence he wielded,

the over-secretary. Mr. Stephen little foresaw the epistolary
conflicts he was destined to wage with the gentleman from
Kent, who in argument was nearly his match, or he might
not have spent much effort in inducing him to accept the
position. The result of the interview was that Head accepted
the appointment determined to see whether the qualities
which had carried him through many difficulties in the past
and which were serving him in good stead in the official
work in which he had lately been engaged, would not sufficiently atone for his lack of experience in colonial affairs
and the technique of civil administration. Stephen handed
him the Grievance Report – whether with a smile or with a
sigh is not recorded – as being a comprehensive embodiment
of the woes of Upper Canada as seen and affirmed by the
house of assembly, or at least the reform majority thereof.
Grasping the substantial volume Head promised to do his
best: it was a great thing to have the wrongs of the province
so fully set forth; he would know just what to set to work
upon, and how to direct his enquiries. He was then in his
forty-third year, two years younger than Chief Justice
Robinson, two years older than Mackenzie – just the age
when a man's powers ought to be at their very best.

It may be assumed that Sir Francis availed himself of
the leisure afforded by a sea voyage in those days to
familiarize himself with his brief, the Grievance Report, as
well as with the instructions of the colonial secretary founded
thereon. As he was a man of acute mind its peculiarities
could not fail to strike him; and this may account for the
strong desire he showed on arriving in Upper Canada to
discuss it with those who might be regarded as its sponsors.
The legislature, as we have seen, was in session when he
arrived, and the rather unhappy idea occurred to him that
he ought to proceed to parliament, make his presence known
and broadly announce his position. This he did on the
twenty-seventh of the month when he informed the two
Houses that he was commanded by the King to lay before
them his Majesty's answers to their addresses of the last
session. This, he said, he would do by message. "As regards
myself," he continued, "I have nothing either to promise or
profess, but I trust I shall not call in vain upon you to give
me that loyal, constitutional, unbiased and fearless assistance
which your King expects, and which the rising interests of
your country require."

The members of the reform phalanx looked at one another dubiously. Could this really be the "tried reformer?" The tone was rather that of a man about to make demands upon them, than of one who had come to yield to all their demands. Then he had nothing to profess or promise. Why did he come down to the House anyway? Was it constitutional for the representative of the sovereign thus to interrupt their proceedings in the middle of a session? The point seemed worth looking into, and a committee was appointed for the purpose. Their report was that they had to go back as far as the year 1765 to find anything that looked like a precedent. Of this ancient occurrence the report said: "Your committee are willing to recognize it as applicable to the case before them, without, however, any prejudice to that freedom of parliamentary debate which might be impaired by any unusual declaration from the Throne."

On the thirtieth of the month his excellency sent down a complete copy of the instructions he had received from the colonial secretary. They were comprehensive, inasmuch as they attempted to deal with all the matters of complaint mentioned in the Grievance Report. The tone of the despatch was most conciliatory. Lord Glenelg was evidently quite as anxious as Lord Goderich had been just three years before to allay irritation and remove every valid cause of complaint. He did not assume that the evils described in the report existed to the extent alleged; but whatever might on enquiry be found to be wrong, he wished to have put right. The most interesting part of the despatch is that relating to the question of responsible government.

A very considerable part of the report is devoted to the statement and illustration of the fact that the executive government of Upper Canada is virtually irresponsible; and the conclusion drawn from this statement is that, under the present system there can be no prospect of a good and faithful administration of public affairs.

In this view of the matter the colonial secretary could not concur. "Experience," he observed,

would seem to prove that the administration of public affairs in Canada is by no means exempt from the

control of a practical responsibility. To his Majesty and
to parliament the governor of Upper Canada is at all
times most fully responsible for his official acts. . . . It
is the duty of the lieutenant governor of Upper Canada
to vindicate to the King and to parliament every act
of his administration. . . . This responsibility to his
Majesty and to parliament is second to none which
can be imposed on a public man, and it is one which
it is in the power of the house of assembly at any time,
by address or petition, to bring into active operation.

On the delivery to the House of his excellency's message
Mackenzie moved that one thousand copies of it and of
the instructions and appended documents should be printed
for the use of members in the form in which the journals
of the House were usually printed. MacNab, who must have
thought that the whole would not make bad reading for
loyal subjects, moved in amendment that two thousand
copies should be printed in pamphlet form. The amendment
carried.

If his excellency's private perusal of the Grievance Report
had led him to recognize in it very much the same characteristics to which Lord Goderich had called attention, in
the documents emanating from Mackenzie which he had
transmitted to Sir John Colborne, his opinion would have
received additional warrant from a discussion that took
place in the Assembly just two days after his visit to the
legislature. As this discussion, however, was a sequel to one
that had occurred a few days earlier, the matter will be
better understood if we take it from the beginning. On the
nineteenth of January Mackenzie moved for the appointment
of a Finance Committee to enquire into everything connected with the finances of the province, including public
works and especially the Welland Canal. In the course of
a very discursive speech he had violently attacked Mr. W.
H. Merritt, the member for Haldimand and president (as
before mentioned) of the Canal company. Perry, stout
reformer though he was, growing weary of these harangues,
felt compelled on this occasion to utter a few plain words.
He generally agreed, he said, with the honourable gentlemen
in his political views, but

his common sense admonished him to deprecate that
gentleman's frequent long speeches which, so far from

promoting the objects he had in view, had often a precisely contrary effect. They generally embraced so many subjects foreign to the matter before the House that they both fatigued and confused the members, and retarded business in a sad and lamentable manner.

He then moved an amendment the effect of which was to name a Finance Committee "without giving it the cognizance of all the affairs of the province at one fell swoop." He also begged Mr. Merritt "not to say anything in reply to his honourable friend from the west riding of York who, he was sorry, had mixed up such a multitude of matters that had nothing to do with the appointment of a committee on finance."

This was the prelude. Eight days later the House was in committee of the whole on a bill for the incorporation of the St. Catharines Bank. Banks in general were at this time Mackenzie's abhorrence, and in discussing the question he spoke of his Grievance Report as having "received the sanction of a large majority of the House; whereupon Perry again took the war-path and vigorously denied the statement." To quote the report published at the time by the *Christian Guardian*:

Mr. Perry said that there was about as much truth in that assertion as there is in nineteen-twentieths of what that honourable gentleman states on the floor of the House. There was not a shadow of truth in the assertion that the Grievance Report received the sanction of the House, and he wished it to be distinctly understood by the country that the House never sanctioned it, and that they never could. He would admit that there was some valuable information in it, which it was important for the country to know; but there was a great deal of falsehood and shameful misrepresentation. The quotations from various documents contained in that report, so far as they were quoted correctly, were calculated to do good by spreading useful information; but where the honourable member's sentiments were given, couched in his own language, that language often contained a meaning directly contrary to the truth. But he would again declare that the House had never sanctioned it. . . . Bills were frequently ordered to be printed before they were read, and it was not to be expected that a document so voluminous as that report would be read in the House; and as for misrepresentations in it, the honourable member for York was alone accountable for them.

Mackenzie replied the following day accusing Perry of having changed his politics, and reminding him that when he (Mackenzie), as chairman of the Grievance Committee, moved to print a thousand copies of the report, he (Perry) asked that two thousand should be printed. This Perry explained by saying that he knew the report would be much sought after, and that one thousand copies would be totally insufficient to meet the demand, and jealousies were apt to be created when a member was unable to supply a public document to certain persons after having given it to others whose claims were no better. He strenuously denied having changed his politics; and how unjust the accusation was plainly appeared a very few weeks later when Perry took the leading part in opposition to the lieutenant-governor. He "weakened," however, on the subject of the Report, declaring that, instead of saying there was some valuable information in the report and a great deal of falsehood and misrepresentation, he should have said that there was a little misrepresentation and a great deal of valuable information. In fact he thought he *must* have said that; but if he did put it the other way, it was only his opinion and he was not infallible. Perry, big, burly man as he was, might have learnt a lesson from Mackenzie in sticking to his guns. Allowing for a certain amount of exaggeration in the language he first used, it was probably nearer to his real conviction than the revised version. It was certainly in line with what he had said in the previous debate on the Finance Committee. Still he had the consistency, when his party sought to repair the effect of his outburst by a resolution sanctioning and confirming the Grievance Report, to vote nay. The yeas had it, however, twenty-four to fifteen.

Sir Francis Head tells us that he was very anxious to come to close quarters with the reform leaders on the subject of the report, but found it extremely difficult to do so. It had been mentioned that he had a gift for lively writing, and it may be well to bear this in mind in reading the following extract from his "Narrative:"[1]

Among those who in private audience presented

themselves to me was Mr. Bidwell, the Speaker of the House of Assembly. To this gentleman who was the leader of the republicans, I expressed the same language I had addressed to the leaders of the opposite party. I told him plainly that I was an inexperienced man, but that I would deal honestly toward the country; and being resolutely determined to correct the grievances of the province, I at once took up the book which contained them, and invited Mr. Bidwell to converse with me freely on the subject. To my utter astonishment he told me there were grievances not at all detailed in that book, which 'the people' had long endured, and were still enduring, with great patience. . . . "What do you mean Sir," said I, "that this book of grievances, which I have been especially sent to correct, does not contain the complaints of the provinces?" Mr. Bidwell repeated his former answer, and from that day to the hour of his leaving the country, *never* could I get him to look at the book of grievances, but whenever I referred to it he invariably tried to decoy me to some other Will-o'-the-wisp complaint which in like manner would have flown away before me had I attempted to approach it.

When Mr. Mackenzie, bringing with him a letter of introduction from Mr. Hume, called upon me, I thought that of course he would be too happy to discuss with me the contents of his own book, but his mind seemed to nauseate its subjects even more than Mr. Bidwell's. Afraid to look me in the face, he sat . . . with his countenance averted from me, at an angle of about seventy degrees; while with the eccentricity, the volubility, and indeed the appearance of a madman, he raved in all directions about grievances here and grievances there, which the committee, he said, had not ventured to enumerate.

"Sir," I exclaimed, "let us cure what we have got here first," But . . . nothing could induce him to face his own report; and I soon found that the book had the same effect upon *all* the republican members, and that, like the repellent end of a magnet, I had only to present it to the radicals to drive them from the very object which his Majesty's government expected would have possessed attraction.

Whether the "tried reformer" knew it or not, he was essentially a tory. Still, there is no very good reason to doubt what he states as to the unwillingness of the leading reformers to enter into a discussion of the grievances of the province *on the basis of the Report*. The grievance business had in fact been very badly managed by them. It had been left wholly to a committee of Mackenzie's own choosing, and he had chosen three entirely new members – *un*tried reformers in the sense of having had no parliamentary experience whatever; all that was known about them was that they were strong Mackenzie men. This threw the whole matter into his hands, and at the end the report he had put together *more suo*[2] was rushed into print without discussion. If Mackenzie had been a man whose judgment inspired general confidence, all this would not have been so extraordinary; but it is perfectly evident that such was not the case. When Perry was denouncing the report, he should have asked himself why the reform party ever allowed such a report to be made, and whether he was not himself in a large measure responsible – exercising the influence in the House that he did – for the shape things had taken.

The appointment of Sir Francis Head, which the reformers at first hailed with joyful anticipation, created in the opposite camp no small amount of doubt and apprehension. "They shrewdly guessed," says Sir Richard Bonnycastle, "that the whig ministry had some powerful reasons of their own, and that they had let loose a tiger who would perform his duty without flinching."[3] The original and striking idea of a tiger let loose and performing his duty without flinching was probably Sir Richard's own. The metaphor is twisted but luminous. The stories cannot have had the best of consciences or they would not have had any dread of tigers from the colonial office. However, they shortly got over their fears; and some of them went so far as to take the tiger in hand, and point out to him what he ought to do, and what he ought to avoid doing, in order to maintain a proper influence in the province.[4] To this teaching he seems to have taken very kindly, and it was not long before he came to the conclusion that, whatever abuses there might be to correct in Upper Canada, his chief mission would be to resist the advance of what he called republicanism, which seemed to him to be the proper name for the principles of the reform party.

A passage in the celebrated "Narrative" throws light on the relations between the lieutenant governor and the party in question.

> Although the well-known blue-bound Grievance Book, which I constantly kept on my table, acted as a talisman in driving from me the republican party, who apparently could speak no language but that of indefinite complaint, yet I clearly foresaw that they would not submit to be thus easily defeated. Although nothing but polite expressions had passed between us, it was perfectly evident to me that the republicans were sorely mortified at being on all occasions 'brought to book,' and . . . that they were not merely waiting, but were eagerly seeking for an opportunity to pick any quarrel with me that would enable them to join with Mr. Papineau and the house of assembly of Lower Canada in open rebellion.

Sir Francis here does signal injustice to the reform party; for when "open rebellion" came, only a small portion of that party took any share in it or manifested any sympathy with it.

If anything like a fight was toward, Mackenzie was not the man to lurk in the background. His journalistic partner, Dr. O'Grady, had predicted that Sir Francis would not find the lieutenant governorship of Upper Canada a bed of roses; and to help the prophecy a bit Mackenzie on the fourth of February moved an address asking his excellency for copy of the correspondence relating to the removal of the attorney and solicitor general in 1833, and concerning his own several expulsions from the house of assembly, as well as any despatches that would serve to explain the retention in office of persons composing the executive council and legal advisers of the government, notwithstanding their opposition to many urgent and beneficial reforms recommended by the Earl of Ripon in his despatch of November, 1832, etc. Sir Francis tells us in the "Narrative" that he regarded this proceeding as the advance of the reform skirmishers; he nevertheless replied in language of great propriety and good temper. He sent to the House all the documents in his possession which he was at liberty to communicate relating to the various subjects of enquiry and informed it that

Lord Goderich's order for the retirement of the solicitor
general was subsequently reversed on consequence of excul-
patory explanations which that officer made during his visit
to England. There was no despatch in his office, he stated,
which would serve to explain the retention of certain persons
in office. He declined in terms of studied and almost deferential moderation to discuss appointments made to the
executive council by his predecessor. With respect to the
power conferred to remove officers in high places who
oppose the policy of the government he said:

> The lieutenant governor will certainly not hesitate to
> avail himself of this power should he ever feel it his
> painful duty to do so; but he considers it would not be
> a fruitful application of his time were he now retro-
> spectively to attempt to determine whether these
> individuals ever had, or had not, opposed any measure
> of the government of his predecessor.

After discussing one or two other questions he concluded
by appealing to the liberality and good sense of the house
of assembly, and asking them to consider that he had but
lately arrived in the country, and that, as a stranger to the
province and totally unconnected with the politics even of
Great Britain, his main object must be to grapple practically
with the problems indicated to him in his instructions.

The date of this message was the fifteenth of February.
Six days later his excellency took a step which, there is no
reason to doubt, was dictated by a desire to put the administration of the government on a better and broader basis,
but which was unfortunately destined to prove abortive.

The executive council at this time consisted of only three
members, the honourable Messrs. Peter Robinson, Land
Commissioner; George H. Markland, Inspector General,
and Joseph Wills. One of these – it is not stated which one –
suggested to his excellency the great necessity that existed,
in connection especially with the proper auditing of accounts,
that the council should be increased in number. Sir Francis
would rather have delayed making any new nominations till
he was better acquainted with the leading politicians of the
province.[5] He says that the tories at this time were still
standing aloof from him; but that, in any case, he was not
disposed to appoint extreme men of either side. After
consulting the Speakers of the two Houses, Chief Justice

Robinson and Mr. Bidwell and the members of the executive council themselves, he sent for Mr. Robert Baldwin whom all united in recommending and proposed to him that he should join the council together with Mr. John Henry Dunn, at the time receiver general and a member of the legislative council, and Dr. Rolph. Mr. Baldwin, after consulting Mr. Bidwell and some other friends, declined to accept the office unless the existing councillors were dismissed. His attitude indeed was much the same as it was five years later under Lord Sydenham; already we see the outlines of the severely authoritative party leader, who took his politics as seriously as Mrs. Battle took her whist and insisted on "the rigour of the game." Sir Francis, however, could be quite as firm as Mr. Baldwin at his best, and he absolutely refused compliance with the demand. On the following day Mr. Baldwin, having reconsidered the matter, agreed to dispense with the condition in question, and to put understanding on record, Sir Francis wrote him a note, of which two copies were made for Dr. Rolph and Mr. Dunn respectively, expressing pleasure at his acceptance, stating that he would give his councillors his implicit confidence, that there were no conditions to be made on either side, and that he would rely on their giving him their unbiased opinion on all subjects on which he might require it.

What consultations or communications, if any, took place between Sir Francis and his enlarged council, between the date of this note (nineteenth of February) and the fourth of March following, there is nothing to show, but on the latter date his excellency received a document, signed by all six members of that body, the tenor of which caused him no slight astonishment. Quoting the words of Lord Glenelg that "the present is an era of more difficulty and importance than any which has hitherto occurred in this part of his Majesty's dominions," the councillors gave it as their opinion that this was to be ascribed "in a great degree to the hitherto unconstitutional abridgement of the duties of the executive council." They added an expression of their belief, founded on

the proceedings of the Assembly and the reiteration of established opinion in the country, that neither will public expectation be satisfied nor contentment be restored, until the system of local government is altered and conducted according to the true spirit and meaning of the Constitutional Act.

They spoke of the false position in which the council had been placed through being supposedly responsible for measures which in many cases had never been submitted to their approval. "The consequence of this silent endurance of political odium has been the perpetuation of the misbelief that the executive council are conversant with the affairs of the province upon which they are appointed to advise." The councillors then referred to those parts of the Constitutional Act which they considered supported their view as to the proper function of the executive council, and hinted that further delay in putting the government of the province on a right footing would "increase public dissatisfaction and lead to the adoption of other views uncongenial to the genius of the constitution and dangerous to the connection with the parent state." Finally they asked that if the lieutenant governor could not give effect to their recommendation, he would permit them to disabuse the public mind as to the extent of their responsibility.

That a document of this nature should have proceeded from the reform members of his council would not have utterly astonished Sir Francis Head, but what spell had been cast upon such veterans as Messrs. Robinson, Markland and Wills to induce them to subscribe to it? That was something he could not see through. Sir Francis, however, was a man of action and possibly not quite so innocent of politics as he had made out: the council had their answer the very next day, and it was one in which there was no note of surrender. He joined issue with them as to the status of the Council under the Act of 1791, and argued the point with no little acuteness. He denied that the constitution of Canada was in all points a copy of that of the Mother Country. In England, he asserted, the King can do no wrong, though his ministers may: in Canada it is just the reverse – the councillors can do no wrong, but the governor may. If the governor takes their advice and it is bad, he cannot throw the blame on them either to the King or to the country; he must assume the whole responsibility himself.

The result of this correspondence was the resignation of the whole Council. Sir Francis had no difficulty, however, in supplying their places for within a day or two he had sworn in a new Council consisting of Mr. Robert Baldwin Sullivan, (cousin of Mr. Robert Baldwin); the Hon. John Elmsley, Captain Augustus Baldwin, R.N. (uncle of Robert Baldwin) and the Hon. William Allan. Messrs. Baldwin and Allan were members of the legislative council; Elmsley was at one time a member of the executive council under Sir John Colborne, but had resigned in 1833. Whether Sir Francis could have worked long, in any case, with the former council is open to doubt; still with careful management on his part and a little less impatience on theirs, the experiment might have lasted longer than it did, and some progress might possibly have been made towards accommodation of views. Sir Francis states that he was preparing a number of remedial measures which he meant to submit to their consideration; it might have been better if he had asked them to prepare the measures, and submit them to *his* consideration. He does not appear to have kept in touch with them as he should have done during the first days after their appointment. He lacked the true politician's eye for all the minor means – scarcely less important than the major – of safe-guarding a position. He trusted too much to broad general principles and to his own personal influence. His natural good spirits and gay self-confidence carried him far in the general intercourse of life, but even in Upper Canada there were men with whom the spell did not work. It seems probable that he under-rated the intellectual value of Baldwin and Rolph, the former of whom, particularly, had in him the stuff of a statesman of no ordinary capacity. As he escaped on this occasion from Sir Francis so five years later he was destined to break through the meshes of a far mightier hunter of men than ever Sir Francis could pretend to be – Lord Sydenham.

Great was the commotion in the Assembly when the resignation of the council so lately appointed was made known. Explanations in the House itself were impossible as not one of the ex-councillors had a seat in that chamber; but Mr. Perry read a letter, which he had received from Mr. Baldwin, giving his version of the matter.[6] At once a resolution was passed for an address to his excellency requesting full explanations. This resolution, which was carried by the sweeping vote of fifty-three to two,[7] laid down the principle that "a responsible executive council to

advise the lieutenant governor on the affairs of the province"
was "one of the most wise and happy features in the
constitution and essential in our form of government as
being one of the strongest securities for a just and equitable
administration of the government, and the full enjoyment
of our civil and religious liberties." When men like MacNab,
McLean, and Hagerman were found supporting such a
resolution it was evident that opinion was developing on
liberal lines. When it came, however, to voting on the
adoption of the address five of those who had supported
the resolution fell away, the vote standing forty-two to
seven. His excellency's side of the case was not as yet fully
understood even by his own friends. In any case it is clear
that the country at this time was ripe for a reasonable
discussion of the whole question of responsible government.
The explanations desired by the House were promptly
supplied by his excellency, who with the greatest possible
frankness took his stand upon his own sole responsibility as
executive of the province. It was he who was responsible
for his advisers, not they for him. He stated in fact the
true principle of the colonial system more distinctly and
undisguisedly, probably, than any of his predecessors had
done. Sir Peregrine Maitland and Sir John Colborne particularly had had many opportunities of joining issue with
the champions of the new political ideas, but had more or
less shrunk from doing so. They preferred to disguise rather
than to reveal the widening breach between the colonial
theory as held by the home government and the larger
demands of the progressive party in the province. True it
was that when, in 1830, the house of assembly informed
Sir John Colborne that they had no confidence in his
advisers, he contented himself with replying, "Gentlemen, I
thank you for your address." By not dismissing his advisers
he practically denied the right of the assembly to call for
their dismissal; still, he shrank from avowing the principle
on which he acted. Sir Francis Head shrank from nothing:
to him it was a joy to declare and uphold a principle that
he believed in. He was not very unlike William Lyon
Mackenzie in this respect.

His frankness, however, won him no friends on the reform
side of the House, but only caused him to encounter the
full violence of the storm that his predecessor had escaped.
Perry worked himself into a towering passion. "If," he said,

Sir Francis Head has come out here with the belief that we could be put down by his saying the word; if he thought that he could place his foot upon the necks of the people of Upper Canada, he would find himself most grievously mistaken. . . . If his excellency expects to have a council whom he is to consult just when he pleases and how he pleases – if he has come out here with these views and to practice such a course of policy, he will find himself unable to get along.

The final words of his outburst do not recall the cadences of Edmund Burke; but Perry was an everyday man and spoke the language of the market place. He moved the appointment of a committee consisting of Messrs. Norton, Roblin, Charles Duncombe, Morrison and himself to report upon the correspondence submitted to the House. Considering the prominent part that Mackenzie had taken in the advocacy of constitutional reforms, it is surprising not to find his name on this very important committee.[8]

On the twenty-fourth of March, before the committee had concluded its investigations, Perry moved an address to his excellency declaring an entire want of confidence on the part of the House in his present advisers, and calling upon him to remove them immediately. After two amendments, favoring suspense of judgement till the committee should make its report, had failed, the main motion was carried by a vote of thirty-two to nineteen. His excellency's reply was moderately but firmly worded. The address had spoken of the excited state of public feeling, and in regard to that he says he is entirely guiltless. He was sincerely sorry that his new council did not possess the confidence of the House, as he had chosen persons who he thought would be most acceptable to the House and to the people. He recalled the fact that he had distinctly informed Mr. Baldwin that the council he was joining was not to be responsible to the people, and that that gentleman, after first declining, had, upon a further consideration, consented to accept office upon that understanding. Mr. Baldwin's conscientious scruples had, however, revived and he had succeeded in making four members of the council completely change their attitude. For his part, his excellency said, his attitude was unchanged, and he still appealed for his justification to the good sense of the Assembly.

In times of excitement, however, what is "good sense" and what is not is a question on which persons who ordinarily possess the quality themselves may seriously differ. The Assembly seemed to think that good sense called for a strenuous and uncompromising resistance to the pretensions of the lieutenant governor. A society called "The Reform Society of Toronto," of which Mr. Mackenzie was secretary, sent out [to] a number of country constituencies the heads of a petition to the house of assembly siding strongly with the late council and recommending a stoppage of supplies by way of protest against his excellency's proceedings. In these petitions, which were true to their origin in being of great length, the people were made to say that "while his excellency has thus resolved to hold the powers intrusted to him by his sovereign to reduce British subjects to a state of vassalage . . . the public lands, made valuable by their industry, are being sold or given away to favourites." The first statement may pass as rhetoric; the second was wholly without foundation. This, however, proved no obstacle to the signing of the petitions, which like doves to their cotes, came back promptly to Toronto. It was anticipated in these documents that the stoppage of the supplies would lead to the dissolution of the House, and the signers pledged themselves to use their best endeavours to secure a reform victory in the ensuing general election. Mackenzie having moved that one of these petitions – that from the township of Pickering – should be entered at length on the journals of the House, MacNab moved in amendment

> that this House does not think it proper to take any notice of petitions avowedly sent by members of it to their constituents *dictating* to them an opinion . . . on the late changes and differences between the executive council and the lieutenant governor, be before a committee of the House has reported, and before the people have had an opportunity of seeing the documents relating to these matters, a motion for printing them and sending them to the country having been negatived by a large majority.

This seemed so fair that it narrowly missed carrying, the vote standing twenty-two to twenty-three.

A week later (April 15th) the committee made their report. The document contained the draft of a memorial to the House of Commons most hostile to Sir Francis Head, accusing him, amongst other things, of duplicity in connection with a certain statement he had made relative to his new council.[9] A fear is expressed that "his Majesty's ear will be so abused by secret despatches and personal detractions as almost to set at defiance the best-directed intentions of his Majesty to arrive at the truth." The main demand of the address was for a system of "responsible government." A change had by this time come over the views of those members of the conservative party who, some weeks before, had joined in declaring that a responsible executive council was one of the happiest features of the constitution;[10] for ex-Speaker McLean now moved in amendment

> that any attempt on the part of the executive council to assume control over the affairs of the province or to interfere with the administration of the government thereof, without the sanction of his Majesty or his representative, would be justly regarded by the people of this province as an illegal assumption of power, and in direct violation of the declared object for which such a Council had been appointed.

This was not all: the amendment went on to speak of the "unfeigned satisfaction" with which the House had witnessed "the firm, consistent and constitutional resistance of his excellency to this unwarrantable attempt to subvert those principles of government upon the preservation of which . . . the stability of our social and political institutions entirely depends." The vote upon this stood yeas twenty, nays thirty-one. It is deserving of note that these were the political opinions upon which twenty members of the House were prepared to face their constituents and upon which in point of fact a large majority of the next House was elected. So foreign are such sentiments to the common political thought of to-day as to be well-nigh unintelligible to those who have not studied the question historically. It must, however, be assumed and understood that there were those at the period now under consideration, neither few in number nor inferior in intelligence, who deliberately preferred the thought of a chief executive aided – not controlled – by counsellors of his own choosing and responsible to him alone, to that of government by a cabinet or junto responsible to, and absolutely dependent on, a political party.[11]

A somewhat memorable incident occurred at the very end of the session. "Mr. Speaker," to quote the journals of the House (April 19th, 1836), "reported that he had received a letter from the Speaker of the house of assembly of Lower Canada with certain resolutions accompanying the same." The letter was dated Quebec, fifteenth of March, 1836. After assailing in bitter terms the British government, and detailing the efforts Lower Canada had made to secure a more liberal system of administration, it proceeds as follows:

> Were we to resign ourselves to a degrading system of servitude, do you hope, do you believe, that the ministerial policy which would degrade us would consent to concede to you an ennobling system of freedom to the extent you deserve? . . . If you are free from improper and unconstitutional parliamentary legislation we rejoice that such is your happier lot. If you have to complain of evils similar to ours, or of any other evils, all constitutional means in the power of the people of this province would readily be resorted to to aid you in their removal. Such good offices it is the duty of every colony to tender and to accept in return.

MacNab moved that this very significant communication with the accompanying resolutions contained "sentiments and opinions subversive of the true principles of the British constitution, which this House, representing the loyal inhabitants of Upper Canada, does not respond to, but most decidedly and distinctly dissents from," and that therefore it "be not entered in the Journals of this House, but be returned to the honourable the Speaker of the house of assembly of Lower Canada." The debate, which would hardly have terminated favorably to the motion, was cut short by a summons to attend upon his excellency who had come down to prorogue the legislature (20th April, 1836). This he did in a speech of a very argumentative character and of unusual length. One point was neatly made. He had been accused, he said, of overthrowing the constitution because he could not recognize his council as a cabinet in the full English sense of the term; and yet their own Grievance Report of the year before had contained a paragraph to this effect. "It appears that it is the duty of the lieutenant governor to take the opinion of the executive council only in such cases as he shall be required to do so by his instructions from the imperial government, and in such other cases as he may think fit." For his part he considered that he had protected the constitution "by refusing to surrender at discretion the patronage of the crown to irresponsible individuals." For the future, he said:

> I will continue to hold in my own hands, for the benefit of the people, the power and patronage of the crown. . . . I will continue to consult my executive council upon all subjects upon which, either by the Constitutional Act or by the King's instructions, I am ordered so to do, as well as upon all other matters in which I require their assistance. I will continue to hold myself responsible to all authorities in this country, as well as to all private individuals for whatever acts I commit either by the advice of my council or otherwise, and will continue calmly and readily to afford to all people every reasonable satisfaction in my power.

In accordance with the suggestions made in the petitions which had poured into the Assembly, the House refused to vote any supplies for the support of civil government. It had, however, made liberal appropriations for various local expenditures, which were to be supervised by the persons named in the several bills, some of them members of the legislature. It had not occurred, apparently, to the reform party that, if they refused the lieutenant governor his supplies, he might refuse to sanction their money bills. This, however, was what he did in the hardness of his heart. It would have been better if he had not done it. Occupying the position he did, generosity should have been the keynote of his conduct even towards opponents.

On the twenty-eighth of May the legislature was dissolved, and writs were ordered for a new election. The reformers counted on a glorious victory and so did Sir Francis Head.

CHAPTER SIXTEEN

FORESHADOWINGS OF REBELLION

There was now a well-defined issue between the lieutenant governor and the reform leaders of Upper Canada. The question was: Where shall the real power in the government reside? Sir Francis held that it should reside with him, aided and enlightened by the advice of his council. The assembly held that it should reside with them. This of course meant that it should be wielded by a party, for it was not to be expected that the assembly, save on rare occasions, would act as a unit. Yet, for some reason or other, *party government*, which was what the reformers were driving at, was never mentioned as their objective point. The views of the assembly were the views of the future; the views of the lieutenant governor were the views of the past. They had to increase and he to decrease, whatever might be the immediate result of their struggle. The probability is that, had it not been for the events of the next two years, "responsible government," *alias* party government, would have been established in the province earlier than it was. In support of this opinion may be cited the despatch addressed by Lord Glenelg on the fifth of September of this year to Sir Archibald Campbell, lieutenant governor of New Brunswick, instructing him that his executive council was to be composed of "gentlemen representing all the various interests which exist in the province, and possessing at the same time the confidence of the people at large." A copy of this despatch was sent to Sir Francis Head a few weeks later, with an intimation that he was to consider it equally applicable to Upper Canada. The answer of Sir Francis was a cry of indignation and alarm; and the colonial secretary then pointed out that he had spoken of responsibility to "the people at large," which he did not consider was at all the same as dependence on a vote of the popular chamber. Still, the despatch was a decided step in the direction of the party system.

The Assembly would therefore have done better if, instead of maligning Sir Francis Head for his straightforward declaration of principles on which, undeniably, his predecessors had acted, which were recognized in his instructions, and from which he had no authority, even if he had had the will, to depart, they had simply availed themselves of his language to give distinctness and point to their demand for a different system. Sir Francis Head gave them the best possible opportunity for raising an issue with the home government. "These," they could have said, "are the views of your Majesty's representatives, but they are not the views of this House, nor, as we believe, are they the views of the people of this province. We ask for a much nearer approach to the system of cabinet responsibility which exists in Great Britain." This could have been done in perfect good temper without refusing the supplies. Had the supplies not been refused, the House would not have been dissolved, and in all probability the home government, which was disposed to over-estimate, rather than underestimate, the degree of interest taken in the question by the people of the province, would have given satisfactory assurances of the gradual introduction of the system desired. As it was, the reform party, by proceeding to extremes, brought on a violent reaction in the politics of the province at the very moment when it was most important, from their point of view, that their cause should be sustained. Then followed the events of 1837-38, and "responsible government" was practically thrown back eight or ten years, for it was not till Lord Elgin's time that it can be said to have been placed in full and acknowledged operation.

From the first Sir Francis Head had anticipated triumph in the elections. He was convinced that the average Upper Canada farmer did not really care very much for the principle for which the reform leaders were contending; and that he would, on the other hand, be readily accessible to an appeal to his feelings of loyalty to his sovereign and attachment to the mother country. In a despatch written on the day after the prorogation of the legislature, he informs Lord Glenelg that "the loyal feeling which is now rising up to support me in all directions is greater than I dare describe." He states that at the conclusion of his prorogation speech, "contrary to all custom, a burst of acclamation resounded; cheers were several times repeated, and a crowd of most respectable people of all parties actually endeavored to take the horses from my carriage to draw me to government house." His excellency's friends found it as hard, apparently, to restrain their feelings as Mr. Mackenzie's had done on more than one occasion; for they too had made demonstrations within the walls of parliament, and had carried him on their shoulders through the streets. In the same despatch Sir Francis enclosed copies of fourteen addresses which he had received from different places, signed in the aggregate by 6782 persons, warmly approving of his policy.

But if there was a rising tide of loyal feeling, there was also a man who, though he professed to have sat down to a game he did not understand, knew uncommonly well how to draw the tide on. He set out to write, he tells the colonial secretary, long replies to every address that reached him – like Mackenzie he believed in *longueurs* – "and observing," to quote his own words,

> that these answers not only produced great excitement in both the Canadas, but that the more addresses I answered, the more I received, I determined to continue the controversy in order that the republicans should, in the most public manner possible, be forced to measure their strength with the supporters of the British constitution.

Ab Sin was here raising a false issue, for the "republicans" were demanding the British constitution as carried into practice in England; but, like many another false issue, it worked with the people. Practically, it may be said, the false issue was a means of raising two previous questions: first, Are these enlargements of political liberty demanded by the reformers in the interest of the province at the present time? and, second, Are these the men whom you would like to see taking over the administration of the country and controlling the patronage of the Crown?

To these questions the country, in the general election which began on Monday the twentieth of June 1836, and ended on Saturday the twenty-fifth, answered emphatically – No. Sir Francis sums up the result as follows:

> In the last House the republicans had a majority of eleven; in the present one the constitutionalists have a

majority of twenty-five, there now being forty-five
constitutionalist members and only seventeen republicans. In the late House there were thirteen American
members, in the present House there are only seven,
of whom one is a constitutionalist. Among the republicans who have lost their elections are: Mr. Speaker
Bidwell, the twin or Siamese companion of Mr. Speaker
Papineau; Mr. Peter Perry, the leading as well as the
most powerful speaker of the republicans; Mr. W. L.
Mackenzie, the chairman of the Grievance Report and
the arch-agitator of the province.[1]

The use here of the term "republican" is both absurd and
unjust: but Head had got the idea into his head that
responsible government could work out to no other end
than the separation of Canada from Great Britain, and it
would have taken no little braying to get it out.

Mackenzie presented himself to his former constituency,
the second or western riding of York, his opponent being
Mr. E. W. Thomson, described by Mr. Lindsey as "a
negative sort of man without decision enough to make him
a very decided partisan," and without "energy enough to
be bitter." The voters on this occasion do not seem to have
been hankering after a bitter representative, and so they
elected Mr. Thomson by a majority of one hundred, the
vote standing Thomson 489, Mackenzie 389. On the first
day of the election Mackenzie delivered a speech in which
he said that he had little hope that the petitions sent to
England would be of any avail. "I dare not conceal my
fears that the power that has oppressed Ireland for centuries
will never extend its sympathies to you." Should the petitions
be favorably answered it would be their duty "to uphold
the system of monarchical government." If not, then "the
Crown will have forfeited all claim upon British freemen,
and the result it is not difficult to foresee." A less prejudiced
person than Sir Francis Head might have detected a lurking
thought of rebellion in these utterances.

On the fourth day of the election according to a contemporary account, Mr. Mackenzie made another speech
before a large gathering at the polling place at Streetsville,
in which he stated that so far everything had been done
with perfect fairness and impartiality, and that, if he was
beaten, he was fairly beaten.[2] Two days later his mind had

changed – possibly owing to subsequent circumstances; for, on the final announcement of the poll, he read a long document containing thirteen reasons for protesting the election of Mr. Thomson. The returning officer was charged with unfairness and partiality, and Mr. Thomson with bribery. The hustings, it was declared, had been surrounded by a profligate and abandoned mob; while the governor was accused of having issued deeds to a large number of persons to enable them to outnumber the voters. Mr. Thomson replied, it is stated, in very warm language expressing great surprise and indignation at Mr. Mackenzie's conduct, especially in view of his voluntary acknowledgments of two days before.

Mr. Lindsey tells us that "Mr. Mackenzie's mortification at a result which he believed to have been brought about by improper means was extreme," and that, having "retired with a few of his supporters to the house of Mr. Graham in Streetsville, he wept like a child."[3] And yet in the speech which he delivered on the first day of the election, from which quotations have already been made, he had said: "I have taken less pains to be elected by you this time than I ever did before, and the reason is, I do not feel that lively hope to be able to be useful to you which I once felt." From this time forward Mr. Mackenzie did very little to promote reform by constitutional means.

On the fourth of July, 1836, – "A significant date," Mr. Lindsey says – Mackenzie, whose relations with Dr. O'Grady had not of late been quite harmonious, published the first number of a new paper of his own under the admirable name of *The Constitution*. Its tone was aggressive in the extreme. The paper was not a week old before Lord Glenelg and the British ministry were accused of having "employed a mean person like Sir F. Head, and secretly authorized him to use every method in the power of a despotic government to crush the spirit of freedom in Upper Canada." The writer of course knew nothing of any secret instructions to that effect or to any other effect, but – he made the statement without a qualm. An article published in the following month was more violent still. Speaking of desertions from the troops stationed in Canada he said:

The orderlies, non-commissioned officers and officers' servants are taking leave, and why? These men hear and see most. Perhaps these men expect the days to return when they may again be called upon to fire upon their peaceful neighbours, while peacefully exercised meeting to petition our lords and masters for a redress of grievances! Perhaps they shudder at the very idea of being asked to prepare for warfare . . . under the major of the baggage train, whose laurels were gained in book-making, defaming the catholic religion and its ministers, and in feeding the ill-fated peasantry of Kent with provisions at which a country pig in Canada would turn up his nose. Perhaps they think desertion to the United States a less crime than it would be if they were again called upon to level their muskets and shoot down their fellow Christians.[4]

A remark made by Mackenzie some seventeen years later throws a backward ray of light on the state of his mind at this time. It was generally acknowledged that in the election of 1836 the reform side had lost a considerable number of votes through the offence given to the Rev. Egerton Ryerson and the Methodists by the publication of Joseph Hume's violent letter and also by Mackenzie's own writings of that period. Referring to this fact Mackenzie, in his *Message* of August 25th, 1853, says: "There would have been no revolt – no need of revolt – but for Ryerson's defection." By this we must understand that, but for Ryerson's "defection," the reformers would have won, and that, if they had won, they would have carried their point against the lieutenant governor. But Ryerson drew off a large part of the Methodist vote; and *therefore* a rebellion became necessary. It is a good thing that political parties do not always feel it necessary to redress the loss of a general election by a rebellion.

During the summer of 1836 two prominent Upper Canadians made their way across the Atlantic on political errands. Mr. Robert Baldwin wished to discuss with the colonial secretary the question of responsible government, and to call attention to what he considered the serious condition of the province. Dr. Duncombe, who had been re-elected for Oxford, went home, partly on private business and partly to complain of the exercise of undue influence by Sir Francis Head in the general election. The colonial secretary declined to have any verbal discussions with either of them; he invited both to lay before him in writing any statements they had to make or views they wished to express. Mr. Baldwin responded in a paper of great ability in which, perhaps for the first time, the question of responsible government in Canada was dealt with in a really comprehensive and statesmanlike manner. He said very aptly that it really signified nothing whether responsible government was or was not provided for by the Constitutional Act; it was enough that it was required by the circumstances of the time and the state of development which the province had reached.[5] In any case there was nothing in the Act to stand in the way of its application to Upper Canada. Mr. Baldwin was a lawyer, however, and his letter is not quite free from special pleading and what might almost be called tricky argumentation. For example, speaking of the lieutenant governor's patronage, he says:

> But suppose that it (the establishment of cabinet government) deprived the lieutenant governor of every vestige of patronage, the simple question is – Is the patronage in the hands of the lieutenant governor the great object for which England desires to retain Upper Canada? If this be indeed the chief or only object, let it be candidly avowed.

With quite as much point, or even more, Lord Glenelg might have asked him whether the grasping of the patronage was the chief or only object which the reformers of Upper Canada had in view in desiring responsible government. There are many to-day who would declare that the main significance of responsible government lies precisely there. The question posed by Mr. Baldwin was not "the simple question": it was a question, and not really a very pertinent one. It *assumed*, what the colonial secretary would most strongly have denied, namely that the home government had a selfish object in desiring, so far as it did desire, that patronage should rest in the hands of the lieutenant governor as representing the Crown. The true "simple question" springing out of the situation supposed by Mr. Baldwin (namely the complete control of patronage by *party*) was whether the change would make for the good of the province and the purifying of its political life. To that "simple question" Mr. Baldwin should have been brought back, with a request for a full and deliberate expression of opinion upon it. Had he placed such an opinion upon record there would to-day be no little interest in comparing it with the teaching of that wisest of all instructions – Time.

There is reason to believe that the carefully drawn plea of Mr. Baldwin exercised considerable influence in Downing Street. Mr. Baldwin himself was an argument for responsible government. If Upper Canada produced men of this type surely the materials for statesmanship and wise administration were there. The letter he addressed to Lord Glenelg was dated the thirteenth of July. The despatch to Sir A. Campbell, previously referred to, bore date the fifth of September. In the meantime the colonial secretary showed a decided disposition to check the somewhat too ebullient spirits of Sir Francis. The latter was in a state of great excitement over his victory in the general election. Lord Glenelg thought he was making too much of it. "At this distance," he wrote (September 8th, 1836), "it is more easy, perhaps, than on the scene of action itself to look dispassionately at the triumph of the moment, and to estimate with a sober and cautious foresight the ultimate results of what is now passing." Sir Francis, having his enemies down, thought the moment favorable for acts of a "stern and decisive nature," but the colonial secretary was of a different opinion. He thought that such a course of action would destroy all the good effects of the victory won, and "provoke a second reaction to which I know not how any effectual resistance could be presented."[6] From the point of view of the colonial office Sir Francis Head was labouring under a considerable excess of that quality to which Talleyrand so strongly objected – zeal. In a despatch written a few months later Lord Glenelg expresses the hope that "the just and lively estimate which you have formed of the importance and responsibility of your own duties will be combined with a due allowance for the not less arduous and responsible nature of mine."

Notwithstanding the odium excited by Mr. Joseph Hume's "baneful domination" letter – an odium not confided to the conservative party in the province – both Mr. Baldwin and Dr. Duncombe sought the good offices of that gentleman in their endeavours to come into relation with the colonial office. Taking Dr. Duncombe's word for it, Mr. Hume introduced him to Lord Glenelg as having "come to England expressly, at the request of the reformers of Upper Canada, to state circumstances connected with the elections in that province very important to be made known to the colonial office here." When the matter came to be investigated a few months later by the legislative assembly of the province, it was found quite impossible to ascertain by whom the member for Oxford had been deputed, all the leading members of the reform party denying any responsibility for his mission. Deputed or not the Doctor had a tale to relate almost as dire as that which the ghost in *Hamlet* might have unfolded, but did not. The Doctor unfolded his in the double form of a petition to the House of Commons, which the ever-serviceable Mr. Hume took in charge, and a direct communication to the colonial secretary. The gist of both was that the lieutenant-governor had perpetrated almost every conceivable enormity in connection with the elections with the result of completely falsifying the verdict of the country.

Both documents were promptly sent to the villain of the play for such answer as he might find it in his power to make. The facts alleged were all such as lent themselves to investigation; and just one week after the meeting of the new legislature, which took place on the eighth of November, his excellency by message laid all the papers in the case before the house of assembly. On motion of Mr. Allan MacNab they were at once referred to a special committee consisting of Draper,[7] Woodruff, Sherwood, Parke and the mover – three conservatives and two liberals. On the first of December the committee was strengthened by the addition of Jones (Jonas) and Norton, one conservative and one liberal; and three weeks later Prince and Burwell were added, and Draper's name was struck out. This gave the undue proportion of five conservatives to three liberals, though it fell short of representing the conservative preponderance in the House as a whole.

The report of the committee was presented on the twenty-third of January 1837, and was accepted by the colonial office, which at this time was watching Sir Francis very closely, as a complete and conclusive answer to the charges brought against him by Dr. Duncombe. The documents, though, like all committee reports, representing the views of the stronger party, speaks for itself, and only inveterate prejudice could lead any one to deny that it placed the author of the accusations in a very damaging position. One by one his statements are taken and confronted with the facts, and in no case are they found to be sustained; in nearly every case they are proved to be grossly and inexcusably inaccurate. The Doctor himself on his return from England took his seat in the House on the twenty-ninth of November. For a few days he attended the sittings of the committee; then on the sixth of December he notified the chairman, Mr. MacNab, that his son-in-law had come to town to take him to his home in Burford, and that, as he had not been at home since his return to Canada, he felt justified in leaving for a few days, notwithstanding his great desire to be present at all the meetings of the committee. The chairman answered at once, saying that the enquiry so far had negatived every one of his charges and allegations, and that it was for him to consider the propriety of immediately submitting any evidence he could produce in support of them. The admonition had no effect, for although the committee sat for over six weeks longer Dr. Duncombe did not again appear before it.

If Sir Francis Head exceeded his duty in any respect in regard to the elections, he had already made a clean breast of it to the colonial secretary in saying that he had so worded his replies to addresses as to work upon public feeling, but whether, considering all the circumstances of the case, there was anything very reprehensible in this is a debatable question. That this was his main offending was practically confessed by Mr. John McIntosh, member for the fourth (or north) riding of York, who testified before the committee that he had no knowledge of Sir Francis Head having interfered personally in his election, but that he was decidedly of the opinion that "the answers given by him to the several addresses from the people prior to that time had an evident influence, and perhaps more so than had he personally interfered." Mr. McIntosh might have left out the "perhaps": for by any kind of personal interference his excellency would not only have defeated any object that he had in view, but would have procured his immediate recall. As it was, the people not only did not resent, but very widely responded to, the constitutional principles which were laid down with so much vigor and art.

Two prominent Upper Canadians only were mentioned on a former page as having visited London in the summer of 1836; but there was a third – a man who, though he had

some other important business in hand, had formed in his
much-planning mind a deep design to have it out once and for
all with the benevolent Joseph Hume. That man, need it be
said ? was Egerton Ryerson, the greatest pamphleteer of his
time in the two Canadas. With Mr. Hume he associated
Mr. Roebuck, who was filling practically the same role in
relation to Lower Canada affairs that Mr. Hume had been
doing in relation to those of Upper Canada; and to these
two gentlemen he addressed a series of six letters which he
published in the London *Times*, beginning in the month of
June. The letters contained a strong defence of the policy
of the home government since the year 1828, and strong
denunciation of the attempts made by Messrs. Hume and
Roebuck to promote discontent in the colonies. In the second
letter we read:

The royal despatches, which have from time to time
been sent out, have been most Liberal in their character,
and have afforded ample proof of the anxious attention
bestowed upon the interest of those provinces (the
Canadas) on the part of his Majesty's government. The
local administrations, under the direction and influence
of successive royal instructions have undergone an
entire change in their spirit and character, and to some
extent in their very composition. In Upper Canada the
appointments to the office of magistrates etc. have, for
several years past, been impartial, even upon the confession of the majority of the radical journals; no
complaints of any importance have been made against
the administration of justice; civil disabilities on account
of differences of religious faith have been entirely
removed. . . . This improved spirit in the government
has been so apparent, and the former grounds of complaint have been to so great an extent removed, that
a great proportion of those who formerly complained
of grievances have gratefully acknowledged the obvious
intentions and efforts of his Majesty's government to
redress these grievances and have become its decided
supporters.

The third letter, dated fifteenth of June – before the writer
was aware of the dissolution of the Upper Canada legislature –,
contains a statement and a prophecy:[8]

The people of Upper Canada are not republicans, nor

do they desire a government purely democratic. They desire nothing but a monarchical colonial government, well administered; and the truth of this assertion they will assuredly prove by an almost unanimous elective voice whenever any British government puts the question to them.

Mr. Ryerson followed up his six letters to Messrs. Hume and Roebuck by two addressed to Lord Glenelg, likewise published in the *Times*. In the first of these he discusses the result of the elections. That result he says was not unforeseen:

One gentleman (not a political man) who had travelled during the month of April through the Midland, Prince Edward, and New Castle districts . . . stated to me in a letter dated the thirtieth of that month (a month before the late Assembly was dissolved) that Sir F. Head had already become very popular among the people; that the proceedings of the majority of the Assembly appeared to be generally reprobated; that there even seemed to be a general and strong desire for the dissolution of the Assembly; that in case of a dissolution there appeared not to be the slightest prospect of one of the majority being re-elected in any of the counties through which he had travelled. And it is worthy of remark that constitutionalists only have been elected in the counties mentioned by my Canadian correspondent.

The writer draws the conclusion that "the returns made in the recent elections are the true results of executive corruption and coercion."[9] The latter remark was made with reference to the charges contained in Dr. Duncombe's petition to the House of Commons, which had been made public. These letters were afterwards published in pamphlet form under the title of "The Affairs of the Canadas – Letters by a Canadian." In a footnote on page 68, the writer observes:

If any proof were wanting that the present house of assembly truly represents the feelings and character of the people of Upper Canada, it may be formed in the unprecedentedly harmonious, rapid and statesmanlike manner in which that body is proceeding with the accumulated business of the country, and the present tranquil and already prospering condition of the province.

It is true that the session was a very businesslike one, and that it was fruitful in useful legislation. The tale of its labours was represented by one hundred and ten acts assented to by his excellency and a dozen more which were reserved for his Majesty's approval.

An attack of illness about the time of the meeting of parliament prevented Mr. Mackenzie from presenting his petition against the return of his opponent in the recent election.[10] Such petitions were required to be presented within fourteen days after the commencement of the session; but it was not till the House had been five weeks in session that Dr. Morrison presented medical certificates on Mr. Mackenzie's behalf, and requested an extension of time. Seven additional days were granted, and on the seventh day (20th December, 1836) the petition was presented. Fourteen days were then allowed by law for preparing recognizances. The law also required that the petition should lie two days on the table before being read. Mr. Mackenzie appears to have assumed that, when the law said that fourteen days were allowed after *presentation*, it meant fourteen days after the *reading* of the petition. He accordingly allowed fourteen days after presentation to elapse without filling his recognizance, and on the day after its expiry the order relating to his petition was discharged, notwithstanding that objections were made, not only by his friends, but by one or two of his strongest opponents who, thought he was fairly entitled to the extra two days. The letter of the law was undoubtedly against him; for it was impossible seriously to maintain that, when the law spoke of the presentation of a petition, and then provided for its reading two days later, it made one act of the two; at the same time it is to be regretted that the petition did not proceed to trial. Dr. Morrison had handed in on the twenty-second of December a list of not less than one hundred and seventy-four witnesses whom Mackenzie wanted to have examined; and the evidence of even a small proportion of these, carefully sifted, might have thrown a good deal of light on the question as to the manner in which the elections were actually conducted.

As it is, there is little detailed information on the subject apart from that furnished by the parliamentary committee which investigated Dr. Duncombe's petition. Mackenzie in his *Constitution* (August 24th, 1836) told how the government had "resolved to dissolve parliament, issue six thousand Kite deeds, and spare no pains to destroy the popular voice." The committee showed that the total number of land patents issued between the prorogation of the legislature (April 20th) and the close of the election (June 25th) was 1478, "of which number 1245 were issued in pursuance of orders in council made prior to Sir Francis Head's arrival in the province, and with which he could no more have interfered than any other officer of the executive government." Dr. Ryerson, in advance of all official enquiry, had entered somewhat fully into this matter in one of his letters, and showed that there was little in it beyond the fact that, when a general election came on, there would naturally be a rush for qualifying deeds or patents on the part of those who were entitled to them but had not taken them out. This, he said, would be particularly the case where the interest of the people had been aroused in an unusual degree, as it certainly had been on this occasion.

It is impossible to turn over the pages of *The Constitution* without being convinced that Mackenzie was more and more accustoming himself to the thought of separation from Great Britain, to be obtained peaceably if possible – if not, otherwise. In September, 1836, he writes:

> Whether we are the party of the few or the many, this great truth should be our rallying point: Upper and Lower Canada to be great and happy *must* be independent; and we should use all lawful means by petition and address to attain that noble end. . . . Permit us to part in peace, and send the mean men who are placed over us back to their humble stations, whence they were unhappily brought to our shores to disgrace our country and theirs.[11]

In the same month he speaks of Upper Canada being "involved in distress and dissension, destitution and faction, pitiless, pelting oppression and misery in every shape and form, evils great and pressing for the present, miseries fearful and appalling in the prospects of the future." A week later (September 14th) he publishes the speech of Patrick Henry

before the convention of delegates of Virginia, containing
such expressions as "There is no longer any room for hope.
We must fight, I repeat it, Sir, we must fight; an appeal to
arms and to the God of Hosts is all that is left us." – "The
war is inevitable and let it come; I repeat, Sir, let it come."
A week later he writes: "The tories were bad, but the whigs
are famine and pestilence itself." On October the nineteenth
he publishes the speech delivered by Robert Emmett when
on trial for high treason. One passage is as follows:

> I wish that my memory and my name may animate
> those who survive me, while I look down with com-
> placency on the destruction of that perfidious govern-
> ment which upholds its dominion of blasphemy of the
> Most High; which displays its power over men as over
> the beasts of the forest; . . . which is steeled to barbarity
> by the cries of the orphans and the tears of the widows
> which it has made.

There was at this time in England, notwithstanding the
passing of the Reform Bill, a great deal of strong and bitter
radical feeling, and Mackenzie was able to transfer to his
paper from one or two London journals matter of a very
inflammatory character. Thus he reprinted from the London
Morning Chronicle such patriotic verses as the following:

> The people, the people, remember them too,
> When America vanquished the Red and the Blue,
> And raised with her stars full of freedom and light
> A firmament blazing through slavery's night.
> The people, the people, can hurl in an hour
> The King from his throne and the ruler from power;
> the good and the evil is theirs, they can be
> The basest of slaves or the first of the free.

He omitted nothing that could excite hatred or contempt
for Sir Francis Head. Under the heading of "News from
Kent" he copies from an English paper a description of the
funeral of a pauper in that county, and exclaims: "Sir F.
Head, hearken to the history of one of your pauper
funerals!" He cites passages from Head's South American
travels in order to show that he had an intolerant hatred
of the Roman Catholic religion, and accuses him of having
far surpassed Maria Monk[12] in the offensiveness of his
allegations. Then remembering that the catholics as well

as the orangemen had mainly supported Sir Francis in the elections, he breaks forth in language certainly not calculated to propitiate either catholic or orange feeling:

> What a degraded despicable race those catholics are whose support of Head and his Orange brigade carried them through the late elections. The orangemen have been to them in Ireland as the Egyptian task-masters were to the Israelites, and Head is the public ravisher of all they hold sacred. Yet it is believed that the majority of these poor soulless beings actually kissed the rod all over the Province.

The colonial minister is accused of contradicting and countermanding, in private despatches, what he puts forth in public ones.

> Head was told in the (public) despatch to enquire, and to recommend a commission to diminish useless offices. In the *private* despatch he was bid to call into requisition all the means of bribery and corruption possible. . . . The public said that the governor would have to vindicate every act of his administration in England; the private told him to keep the Canadians poor, and Glenelg would share the mock responsibility. . . . New Brunswick has tested the government and found it a lie. Every Britain [sic] of manly feeling, every Canadian of honourable pretensions must turn with abhorrence and disgust from a system which could only be carried into execution by the scum and offscourings of the human race. (March 15th, 1837)

The Methodist Conference is dealt with as follows: "God sent down fire and brimstone and burned Sodom and Gomorrah four thousand years ago; and it is to us a matter of surprise how your conference, fallen as it is, escapes an open manifestation of the divine vengeance." (22nd March, 1837) Would it be going too far to question the complete sanity of these utterances?

On the twenty-second of June, in an address to his readers, Mackenzie glances back over the course of his paper during the previous year. "It has many faults," he says,

> and so has its conductor: but its columns have been sincerely and earnestly devoted to the cause of the

people. . . . I know that the press is preparing the
public mind for nobler actions than our tyrants dream
of. I have exposed their oppressions, their peculations,
their tricks of state, their conspiracies against freedom,
their hostility to truth, their bribery, favoritism, rotten-
ness and corruption. Canadians! I pray you to lend
me your aid in continuing this bold, dangerous, but
delightful course.

About this time he was urging the public to make a run on
the banks and get out their money while they could. One
of these notices printed in double great primer reads:

The Montreal Banks are all broken; so are all the New
York Banks; so are all the Boston Banks; so are the
Rochester Banks; and the Bank of Upper Canada is
employing but one man to count the money, shutting
its doors every day at three o'clock, and not opening
them till ten! It has evidently very little to pay with!!

The course of events in Upper Canada was precipitated
by the action taken in the Imperial parliament with respect
to Lower Canada. The respective situations of the two
provinces could not well have been more different than
they were. In the lower province the Assembly, after long
refusing supplies, had ceased its functions altogether. In
the upper province on the contrary the most harmonious
relations existed between the popular chamber and the
executive. It was precisely the fact that these relations were
so harmonious, and that the government was so powerfully
sustained by the representatives of the people, that exasper-
ated the extremists of the reform party: they would not
bow to the popular verdict. Advantage was accordingly
taken of the excitement caused in Lower Canada by certain
resolutions introduced in the imperial parliament by Lord
John Russell on the sixth of March 1837 providing for the
application of the revenue of the province to its most
pressing needs. To try to create a kind of parallel excitement
in Upper Canada Mackenzie lost no time in giving his
version of the matter:

The secret is told at last. The screens and councils and
constitutions, the pledges and kingly decorations, the
declarations and acts of parliament and ministerial
statements to which the judge on the bench, the repre-

sentative in the legislature, and the loyalist in the family referred as proofs that colonists were freeman [sic], are swept away in one instant by an almost unanimous resolution of the House of Commons of England, agreeing to rob, plunder, steal and defraud the people of Lower Canada of their money, the produce of taxation: to apply that money to purposes the people by their representatives would not consent to apply it; and to refuse them all substantial redress of the grievances under which they have so long and so patiently laboured. . . . They (the resolutions) show the true character of the plausible villains who were enabled to ride into power by offering England a reform bill, but were kicked out of it again for offering to gag and coerce Ireland; and who screamed against negro slavery in the West India colonies, while they were forging the fetter for the bondsman with a white skin in conquered Canada.

Mr. Joseph Hume in England offered an example of language of nearly equal violence, declaring in the House of Commons that "the Canadians were men like their fellow subjects here; and, if they did not resist oppression, they would deserve the slavish bonds which these resolutions would prepare for them." He also expressed the hope that, "if justice were denied to Canada, those who were oppressed would achieve the same victory" as the Americans had done. The words quoted were transferred to *The Constitution* and printed in large capitals.

Events were developing rapidly in the Lower Province. A proclamation which Lord Gosford[13] had issued for the purpose of appeasing the public mind totally failed of its effect. In many places it was torn to pieces by the habitants in indignation and contempt. Tumultuary meetings were held in different places, and arms were openly displayed. Mackenzie discussed in his paper such questions as "Will the Canadians declare their independence and shoulder their muskets?" and "Can the Canadians conquer?" His reply to the latter question was a very hopeful one for the Canadians: he saw many reasons why they should conquer. They were better workmen than the British soldiers; they had both better organization and better leadership than the authorities were at all aware of; and they would certainly receive help from thousands of sympathizers in the United States. To familiarize the minds of his readers with the thought of armed conflict, he published rude wood cuts showing battle scenes, troops on the march and other warlike incidents and emblems.

On the second of August there appeared in *The Constitution* a "Declaration of the Reformers of Toronto to their Fellow Reformers in Upper Canada." This document Mr. Lindsey describes as "virtually a declaration of independence." The document was signed by T. D. Morrison, as chairman of the committee, and John Elliott as Secretary; while sixteen other names were appended to it of those forming the committee. Among these were David Gibson and John McIntosh, members for the first and fourth riding of York respectively, and W. L. Mackenzie. Some other prominent members of the reform party, after discussing the matter, declined to append their signature. In imitation of the American Declaration of Independence the alleged wrongs of the province were recited; and the reformers of Upper Canada were "called upon, by every tie of feeling, interest and duty, to make common cause with their fellow citizens of Lower Canada, whose successful coercion would in time be visited on us; for the redress of whose grievances would the best guarantee for the redress of our own." To make this co-operation more effectual political associations were to be organized, public meetings were to be held throughout the province; and a convention of delegates was to meet at Toronto to take into consideration the political condition of Upper Canada, with power to appoint commissioners to meet similar commissioners from Lower Canada and any other of the colonies; and so to constitute a Congress "to seek an effectual remedy for the grievances of the colonists." Such was the scheme devised to introduce the virus of disaffection and rebellion into a peaceful province which at the moment had no quarrel, and never had had any kind of a quarrel with the Mother Country. Small wonder is it that Lord Durham should have found it "really hard to understand what justification there was for rebellion." Nor is it surprising that the loyal portion of the population on whom that rebellion, with all the confusion that it entailed, was forced, should long have entertained feelings of bitter antagonism to those who were its authors and abettors, or even merely its dupes.

CHAPTER SEVENTEEN

THE OUTBREAK

Meantime there had been trouble between Sir Francis Head and the colonial office. It did not take that very correct and judicious establishment long to discover that the administrator it had sent to Upper Canada was one of a hitherto unknown species; and the anxiety with which it watched his lively proceedings was not unlike that with which a respectable and experienced hen watches the acquatic performances of a duckling hatched indeed by her but not of her ancestry or habits. As early as the month of July, 1836, the colonial secretary, referring to those replies to address which Sir Francis thought were doing so much good, said that he felt "compelled to express, however reluctantly a wish that some of the expressions contained in them had been more carefully weighed, and that you had more studiously maintained the temperate forbearance and reserve by which such compositions are usually distinguished." The criticism was not all on one side, however. Sir Francis expressed his strong dissent from some of the views expressed by the Lower Canada commissioners – "the three G's" as Mackenzie called them, with a hint that a hard sound should be given to the G – and tendered his resignation in case there was any intention to apply those views to Upper Canada. He also criticized the appointment of M. Bedard, author of the Ninety-two Resolutions, to the bench of Lower Canada; and drew forth from Lord Glenelg the dry reply: "It may be sufficient to observe that you are very imperfectly acquainted with the circumstances of the case, and with the motives which influenced Lord Gosford's conduct. On much more ample information his Majesty has been graciously pleased to approve and confirm that choice."

It was not, however, upon any large political question that the rupture occurred which brought the career of Sir Francis as lieutenant governor to an end, but upon an altogether minor point of administration. In the official gazette of the sixteenth of July, 1836, the two following notices appeared:

"His Excellency has been pleased to appoint John Y. Spragge, Esquire to be Surrogate of the Home District in the room of William Warren Baldwin, Esquire, removed;

"And Robert E. Burns, Esquire, to be Judge of the District Court of the Niagara District, in the room of George Ridout, Esquire, removed."

The removal of Dr. Baldwin was consequent upon his having signed a placard as president of the Constitutional Reform Society, formerly the Alliance Society, founded by Mr. Mackenzie in the year 1835, in which the following words were used; "It is our duty solemnly to assure you that the conduct of Sir Francis Bond Head has been alike a disregard of constitutional government and of candour and truth in his statements to you." The case was a simple one, and no objection was raised by the colonial office to the action taken: no objection indeed seems to have been raised by Dr. Baldwin himself. Not so simple was the case of Mr. Ridout. He was known to have frequented meetings of the society in question, and taken part in its discussions, and it was assumed that, as a member, he was responsible for the placard put forth in its name. He protested, however, that he was not a member of the society, and offered proof to that effect. Being unable to obtain satisfaction from Sir Francis Head, he appealed to the colonial secretary, who ordered his restoration to the positions[1] from which he had been removed, unless there were other reasons for his dismissal, in which case those reasons were to be fully communicated to Mr. Ridout. Sir Francis maintained that, although Mr. Ridout might not have been a member of the society in question in a technical or legal sense, he was practically one. In any case there were other reasons, he said, which fully justified his course; but these he did not choose to communicate to Mr. Ridout or make matter of discussion, as they turned on the violent opposition which that gentleman had in various ways manifested to his policy as head of the government. The despatch instructing Sir Francis to communicate such additional reasons to Mr. Ridout was dated fifth of April, 1837. After an unreasonable delay of about four months, he refused to comply with the instructions and tendered his resignation, which was accepted by a despatch dated the twenty-fourth of November. Before that despatch reached Upper Canada grave events had taken place, and these must now be taken in order.

The "Declaration" referred to in the last chapter was discussed at the meeting of reformers held at Elliott's tavern on the north-west corner of Yonge and Queen Streets on the afternoon of the twenty-eighth of July. On the evening of the same day another and larger meeting was held at Doel's brewery on the north-west corner of Adelaide and Bay Streets.[2] At this gathering a resolution was unanimously passed, expressing sympathy with Papineau and his party, and declaring that the reformers of Upper Canada should make common cause with them.[3] It had been proposed that the "Declaration" (not as yet published) should be adopted at this meeting; but, as the finishing touches had not been given to the document, this action was postponed to an adjourned meeting to be held at the same place three days later. If Dr. Rolph was in part the author of the manifesto, as Mr. Lindsey states, his name was never appended to it: nor did he, according to Mr. Dent, who has followed his career with close and particular attention, take any active part up to this time, in the deliberations of the radical leaders, or attend any of their secret meetings. The learned and eloquent doctor had his own ambitions; and, if the rebellion had succeeded, could have occupied with much grace some prominent position in the reconstructed province; but he was not a man to burn his bridges or his boats. Mackenzie on the other hand threw himself into the breach. To him was assigned the post of "Agent and Corresponding Secretary." "He was," says Mr. Dent,

> in so far as his abilities enabled him to do so, virtually to play the same part in Upper Canada that had long been enacted by Papineau in the lower province. He was to be a supreme itinerant organizer, and was to go about the country stirring up opposition to the government. This would involve the arranging and holding of public meetings and secret caucuses, the selection of local correspondents, the supervision of local reports, and various duties not definitely specified.[4]

The scheme which was adopted in order to give effect to the "Declaration" was briefly as follows: To form in as many different neighborhoods as possible local societies consisting of not less than twelve, nor more than forty, persons; each such society to appoint a secretary; the five secretaries of as many societies to form a township committee; ten township committees to form a County committee, a district committee to be composed of one representative from each county committee within the district; each district committee to send two or three members to a divisional committee; four of these to be created for the whole province: finally an executive consisting of three persons chosen from the divisional committees, which should have full powers for carrying out the objects of the organization. This plan was Mackenzie's; and when he unfolded it at the meeting held at the brewery on the twenty-eighth of July, he pointed out how the whole system might be changed from political to military purposes. The secretary of a mere local association might become corporal or sergeant, and those of larger units take higher and higher rank according to the area represented.

It is needless for the purposes of this work, which is essentially a political study, to detail the meetings held or the resolutions passed under Mackenzie's vigorous impulsion. At one meeting

> The emblems, devices and mottoes displayed were even more significant than the resolutions. On one flag was a large star surrounded by six minor lustres; in the centre a death's head with the inscription 'Liberty or Death.' Another bore the word 'Liberty' in large letters with figures of pikes, swords, muskets, and cannons by way of relief to the eye.[5]

In doggerel verse it was asserted that Canadians never would be slaves, and that "one short, sharp hour" would free their country. Mr. Lindsey has extracted from Mackenzie's paper a striking example of the kind of language he was using about this time. Upper Canada in 1837 was passing through a very severe commercial crisis, which, however, was affecting the United States still more disastrously. The banks were making a desperate fight to keep up specie payments in spite of a constant drain of coin to the famishing republic. In order to devise some means of relieving the strain, Sir Francis Head had called a special summer session of the Legislature. Mackenzie describes the situation as follows:

Canadians! Your mock parliament has done its duty.
. . . The end of the farce is that the banks and the
province have been handed over by a sham legislative
enactment to Sir Francis, like a Jamaica or other bank-
rupt estate, to be made the most of for the use of its
foreign owners and creditors, or like a farm held for a
term of years at rack rent, to be impoverished in every
possible shape by the holder before it be given up.
Ye false Canadians! Tories! Pensioners! Placemen!
Profligates! Orangemen! Churchmen! Spies! Informers!
Brokers! Gamblers! Parasites and knaves of every caste
and description, allow me to congratulate you! Never
was a vagabond race more prosperous. Never did successful villainy rejoice in brighter visions of the future
that ye may indulge. Ye may plunder and rob with
impunity – Your feet are on the people's neck; they
are transformed into tame crouching slaves ready to be
trampled on. . . . Your country is taxed, priest ridden,
sold to strangers, and ruined. What then? Ye share the
plunder. Like the lazzaroni of Italy ye delight in cruelty
and distress and lamentations and woe.[6]

There was little or no meaning in it at all? Yet thus it
was that the spirit of rebellion was roused in Upper Canada.
Rolph did not do the work, nor Baldwin, nor Morrison, nor
Perry, nor all of them put together: Mackenzie could stand
forth and declare with Coriolanus, "Alone I did it!" To
say "No Mackenzie, no Upper Canada rebellion," is to
utter the most elementary historical truth. With many it
has hitherto passed for a truth to say "No rebellion, no
responsible government;" but a careful and dispassionate
reading of history is far from supporting such a view. More
than one writer, including Lord Durham in his celebrated
Report, has remarked upon the independent tone of the
very parliament to which Mackenzie referred in the whirl-
wind of denunciation just quoted. The simple fact is that
organized public opinion, suitably expressed, is a force
which no individual power can long withstand; and the
thirteenth parliament of Upper Canada had the advantage
of feeling that it had been called into existence by a real
wave of public feeling, however produced. Bitterly as Mr.
Dent condemns, and, it might almost be said, vituperates,
Sir Francis Head, he states that "he had to a large extent

been accepted by the country at the valuation" set upon him by the tory party who "had sounded his praises with stentorian lungs."[7] If the country largely took him at this valuation, it is needless to seek in corruption and intimidation for an explanation of the election returns of July 1836. But what does Mr. Dent go on to say of the action of the two branches of the legislature in the session which followed?

> Neither the majority in the Assembly nor the members of the Legislative Council were prepared to slavishly accept his dictation, or to follow him blindfolded withersoever he might choose to lead them. Some of the official utterances of those bodies during the session had been as strongly assertive of their own dignity and independence as the deliverances of the former Assembly had been.

If Mr. Dent had only added that Sir Francis made no attempt to dictate to either chamber of the legislature, or to lead any one blindfold, he would have dulled the edge of his previous remark, but he would have put himself right with the facts. The messages and other communications of his excellency with the legislature may be searched in vain for any trace of dictation or undue assertion of authority. He was in fact *far more deferential to the representatives of the people than he was to his official superior, the colonial secretary*.

Mackenzie's ideas were ripening fast where suitable soil had been found for them; and one afternoon in the early part of October he unfolded to a number of trusty friends assembled at Doel's brewery a scheme for seizing the lieutenant governor that very day. His excellency had just come in from his daily ride; he was guarded by only one sentry; the regular troops had all been drafted to the lower province; a few resolute men could do the business; and these could be had from a couple of manufacturing establishments in the town. The capture made, they would proceed to seize the city hall where some six thousand of stand of arms were stored. His excellency would be ordered to dissolve the legislature so that "a new and fairly chosen" one might be forthwith elected. If he refused to comply, then – "go at once for independence and take the proper steps to obtain and secure it." In the speech with which he introduced his proposal Mackenzie remarked that "there was imminent danger that leading reformers would be seized and sent to the dungeon." When leading reformers discuss measures of that nature it is difficult to see how such danger is altogether to be avoided. He also gave a recital, which cannot have been altogether new to his hearers, of the wrongs of the country – how "the government had been converted into a detestable tyranny," and law had become "a mere pretext to plunder people systematically with impunity."[8] It is rather strange, considering his low opinion of the law, that only a couple of weeks before, in connection with an action for libel that had been brought against him by the bookkeeper of the Welland Canal Company, he had publicly challenged the president of the company, Mr. Merritt, to bring all he (Mackenzie) had written on the subject of the canal before the courts and charge it was libellous. If he would do that he (Mackenzie) would meet him there, and let him have the benefit of all the counsel, whig and tory, in the province, while he would conduct his own defence. The idea that law was "merely a pretext to plunder people systematically with impunity," could not have been present to his mind at that exact moment.

The scheme for the immediate seizing of the governor appeared a little too Nicaraguan even to the resolute souls to whom it was proposed; and two or three weeks were consumed in consultations and deliberations. During this period Mackenzie had more than one interview with Dr. Rolph and Dr. Morrison; and on the last occasion, towards the end of the first week in November, he appears to have persuaded them that the prospects were good for a successful rising. It is claimed on his behalf that he did more than this – that he obtained the sanction of Rolph as "executive" to the plan on which he at once proceeded to work, namely, to collect men and arms in the townships north of Toronto for a descent on that city on the seventh of December. It must be stated here that, ever since the appearance of Mr. Dent's *Story of the Upper Canada Rebellion* in 1885, there have been two conflicting versions of the facts connected with the outbreak – the Mackenzie version and the Rolph version. It would not be without interest to analyse the facts presented on either side and endeavour to discover the exact line of historical truth; but this cannot be attempted here, nor does it much concern the main object of this work to unravel the extremely tangled relations between the two men. On Rolph's side it is contended that he did not sanction the measures taken by Mackenzie, and moreover, that he was *not* the "executive" of the movement. He was to stand in the shadow, ready to emerge if the movement proved successful, and take the lead in it. It certainly was a *beau rôle* that he was reserving for himself.

With or without the concurrence of Rolph, Mackenzie took the task in hand with the intense and feverish energy that was characteristic of him; and towards the end of November he had most of the arrangements made for the uprising. It is remarkable that, in the midst of his prodigious exertions in the direct promotion of insurrection, Mackenzie was still able to contribute to his paper. An article which he published on the twenty-ninth of November was of special significance, as it contained a warning to those who might be disposed to support the government. After stating that Head was detested throughout the province, and that it was ridiculous to suppose that Sir John Colborne[9] would be able to cope with the rebellion in Lower Canada, which by this time had broken out, the article proceeds:

> We do not mean to deny that there are tories. But will they dare to lift a musket against their country? Will they touch Head's guns and pikes, swords and spears imported to shed the blood of their friends and neighbours? No not they. They are proprietors. They have read the lessons of history. They well know that reformers seek no man's wealth, no man's substance, no man's fair fields. But they also know that, *if found in the act of fighting against the people to uphold a despotism, they would lose their lands, be banished the country as traitors, and their wealth used to defray the expense of the unnatural and cruel contest their covetousness had given rise to.*[10] . . . The Orangemen, as compared to the whole people, are but a handful; and many of them own land, which it would be inconvenient to part with by fighting against the cause for which their forefathers spilt their blood.

As it happened, the opportunity to deprive the tories and orangemen of their lands did not present itself; but, considering the intentions he had announced, it is singular to find Mackenzie, not long afterwards, calling heaven and earth to witness the wrongs inflicted on himself and those who, having taken arms at his instigation against the government, were compelled to follow him into exile, even though in no case were any lands confiscated. The measure he had intended to mete was not measured either to him or to them.

It is impossible not to impute serious blame to Sir Francis Head for his almost ostentatious neglect of the precautions necessary to give a reasonable degree of security to the capital of the province. Sir John Colborne in one of his despatches had spoken of Mackenzie as "a dangerous demagogue." Sir Francis refused to consider him dangerous – refused to pay any attention to him at all. News was brought that men were drilling, that meetings of a seditious character were being held throughout the country, and Mackenzie's own utterances breathed almost undisguised rebellion; but none of these things moved Sir Francis. He considered it impossible that any movement of the slightest consequence could have Mackenzie for its leader. Another consideration, moreover, restrained him. He had boasted in his despatches to the colonial office, and, we may well believe, to no small extent in daily conversation, of the great moral victory he had achieved in the election of the new legislature: how would it match with these claims and declarations if he should now put Toronto in a condition of defence as a precaution against rebellion? He might, however, have considered that, with a rebellion visibly brewing in Lower Canada, with Upper Canada depleted of regular troops, and with a man of Mackenzie's powers of agitation actively and continually at work in creating disaffection, the situation justified measures of reasonable precaution; nor need he have feared that his moral victory would lose all its significance were such measures taken. It is dangerous to have a moral victory on your hands which compels you to run the risk of another kind of defeat. It is dangerous also to despise an enemy; it is best to recognize and watch him, however low your opinion of his personal worth may be.

There was one public officer who could conscientiously say that he at least was not responsible for the supineness of the authorities, or their insensibility to the threatening condition of affairs. That was Colonel James Fitzgibbon, formerly a captain in the British army, who had fought in the war of 1812, and had never ceased to take a strong interest in the military security of the country. For some years past he had held the position of clerk of the legislative assembly; but while his principal duties were of a civil character, his military instincts were always predominant. When the gallant colonel heard of what was going on in the north country, he was like a war-horse, scenting battle, and loud and incessant were the neighings with which he strove to arouse a listless executive. In fact, in vice-regal surroundings, if the question had been asked, who was the true disturber of the peace, the answer would probably have been – Colonel Fitzgibbon. More than once he did actually disturb his excellency's slumbers, in order to impart his apprehensions. Nor was his excellency alone in his invincible incredulity as to the power of Mackenzie to organize an attack on the government of the province; to many of his principal advisers and associates the thing seemed equally impossible. Finally on Saturday the second of December the evidence that trouble was really brewing became overwhelming. A meeting of the council was held, at which it was resolved to call out two regiments of militia and to arrest Mackenzie; Col. Fitzgibbon was at the same time appointed Acting Adjutant General of Militia, and instructions were given for placing a small militia force in charge of the fort. These measures were taken, it will be observed, exactly five days before the intended descent on Toronto, and when some of the insurgent bands were already on the move.

Even this belated activity however, threatened to interfere seriously with the plans of the rebel leaders, who were hoping that the government would maintain its dignified passivity to the very end. On the afternoon of Saturday an agent of Mackenzie's, Silas Fletcher, had called upon Rolph to inform him that things were going well in the north. According to Fletcher's statement, made in a letter to Mackenzie in the month of July 1840, he enquired of Rolph, "as executive," as to whether he had any change of plan to suggest, and had received a reply in the following "exact words" – "No, by no means; I shall expect every man to be active and vigilant, so as to be able to get up the expedition and come in on the seventh and take the city." We may admit with Mr. Dent, who impugns the genuineness of this letter, the extreme improbability of Fletcher's having remembered, from the second of December, 1837, to the twenty-ninth of July, 1840, a sentence of thirty-four words. On grounds of higher criticism also it might be questioned whether Rolph really expressed himself so awkwardly; but there is little doubt that Fletcher was the bearer of a message to the general effect. Rolph, however, had not then heard all the news of the day, and after Fletcher's departure he was considerably disconcerted, and no doubt distressed, over what he did hear – that witnesses had been examined before the Council; that cognizance was at last being taken of Mackenzie's doings: that his arrest had been decided on; and that measures of defence were being concerted. He concluded that to delay the attack till Thursday would be fatal; and accordingly he despatched a verbal message the same night, to the house of David Gibson three miles north of the city, to be forwarded to Mackenzie wherever he might be found. That message, according to the Dent (Rolph) version, was not in the form of an order, but was a warning as to the danger which might be involved in delay, and a recommendation to make the attack, if possible, on Monday, even if it had to be done with a smaller body of men; as the city would certainly then not be in a condition of defence. The Mackenzie version is that the message was a formal order from Rolph, as executive, to make the attack on Monday instead of on Thursday. Gibson did not know where Mackenzie was, so he sent the message on to Samuel Lount of Holland Landing, who was directly controlling the movements of the insurgent forces. The message reached Lount early on Sunday morning, and the fact that he proceeded to act upon it without seeing or consulting Mackenzie lends force at first sight to the contention that he recognized it as authoritative. On the other hand, Mackenzie was not within reach; some decision, one way or the other, had to be come to immediately – for if the men were to descend on Toronto *next day*, there was not a moment to be lost – and Lount may well have thought there was less danger in acting on the message than in disregarding it. Mackenzie arrived at Gibson's some time on Sunday and learnt the position of affairs. Foreseeing trouble and confusion, particularly as no commissariat arrangements had been made for Monday, he tried to countermand the instructions given. A messenger despatched for that purpose returned, however, on Monday afternoon, with the information that it was too late; that the intended rising was publicly known all through the north; that the men had been ordered to march and were already on the road.

Early in the afternoon of Monday, while the men of the north were trudging weary miles through the mud of December roads towards their destination at Montgomery's, Mackenzie and Gibson had an interview with Rolph at the house of Dr. J. H. Price a mile or two beyond the city limits. The fact of the interview is barely mentioned by Mr. Lindsey.[11] Mr. Dent deals with it at some length, and states that Rolph, discouraged over the very unfavorable turn (for the rebels) which the rebellion in Lower Canada had taken, told Mackenzie that he thought it would be advisable to send the men to their homes, and dismiss, for the present at least, all idea of a rising in arms. To this Mackenzie utterly refused to assent. In that case, Rolph said, the only thing to do was to act with promptitude and vigour. "During this interview," Mr. Dent states, "Mackenzie made no pretence whatever that Rolph was entitled to act in an executive capacity."[12]

It would be beyond the scope of this narrative to enter into the many perplexing details connected with the management and mismanagement of the rebellion organized by Mackenzie and, according to his narrative, disorganized by Rolph; the main outlines can alone be given. On Monday evening the various bands which had been set in motion by Lount's orders began to arrive at Montgomery's, weary with long marching, foot-sore, mud-bespattered, and hungry. Having reached their rendezvous they hoped that a substantial meal was awaiting them. On the contrary, there was nothing in the house for them to eat; for Montgomery, the proprietor of the house, had declined up to this point to undertake any commissariat business; and Linfoot, the lessee of the establishment, was standing equally aloof. By dint of scouring the neighborhood a supply of provisions consisting chiefly of bread and cheese was obtained. The hunger of the men having thus been appeased, the question arose, were they to march on to Toronto the same night according to Rolph's advice, or not? Some were ready to go, and Mackenzie was ready to lead them; though he was disappointed and perplexed, as we read, at not having any word from "the executive" in the course of the evening as to the exact situation of affairs in the town. "The executive," it may well be surmised, was having a desperately anxious time of it that very evening. The man who had been dallying in thought with rebellion, and lightly touching it with delicate fingers; giving aid and counsel, but taking infinite precautions against putting it in anyone's power to say, as was said to Peter, "Surely thou also art one of them" found himself all at once confronted with the spectre he had invoked. The time had come for action – that most distressing time to a man of contemplative habit. Whom could he trust with a message to men actually in arms? What step could he now take that might not be fatal to him?

After much discussion and not a little wrangling, it was decided to postpone the attack on the town till the morning; yet the night was not destined to pass without bloodshed. The death of Colonel Moodie is one of the best known incidents in Canadian history. The colonel was a veteran of the Peninsular war, who had also fought in the war of 1812. After the conclusion of that war he had returned to England, but a few years later had come out again to Upper Canada, and settled on a large property on Yonge Street not far north of Montgomery's. On that fatal Monday evening he had seen bands of armed men passing his door going south, and heard that they were halting at Montgomery's. It did not need much divination to recognize rebellion, and he determined to gallop into town and give the alarm. Three guards had been set at different points on the road. Disregarding the challenge of the first, he rode on only to be stopped by the pikes of the second, stationed close to the inn. Enquiring who dared to stop him on the Queen's highway, he fired his pistol, when at once two or three guns were levelled at him, and he fell mortally wounded. He was carried into Montgomery's, where he died after two hours of great anguish.

The night had not advanced very far before a victim fell on the side of the insurgents. Mackenzie, taking with him Anthony Anderson of Lloydtown and three others, started on horseback to reconnoitre the road leading to the city. Anderson, it appears, possessed some military knowledge, and it was he who had drilled the insurgent bands of north York, and who up to this point had been the chief military adviser and organizer of the movement. Vague rumours had by this time reached the city of the war cloud gathering to the north; and, as Mackenzie and his companions proceeded south, they met two men riding north on a similar errand but in a different interest. These were John Powell, afterwards mayor of Toronto, and a Mr. Archibald Macdonald. Mackenzie and his party being five in number compelled the two to surrender. Powell was asked whether he had any arms, and not considering that in war strict veracity was required, replied in the negative. He and his companion were then handed over to Anderson and another man named Shepard to be conducted as prisoners to Montgomery's, Powell being in charge of the former, and Macdonald of the latter. As they proceeded up the road Powell made two or three attempts to fall behind, and was threatened by Anderson with having a bullet put through his body if he did not desist. A few moments later he made up his mind to act, and sharply pulling up his horse, he discharged his pistol at Anderson, the bullet striking him in the back of the neck with instantly fatal effect. The two prisoners then wheeled round and put spurs to their horses. Shepard fired, but harmlessly, at their retreating figures. As they rode south for their lives they had to pass Mackenzie and one or two of his men. Mackenzie fired without effect, and then Powell fired within a few feet of Mackenzie's head; but this time the powder merely flashed in the fan, and the leader of the rebellion was saved. Pursuing his way to town Powell roused Sir Francis Head from his slumbers, and informed [him] that a rebel force was on the outskirts of the town.

On the following day, Tuesday, uncertainty still prevailed in the rebel ranks. Men were continuing to arrive, but the death of Anderson, in whom all seem to have had great confidence, had a very discouraging effect. There was really at this moment no military leadership. Col. Van Egmond of Huron county, who had served under Napoleon, and was a man of some real military competence, had been summoned, and had agreed to take the command; but he had not yet arrived. The morning passed in fruitless debate; and about one o'clock in the afternoon a white flag was seen approaching from the town. Sir Francis had sent a message to the rebels, and his envoys were men of no less mark than John Rolph and Robert Baldwin. Up to this there was evidently no suspicion on the part of the authorities of any guilty relations between Rolph and the rebels. So far the Doctor had covered up his tracks with uncommon skill; but twenty-four hours had not elapsed before the authorities were wiser. The substance of the lieutenant governor's message was the offer of an amnesty for past misdeeds provided the men would return peacefully to their homes. The reply returned was a demand for a convention to decide on the affairs of the province; it was also requested that the lieutenant governor would reduce his propositions to writing. Sir Francis says that his rejoinder was conveyed in the one word "Never!"

An extremely bitter controversy has arisen over Rolph's action in this matter, yet the essential facts of the case do not admit of much dispute. It is charged by Mackenzie that Rolph on his *first* visit to the insurgents, after delivering Sir Francis Head's message, made a sign to Lount to step aside, and that he then bade him not to heed the governor's message, but to advance upon the city with as little delay as possible. Mr. Dent considers it of much importance to prove that Rolph did not do this on his *first* going out; but admits that he did so on the *second* occasion, when he brought back the governor's refusal, after the delivery of which he considered the truce to be at an end. The point does not really seem to be of great importance. The truce, which was supposed to have been for one hour, may have been at an end; but Rolph had consented to act as Sir Francis Head's envoy; and that he should, after delivering the latter's final message, have directed the insurgents to move at once on the city was as much an act of treachery *to the governor* as if he had given the same advice on the first occasion. Tennyson has described the case of one whose "Honour rooted in dishonour stood." It was so with Rolph. To be honourable with the insurgents he had to be dishonourable to Sir Francis Head; to be honourable to Sir Francis he had to be dishonourable to the men whom he had done much to lead into the desperate position in which they stood. He was honourable to neither. The deposition made by Samuel Lount in prison in the month of January, 1838, supports Mackenzie's statement, that it was on the first occasion that the communication was made. On the other hand the evidence given at the same time by Robert Baldwin indicates that the thing must have been done on the second occasion. Mackenzie furnishes besides a letter written by Silas Fletcher, one of his co-rebels, in July 1840; and Rolph, on his side, a statement made in August, 1852, by Hugh Carmichael who carried the flag. Mr. Dent doubts the genuineness of the Fletcher letter and Mr. Lindsey that of the statement made by Carmichael. In each case it is suggested that the document was inspired and dictated by the party interested. But from the standpoint of history it really seems to matter very little *when* Rolph dropped his hint to the insurgents, if it be admitted, as it is, that he did it. Bidwell stood aloof absolutely from all projects and suggestions of rebellion; and so, it need hardly be said, did Baldwin. Rolph coquetted with the idea, and applied his subtle mind to the problem how he might promote it without fatally compromising himself. Better would it have been for his reputation had he taken the field with Mackenzie and Lount, even though he had gone with the latter to the scaffold.

One of the first acts which Mackenzie performed after the departure of the messengers was to set on fire the house of Dr. Horne, a little north of Bloor street. The reason assigned for this by his biographer is that Dr. Horne was a tory, and his house a resort of spies. The evidence of the latter fact was that a certain young lady had been seen to leave the house, pass the camp and return. Samuel Lount, in the deposition above referred to, said that he disapproved of many of the rebels' acts, "particularly the burning of Dr. Horne's house." Mackenzie, in a statement published in New York in 1838, declared that the burning was done by "the distinct and explicit orders of our executive, Dr. Rolph, which were to do so before we set off for the city." But Dr. Rolph's "orders" were given to Lount, and it is singular that Lount should have blamed "the rebels" if the order was communicated to them by himself. Mackenzie also wished to burn sheriff Jarvis's house; but in this case both Lount and Gibson interfered with effect. This, he states in his "Message" extra on "The Flag of Truce," he was also ordered to do by Rolph. If so, Rolph's authority did not go far with two of his chief coadjutors. But there is nothing to show that he appealed to or quoted Rolph's authority in the matter; any evidence that exists makes against this supposition.

On the evening of Tuesday Mackenzie attempted to lead his men into the city, and they had arrived at the toll bar on Yonge street when they were fired upon by an advance picket under the command of Sheriff Jarvis. This threw them at once into confusion. The front rank consisting of riflemen under Lount fell on their faces, which caused those behind to think they had been mowed down by the fire of the loyalists. "In a short time nearly the whole force was on the retreat."[13] Mackenzie did his utmost to arrest their flight, but expostulation and vituperation were alike in vain. They would not advance again in the dark.

The whole insurgent force on Tuesday morning had numbered some eight hundred men, but of these a considerable number were only armed with pikes. After the repulse of the evening the majority returned to their homes; and, though a couple of hundred more arrived during the night, the number on Wednesday morning did not exceed from five to six hundred.

Meantime the loyal forces in the city had been considerably augmented. The number of men available on Tuesday morning, according to Sir Francis Head, was not over three hundred, which does not point to any great zeal for the fray on the part of the citizens. About nine o'clock in the evening a detachment of militia marched in from the east; and very shortly afterwards a steamboat arrived from Hamilton, bringing sixty or seventy picked men from the Gore district, known since to Canadian history as "the men of Gore" under the command of Mr. Allan MacNab. Sir Francis acknowledged in his official despatch that he was considerably overcome by the sudden appearance of this very timely succour. Mr. Dent, "on the authority of an eye-witness," says that he became well nigh hysterical. A little manifestation of feeling might be excused even in a lieutenant governor on such an occasion; though a proper exercise of prudence – that virtue which Jean Jacques Rousseau says renders all other virtues superfluous – would have saved all necessity for an emotional overflow.

On Wednesday the insurgents did nothing worth mentioning. Mackenzie, according to his own account, harangued them a good deal, but did not succeed in raising their spirits to a very high pitch. On Thursday morning Van Egmond arrived to take command, and a council of war was held at Montgomery's, at which a violent opposition of opinion broke out between Mackenzie and the professional soldier. The latter wished to wait for reinforcements expected to arrive in the forenoon, and a portion of which did actually arrive. Mackenzie was for immediate action. The veteran's counsel prevailed; and meantime Peter

Matthews of Pickering was ordered to proceed with a small body of men to the east end of the city and cut off communication in that quarter by destroying the Don bridge. Before the main body of the rebels got into motion word was brought, about one o'clock in the afternoon, that the government troops were advancing. The report was not believed at first, but it was true. Sir Francis, in his despatch of the nineteenth of December, says that he might have attacked a day earlier, but postponed doing so, being sensible of the strength of his position, and feeling extreme reluctance at the idea of entering on a civil war. "At twelve o'clock," he writes, "the militia force marched out of town with an enthusiasm which it would be impossible to describe." The force as a whole was under the direction of the Acting Adjutant General, Colonel Fitzgibbon. The main body was led by Colonel Allan MacNab, the right wing by Colonel Samuel Jarvis, and the left by Colonel William Chisholm; while two pieces of field artillery were under the charge of Major Garfrae of the militia artillery. The force thus embodied was composed exclusively of militia men and militia officers. There were two or three regular officers available and eight artillery-men; but Sir Francis did not wish to have it said that even so small a contingent of British troops had been employed against the insurgents. If they were to be put down, it must be by their fellow provincials.

There was arming in hot haste when the rebels learnt that it was no longer a question of their descending on Toronto to overturn the government, but of sustaining the attack of the government forces. Mackenzie, according to his own account written at Navy Island under date the fourteenth of January, 1838, when the events were certainly very fresh in his recollection, says that he addressed the men and asked them if they were ready to fight a far superior force, well armed, and with artillery well served. These were not very encouraging words for his raw levies; but the men having replied, as we are given to understand, that they were ready, he told them to go to the woods and do their best. He then described "the extraordinary bravery with which the men fought against an enemy twelve hundred strong, and who had plenty of ammunition, with new muskets and bayonets, artillery, first rate European officers,[14] and the choice of a position of attack." Although Mr.

Lindsey quotes this eulogy of the "patriot force," as he calls it, he hardly seems to give it full credit. "Gibson," he says, "was unanimously elected captain of one of the companies, but he left his post the moment the enemy appeared in sight. In this respect he was neither better nor worse than about one half of the patriot force."[15] The narrative referred to states that the rebels "stood their ground firmly and killed and wounded a large number of the enemy." They themselves, it is declared, had only three killed and four wounded, and yet they "were at length compelled to retreat." On what compulsion did they, when they were doing so well? The facts as regards killed and wounded are given by Mr. Dent, apparently after careful enquiry.[16] One man only was killed outright on the side of the rebels; but several were wounded, four fatally. On the side of the loyalists no one was killed; nor was any one, it would appear, seriously wounded. In the affair on Tuesday night, when the advancing rebels were fired into by Jarvis's picket, two were mortally wounded.

The skirmish lasted from twenty minutes to half an hour and ended in a complete stampede of the insurgent forces. Mackenzie, Lount and Gibson made their escape – the second only to be captured a few days later; but Van Egmond was taken the same evening in a farm house about four miles up the road; and Matthews, whose attempt to burn the bridge had been foiled by a party of militia, was made prisoner on the following Saturday at a house in which he had taken refuge near the township line of Markham. Mackenzie in his flight left behind him at Montgomery's a carpet bag, which fell into the hands of the government, and which was found to contain "an approximately complete set of the 'rolls of revolt,' in which were inscribed the name and address of almost every insurgent in the province"[17] – information which naturally assisted the authorities in the discovery and prosecution of those who had lent or promised aid to the rebellion.

Mackenzie's stronghold had always been the Home District; but further west, in the London District, he had also a considerable number of partizans, and to Dr. Duncombe, the author of the famous indictment of Sir Francis Head in connection with the general election of 1836, was entrusted the task of organizing an uprising in that part of the province, as nearly as possible simultaneously with that in the neighborhood of Toronto. The Doctor did not add to his reputation by his exploits in the character of rebel chieftain. He managed to set a number of men in motion, ordering them to concentrate upon Scotland, a village not far from the present city of Brantford. The government seems to have been apprised of what was going on; for, immediately after the dispersal of the rebels at Montgomery's, a well-equipped militia force of about five hundred men under Col. MacNab was despatched westward, to stamp out whatever vestiges of rebellion might be found in that quarter. Duncombe's followers did not await the coming of the expedition, which, already more than sufficient for its purpose, had been strengthened by accessions of volunteers from different western towns. Some, including Duncombe himself, made their escape to the United States; others returned to their homes to await results.

The rebellion, so far as internal resistance to authority was concerned, was at an end; but there was an aftermath of frontier troubles of which something must be said in the next chapter.

CHAPTER EIGHTEEN

THE ACTIVITIES OF AN EXILE

In the dispersal of his unhappy followers Mackenzie took flight with the rest. He was not the first to leave the field, however, for as he sped on his way he overtook first Van Egmont and then Lount. Questions have been raised most unnecessarily and unjustly as to his personal courage; up to this point he seems to have been in the forefront of every dangerous position; and it is undeniable that if a sufficient number of his followers had been of his mind and temper, the rebel force would have moved on Toronto early in the week, if not on the very night of their arrival at Montgomery's, – with what result it is vain to conjecture.

All that was now left for the leaders in the revolt was to flee the country if by good fortune they were able to do so. Their crime was treason undisguised, and they had no reason to count on the weakness of the law. The narrative of Mackenzie's escape to the United States is given, mainly in his own words, by Mr. Lindsey. It is a tale of endurance and address on his part, and of touching fidelity on the part of the friends from whom he sought shelter and assistance on the way. Sir Francis Head had immediately offered a reward of one thousand pounds for his apprehension; but this did not tempt one of the many to whom the fugitive had to entrust himself before he finally crossed the frontier. The narrative in question was written in the year 1847, and was first published in the Toronto *Examiner* in the month of October of that year.

The author tells how one of the persons who befriended him during his flight visited him afterwards in Monroe county (N.Y.) prison and wondered greatly to see him there. "I too," says Mackenzie, "in those days had taken but a surface view of the conduct of a cold-blooded reptile band, who pretended to love liberty that they might thereby more effectually hoodwink and betray 'a working majority' of their trusting countrymen." By the "cold-blooded reptile band" must apparently be understood the Van Buren or democratic party, under whose auspices he had been committed to prison for infraction of the neutrality laws of the United States; but a man is truly unfortunate who only escapes from the "reptiles" of one country – for the word was not one which Mackenzie spared in speaking of the friends of the administration in Upper Canada – to find "reptiles" still more venomous awaiting him in another. The reflection is also forced on the reader how lamentable it was that a man who, by his own confession, was continually taking "surface views" should have had such unbounded confidence in them.

It was in the afternoon of Monday the eleventh of December, that Mackenzie stood secure from arrest on United States soil at Black Rock, just north of (now included in) the city of Buffalo, having in broad daylight eluded the vigilance, or rather profited by the lack of vigilance, of the Canadian customs officer at Fort Erie. It must often have occurred to him in after days upon how slender a thread his life hung at that moment; for certainly, judging by the fate of Lount and Matthews, he had no mercy to expect had he then been arrested. Proceeding to Buffalo he was entertained by a prominent and very respectable citizen, Dr. Chapin. And here opens a new chapter in an eventful career.

To what extent Mackenzie had, before the outbreak, endeavoured to conciliate support in the United States, there is nothing to show; but on the evening of the fifth of December, the same evening on which the rebels were repulsed by Jarvis's men at Bloor street, a meeting was held at Buffalo "to express sympathy with the Canadian revolution;" and two days later a similar meeting was held at Oswego. On the sixth of December Mackenzie addressed from Montgomery's the following letter to the Buffalo *Whig and Journal*: "The Reformers of this part of Upper Canada have taken arms in defence of the principle of independence of European domination – in plain words they wish this province to be a free, sovereign, and independent state. They request all the assistance which the free citizens of your republic may choose to afford." To this letter was appended a note: "American editors will be pleased to copy this letter, whether they are or are not favorable to Canadian freedom." The meeting of the fifth at Buffalo had appointed an executive committee of thirteen; and, at the call of this committee, a meeting was held on the evening of the very day on which Mackenzie had arrived in the city. Exhausted with the fatigues, privations and excitement of the previous week, he was sleeping profoundly; but his host, Dr. Chapin, attended the meeting and mentioned the fact that the leader of the Upper Canada rebellion was then under his roof. The meeting demanded that the hero himself should be produced. "Not tonight," said Dr. Chapin, "he is too fatigued; but tomorrow night he shall address you." The meeting broke up with cheers for Mackenzie, Papineau and Rolph.

On the following evening Mackenzie, completely refreshed, mounted the rostrum and set forth, with great wealth of words, the woes of Canada, which, he stated, were of the same nature and fully as grievous as those which had caused the Thirteen States to throw off their allegiance to England. A recent writer has spoken of the period with which we are now dealing as "the saddest part of (Mackenzie's) career." It certainly is a part which even his strongest sympathizers must regret, and for which it is hard to find a shadow of excuse. His hand was turned against the country which for seventeen years had been his home, and to the interests of which he had often most effusively professed to be devoted. He was willing to make it the theatre of civil war; he invoked the aid of foreigners to put down its government by force, and meantime to devastate its frontier. He uttered words of intensest bitterness and contempt against both the provincial and the imperial administration. Even the girl Queen on the throne was not spared in these onslaughts. As a means to the overthrow of the party of his hate in Upper Canada, he desired, and did what in him lay to bring about, a war between Great Britain and the United States. A more desperate career, or one more completely swayed by feelings of enmity and revenge would be difficult to imagine.

The result of the Buffalo meetings was the organization of an expedition for the occupation of Navy Island on the Canada side of the Niagara river, just above the point where the Chippewa or Welland flows into it. A certain Mr. Thos. J. Sutherland appears on the scene at this moment, a man who evidently believed that he was called to high destinies as a military leader. If his statement is to be credited, the idea of occupying Navy Island was a stroke of his military genius, and Mackenzie had very little to do with it. He was in fact the first signer of a document, to which ninety-seven names were appended, of persons who pledged to one another their mutual support "for the commendable purpose of aiding and assisting our Canadian brethren in their present struggle for liberty and those principles which have given to the world that asylum which we have the honour of calling our home, and which pronounces to mankind the sacred dogma of equality."[1] This document might well have proceeded from the pen of Sutherland, who was nothing if not pompous and oracular. The chief command of the expedition was entrusted to a young man named Rensellaer Van Rensselaer, of the same family at the Van-Rensselaer who commanded the New York militia in the war of 1812. His qualifications were a certain amount of military ability and a good address; a serious disqualification was his addiction to intemperance. Probably, even with this drawback, he was the best available candidate. Between the commander-in-chief and Mackenzie serious dissension soon broke out.

So noisy was the enthusiasm at Buffalo, and so numerous were those who expressed a readiness to take the path of glory leading to the farms and other possessions of loyal Canadians, that it was a severe disappointment to Mackenzie and his general when, on the thirteenth of December, the day appointed for the descent on Canadian soil, only twenty-four volunteers were found ready to accompany them. Mackenzie, according to Van Rensselaer, had another fit of depression and collapse similar to that which had followed his defeat in West York the year before. "He sank inert and spiritless upon the frame of a cannon, where he passively reclined until aroused by a false alarm." Still, small as the band was, they carried out their purpose of landing on the island, and proceeded to organize a provisional government for Canada, as attested by a proclamation bearing date the same day and signed by Mackenzie as Chairman of that government, *pro tem*.

Addressed to the inhabitants of Upper Canada the proclamation told how, for nearly fifty years, the province had "languished under the blighting influence of military despots, strangers from Europe" – Mackenzie loved to call

Great Britain "Europe" – "ruling us, not according to the laws of our choice, but by the capricious dictates of their arbitrary power." "We are wearied," it continues, "of these oppressions and resolved to throw off the yoke. Rise as one man and the glorious object of our wishes is accomplished." To invite a province to "rise as one man" for objects which commended themselves only to a small minority – a minority that had just been chased utterly from the field by a small portion of those otherwise minded – suggests the inconsequence of a rich Hibernian imagination rather than the sober practicality of the Scot. But of course there are Scots and Scots, and Mackenzie, as we have seen from the first, was a man to whom the impertinent opposition of mere facts was never of much account. To Mackenzie a fact that stood in the way of his views was much like the "coo" in the way of Stephenson's engine – in a very unlucky position. Upper Canada was to rise, not as *two* men, one very much bigger than the other; but as one man; and the small man was to be that one – all because he wanted it so. Then he went on to tell how he would have the country governed – "an executive composed of a governor and other officers elected by the people;" vote by ballot, perfect free trade, and "a frugal and economical government in order that the people may be prosperous and free from difficulty." "Frugal and economical!" – how strangely these words, relics of a primitive faith, do fall upon the modern ear! It is worthy of remark that no hint of "responsible government" is given in this manifesto, probably because Mackenzie had in his mind the constitution of the United States in which the government of the day is not subject to the vote of the legislature.

The gallant twenty-four had not been more than a few days on the island when their numbers were materially increased. The whole expedition had been organized very hastily and it took a little time to get things under way. Arms had to be collected or stolen from the state armouries, money had to be raised, provisions purchased and transport secured. Within a couple of weeks the entire force on the island numbered between five and six hundred men. The burden of the correspondence relating to the affairs of the expedition fell upon the chairman of the provisional government. A large number of the letters addressed to him at the time have been preserved. In some cases personal service is offered; in others enquiry is made as to what rank the writer might expect to have amongst the embattled "patriots;" others relate to the supply of munitions of war or to contributions of funds; others give suggestions as to how the campaign may best be conducted. Few of the letters, comparatively, evince anything like superior or even respectable education. A Mr. Havens writes introducing "a patriotic gentleman of good Famely and Charicter who wishes to enter the services as asst sergeant." Another is expressed in terms as follows:

Dear Sir,

I am willing to Lende you my Assistants in this Campaign Against the Queen and the Loyalists Nagestes Government. I feel myself at Liberty to say to you that I can done my duty at the Cannon by Giving the Word of Command as a Officer and Drilling the Soldiers under the Soard Exercise and the Cannon in every pointe, and if you air in want of me to Command one of your Largestest pices you will obleage Me by Dropping a Loin to me to morough.

(Signed) J. S. Martin.

Tonawanda, 26th, 1837.

As experience and valour were more wanted in this grave crisis than orthography Mackenzie wrote Mr. Martin to come.

Another letter enclosed the minutes of a meeting held in the town of Clarendon, at which a resolution was passed expressing sympathy with the Canadians who were struggling to escape from "the gallin yoke of Briton" – A Mr. John Henderson writes from Ogdensburg to say that he is "a natural boarn sitizen of the state of New York," but that he went to Canada some years before, and entered into partnership with a man called Bowman, who robbed him of all his money. He does not say whether Bowman was a reformer or a conservative, but, as he was a Canadian, he wants revenge on the country and would go to Mackenzie at once were it not that he is destitute. If Mackenzie can contrive any means to get him to Navy Island he expresses willingness to take any position "agreeable to my deserts." Andrew Robinson sends "for the good of the cause 117 loves of bread." The loaves would not be the less acceptable because the writer had anticipated the spelling reformers in omitting "a" from the word. It would be very unreasonable, and indeed uncharitable to doubt that many, if not most, of the gifts sent to Navy Island were prompted by real kindness of heart and a desire to help what the donors sincerely regarded as a good cause. They had heard the version of the Canadian troubles given by Mackenzie and other refugees, and had heard no other. What could they think but that Canada was writhing in the grasp a cruel tyranny, and that to aid in its liberation was the simplest and most binding of human duties? The widow's mite and the "loves of bread" may well be entered in the same record.

A letter of a different kind is one from a graduate of West Point who writes to give Van Rensselaer his ideas as to the best means of protecting the landing places on the island against the approach of boats. Another gentleman, who described himself as a surgeon and medical man of eight years standing, offered his services with the remark that "the Rheubicon is past, the Canadians will be freed from the yoke of Teriny." The very spelling here smacks of medical studies for nothing but a recollection of "rheumatism" could have suggested the spelling "Rheubicon."

To watch the operation of the patriots on Navy Island, whose intention was to cross to the Upper Canada side of the Niagara River as soon as they were in sufficient force, a body of militia under Col. MacNab was stationed at Chippewa; and it was while the two forces were thus facing one another and exchanging, for the most part, ineffectual shots, that the thrilling incident of the *Caroline* occurred. The story was told at the time, and even long after, with every species of exaggeration; but the bare facts of the case are sufficiently interesting and memorable, and cannot be omitted from our narrative.

On the afternoon of the twenty-ninth of December as Col. MacNab was surveying the American shore through a telescope he saw a small steamer set out from Fort Schlosser, nearly opposite, and make for Navy Island. As it approached it was seen to be crowded with men and to have two field-pieces on its deck. A number of men and the field pieces, together with other freight, were landed on the island, after which the vessel returned to her moorings at Fort Schlosser. This was not a sight which so loyal a man and ready a fighter as MacNab could view with equanimity. If the neutrality of the United States was being so openly violated by its own citizens, why should it be scrupulously respected by the subjects of her Majesty? Turning to Captain Andrew Drew, R.N., who had been put in charge of a naval brigade for such operations as might be necessary on the river, he asked him if he could "cut out that vessel." "Nothing easier," said Drew, "but it must be done at night." "Do it then," said MacNab. Though Drew had said "Nothing easier," the task was one both of difficulty and of peril. Still, when volunteers were called for, a far larger number offered than could be accepted. The best men were chosen, about fifty in all. The crossing had to be made between the north end of Navy Island and the Niagara rapids. To go too near the island was to run the risk of being fired upon and sunk; to go too near the rapids was to risk being carried over the cataract. The maxim *"in medio tutissimus"*[2] was hardly applicable to the case, for the middle itself was ambiguous and full of danger. Seven boats, with seven or eight men in each, started. Two which went too near the island were fired upon and turned back; the other five went on. The crews had to put forth great effort to stem the current; but they crossed safely, boarded the steamer and drove ashore at the point of the sword one or two men who were on watch, as well as some who were sleeping on the boat; after which they cut out the vessel from her moorings, set her on fire, and let her drift down the river towards the cataract. This was not done without loss of life. One man was killed on the wharf by the attacking party, and one or two others were wounded; while Lieut. McCormick, R.N., second in command to Captain Drew, received wounds which proved mortal. A result which might have been foreseen was that a serious international difficulty was created.

On the same day on which the Caroline was destroyed Mrs. Mackenzie arrived at Navy Island, desirous of sharing the fortunes of her husband. She remained nearly a fortnight, "making flannel cartridge bags and inspiring with courage, by her entire freedom from fear, all with whom she conversed."[3] Ill health then obliged her to leave; and Mr. Mackenzie accompanied her to Buffalo. On his way thither he was arrested in a railway car for breach of the neutrality laws of the United States. Giving bail for his appearance, he returned, his biographer tells us, to the island, "where he remained till Van Rensselaer announced

his intention to evacuate it on the thirteenth of January."
Van Rensselaer, in his account of the occurrences on Navy
Island, written in Albany jail in March 1838, and published
in the Albany *Daily Advertiser*, makes no mention of
Mackenzie's return to the island; in fact he distinctly implies
that he did not return. This is his statement: "At this
trying crisis where was William Lyon Mackenzie? He left
the island when the bombardment and cannonading was
commenced against us in real earnest;[4] and, in spite of my
remonstrances and entreaties to the contrary, he pushed
off for Buffalo, where he remained safely ensconced in the
house of a friend." If Mrs. Mackenzie arrived on the
twenty-ninth and remained "nearly a fortnight," we may
perhaps place the date of her departure at the tenth of
January. The evacuation took place actually on the fourteenth, just four days later, and it must be these days that
Van Rensselaer refers to when he says that Mackenzie
"remained safely ensconced in the house of a friend." A
letter in Mackenzie's own hand, written at the house of
one Capt. Appleby (to which he had conducted Mrs.
Mackenzie), and dated fourteenth of January, 1838, seems
to confirm Van Rensselaer's statement. It is addressed to
Dr. E. Johnson the chairman of the Buffalo committee. In
it he says: "Since I came to the city I have answered a
hundred letters many of them of consequence." It would be
good work to answer a hundred letters in three or four
days, and it is difficult to understand how any part of the
period could have been spent on Navy Island.

It has been mentioned that Van Rensselaer and Mackenzie
did not work together very harmoniously. The account which
the former gives of their differences is worth reproducing,
especially as it is given neither by Mr. Lindsey nor by
Mr. Dent:

> During the period we remained on the island, of the
> thousands who visited us for business or curiosity, all
> are witnesses of the extent of the duties, fatigues and
> perils which devolved upon me. . . . But among all
> the perplexities incident to the organization of a repub-
> lican army for invasion . . . nothing was more perplexing
> than the conduct of William Lyon Mackenzie. I had
> known him long to have the reputation of a firm and
> consistent opposer of monarchical abuses; as such I

respected him so much that many little disagreements
occurred between us before my confidence in him could
be shaken. A breech, however, did occur which grew
wider as my knowledge of his disposition and character
increased. I found him governed by the impulses of
the moment, fickle, arbitrary, and impatient. He would
suggest fifty plans for effecting the object in view in
as many minutes, and abandon them as often; but he
could fix upon no single one and follow it out. If I
presumed to differ or remind him of his stipulation not
to interfere, his potent ire would immediately arise and
a quarrel ensue. . . . To keep his restless spirit quiet
while our reinforcements were coming in, the general
correspondence was entrusted to his charge. How well
or how badly he performed the duty I am not able to
judge, for he scarcely ever thought it necessary to make
any reports.

There are, in the statements from which these quotations
are made, slurs upon Mackenzie's courage which it has not
been thought necessary to reproduce.[5] The remarks actually
quoted reveal, it must be acknowledged, a character that
has already become very familiar to us.

The letter written by Mackenzie on the fourteenth of
January at Buffalo to the chairman of the local committee
possesses interest apart from the light it throws upon the
question of his whereabouts during the last days of the
Navy Island fiasco; for in it he made a proposition respecting
the establishment of a newspaper to be the organ of his
liberationist views with regard to Canada. It is thus that he
unfolded his proposition:

Since I came to this city I have answered a hundred
letters – many of them of consequence – and am decidedly
of opinion that, as there is now no confidential writer
either in Upper or Lower Canada to whom the sufferers
across the line can express their grievances and wrongs –
as large sums would be subscribed and paid on their
behalf, if their situation was fully understood – as some
journal officially known through the Union as expressing
their wants and wishes is absolutely required – as the
arguments against their cause should be deliberately
met and answered – and as a weekly sheet under the
management of a trusty person could be published here

so as to be profitable and highly useful to our cause, that such a paper should be instantly set on foot. I will, whether here or in Canada, do all I can to uphold it, and so will Dr. Rolph doubtless. I have found the press in Canada my most useful and efficient weapon, and that it will be so here I cannot doubt. . . . I am keeping as retired as possible;[6] it seems to be the opinion of some who have the means of knowing that that is the wiser course. But I should be glad to find that no serious objection can be raised against the project of a journal to express the opinions of the reformers of Canada.

The significance of this letter lies on the surface. Mackenzie's activity on Navy Island, such as it was, had not been satisfactory to his associates, and some of his public utterances on the occasion of his arrest are said by Van Rensselaer to have been very indiscreet. He had therefore been urged to keep as quiet as possible. But some outlet for his chafing energies he must find, and what more suitable than the old familiar channel of newspaper agitation? The committee appears to have taken his suggestion into consideration, for on the twelfth of May, 1838, the first number of *Mackenzie's Gazette* made its appearance, just fourteen years less six days after the first number of his *Colonial Advocate*. The place of publication was New York, to which city Mackenzie removed his family, who up to this time had remained at Toronto. It is hardly too much to say that the real, though disavowed, object of this paper was to make trouble and, if possible, bring on war, between England and the United States;[7] while meantime it served the purpose of inviting sympathy and assistance for those who were organizing attacks on the Canadian frontiers. In less than two months after the paper was established he was able to quote the opinion of the New York *Journal of Commerce* to the effect that his powers of agitation were almost equal to O'Connell's, and that, were his paper generally read in the United States, war could not be prevented between that country and England. This was a tribute to be proud of; and the editor was probably not much abashed by another opinion which he quoted from the New York *Commercial Advertiser*: "He (Mackenzie) is a criminal in the United States . . . and the impunity with which he plants himself in the midst of a community which he has outraged is discreditable to our authorities and an insult to our citizens." The New York *Sun* spoke of the *Gazette* as "one of the most interesting sheets issued from the New York press;" while the Detroit *Morning Post* acknowledged that the editor wielded "no common pen."

The *Gazette* of the fourth of August, 1838, contains one of those many-headed manifestoes in which Mackenzie delighted. It is an address to the friends of freedom in Upper Canada. "I rejoice," he says, "at the progress we have made, and am firmly resolved to continue by every means in my power, to harass the minions of England in Canada until we drive them from the continent. I am satisfied it can and will be done." By this time, however, he had begun to interest himself in United States politics and had strongly espoused the democratic side represented by the President then in office, Mr. Van Buren. As might be expected he had conceived an intense contempt for the opposite party; and consequently we find him interjecting into the address referred to the following interesting observations:

> He (Van Buren) is opposed by the whigs here most violently; and the more I see of their leaders, the more fully convinced I am that Canada would gain little by exchanging the plundering band of Lord Glenelg for the still meaner retainers who rally around such men as Daniel Webster. One swarm of locusts would leave us, it is true; but another, keen in their bite, would light in their places. I have not struggled sixteen years in Canada to exchange American whigs for those of Europe. To us this faction would be the same, greedy, selfish, and unfeeling.

It is not every man who, taking refuge in a foreign country, would so soon have entered into its domestic politics, or allowed himself so much licence in speaking of one of the great parties into which the country was divided. And besides it was all to be unsaid later, and his support to be given to these very "whigs."

Meantime the Canadian refugees and their American sympathizers were not idle. On the twenty-ninth of May, 1838 (the day on which Lord Durham landed at Quebec), the fine Canadian steamer, *Sir Robert Peel*, was burnt at her moorings at Wells' Island, N.Y., nearly opposite the Canadian town of Ganonoque, in alleged retaliation for the destruction of the *Caroline*. The cases were in no way parallel. The Canadian vessel had committed no act unfriendly to the United States government, or even to any party or faction in the United States.[8] She was, moreover, a passenger vessel employed at the time in the conveyance of passengers, several of whom were women, and trusting to the protection of United States law. Nor was there any risk involved in the perpetration of the outrage, which was committed at night by a large band of masked men. A few days later a considerable body of armed men passed over from Grand Island in the Niagara river to the Canada side, and established themselves in a very difficult piece of country known as the Short Hills in the township of Pelham. A few miles distant at St. Johns, quartered in Overholt's tavern, was a detachment consisting of ten men of the Queen's lancers, a volunteer corps. These they attacked and captured about three o'clock in the morning of the twenty-first of June, releasing them shortly afterwards, but appropriating their horses and arms. Retreating then to the Short Hills they were pursued and dispersed by another body of militia which had arrived on the scene. Their leader, James Morrow, and several others were captured. That unhappy man had prepared a proclamation commencing, "Canadians! we have at last been successful in planting the standard of Liberty in one part of our distressed country – Fort George and Fort Missasauga are now in our possession." Morrow spoke of "our country" for the sake of effect probably; but he had, as a matter of fact, been joined by a few Canadians. The statement that he had captured the forts mentioned were absolutely false; possibly it was a mere premature counting of chickens, his intention being to issue the proclamation *after* they had been captured. Morrow had cast the die and lost; on the thirteenth of July he was hanged. His leading associates were condemned to the same fate, but their sentences were afterwards commuted to transportation for life.

A more important descent on Canadian territory was that made near Prescott in the month of November by an armed force of something under two hundred men, commanded by one Von Shoultz, a Pole, a man apparently of real merit, who had too easily been led to believe that, north of the

St. Lawrence, lay a country that was groaning to be delivered
from a tyrannical government. The invaders took up their
position in a stone windmill three miles below Prescott,
which they held for some days and defended with no little
courage. On the sixteenth of November they were dislodged
by a combined force of regulars and militia. The losses on
both sides were the most considerable that occurred at any
time in Upper Canada during the rebellion. On the Canadian
side the killed and wounded numbered forty-five; fully
double that number fell on the side of the invaders. The
remainder were taken prisoners; of these some were
pardoned on account of their extreme youth, or other
extenuating circumstances, but ten, including Von Shoultz
himself, were sentenced to be hanged, a sentence which was
rigorously carried out.[9]

Brief mention must be made of the operations of the
patriots on the western frontier of the province. Simultaneously with the occupation of Navy Island, a force consisting
almost exclusively of American citizens had been organized
on the Detroit river. The intention was to land at some
convenient point on the Canadian side, and then to march
east, augmenting their numbers as they went by gathering
in the disaffected. Van Rensselaer, who seems to have been
impressed by Sutherland's abilities, gave him a commission
as commander of this army, with the rank of brigadier-
general. Armed further with a letter of introduction from
Mackenzie, the new brigadier proceeded at once to the
scene of his intended exploits. Mackenzie's letter, which was
addressed to T. Dufort,[10] Detroit, read in part as follows:

> For the purpose of co-operating with the patriots now
> on this island in their intended descent upon Canada,
> and of giving greater strength and more full effect to
> their plan of operations for the deliverance of that great
> country from the horrors of despotism, the bearer
> proceeds immediately [sic] to Detroit to take command
> of an army which his efforts and those of his friends
> may raise for the invasion of Canada.

An army had, however, been raised and had chosen their
own commanders, so that the advent of Sutherland with
pretentions to the chief command was not altogether
welcome. After no little wrangling it was decided to let
Sutherland take command in an attack about to be made

on Amherstburg. As a preliminary to a descent on that town, the neighbouring island of Bois Blanc was occupied. The patriots had chartered a schooner "Anne," on which they embarked all their warlike stores. While this vessel was manoeuvring in front of Amherstburg she grounded within gun shot of the town, when a duel ensued with the local militia which was all in favor of the latter. A number of men were killed on board the schooner, and the rest, several of whom were wounded, were made prisoners. Sutherland, who had remained on the island with the bulk of his command, ordered an immediate and precipitate retreat. His heroism on the occasion was by no means marked. The schooner and its stores, which were of some value, fell into the hands of the militia.

The next movement of consequence was the invasion of Pelee Island by a force of over three hundred men under a Col. Bradley, about the first of March, 1838. On the third they were attacked by Col. Maitland, with four companies of regulars, a few volunteer troops and Indians, and two six pounder cannon. The ice had been strong enough to permit the passage of the troops with their cannon; but the snow was deep on the island and movement was difficult. The invaders were dispersed by a bayonet charge and escaped to their boats, leaving their colonel, major, two captains and seven others dead on the ground. On the British side three were killed and many wounded.

There was scant encouragement so far for the sympathizers, nor was the Short Hills affair in June, or the Prescott disaster in November calculated to raise their hopes; nevertheless, on the fourth of December, 1838, a force consisting of four hundred men crossed over, in the most open manner, from Detroit to Windsor, amid the plaudits of a vast crowd that had gathered to witness their departure. The town of Windsor was, at the moment, almost wholly unprotected, and at first the invaders had all their own way. They fired several buildings, burnt the steamer *Thames* lying at the wharf, overpowered a small militia force, killing the officer in command, Captain Lewis, and two or three others; and then marched towards Sandwich. Here, however, their luck was at an end, for they were encountered by Col. Prince with a body of Canadian militia and vigorously attacked. They took to flight leaving behind twenty-one dead. A severe frost set in, and several of those who took to the woods were afterwards found frozen to death. It was on this occasion that Col. Prince ordered the shooting of four prisoners, an act which has been much criticized, but which writers as humane as Dr. Kingsford and Major Richardson have hesitated to condemn.[11]

It is doubtless true that Mackenzie had very little to do with the planning or carrying out of any of these justly ill-fated enterprises. Mr. Lindsey informs us that

> in 1839 Mr. Mackenzie made affidavit that, when he heard of these intended expeditions at Short Hills and against Prescott and Windsor, through the public press, he wrote to Lockport, N.Y.,[12] earnestly urging those whom he thought likely to have influence with the refugees to abandon all such attempts as injurious to the cause of good government in Canada.

If such were his views as early as the date of the Short Hills attack, he had made a *volte face* since writing his letter of introduction for Sutherland in the previous December. If he was really opposed to the frontier warfare, he had a journal under his control which afforded him the best possible means of discouraging the business; but its columns will be searched in vain for any condemnation of it. On the contrary we find in the *Gazette* of the twenty-first of July, 1838, exactly one month *after* the Short Hills affair, a letter from Mackenzie to "William Johnson, now encamped in Upper Canada on the islands in the river St. Lawrence contending for the liberty of his native country," in which the following passage occurs: "Some of our friends here are discouraged because of late events at the Short Hills and with you. So am not I. If the system of harassing our enemy be steadily adhered to, the time will come for more powerful operations; and we must be successful to the extent of our warmest aspiration." This William (better known as "Bill") Johnson was one of the leading actors in the burning of the *Sir Robert Peel*, and later promised help, which at the last moment he failed to give, to the expedition under the brave an misguided Von Shoultz.

Again, in an article published on the twenty-fourth of November, after the news had been received of the result of the last named expedition, he says: "Two years more of even such warfare as we have already seen will make England and her millions heartily sick of both the Canadas."

The "bounden duty," he declares, of "the friends of Canadian freedom" is "by harassing the enemy in large and small bodies – by cutting off their forces – by coming on them by day and night, and striking terror and panic into them, to render the country whose freedom they have destroyed too hot for them." By "they" the British are to be understood, the constant effort of the *Gazette* being to represent Canada as held down by British troops, while the truth as regards Upper Canada, as Mackenzie well knew, was that the rebellion set on foot by him had been quelled by the unaided and voluntary efforts of the provincial militia. The regular troops were solely employed (in connection with the militia) to repel attacks on the frontier made almost entirely by foreigners.

Mackenzie must have forgotten these utterances when he made his affidavit in 1839 as to his attitude as early as June 1838; and possibly he had forgotten the affidavit when, on the seventeenth of June, 1840, he wrote from Pine Orchard House in the Catskill Mountains to a fellow refugee a letter the significant portions of which are as follows:

I may say to you that a war is to be waged with British commerce, British goods, British shipping &c., that may tell fearfully, yet do those engaged in it little harm. We ought never to have given the European robbers a moment of rest – it is attended with bad consequences. . . . The weak point in British power is her commerce; there we'll try to cripple her; see if we don't. . . . If you know of any shrewd and daring fellows who would repair to the frontier when wanted, to burn a church of England, a fleet, a barrack, or a warehouse, let me know directed to Rochester as usual. But burn or conceal this letter, *show it to no one*. . . . I believe you will find that the Kingston fire ($50,000 loss) was not accidental. A person (patriot) left the town with the heat to prevent apprehension, and came over to Montgomery's.[13] He was a relative of some banished.[14]

This does not read quite like the letter of a person in full possession of his reasoning faculties, and some allowance may perhaps be made for it on that ground.

If such an excuse can be urged, it would apply also to his *Caroline Almanac and American Farmer's Chronicle*, produced in the fall or early winter of the year 1839, the

year of the affidavit. "Remember the Caroline" was the
lesson of the title page, on which appeared an excessively
rude wood-cut representing the dead body of a man lying
on a wharf just above the falls of Niagara, while the steamer
Caroline in flames was in the middle of the stream on the
point of plunging into the abyss. In point of fact Fort Schlosser, where Amos Durfee was killed, was fully two miles
above the Falls; but the Falls were wanted in the picture
for the sake of the *Caroline*; and as the corpse would not
have shown to any advantage at a distance of two miles, it
was brought into the foreground at the expense of the
topographical truth. Another picture is meant to represent
the double hanging of Matthews and Lount, with Indian
savages employed to guard the scaffold. The first item of
general information given, after the astronomical date for
the year, is an account of the British cabinet. The salary
received by each member is mentioned, with whatever, true
or false, can be alleged to his discredit.[15] Under successive
dates throughout the year various calamitous events are
recorded in a manner intended to excite hatred against the
British nation and British authority in Canada. A very few
examples must suffice. Under January 5th, we read: "Von
Shoultz' murder sanctioned by the bloody Queen of
England." Under January 7th, it is stated that the men
composing the court martials in Canada were chosen
"because they would hang their nearest friend for profit and
promotion." The burden of January 8th is in part as follows:

> No treaty can bind the faithless and brutal government
> of England. We have read the mystery of Babylon in
> the seventeenth chapter of Revelations attentively, and
> are satisfied that 'the mother of harlots and abomina-
> tions of the earth' there spoken of is England, the
> bloody English power, which has ascended out of the
> bottomless pit; and that the prophesy of its destruction
> will be speedily fulfilled.

Ten days later, with reference to some executions that had
taken place in Lower Canada, the *Almanac* records that "all
these murders of the virtuous Canadians are urged on by
the bloody Queen of England, who is as keen for spilling
Canadian blood as her mad old grandfather, George the
Third." The *Almanac* was meant for circulation in the
United States; and, if it did not intensify whatever hatred

towards England already existed in that country, it failed of its object.

In quoting from the *Caroline Almanac*, we have have anticipated matters a little, for when it appeared, towards the close of 1839, Mackenzie was an inmate of a United States prison. The intervening events must be taken up in the next chapter.

CHAPTER NINETEEN

IMPRISONMENT AND OTHER VICISSITUDES

In following the fortunes of Mackenzie after the collapse of his attempt at armed rebellion, we have lost sight of his chief coadjutors. It is time now, for the connection of the narrative, to pick up some dropped threads. The skirmish of Tuesday night, the fifth of December, was enough for Rolph. He had no part in it, but he did not think it wise to await further developments. Wednesday morning saw him making for the west on the plea of an urgent professional call. The call was urgent enough, whether professional or not, to take him clean across the border; and the news he received a couple of days later must have made him thankful that so valuable a life as his had been plucked from the gallows. He paid a flying visit to Navy Island while the "patriots" were in occupation, but, if Mackenzie is to be trusted, he was so nervous that he could hardly be persuaded to sit down; and he did not remain more than an hour. He does not seem on that occasion to have incurred any reproach of treachery from Mackenzie or anyone else. On the contrary the patriots were extremely anxious to make use of him. It was proposed to employ him to collect money for the cause; and the following public notice was prepared:

Dr. John Rolph of Upper Canada, now at Buffalo, is authorized by the General Commanding the forces on Navy Island, and by the members of the Provisional Government established there, to receive all money that may be subscribed within the United States on behalf of the patriots striving to establish the independence of the Canadas.

Flattering as was this expression of confidence, the learned Doctor did not seem to think that he would shine with much lustre in the character of a collector even for so noble a cause; and across the document is written the disappointing note – "He declined." If we seek for the Peer Gynt of the Upper Canada rebellion, we need not go beyond John Rolph.[1] At the same time it may well be believed that a close view of the "Commander-in-Chief," who may possibly not have been sober at the time, and a further insight into the views of the "Chairman of the Provisional Government of Upper Canada" may have furnished him with pretty solid reasons for not committing himself to their schemes. Settling in Rochester, N.Y., Rolph carried on his profession there till the summer of 1843 when, on the recommendation of the council which Sir Charles Metcalfe had inherited from Sir Charles Bagot, commonly, but not accurately, called the first Lafontaine-Baldwin government, he, with a number of other refugees, received a free pardon, whereupon one and all hastened to return to Canada.

The capture of Lount, Matthews and Van Egmond was mentioned in a former chapter. The first two were put on trial for high treason, and condemned to death. Whether if Head, who, in his own way, understood the country, had remained as lieutenant governor, the sentence would have been carried out, may at least be doubted; though he could not have interfered to save them without going counter to a very strong popular sentiment. It is true that petitions were numerously signed, and not by reformers alone, praying that their lives might be spared; but the feeling of a much larger number was that an open attempt to subvert the institutions of the country by force of arms called for nothing less than capital punishment in the case of its chief promoters. As Mackenzie had escaped, Head might possibly have made successful appeal to a more generous and humane instinct; and no one can doubt that he would have been disposed to do so. This could hardly be expected, however, of General Arthur, a quite new man – he arrived at Toronto only on the twenty-third of March – and one much less indulgent by nature than his predecessor.[2] He consulted his council, and they were unanimous for letting the law take its course. He then called in the chief justice and the attorney general, and asked them separately to state their views: both agreed that there were no grounds whatever on which the condemned men could be recommended to mercy. In such circumstances what could he do – what could he be justified in doing? It has been charged against him that he appeared unmoved when the wife of Lount presented a petition praying that her husband's life might be spared, and threw herself at his feet in a passion of entreaty. A man of firm character, accustomed to self-repression, may appear externally unmoved, while struggling with the strongest impulses of sympathy and compassion. If, on this occasion, Arthur could not conscientiously yield, of what advantage would any show of emotion have been?[3]

There was no stay of the law, and the sentences on both men were carried into effect in front of the jail, which then stood on the corner of Court and Toronto street, at eight o'clock on the morning of the twelfth of April. Both met their fate with fortitude – a fate which, to this day, excites no small amount of commiseration. The despatches from the colonial office, written after the news had reached England, showed plainly that the Home government did not view the resort to capital punishment with approval; but all authorities up to the present time have insisted that Canadians on the spot are able to form a vastly corrector judgment of matters of immediate concern to themselves than the officials of Downing Street four thousand miles distant. Was this case an exception? If so, perhaps there were others.

Van Egmond, as commander in chief of the rebel forces, would probably have shared the fate of Lount and Matthews, had it not been that, in the cold cell to which he was consigned, he contracted inflammatory rheumatism, which necessitated his removal to the hospital, where not many days afterwards he died.

Feebly as the Upper Canada rebellion – if it must be called by that name – represents the horrors of civil war, if all the sorrowful and pathetic incidents to which it gave rise could be told the narrative would constitute a very painful chapter of history. Most of these today are buried in oblivion. The wounds are healed, the tears are dried, the hearts are stilled; and all the ache and burden of calamity are now part of the silent past. Was it all for naught? *That* some deep instinct forbids us to believe. In the greatest of the prophets it is declared: "I form the light and create darkness; I make peace and create evil;" while a lesser prophet boldly puts the question: "Shall there be evil in the city, and the Lord hath not done it?" Our own poet strikes a like note of faith when he affirms

That not a worm is clov'n in vain;
That not a moth, with vain desire,
Is shrivelled in a fruitless fire,
Or but subserves another's gain.

The mystery of pain outruns human understanding; but this at least it is permitted to believe, that in what we call evil, all is not evil, and that in the deepest darkness the seeds of light are sown.

The support given to *Mackenzie's Gazette* was not encouraging. Two months after its establishment, as Mr. Lindsey tells us,[4] "the publisher complained that, of the subscribers, about one fifth had paid from one dollar to three each – the annual subscription price was three dollars – and that the remaining four fifths had paid nothing." After a further trial of six months it was decided to transfer the paper to the city of Rochester, N.Y., as being nearer to Canada, as well as to the localities in which the Canadian refugees and their sympathisers chiefly congregated, and thus more distinctly the centre of interest in Canadian affairs and filibustering enterprises than the great commercial metropolis, where Canada was not really an absorbing topic. Mr. Mackenzie's family at this time consisted of a wife and six or seven children. Removing with him to Rochester they entered there upon a very distressing chapter of experiences. Strangers in a strange land, they had to encounter the extremes of poverty. Sickness and death cast an additional shadow over the household; and, to crown their misfortunes, the wife had to witness the imprisonment for eleven months, under rigorous conditions, of her husband, the father of their children. It is indeed impossible to read of their situation without deep commiseration and sympathy. In the mind of Mackenzie himself it was clear whence all this trouble and wretchedness flowed: it was purely the fault of the loyalists of Upper Canada, those despicable men who were mean enough not to be dissatisfied to the point of rebellion with the institutions under which they lived. A singular trait in Mackenzie's character was the lack of any sense of responsibility for his own actions and their results. He was ready enough to acknowledge errors of opinion, and was continually doing so; but there the thing ended: it never seemed to lie on his conscience or his heart that, through the vehement expression of ill-natured or ill-grounded opinions, he had led others into deep distress, and had brought some to their death. The misfortunes of these were all laid to the charge of the government of Upper Canada and its supporters. Mackenzie himself, in his own estimation, stood absolutely clear.[5]

In the fall of the year 1838 Mr. Mackenzie made a tour of some of the principal cities of the United States in order to advocate on the platform the "independence" of Canada. Mr. Lindsey compares his mission with that of Kossuth[6] in the early fifties, but the resemblance is certainly not close. Kossuth had been a responsible minister, and, in the hour of trouble, had been named dictator of a country in arms which for a time had withstood the combined forces of two first class powers, Austria and Russia; and which, in the end, only yielded to overwhelming military compulsion. Mr. Mackenzie did not represent Upper Canada; Upper Canada was not, and had not been, in arms, except to the extent necessary to disperse the internal disturbers of her peace (which had been done with less loss of life than frequently attends a street riot), and to repell the foreign foes who were assailing her frontier in the interest of the defeated faction; finally Upper Canada had not been crushed by military power, but had simply employed a small portion of her own military power to crush an unjustifiable and feeble insurrection. It is doubtful whether under quite similar circumstances Kossuth would have gone in quest of aid to the United States.

The response to Mackenzie's appeal, save in the matter of cheers and cries of "Go On!," was remarkably slender.[7] "You have seen," a correspondent writes to him in December, 1838, "splendid assemblies in Albany and New York – large committees appointed to make large collections. Not a man of them has moved, not a farthing has been obtained." The reason assigned by the writer was that the government at Washington had expressed disapproval of the proceeding; but surely what kind of liberty was enjoyed in "free America," if the government at Washington could browbeat its citizens into refusing financial aid to the sacred cause of liberty in an adjoining country? The family compact should have gone to Washington to take a few lessons in the art of curbing the people.

Mr. Mackenzie, as we have seen, on leaving Navy Island with Mrs. Mackenzie was arrested at Buffalo for breach of the United States neutrality laws. In May of the following year a true bill was found against him at Albany. He declared himself ready for trial, but the state attorney was not ready to proceed, and the case was adjourned till October. At the appointed time he repaired to Albany only to find that, by a statute passed in the interval, it had become necessary further to postpone the trial till June of the following year (1839), and then, to hold it at Canandaigua, the chief town of Ontario county. Finally the trial came off on the twentieth of that month, and lasted two days, Mackenzie as usual defending himself. The main charge was that he had, on United States territory, set on foot, or aided in setting on foot, a military expedition against a part of the dominions of Great Britain, a power with which the United States was at peace. The first witness for the state, one Joseph B. Lathrop, testified that, at the Buffalo meeting on the twelfth of December, Mackenzie "proceeded to give the grievances of the Canadians, and, in reading our Declaration, drew a parallel between the grievances set forth therein and those complained of by the Canadians; alluded to the succour this country had received from other nations and called upon the people to give aid." Mackenzie took his innings in a six hour speech which, of course, wandered very far from the simple issue which the jury had to try, whether he had, or had not been concerned in setting on foot a military expedition against Canada. In addressing the jury the prosecuting attorney stated that, on the very night of the meeting at which Mackenzie spoke, "violence was done to the court house, and two hundred stand of arms belonging to the state, or to the city of Buffalo, were clandestinely taken and carried away."

The six hours that Mackenzie took gave him ample time for irrelevant matter and futile objections. One of these objections was that the witness Lathrop did not swear to "the exact words" he (Mackenzie) had used at the meeting. Another was that Canada was not rightly described as "a province of the Crown of England." "If I can prove," he said, "that Canada is *not* a province of the Crown, then every count in the indictment fails." The court said that it was enough that Canada was recognized as such by the federal government, which controlled all foreign relations. He also wished to prove by Lord Durham's report that anarchy reigned in the province, and that there was no government at the time of the outbreak. He "objected absolutely" to the admission that Queen Victoria was sovereign of England and the Canadas. "I affirm," he said, "that the girl has forfeited all right to rule over any part of what she claims as her dominions. I was born," he went on to say, "under the reign of her uncle,[8] and have long been tired of their usurped tyranny." He referred to the fact that, as yet, not a single American citizen had been put on trial for violation of the law which he was charged with having broken, in spite of their notorious participation in military enterprises against Canada. "We," he exclaimed,

> are poor exiles, refugees, wanderers in your land, little cared for and indeed despised, and is not this misery enough? Must we be placed as felons and criminals before your people, and singled out for the cell, the victims of British interest, British influence, and British gold. Surely you will never say it. Such a verdict could consign me to a prison, and leave my children without bread; but to you it would be perpetual infamy.[9]

The jury did not decide hastily. They took three hours to digest all they had heard and then brought in a verdict of guilty. Judge Smith Thompson, who presided, found some extenuating circumstances in the case, and imposed a sentence of eighteen months imprisonment in Monroe county jail with a fine of ten dollars: the maximum sentence would have been three years imprisonment and a fine of three thousand dollars.

It was Mackenzie's expectation that, as his offence was of a political character, his incarceration would be accompanied by privileges not accorded to ordinary criminals. In this he was disappointed. We have descriptions of his situation from his own pen in letters addressed to the secretary of state and the secretary of the treasury at Washington. In the letter addressed to the former, a copy of which was sent to every member of Congress, he says:

> The prison is on a small island on the marshy flats of the Genessee river, so low that, while I write, all around the jail is overflowed. Under my windows are floods of standing water, which became very unwholesome in the warm weather; and when I add that a soap

and candle factory, a variety of dwellings for pigs, and other filthy dwellings are on the island under my window, you will agree with me that, apart from constant confinement indoors, there is a source of malaria enough to sicken an army. . . . My family are not prevented from coming to see me, and the sheriff and jailer have stated that they would have much pleasure in allowing me to take exercise in the open yard if they could have obtained a shadow of permission from the marshal. He says he has written you repeatedly for orders and cannot get a syllable from you in return.

In another part of the same letter he says:

When I was locked up in prison, a felon's night pail and a seat or bunk were all the furniture allowed me, to which a stove was afterwards added. Food, bed, bedding, night-light, everything else but wood, had to be provided from the scanty means left my family by the loyalists.

This fling at the "loyalists" was in no way creditable to Mackenzie. As we have seen, he himself had distinctly threatened all who might oppose his movement with confiscation of their property.[10] The "loyalists" confiscated no man's estates, not even Mackenzie's.[11] By his own act he had deprived himself of his Canadian citizenship, and the verdict of a United States jury had consigned him to prison. Save by process of law for debt, his property was untouched; and, when he returned to Canada some years later, he was still in possession of some real estate at Dundas, if not elsewhere.

What answer or acknowledgement the secretary of state gave to this letter there is nothing to show; but it received some consideration, for, on the twenty-third of October, just as Mackenzie, despairing of the success of his appeal, was indicting a memorial to the President, the secretary wrote to the marshal, N. Garrow by name, instructing him to see that no unnecessary severity was inflicted on the prisoner.[12]

There is a letter extant from the latter functionary dealing with the question whether the jailer should receive compensation for Mr. Mackenzie's board seeing that his food was entirely provided by his family. It may be quoted as throwing a little light on Mackenzie as a prisoner:

> The jailer claims that he has great trouble with Mr. Mackenzie, and that he should have full compensation as if he had furnished him with food, inasmuch as he is put to as much extra trouble by the food being furnished from without as if he did the whole thing himself. . . . I had hoped that Mr. Mackenzie would have suffered himself to have conformed to the circumstances of his case; for I am persuaded he would have engaged more sympathy in his behalf by a reasonable yielding to the mandates of the law than by continued complaints.[13]

The main object of the letter to the secretary of the treasury, Mr. Levi Woodbury, which was written on the nineteenth of January, 1841, some eight months after Mackenzie's liberation, was to obtain a refund of expenses for food, &c. incurred during his imprisonment. "Here, in free America," he writes, "I was imprisoned on the criminal side of the jail in June, 1839, and for months kept close in one apartment, bolted and barred and grated, and never for an instant suffered to quit it, to breathe the fresh air, nor for any purpose." The food tendered to him, he says, was the ordinary prison fare, consisting of "mush and molasses once a day and soup and offals once a day." This he would not touch: his family were allowed to provide his food and did so. "It is submitted whether the United States or the family of a broken-down exile, invited to your shores under the seal of friendship . . . ought to pay the expenses after eleven months confinement on a marsh." There is a decidedly feminine touch in some of the utterances of Mackenzie, and this about being "invited to your shores under the seal of friendship," and also his statement about the loyalists having stripped him of all his possessions, are certainly cases in point. History has it that he, Rolph, and other leaders in the rebellion issued very urgent invitations to themselves to visit the shores of the United States; and lucky were they who succeeded in gaining those shores. It seems to have been simply impossible to Mackenzie to take the facts and laws of life seriously.

The result of the intervention of the Washington authorities was that Mr. Mackenzie was first permitted to take exercise in a large attic extended over the entire building, and subsequently in the jail yard. Apparently he was able during the whole period of his imprisonment to write for his paper, which, beginning with the issue of the twenty-ninth of June, bore on the date line, as the place of publication, "Monroe County Jail." This was changed a few weeks later to "The American Bastille." Possibly the word "American" may have given offence, for it was shortly dropped, and the place of publication styled simply "The Bastille."

During Mr. Mackenzie's incarceration an event occurred which he felt very deeply – the death of his mother, who for years had been a member of his household. As it appeared that no permission could be granted for him to go and see her in her last illness, he wrote her a farewell letter in which he said: "If all the wealth of the world were mine, and it would carry me to your bedside, I would give it freely; but wealth I have none, and of justice there is but little here." A means was, however, devised, with the connivance of the authorities, by which he was able to see his dying parent. His friend, Mr. John Montgomery, who, as already mentioned, had resumed in Rochester his former occupation of hotel keeping, brought suit (by agreement) against one of his boarders for money due, and Mr. Mackenzie was summoned as a witness. The state attorney gave permission for the holding of the court in Mr. Mackenzie's house. But Mr. Lindsey, from whom these facts are borrowed, should be left to tell the tale:

The magistrate was not very punctual in arriving; he was very kind and very cold when he did arrive, and was some time before he was sufficiently warmed to open his court; and, when it did open, witnesses who had nothing particular to say were examined at a considerable length. By this stratagem, Mr. Mackenzie's last interview with his aged and dying mother was protracted five or six hours. It was an affecting scene. The mother was leaving an only son overwhelmed with calamities: failing health – for the ague had again returned upon him – increasing poverty; a helpless family dependent upon him; and a prison for his home. The jailer and the sheriff were waiting, and the interview must come to a close. Summoning for the last time all her fortitude, the dying mother pronounced her last farewell, bidding her son trust in God and fear not. . . . She never spoke after he had gone back to his dreary prison.[14]

A few days later Mr. Mackenzie gazed on his mother's funeral as it passed his prison window.

In the fall of 1839 petitions for Mackenzie's pardon began to be sent to the President. For a time they produced no effect. Neither Mr. Van Buren nor the secretary of state, Mr. Forsyth, seemed at all disposed to move in the matter. They were willing to ameliorate to some extent the conditions of his confinement, but apparently saw no reasons for abridging his sentence. Finally however, as the movement in his favor grew in importance, it was decided to pardon him, and on the tenth of May, 1840, with over seven months of his sentence unfulfilled, he stepped from the jail at Rochester a free man.

Mackenzie's principal biographer dwells with some emphasis and feeling on the efforts made by the government of Upper Canada "to get Mr. Mackenzie into their power," with the purpose, as he says, "of strangling him." "Rewards for his apprehension," it is stated, "were held out as a premium to kidnappers, and his personal and political enemies clubbed their dollars into blood-money to make the temptation strong enough for some vile man-catcher to undertake the detestable speculation."[15] If it is meant that private rewards were added to the one publicly offered, some details might well have been given of what was actually done, together with a reference to the evidence. As to the government reward, it could only apply to arrest on Canadian soil, as the kidnapping of the culprit on American territory would have been followed by an immediate and peremptory demand by the United States government for his restoration to the protection of their flag. The offering of a reward for a culprit actually on foreign soil could not legitimately be construed as an incitement to kidnapping; for the culprit might at any moment take it into his head to visit, for one purpose or another, the country from which he had fled, as Mackenzie in fact did in the winter of 1838-39, when he made a dash by night across the ice to the neighborhood of Bath on the Bay of Quinte.

The last number of Mackenzie's *Gazette* was issued on the twenty-third of December, 1840. There had never been an effective demand for it; and, now that there was little or nothing doing on the frontier, such demand as once existed had practically come to an end. A year had elapsed since the publication of the *Caroline Almanac*, and six months since the indicting of that letter from the Catskill mountains in which a general war was declared on British commerce, and volunteers were called for to fire Canadian towns; so Mackenzie was now free to write in his valedictory as follows: "A close observation of the state of society here has lessened my regrets at the results of the opposition raised to England in Canada in 1837-38." As usual, a frank confession of change of opinion, and as usual there it ends – no evidence of any of personal responsibility for sorrow caused or mischief done through hasty action, founded (to use his own expression) on "surface views." He could denounce the loyalists for hanging Lount and Matthews and Morrow and Shoultz; but that he should himself have disseminated opinions, excited hopes, and nourished animosities which led directly to these tragic occurrences called for nothing more than an acknowledgment that he had been mistaken; and that he handsomely made.

Shortly before the *Gazette* passed out of existence Mackenzie bethought himself of applying for admission to the bar of Monroe country. A copy of his application has been preserved. He speaks of the many offices he had held in Canada: one of a judicial character, that of mayor and magistrate of the city of Toronto, and others, such as chairmanships of legislative committees, of a kind to render him familiar with the nature of law and legal procedure. He also mentioned that he had pleaded on several occasions in the superior courts of Upper Canada; but did not explain that this was only when defending himself in libel suits. He told, not without exaggeration, of what he had done, as "secretary to fifty thousand Americans," to prevent the first Naturalization bill passing; and states that in 1838 he had taken the preliminary steps towards becoming an American citizen, and "made the usual declaration of adherence to the principles of American institutions, to the sincerity of which his whole life is a testimony." Mackenzie himself informs us of the facts of his application: written in his own hand across the copy are the words: "A few days after, Judge Dayton wrote me that the court had with great unanimity refused my request.

The situation of the exile becomes now for a time a very pitiable one indeed. No one can withhold sympathy from the father of a numerous family who, though straining every nerve, is yet unable to provide them with the necessaries of life. As early as May, 1838, he had been obliged to raise money upon the security of the gold medal presented to him in 1832 by the electors of York. Now in 1841 he had to meet the note then given, and to do it the medal had to go into the melting pot. "During the winter of 1841-42," says Mr. Lindsey,

> the exile and his family drank the cup of poverty to the dregs. One night, when the younger children were crying for food, he went to the cupboard to see whether there was nothing to be found there. All he got was a book, of which, by the light of the feeble embers that formed the only light and the only fire, he discovered that the title was 'The Dark Ages'; at which he could not help indulging in a hearty laugh, after which the family went supperless and breakfastless to bed.[16]

Mackenzie had at all times a keen sense of humour, but it probably never asserted itself under more painful circumstances than these.

Mackenzie was through life a copious letter writer, yet of letters written by himself comparatively few are available for consultation. On the other hand his papers contain a very large collection of letters addressed to him; and many of these are instructive as showing the relations he sustained with the writers and the impression he had made upon them. There are letters extending over a period of fourteen years from General Donald McLeod, a "patriot" who had once been a soldier in the British army, and who afterwards taught school at Brockville. He was an admirer of Van Rensselaer, from whom he got his commission, for, in a letter dated the sixteenth of February, 1838, addressed to that worthy, he says: "When your name is spoken each man appears enlivened, and are (sic) ready to rush on and sustain the shock of bottle." This "despatch" was written at Sandusky, Ohio; he says that he expects to date the next in Canada. His hopes were not fulfilled. On the twenty-fifth of February he and his men occupied Fighting Island near Sandwich; but, instead of "sustaining the shock of battle," they beat a precipitate retreat when fire was opened on them from the Canadian shore. On reaching the American side they were disarmed by the authorities. On the first of November, 1838, McLeod writes to Mackenzie expressing a good deal of dissatisfaction at the lack of interest shown by supposed American friends of the patriot movement. A meeting had been held at Cleveland at which it was resolved to raise $10,000 for the cause. Up to date only $300 had been collected, and the general was in serious doubt whether the patriots would see any portion ever of that modest sum. In a letter dated in April, 1840, he informs Mackenzie that he is keeping up "an active correspondence with the friends, in the London and Western districts," and finds them "very sanguine in the hopes of a war between the British and American governments." In the same letter he speaks of a great revival that had taken place at Cleveland. "I need not," he adds, "ask you, who had so good and pious a mother, whether you are in possession of the pearl of great price. . . . You must surely possess a great portion of religion, or you could never endure so much of torturing and almost insufferable punishments." In the month of August following his tone is changed, and we find him accusing Mackenzie of half-heartedness in the patriot cause if not of absolute treachery. "Shortly after your enlargement," he says,

you wrote me that you were ready to drive ahead and go three steps beyond what I proposed last June.[17] I believed you. From Washington you wrote me, after speaking very unfavourably of Van Buren, as follows: 'There is no shadow of hope for us except in our own exertions. . . . The presidential question should be abandoned, and we should be neutral, for we are weak and want the aid of all our friends.' It seems you have received new light since that. You have now taken the stump for the man who harassed, persecuted and imprisoned you, and who, by his never to be forgotten proclamation published to the world that we were 'a nefarious set of ruffians. It is our abidng interest to ensure Van Buren's election. . . . If he fails, God help us poor exiles! we'll have hard times of it.' Are you *compos mentis*? When had the exiles anything but the worst of usuage from him? Your long imprisonment has impaired your mind. I am sorry for it. You are one moment for Van; the next you are opposed to him; the third you are on the stump for him. One day for war and the emancipation of Canada, the second for peace, the third for half-way measures, the fourth for nothing at all. You go by fits and starts, promising much and performing nothing.[18] Canada must now be abandoned for the election of that cut throat, Van Buren. But perhaps he has thrown some new light into your pockets while you were at Washington. . . . You have urged me for plans; they are no sooner proposed than you reject them. You will not propose any yourself, nor adopt those that are formed; not from their deficiency but from your contrariness. . . . In fact I am sincerely of the opinion that you are inadequate to any great and noble undertaking.

All we know of Mackenzie's reply to this letter is that he said it was "imprudent" – the word being quoted in a further letter of McLeod's dated in the following month – and that he indignantly repelled the insinuation of bribery. McLeod took the ground that the facts did not admit of any other construction. "I am now satisfied," he added,

that your object has been merely to keep the Canadian tories in hot water without any nobler views. Dr. Duncombe has returned disheartened; he believes, as I do, that you never was [sic] intended to direct the movements of so great and momentous a concern as the independence of the Canadas; we must look for some one else, or drop the cause altogether. The latter I think is the better plan. For my own part I am heartily sick of it. I have met with nothing but treachery, deceptions and disappointments from first to last. . . . From this moment and henceforth I renounce all connection with the cause on this side of the lines. It commenced foolish and ended ruinous, at least to me.

He concludes with the remark that, if his letter was "imprudent," Mackenzie's was "pre-eminently so, with interest."

This Brutus and Cassius quarrel was patched up in some way – there is nothing to show how, but probably by the frank withdrawal by McLeod of his insulting insinuations against Mackenzie. On the seventh of December 1841 we find him writing: "It is so long since I have had a scratch of a pen from you that I can no longer rest until I hear from you. Depend upon it, you have not a warmer or sincerer friend in North America than the subscriber." He proceeds to discuss the Canadian situation: "Canada, for want of courage and manly heart has like the sluggard laid [*sic*] down to slumber in the arms of her oppressers" – it did not apparently occur to the ex-schoolmaster that the arms in which you can slumber must make you pretty comfortable –

and prefers to hug the chains of her political degradation to a noble and heroic assertion of her natural rights. At the present moment they are like the sow that was washed (returning)[19] to her wallowing in the mire. Poor devils! They are not worth a serious thought. . . . However you may disagree with me, I nevertheless sincerely, solemnly, and honestly declare that they are a poor, ignorant, miserable, indolent, time-serving set of cravens and poltroons, who talk much and do nothing, and are unworthy of the blessings of liberty. . . . Ah, sir, what fools we were to hazard our lives at the cannon's mouth for such a clownish people!

If McLeod ever hazarded his life at the cannon's mouth, history has let the fact slip: the only military exploit to the *actif* of his Canadian record was his very fugitive occupation of Fighting Island.

Six months later McLeod wrote:

I have travelled much in my time, and seen a great deal of the world; but, in all my peregrinations, I never met but with one true patriot, and that was yourself. Through thick and thin, through evil as well as good report, you never wavered; neither bribes nor threats, the hope of favour nor the fear of punishment, could change your purpose or affect your principles. Posterity will do you justice.

Then follows a really remarkable prediction: "I have a strong presentiment resting on my mind (but you must not laugh at it) that, prior to the year 1853, you will represent a constituency in Canada, and with greater *éclat* than ever." The presentiment came true with more than a year to spare; for on the fifteenth of April, 1851, Mackenzie, pardoned and restored to Canada, was elected to represent the county of Haldimand in the legislative assembly. McLeod himself,

in spite of his excessively mean opinion of the Canadian
people, took the earliest opportunity presented by a general
pardon to return to Canada, where after a time he obtained
some government employment. We find him in 1851 settled
at Sparta in the county of Elgin, several letters dated from
that place being among the Mackenzie papers.

After the discontinuance of his *Gazette* Mackenzie strove
vainly for about a year and a half to make a living for his
family in Rochester. Towards the end of the period he confessed, in a letter to his son, to have been "starved out." In an
earlier letter to the same he had said: "The more I see of this
country, the more do I regret the attempt at revolution at
Toronto and St. Charles." This is an advance upon the statement in his valedictory, in which he merely spoke of lessened
regret at the *failure* of his attempt; now it is increasing to
regret *that the attempt was ever made*. To incur defeat, to
endure misery, and involve in the same misery a dependent
household – to say nothing of the misery caused to multitudes
of others – is bitter enough even in a good cause; but when
one is compelled, on reflection and further acquaintance with
facts, to condemn the cause itself, the situation, one would
suppose, would become almost unbearable. Mackenzie's mercurial temperament enabled him, however, as a general thing,
to make comparatively little of the matter; and, after his
return to Canada, his tone in referring to it was usually one
of levity and jocosity.

Mackenzie now decided to remove to New York, as afford-
ing a wider field and more hopeful opportunities for his
energies and talents; and on the tenth of June, 1842 – friends
having advanced the necessary funds, he took passage to that
city on a canal boat for himself and his family. Before following him thither it may be helpful, towards an understanding
of the times, to glance at the letters of two other correspondents of somewhat more note than "General" Donald
McLeod, namely Thomas Storrow Brown and E. B. O'Callaghan, both prominent in the Lower Canada rebellion. Brown
was in political principle a violent radical, and had sided with
the *Fils de Liberté*, a French Canadian revolutionary club in
an *emeute* which took place in the streets of Montreal on the
sixth of November 1837. Later he found himself, most
accidentally he declares, in command of the rebels at St.
Charles. O'Callaghan was the editor of the *Vindicator*, a
paper which did much to foster the revolutionary spirit.

On the first of July, 1838, Brown writes in terms of high appreciation of the course so far followed by Mackenzie: "You alone of all who have *driven the people of Canada into their present troubles*, are the only one who has done his duty in earnestly devoting all the energy given him by his Creator in aiding, assisting and carrying on everything connected with the work begun." The words we have ventured to italicize seem to express rather more truth than might have been looked for from such a source. "Somebody," the writer continues, "I supposed O'Callaghan, is giving, I am sorry to see, good advice to Durham in the Burlington *Sentinel*. For God's sake don't tell these imported things what they should do to succeed in their mission. Let Durham break his neck like his predecessors."[20] Mackenzie at this time had a high opinion of Papineau and was constantly eulogizing him. Brown too thought highly of his abilities and accomplishments, but considered that he had been proved "unequal to the emergencies of the times." "With these views," he continues, "I do not wish to hear him called the Washington of Canada till he has proved himself worthy of the appellation." The epithet quoted may perhaps have been applied by Mackenzie: Brown was right; Papineau was not much more of a Washington than Mackenzie himself. The temper of this man is further shown in a letter dated Key West, Florida, 25th November, 1838, in which he says:

> You should insist that our people should not be so regardful of property. . . . Why is the St. John railroad not destroyed?[21] I have seen by my own experience that nothing but an excuse is sometimes wanted for stringing up such persons as Brown, Ellice and Ross[22] to the first tree. . . . Depend upon it, a dozen of the leading tories of Montreal or Quebec swinging on the trees would do more to make reasonable men of the rest than all the arguments your *Gazette* could publish in ten years.

The next letter was written in March, 1840, when Mackenzie had been nearly nine months in prison. The writer expresses his surprise that any jury could have found a verdict for breach of neutrality against one who was, "to use your own phrase, 'but a fly on the wheel' of general excitement." Mackenzie, as an innocent fly on a fiercely whirling wheel of excitement, is quite a striking image, considering the many wheels of excitement he set in motion in his day.

Brown by this time had become greatly interested in United
States politics, and a warm partisan of Van Buren. Though
he could blame the jury for their verdict, he could not blame
the President for not interfering with it. "I think," he says,
"he is right. I look upon the power of pardon in a chief
magistrate as a monstrous and dangerous power – a relic of
the principle that the king is master of the life and liberties
of his subjects." He goes on to speak of the way in which the
pardoning power is abused in the United States – usually in
favor of "some scion of our puny aristocracy, whose influential friends get at the governor of the state." It is
singular that this deadly foe of British institutions should not
have drawn his examples rather from Canada and Great
Britain than from the American democracy – that is to say if
he could have done so.

Eight years later this gentleman writes from Montreal,
where he had again found a home in spite of the attractions
of the Great Republic. Popular government has been established, liberalism is in the ascendant, and yet he is horribly
disgusted with the political situation. What he has seen since
his return has been "quite enough to open one's eyes to the
folly of any one man wasting his time or talent against the
current of colonial mismanagement and corruption." Very
similar were the conclusions – as we shall hereafter see – to
which Mackenzie himself came after a brief experience of the
new system. Brown finds that during his absence a lot of
people whom he formerly regarded as opponents have turned
"liberals," and yet he does not at all rejoice, like the angels
in heaven, over these repenting sinners. To him they seem
consummate humbugs. As to responsible government this
critic sees very little in it.

> You have heard that we are blessed with the boon of
> 'responsible government,' and having committed the
> phrase to memory, you know exactly as much about it
> as anybody else; for it is one of those admirable
> mysteries which the muddy headed gentleman who in-
> vented the phrase,[23] and the infants who can repeat the
> sound, can explain with equal clearness.[24]

Further expounding his views he observes:

> If he (the Governor) is to be a mere machine with no
> will of his own . . . let him be a cheap automaton of

wood, and not a living being with $30,000 a year . . . with nothing to console him in his degradation but his salary and the song of the Vicar of Bray. . . . Her Majesty's ministers and others who debated 'responsible government' cautiously decided it were best to attempt no reasonable definition of it.

He also speaks of "the battle between Robert Baldwin and Dommick [sic] Daly *for the possession of the governor.*"

The letter concludes with a high eulogy of Mackenzie. "You are acknowledged to have done more good for Upper Canada than any other public writer; and few men who have written so much have written more truthfully." The important positions and missions which Mackenzie had filled are mentioned, and regret is expressed that he is now (1846) involving himself in newspaper squabbles, and exposing himself to the "undiscriminating jeers of a ribald press."

E. B. O'Callaghan was a man of higher culture than Brown and of more generous temper. He was much troubled, as his letters show, over the censorious and suspicious disposition constantly manifested by Mackenzie – a characteristic with which no fault had been found by Brown. Writing on the sixteenth of October, 1838, he says: "A man that throws as many stones as you do ought to be perfect, . . . but I cannot be brought to believe in your perfection, until I see that you are less suspicious and less given to grumbling." In March, 1841, he has a word to say about American politics:

I have been over three years in these states. Month after month has brought its excitement. One time this, to'ther time that. Yet have they all been raised by vile, interested party politicians for mere party purposes; and when they served these mean ends they have been thrown aside, and the great gaping vulgar multitude again excited by some new soap-bubble.

These revolutionists – Brown who regarded "responsible government" as a kind of humbugging mystification, and O'Callaghan with his poor opinion of the "gaping multitude" – do not seem to have had quite as much faith in "the people" as one could have expected.

Mackenzie had at first conceived a very high opinion of Papineau. Later he became suspicious of him, and O'Callaghan writing in August, 1844, defends the Lower Canadian leader against Mackenzie's criticism. He himself, however, is not an ardent admirer of Lafontaine, of whom he says: "He is not the man to remember you or me. You and the like of us made him what he was, and he has followed the example of Pharoah's chief butler, a description of which you will find in Genesis XI.23." Of the Lafontaine-Baldwin administration (so called) he says:

> No wonder that Metcalfe concluded there was 'no health in it.' It is my opinion that they should have made a general amnesty a *sine que non* before entering into office under Bagot. But they went in making seemingly no condition, but that Mr. Baldwin was to have the management of the patronage in Upper, and Mr. Lafontaine in Lower, Canada.

Shortly before this Mackenzie had been entertaining hopes of getting an inspectorship of customs at New York; but the proposition caused a great outcry in the press. He himself thought the opposition came entirely from the whig party, which he had before opposed; but O'Callaghan assures him that such is not the case. There is a coterie, he says, consisting of men of both parties, amongst whom there is a great hatred of "adopted citizens." He then advises him as follows: "If you could keep quiet, I think it would be better for you; but perhaps this you cannot do. Byron said that 'quiet was a hell' to souls like his; and perhaps 'tis the same with you." He asks him why he could not occupy his mind by learning German or Gaelic. "This would 'consume' your pent up steam, and give you time to breath."

Mackenzie having continued in his letters to asperse the character of Papineau, O'Callaghan replies (12th November, 1844) with some warmth:

> I cannot allow even the better feelings of my nature to lead me into the grave error of countenancing in any way, direct or indirect, the many injustices of which you have been guilty, in my opinion, towards one to whom you know I am attached by every bond that can unite one honourable man to another. . . . The whole course of your reasoning was founded only on surmise, suspicion, distrust. . . . I have long ago told you that you are a prey to this corroding weakness. You tell me that you are more – that you are Scotch: I do not understand the point of the expression.

The writer proceeds to say that he knows Scotland and the Scotch through the writings of Campbell, Burns, Carlyle, Scott and others, and cannot therefore think less favorably of him on account of his nationality. "Believe me," he says, "your own character is liable to suffer more from this disposition than you are aware of." Papineau, however, was not the only one whom Mackenzie had attacked. He had had some bitter things to say about Viger and D. B. Papineau (brother of L. J.) for joining the Draper administration under Sir Charles Metcalfe. Remarking that christian charity made it a duty "to put the most favourable construction on the motives of men who, we know, must entertain at least as warm, and as sincere a love for their fellow countrymen as we possibly can," he renews his general warning in these words:

> Go on if you choose entertaining suspicions of others which you would not wish them to entertain of you. Put as many unfavourable constructions as you please on the actions of others, and deny them love of country, honourable views and sincere patriotism and ring the changes on 'fattening at the public crib.' But believe one who often felt for you, but who never flattered you – believe me when I say that such a course as this will only reflect on your own public character when you are in the grave, and paralyse your efficiency for good while you are living.

It would have been well if Mackenzie, even at this late date, could have heeded his friend's admonition; but the defence which he set up, that he was Scotch, indicates a consciousness that his waters of bitterness came from a very deep spring. And yet the man did injustice to himself, for the deepest springs of all in his nature were springs of humanity and benevolence. He loved his fellowmen in the mass, but his life was twisted and deformed by the enmity he held to a few.

Mr. Lindsey, whose work will always be the chief source of information respecting Mackenzie's private life, tells us that, upon arriving in New York, "he refused situations in two or three newspaper offices, because he would not occupy a subordinate position on the press" –"no bad illustration," his biographer adds, "of his character." He obtained employment for a time as actuary of the Mechanics' Institute, but the emoluments were so small that [at] the end of 1843 he

resigned. Through the influence of a son of President Tyler
he was nominated to an inspectorship of customs, but the
nomination was not confirmed by the United States senate.
The salary was to have been $1,000 a year; and, on the
strength of his expectations, he rented a large and fine house
on William street, for which he was to pay $450 a year.
Young Mr. Tyler continued his interest in him, and shortly
procured a situation for him in the archives office of the New
York customs, but with a salary of only $700 a year. The big
house had to be given up for a smaller one across the East
river. While examining the records of the New York customs
Mr. Mackenzie, we are told, discovered some letters relating
to a defalcation of a former collector of that port, which
formed in part the foundation of a work which he published
in 1846 and the copyright of which he sold for $1000, en-
titled *The Life and Times of Martin Van Buren*. The book
was a heavy onslaught on Van Buren, against whom the
letters in question furnished, Mr. Lindsey states, very damaging evidence.

In the same year (1846) he became connected with the
New York Tribune, having, we must suppose, conquered his
objection to subordinate positions; and from this time forward, his financial position was easier. He wrote important
letters to the *Tribune* as their correspondent at Albany when
the revision of the state constitution was under consideration.
He now received many offers of literary employment. He
could also have obtained control of a large and profitable
printing business, if he would have consented to take a
partner, but as his biographer states, he "disliked partner-
ships." Notwithstanding these comparatively fair prospects
Mr. Mackenzie longed to return to the country whose government he had sought to overturn; and finally the opportunity
to do so was afforded to him by an act of amnesty passed by
the Canadian parliament in January, 1849, and assented to
by Lord Elgin, in the Queen's name, on the first of the following month. An experimental trip which he made to
Toronto in March was the occasion of a disgraceful riot, in
which it was made evident, not for the first, nor for the last
time, that high toryism and rowdyism have some deep affinity.
It must nevertheless [have] been manifest that, so far as the
bulk of respectable opinion was concerned, there was no
objection to the return of the exile; because, in May of the
following year (1850), he moved with his family to Toronto,

and once more took up his residence in that city, not however to play the part in it that he had once played. He was
by no means an old man – only fifty-five – but he was no
longer in touch with the politics of the country; and politics
was the only medium in which, so to speak, he could draw
breath. With its commercial, industrial, or educational interests he had never maintained any relations save through
politics. And now new political leaders had arisen, none of
whom courted his assistance. His position, therefore, was one
of isolation, and became increasingly so as the years advanced.

CHAPTER TWENTY

THE ADVENT OF
RESPONSIBLE GOVERNMENT

Before describing, as it will be necessary to do, the political changes which took place in Canada in Mackenzie's absence, it may be well to notice the changes of opinion which he himself underwent in the later years of that period: though it must be confessed that in his case, changes of opinion were less significant than with most men. With him changes of opinion were normally produced by changes of mood and circumstance; and the latest phase about to be recorded was not his last. His declarations of 1841 and 1842 have been noted; the latter, it may be remembered, being a frank expression of regret that rebellion in Canada had ever been attempted, and this not because it had failed, but because, had it succeeded, the results would have been disastrous. A few years pass, and on the twenty-third of November, 1846, taking as his text an article in the New York *Albion*, blaming the British Cabinet of 1836 for having made the concession it did to the radicalism of Upper Canada, he addressed to .Earl Grey, Secretary for the colonies in Lord John Russell's newly formed administration, what reads like a belated attempt to justify his action in 1837. In this letter he denied that the rebellion which he set on foot "was anything more than resistance to unlawful power for lawful, just and praiseworthy objects;" though he adds, "I really wish that we could have borne a little more of the insults, injuries and oppressions which I vainly endeavoured, as your Lordship well knows,[1] to lessen or mitigate for many years, and at great personal and pecunniary [sic] risks and sacrifices." Sometimes the analysis of a single word will throw a flood of light on the significance of a general statement. "I wish," Mackenzie says, "that *we* could have borne." Substitute for "we" its true equivalent "I and my personal followers" and the "we" no longer seems to stretch over Upper Canada. Make it read

"that I and my personal followers could, like such men as
Baldwin, Perry, Bidwell, Roblin, Hincks, the Lesslies, and the
more solid men of the Reform party generally, have borne
etc.," and the whole thing presents itself in a mightily changed
aspect, and that aspect the true one. Pronouns are very convenient as taking the place of nouns, but it is necessary to see
that they do not stretch their representation unduly.

Proceeding, Mackenzie quotes Lord Sydenham as calling
the government of Upper Canada, as he found it, "an abominable government." Lord Sydenham spoke of "the present
abominable system of government;" but let the whole passage
be quoted, for it is a most significant one. "Think," said his
lordship,

> of a House in which half the members hold places, *yet
> in which the government does not command a single
> vote*;[2] in which *the placemen generally vote against the
> executive*; and where there is no one to defend the
> government when attacked, or to state the opinions and
> views of the governor. How with a popular assembly
> government is to be conducted under such circumstances
> is a riddle to me. I am now more than ever satisfied that
> the Union affords the only means by which the present
> *abominable system of government* can be broken up,
> and a strong and powerful administration (both depart-
> mental and executive) be formed.

Sydenham was a man resolute in action and emphatic in
utterance. He was also a man of strong business instincts, and
a system of government that lacked vigorous leadership
would, in his eyes, deserve to be called "abominable."

A year later Mackenzie wrote in the New York *Tribune* a
very long article on the Canadian troubles. He then said that
he was glad the revolutionary party had not succeeded in
Canada, since, if it had, the poor slave would have been
deprived of the only place of refuge and protection open to
him. In 1837 and 1838 Mackenzie was very indignant with
the escaped negroes in Upper Canada because they rallied to
the support of the government that had sheltered them.

About this time petitions began to be circulated in Upper
Canada praying for the pardon of the exile, and Mackenzie
himself thought the occasion opportune for making a general
statement of his views and feelings in a letter addressed un-
officially to Major J. T. Campbell, secretary to Lord Elgin.

"I do not know," he said in this letter, which was dated *Tribune* office, New York, February 10th, 1848, "what, after an absence from Canada of more than ten years, and being stripped of what means I had, that I would feel at home in it, but I know that I always did feel at home in it, and that I do not and cannot feel so here." He went on to speak of some flattering business offers he had lately received in New York, and added: "My reply was that the longer I lived in this country the more sensible I was of the great error I had committed in my opinions respecting it, much as I admire many of its inhabitants; and that, the longer I lived, the more attachment did I feel for the country of my birth and the people among whom I had passed my earlier and happiest years." He wanted his letter laid before the Governor General, if Major Campbell saw no objections, but "not before any Ministry." The significance of the expression "*any* ministry" lay probably in the fact that the conservative government was then tottering to its fall, and a reform one under Lafontaine and Baldwin was expected to take its place, which it did just one month to a day after the date of this letter. Mr. Mackenzie did not care to entrust his case either to conservatives or to reformers; he preferred to leave it in the hands of the representative of that British government of which he had said so many terrible things not so very long before. He goes on to speak of himself as "convinced that I might have acquired in Canada great additional influence for good by a patient endurance of what then seemed cruel wrong; and that I ought to have stood by my native country, as by my forefather's faith, and tried to reform both, but not to dismember the first, if improvement was needed in either, and I a fit person for the task." He goes so far as to say that, were Sir Francis Head governor, he would equally desire permission to return, facts having come to his knowledge showing "that but for the course that was taken in 1837, much that would have tended to endear the people to the government would have been accomplished." The utterance is a little mysterious, and one would rather have expected him to speak of the *government being endeared to the people*. The evident meaning, however, is that some great good was about to happen to the province when the rebellion of 1837 threw everything into confusion.

A singular statement follows: "I cannot help seeing that, if the events of 1837-8 had not happened, the Mexican war, so fraught as it is with evils, might have been avoided, and much else that has had mischievous effects prevented." The writer then dips into general politics; deprecates Mr. Papineau's election to the Speakership, which he hears is on the cards, in as much as it would help the election of Mr. Cass to the Presidency, in which case "we would have my old neighbour Mr. Bidwell back again, and the old intrigues." This was not a very generous reference to Mr. Bidwell. It is impossible to omit one other quotation from this remarkable letter:

Had I been ten years apprenticed to American politics, and been behind the curtain before the outbreak, as I have been since, no man living could have tempted me to such a movement. As it is *you might trust me with the worst executive Canada ever had*, and I would live it through, and wait, and try for better times. Education to all, and of the right kind, I take to be the only true and permanent way to upraise Canada.

A year passes; Mackenzie learns that an act of amnesty is in contemplation which will permit his return to Canada, and he hastens to address a letter to the colonial secretary, Mr. James Leslie. "I acknowledge with thankfulness," he says, "that long and earnestly desired evidence of the royal favour, which would permit one so undeserving as I am once more to visit the loved land of his boyhood, and the country in which he had passed many of the most active and also some of the very happiest years of his life. I have long been sensible," he continues, "of the errors committed during that period to which the intended amnesty applies. No punishment that power could inflict, or nature sustain, could have equalled the regrets I have felt on account of much that I did, said, wrote and published; but the past cannot be recalled." Whether pardoned or not he hopes that his future conduct will prove him to be a true and steadfast friend to the unity of the British Empire. This letter was dated the third day of February 1849; on the fifth of the month he sent a copy of it to Earl Grey who was still colonial secretary, and who doubtless noticed a change in its tone as compared with the one he had received a little over two years before.

A letter written nine months later to his old friend, Mr. James Lesslie of Toronto (23rd November 1849), brings us very near to the period of Mackenzie's return to Canada. In it he expressed the opinion that such issues as "annexation, elective legislative councils, elective governors, etc. are lures to divert the people from seeking practicable reforms." He hopes that no true friend of reform will fall into the trap. Then follows the very significant utterance: "1837 – it was the more haste the worse speed; and if that error is remedied now, peacefully, by keeping to the moderate constitutional side, *there must be progress*."[3] On the subject of the legislative council he says: "As long as it is not *obstructive let it alone*. . . . As the existing senate gets no pay, and can be improved by additions at pleasure, why not let well enough alone?" There is a word too about Rolph: "I hope Rolph will come forward. He's the man for the times. . . . Reforms must have men to carry them through that have weight and ability."

The Canada to which Mackenzie returned was not the Canada he had left. The probability is that, if he could have had his choice, he would have found himself more at home with Sir John Colborne, or even Sir Francis Head, with the "family compact" such as it was, thrown in, than he did with the new breed of politicians. People do not always know it, but, deep down somewhere, they may even have a lurking affection for foes whom they understand, and whom they can encounter in open warfare on simple issues. Keen, undisguised conflict does not breed half the hatred that is begotten between persons whose professions are alike, but whose ideals and practices are fundamentally dissimilar. It may be questioned whether there is one word on record to show that Mackenzie highly appreciated the boon of responsible government in which, on his return the country was supposed to be rejoicing. There are many to show that he was woefully disappointed in its agents and in its results.

Although Upper and Lower Canada were until 1841 two entirely distinct provinces, presenting very different social and political features, it was not unnatural that, when trouble broke out in both simultaneously, the conclusion drawn in the mother country should have been that both were suffering from the same malady, whatever that might be, and might be cured by the same remedies. Yet so far was Upper Canada from being in the same situation in the year 1837 as Lower Canada, that, while in the latter province the rebellion was the almost inevitable outcome of a prolonged and hopeless quarrel between an overwhelming majority of the legislature and the executive, involving a continued withholding of the supplies, in Upper Canada the executive was on the best possible terms with a large majority of the legislature and the so-called rebellion was solely due to the turbulence and mad spirit of adventure of one man, and the fatuous ignoring by another of the plain beginnings of mischief. The conjunction of William Lyon Mackenzie and Francis Bond Head made the Upper Canada rebellion such as it was. Without Mackenzie there would have been no rebellion; but neither could Mackenzie have made it under such a governor say as Sir John Colborne, or any man of ordinary prudence, firmness and good sense.

On the retirement of Lord Gosford in February 1837, the administration of the government of Lower Canada had, as we have seen, been entrusted to Sir John Colborne, Commander of the forces. This was only regarded as a temporary arrangement; yet whom to send out to Canada, with any hope of his succeeding where so many others had failed, was a difficult problem. The situation in Lower Canada was undeniably grave and the man to cope with it must be possessed of exceptional powers. In the month of July the office was tendered to the Earl of Durham who a few weeks before had returned from Russia where, for a period of two years, he had held the post of British Ambassador. Durham was a son-in-law of Earl Grey, in whose cabinet he had held for over two years the office of Lord Privy Seal. He was a strong advocate of parliamentary reform, and was made chairman of the committee of council to which was referred the preparation of the first reform bill of 1831. Durham, whose political opinions were decidedly more advanced than those either of the head of the government or of any other of his colleagues, laboured to make the bill as liberal as possible, and at times he would urge his opinions with a temper and vehemence that did not conduce to harmony. He was not satisfied with the bill as it finally passed in 1832; but, as better could not at the time be had, he gave it his strong support. In 1833 he resigned from the government on a question of Irish policy. In 1834 the cabinet was reconstructed, Earl Grey retiring and Lord Melbourne succeeding him as Prime Minister. In connection with other changes that were made a place might have been found for Lord Durham, but none was offered him: the fact was that he was somewhat dreaded as a colleague. Even his father-in-law did not very strongly press his claims: he had had his own troubles with him. Being thus left at liberty Durham, during the autumn of the same year, delivered some speeches in Scotland, where his advanced liberalism made him very popular, which did not improve his chances of cabinet position – except possibly as leader of a purely radical government – and which involved him in a quarrel with Lord Brougham, the unhappy results of which were seen some years later in the very crisis of his fortunes.

In spite of his professed radicalism Durham was a proud shy man. With his friends and in the family circle he was affectionate; but he had at all times an intense self-consciousness and an acute, almost morbid, sensitiveness. A man in his station who neither danced nor played cards, and had an absolute intolerance of tobacco, could not have mingled on the freest terms with his fellow men. He earned the nickname in the North of "Radical Jack" but how far his views were practical may be questioned. His political friends, including his distinguished father-in-law, were not altogether unreasonable in complaining of the course he chose to pursue. He knew with what difficulty the Reform Bill, such as it was, was carried, and with what violent antagonism a strong, probably a predominant, party in the country would view any attempt to go beyond the settlement arrived at; and yet after supporting the bill, he went before popular audiences and insisted that matters could not rest there, but that other trenchant "reforms," such as household suffrage, the ballot, and triennial parliaments, must follow, and that without too much delay. The ways of the mere politician are not always admirable, and, as compared with the political dreamer and agitator, he may appear rather unideal, yet sometimes he has common sense on his side.

Durham was, in fact, more a man for special parts than for concerted action; and, so far, the mission to Canada might be considered as suited to his peculiar genius. When first tendered to him, however, he declined it, though the proposition was made by Lord Melbourne in the most complimentary terms; but when the news of the outbreak of rebellion in Lower Canada came to hand, and the offer was renewed with more urgency and a stronger appeal to his sense of public duty, Durham, like the brave and patriotic Englishman that he was, accepted it. If England required his services she must have them.

Landing at Quebec with his civil and military staff on the twenty-ninth of May, 1838, Durham applied himself with signal diligence and in a high spirit of equity and impartiality to the task before him. The work accomplished by himself and his coadjutors during the five months of their stay in Canada was immense; and his report, with its appendices, will always remain one of the most remarkable documents in the whole range of British official literature. As regards the conclusions of the report itself opinions have differed and continue to differ. It would indeed have been extraordinary if a stranger to the country, with assistants equally strange to it, could in the space of a few months have mastered all the complications of the two-headed Canadian problem. The probability was that, coming as a professed reformer – a man with a keen scent for evils to be remedied – he would be disposed to over rate rather than under rate those which fell under his notice. The man who has a specialty likes to have matter whereon to exercise it, and to have found but few grievances in Canada, and these of little moment would, on the ordinary principles of human nature, have been disappointing to the grievance specialist who had been sent out to perform a Herculian labour in their removal. Not more necessary to the chivalrous and slightly cracked Don Quixote were distressed damsels whom he might rescue, than were oppressions and wrongs to the radically reforming Durham. This does not of course mean that there was nothing in Canada to reform; but it does mean that to the eye of exalted chivalry, whether political or romantic, things may not always appear in their true colour or true perspective. There are many errors which may be committed short of mistaking windmills for giants.

The part of Durham's report which is of most interest in connection with the present narrative is that relating to Upper Canada. A recent writer, who has approached the subject in a purely academic spirit,[4] finds reason to believe that this part of his report at least was almost wholly written by Durham's chief secretary, Charles Buller – a young man, as we should call him today, of thirty-two, who belonged, like Durham himself, to the advanced school of British liberals – and that it was prepared on insufficient data and under the influence of preconceived opinions. "The section on Upper Canada," he says (page 247), "is the work of a politician whose views are already determined, and who can only see facts through the distorted medium of personal sympathies with distressed reformers; there is no attempt to hold the balance of judgment even, as in the previous section (that on Lower Canada), and scarcely any indication of a personal acquaintance with the real state of affairs." The account given of the history of the province, he says further, (page 275), reads like an attempt to explain why the people of Upper Canada ought to have been disaffected if they were not; while an unpleasant feature of the section is that charges of jobbery are made, without any evidence to substantiate them.

Considering the general bias of the report, certain statements in it challenge attention. The following may be cited:

> It is very difficult to make out from the avowals of parties the real objects of their struggles; and still less easy is it to discovery any cause of such importance as would account for its uniting any large mass of the people in an attempt to overthrow by forcible means the existing form of government.

> The course of the parliamentary contest in Upper Canada has not been marked by that singular neglect of the great duties of a legislative body which I have remarked in the proceedings of the parliament of Lower Canada.

> The statute book of the Upper Province abounds with useful and well-considered measures of reform, and presents an honourable contrast to that of the Lower Province.

> (The rebellion was) as foolishly contrived and as ill-conducted as it was wicked and treasonable.

When, however, all else that is contained in Lord Durham's report has been forgotten, it will be remembered that the chief remedy which he recommended for the disorders which he recognized in both provinces was Responsible Government. In the Lower Canada section of his report he says:

> The powers for which the Assembly contended appear to be such as it was perfectly justified in demanding. It is difficult to conceive what could have been their theory of government who imagined that, in any colony of England, a body invested with the name and character of a representative assembly could be deprived of any of those powers which, in the opinion of Englishmen are inherent in a popular legislature.

In the Upper Canada section he says:

> The struggle, though extending itself over a variety of questions of more or less importance, avowedly and distinctly rested on the demand for responsibility in the executive government. I would not impair a single prerogative of the Crown; on the contrary I believe that the interests of the body of the people of these colonies require the protection of prerogatives that have not hitherto been exercised. But the Crown must on the other hand submit to the necessary consequences of representative institutions.

Whether his lordship had fully worked out the scheme in his own mind may reasonably be doubted. Some five or six years later, when the difficulties which Sir Charles Metcalfe was having in connection with this very question were under discussion in the British House of Commons, Mr. Charles Buller, Durham's *alter ego* in this whole matter, – Durham himself died in 1840 – approved of the stand Metcalfe had taken as being in accordance with his (Buller's) theory of responsible government. Nevertheless the seed had been sown; the phrase that had been the watchword of the Upper Canada reformers had been adopted, sanctioned, even insisted on, by the most authoritative voice that had ever pronounced judgment on Canadian affairs. With such an endorsation how could the demand be longer denied?

It is impossible here to enter into the circumstances which brought Durham's mission in Canada to an untimely close on the first of November, 1838, when he stepped on board the frigate "Inconstant" to return to England, without waiting for the acceptance of the resignation which he had tendered. There were those who said that he was only too glad to have a pretext for abandoning a task to the real difficulties of which his eyes had been opened. His visit to Canada had in any case not been in vain. His report was well under way before he left the country; early in January it was finished; in February it was published and laid before Parliament. Some time elapsed before the British government could see at all clearly what was the next step to take. Durham had recommended a reunion of the provinces, and this it was proposed to carry into effect. Meantime Sir John Colborne was maintaining peace in Lower Canada and Sir George Arthur was administering the government of Upper Canada with comparatively little friction. It became a question of finding a suitable man for a very difficult and responsible task. Finally the man was found.

Mr. Charles Poulett Thomson had been a member of the cabinet and, as president of the Board of Trade, had earned a high reputation for business capacity. Miss Martineau, in her *History of the Thirty Years Peace*, sketches his character with considerable insight. "He was an able man," she writes, "had a clear head and a strong will, and much knowledge; but there was little that was morally noble in him except his strength of will shown in his industry and endurance of pain. . . . He found his most favourable position when he went to Canada; but he neither entertained nor inspired political faith, nor drew towards himself any high regard or genial admiration."[6] There are shadows in the picture; but admitting that they have not been unduly deepened, a man with a clear head, a strong will, much knowledge and great industry must possess considerable driving force and this is what Thomson or, to give him the title by which he is better known, Lord Sydenham, both possessed and used. Before coming to Canada he had many conferences with Lord Durham, with whom he was on very friendly terms, and who generously gave him all the help in his power towards understanding the Canadian situation; while, as his biographer, Mr. Poulett-Scrope, states, "the mass of information collected by that noble lord and his coadjutors, and embodied in his voluminous report, offered him very material aid in the determination of his future policy."[7]

In appointing Mr. Thomson the home government was far from intending any immediate application of Lord Durham's specific of responsible government to the ailing Canadas; nor had that gentleman himself, in all his interviews with Durham, imbibed any strong belief in the principle. He arrived at Quebec in the latter part of September, 1839. The views of the then colonial secretary, Lord John Russell, were plainly set forth in a despatch dated the fourteenth of October which began as follows: "It appears from Sir George Arthur's despatches that you may encounter much difficulty in subduing the excitement which prevails on the question of what is called 'responsible government.' I have to instruct you, however, to refuse any explanation which may be construed to imply an acquiescence in the petitions and addresses on this subject."

Amongst those who advocated the principle, his lordship went on to say, there was no very definite agreement as to what it meant; "its very vagueness is a source of delusion; and if at all encouraged, would prove the cause of much embarrassment and danger." At the same time the new governor was instructed to administer the government as far as possible in accordance with the well understood wishes of the people. A despatch two days later in date laid down the principle that persons holding positions more or less equivalent to cabinet offices were not, as heretofore, to consider that they had a life tenure of them. They were to retire whenever it was obviously expedient on political grounds that they should do so. The appointment of a new governor might be an occasion for a change. This was intended to ease the situation by enabling a governor to get rid of unpopular members of his council – a kind of timid approach to that complete dependence of ministers on the vote of the popular chamber which was what the reformers of Upper Canada were demanding, and what they were destined before many years were over to obtain.

The question, however, was not likely to become acute until after the union of the provinces had been accomplished; and to that, as the main object of his mission, Mr. Thomson at once applied himself. Lower Canada at this time had no representative institutions,[8] and could therefore be brought in without difficulty, despite the opposition of almost the entire French Canadian, and a portion of the British, population. In Upper Canada the case was different. That province was still in full possession of its legislature; and no small amount of skill in the managing of parties, the combatting of prejudices and the calming of fears was requisite in order to obtain such a vote in favor of union as might justify hope for the success of the scheme. It was no small triumph for Thomson to have achieved this result. In Lower Canada the Special Council had previously passed the necessary ordinance, and the way was prepared for the action of the imperial parliament.

The Act of Union, drafted to a considerable extent on lines suggested by Thomson, received the royal assent on the twenty-third of July, 1840, and came into effect by proclamation on the tenth of February, 1841 – an interesting date as it was the anniversary of the treaty of Paris which gave Canada to Great Britain in 1763, of the suspension of the constitution of lower Canada in 1838, and of the marriage of Her Majesty Queen Victoria in 1840. Writs were at once issued for a general election. In Lower Canada measures not strictly defensible, it seems clear, were used to gain over a few constituencies to the cause of Union; but, if there ever was a case in which a man in a position of great responsibility might be pardoned for straining a point to snatch success for the cause entrusted to him, this was one.

On the opening of the legislature of the now united provinces the Speech from the Throne announced that the British government was prepared to guarantee a provincial loan for the large sum of a million and a half sterling to be applied to the completion and extension of public works in Canada. "May no dissension," said his excellency (now Baron Sydenham), "mar the flattering prospect which lies before us." His great desire was to stave off party quarrels, and for the moment he succeeded; but the session did not close without a declaration by the assembly on the subject of responsible government. This was contained in a series of resolutions moved by Robert Baldwin, and carried with certain amendments proposed, at the instance, it was understood of Lord Sydenham, by the provincial secretary, Mr. S. B. Harrison. The amendments did not materially alter the significance of the resolutions but as these were sure to carry in the House as constituted, his excellency doubtless thought it best, by practically adopting them, to avoid the appearance of their having been imposed on him and his government. It was now, by these resolutions, affirmed that, while his excellency was responsible to the imperial authority alone, the local affairs of the country could only be managed by him "with the assistance, counsel, and information of subordinate officers in the province;" moreover that his excellency's advisers "ought to be men possessed of the confidence of the representatives of the people," and that the people had "a right to expect from the provincial administration the exertion of their best endeavours that the imperial authority, within its constitutional limits, shall be exercised in the manner most consistent with their well-understood wishes and interests." The political creed of Robert Baldwin was thus entered on the journals of the House; but though interesting as a record it cannot be said that the passing of such resolutions was constitutionally an act of any great importance. They did not form any binding rule for the action even of the House itself; and not requiring the concurrence of the executive, they in no way compromised that coordinate estate.

If the question were asked, what party was in power in Canada at this time? the answer would have to be, no party. The effort of Lord Sydenham was to dominate all parties, to hold them in leash as it were, and prevent their flying at one another. He tried to make his council representative of all allowable shades of political opinion, and was greatly disappointed when Mr. Baldwin, after joining it as solicitor general in February, 1841, abruptly resigned just as the legislature was on the point of meeting. His ideal of colonial government did not really differ materially from that of Sir Francis Head. He did not want party struggles; he wanted a business administration of public affairs; he wanted to do everything for the best, but he was to be the chief motive power. Robert Baldwin, on the other hand was eagerly bent on "sitting in" (to use a current phrase) a regular party game, for which he felt himself specially qualified, and after a time Robert Baldwin had his way. No other game has been played since.

Sydenham's successor, Sir Charles Bagot, was a man of quite different type, and, as his correspondence shows, no great admirer of his immediate predecessor; yet would he gladly have continued to conduct the government of the province on the no party principle had it been possible. It was not possible. There was enough virtue in Robert Baldwin's resolutions of the third of September, 1841, to make it impossible to retain an administration against which a formal vote of want of confidence should be passed by the popular chamber; and, in immediate prospect of such a vote, Sir Charles made overtures to Mr. Lafontaine, leader of the French Canadians, to see on what terms he could be got to enter the cabinet and rally his followers to its support. Mr. Lafontaine would not come in without Mr. Baldwin: Sir Charles, on the other hand, who knew how Mr. Baldwin had given Lord Sydenham the slip, and probably had heard more or less about his dry and haughty ways, had registered a kind of vow that he should never be minister of his. What was to be done? There was only one thing to be done, short of plunging the country into the turmoil and perhaps violence of a new general election, – with very little prospect even so, of a better result – and that was to yield to necessity, call off the vow, take in Mr. Lafontaine and with him Mr. Baldwin *tel quel*. And so it was done; Mr. Draper, the attorney general, the most important member of the cabinet though not its official head,[9] retiring in order that his office might be bestowed on Mr. Baldwin. Other necessary changes were made to find places for the new comers; for, in addition to Mr. Baldwin, Mr. Lafontaine claimed seats for a couple more of his party. The cabinet so reconstructed was in office when Sir Charles Bagot's successor, Sir Charles Metcalfe arrived in Canada in March, 1843.

And now there is going to be trouble. Sir Charles Metcalfe was a very amiable man, kindly and unassuming in manner, generous and benevolent almost to a fault, but with an imperturbable firmness that some were greatly surprised to find allied to such qualities. Sir Charles knew India and Jamaica well, but he had had no experience of "responsible government" in a colony. He saw nothing to object to in the Baldwin resolutions – properly understood – and declared himself anxious to govern the country in the interest, and according to the well-understood wishes, of the people. But what he was not prepared to do – though it had to come, and was really covered, and was meant to be covered, by the wording of the Baldwin resolutions – was to leave the entire patronage of the crown at the mercy of the party in power to be used for party purposes. To his advisers this was of the very essence of "responsible government;" and it is not surprising, therefore, that, after more or less playing at cross purposes for several months, an issue was at length created which led to the resignation of the entire cabinet, with the sole exception of the Provincial Secretary, Mr. Dominick Daly (26th November, 1843). Explanations followed in the House – the legislature being in session at the time – and a resolution was carried by a large majority expressing confidence in the retiring ministers. His excellency also put forth a memorandum in which he said:

The governor-general subscribes entirely to the resolution of the Legislative Assembly of the third of September, 1841, and considers any other system of government but that which recognizes responsibility to the people and the representative assembly as impracticable in this province. No man is more satisfied that all government exists solely for the benefit of the people; and he appeals confidently to his uniform conduct here and elsewhere in support of the assertion.

The legislature was prorogued on the eleventh of December. To strengthen his own hands and those of his solitary minister, Mr. Daly, Sir Charles now called to his assistance, Mr. Draper and Mr. D. B. Viger. The adhesion of the latter gentleman, well known for his advanced sentiments in pre-rebellion days, to the cause of the governor brought down on his head no small amount of abuse; but there was really nothing inconsistent in his action, for the absolute control of the patronage by party had never been an article of the liberal creed in Lower Canada. Within this skeleton of a cabinet Metcalfe carried on the government for nearly ten months, not without great scandal and unlimited railing, it need hardly be said. In August, 1844, he was able to fill up several vacancies, one of the accessions being Mr. D. B. Papineau,[10] brother of the agitator. Then he went to the country, and so far as Upper Canada was concerned, swept it very much as Sir Francis Head had swept it in 1836, and upon an appeal of very much the same nature as the gallant knight had made. In the two provinces combined the government had a scanty majority, for naturally enough Lafontaine had things pretty much his own way in Lower Canada. The Draper-Viger cabinet had a hard struggle for its life; but it held its ground until swept away in the general election of January 1848.

And now Lafontaine and Baldwin were again in power, with Lord Elgin, who had been a little over a year in the country as governor general. His excellency, a son-in-law of Lord Durham, was a sagacious person. He had read the signs of the times better than Sir Charles Metcalfe, and had profited moreover by the teaching of recent events. He had seen the weakness of the conservative administration unsupported by a strong parliamentary majority. In the general election it was responsible government that had won, and so responsible government it had to be.

Such was the Canada to which Mackenzie returned with his family, in the spring of 1850. The place that had known the "family compact" knew it no more; the power of Downing Street was broken; the French Canadians were almost ardent in the support of the new regime, of which they plainly saw the profitable side; ministers rose and fell at the bidding of the parliamentary majority; the politicians were revelling in the so-called "patronage of the crown;" the governor general might still yield a social, or even, if, like Lord Elgin, he was a very able man, a certain intellectual, influence; but in all matters of provincial, as distinct from imperial, interest, his executive council was supreme. Robert Baldwin, the man who had stood in the shadow in the days of storm and stress, was at the head of affairs, and Francis Hincks, who had shared many of Mackenzie's political ideas, but had kept carefully aloof from his revolutionary schemes, was, as inspector-general, the next most influential man in the cabinet. John Rolph, who had by no means kept aloof from them, had, shortly after his return, been adopted by the most advanced or "clear grit" wing of the reformers as their leader; and though he was not as yet in the legislature a seat in that body and a cabinet position were awaiting him in the very near future. It was a time of great prosperity for the liberal party, including some who had carried their liberalism very far. Was it going to be a time of great prosperity for Mackenzie? That remained to be seen.

CHAPTER TWENTY-ONE

A FIGHTER TO THE LAST

The tory riot on the occasion of Mr. Mackenzie's flying visit to Toronto in March, 1849, was severely commented on, as might be expected, by the reform press. The Toronto *Examiner*, edited at the time by Mr. James Lesslie, a staunch friend, and formerly a business associate, of Mackenzie's, apart from condemning the riot, devoted a well-written article to a review of the returning exile's career. It referred to "the great political regeneration we have now achieved," and spoke of Mackenzie as one who, with Gourlay, Rolph, Bidwell and Baldwin,[1] had bravely advocated its principles. "Their acts," it continued, "their public labours which stand on record . . . will go down to other ages, we doubt not, an undying testimony, when the present race of inhabitants shall have mouldered into dust." As to Mackenzie in particular, it said:

Let us appeal to every man in Canada or elsewhere, who had been acquainted with Mr. Mackenzie during the whole period of his eventful life, whether he has not sustained a most honourable reputation in all the social relationships of life, not only as an exceedingly intelligent and useful citizen, but as a sober, humane and upright man – as a kind and generous neighbour, and as a faithful and affectionate husband and father. . . . Mr. Mackenzie, like others, has his peculiar failings which have been greatly magnified by his enemies; but he has also great and noble qualities, which have been, and may yet be, employed for the public good. . . . We have known him from his youth, and have had much personal intercourse and some personal difficulties with him; but throughout all we have admired his great intelligence, his herculean mental labours, his manly and straightforward patriotism, his stern resistance to the blandishments of power, and his numerous and mighty sacrifices for the public weal.

This was the loyal testimony of a friend to a friend and may be taken as an offset to the unmeasured denunciation of Mackenzie by his enemies.[2] The prediction that his great qualities might yet be employed for the public good must have seemed to the writer to be on the way to fulfilment when, in the month of March, 1851, only ten months after his definite return to Canada, Mackenzie presented himself to the electors of Haldimand, the representation of which had become vacant by the death of the sitting member Mr. David Thompson. His election address was a little matter of ten columns, showing that the fountain whence had issued, in other days, such copious indictments of Sir John Colborne, and appeals of one kind and another to the people had not run dry. He announced himself as an independent reformer; dwelt on the need for economy in the administration; and pointed to certain still unrealized reforms. He was not without opposition. There were two local candidates, a conservative, McKinnon, and a reformer, Case. But a man of much more note than these ran also; this was Mr. George Brown, already of anti-popery fame, now first seeking entrance to the legislature. Mackenzie at this time was rather cultivating the Roman Catholic vote, and probably received a large share of it. Brown appeared as a supporter and champion of the Lafontaine-Baldwin government; he was not yet the leader of the "Clear Grits." Mackenzie's attitude to the government, while not one of declared hostility, was critical. At the close of the poll on the fifteenth of April the vote stood, Mackenzie 294; McKinnon 266; Brown 165; Case 61.[3]

The victory was a notable one. Defeated in 1836, a rebel and a refugitive in 1837, an exile struggling with misfortune and, at the best, uncongenial conditions for a long term of years, Mackenzie was not only restored to Canada, but again had a constituency at his back and a voice in the legislature of the country. The man who could thus keep his head over the waves of misery was not a common man. There were qualities there which, in happier combination, might have made an admirable, not merely a notable, character, a pillar and not a puller-down of the state.

The session opened at Quebec on the twentieth of May,

1851, and thither Mackenzie repaired primed for renewed activity. In his knapsack he had one or two little things that were not designed to smooth the path of the administration. He had a notion that sheriffs ought to be elected by the people, and he meant to bring the matter up. Mr. Baldwin had lately reorganized the court of chancery according to his best judgment; but the court itself, in any shape, was odious to Mackenzie, who had recorded in his own mind a *Delenda and Carthage* against it. He probably little thought that what he would accomplish in this matter would be, not the abolition of the court, but the downfall of Baldwin; though it is not at all likely that he would have stayed his hand on that account. Then he had his own views, and strong ones, as to the way in which the public money was being spent under the "great political regeneration" of which his friend Lesslie had spoken. Some of his ideas were undoubtedly sound, but he soon discovered that he was living and moving in a totally different medium from that of the thirties. The King Lag of the old fixed administration had given place to an extremely active and vigorous King Stork. The old administration could not command votes – *teste* Lord Sydenham – and had to make the most it could of moral influence. The new administration *could* command votes, and therefore did not need to trouble much about moral influence. Of course it was "responsible government;" that is to say the government had to consider where and how it was going to get the votes necessary to its existence, and shape its course accordingly. *How* it got them was a thing that soon began to trouble Mackenzie exceedingly.

When Joseph Hume of "baneful domination" fame heard that Mackenzie was a candidate in Haldimand he wrote him a letter of warm congratulation.[4] Referring to Mackenzie's mission to England in 1832 he said:

> The influence you possessed in the house of assembly, and the industry which you bestowed on explaining fully the grievances of the Canadians, entitled you to more attention that you received from the colonial minister. . . . If the representations you then made of the great discontent of the Canadians . . . had been listened to, the misfortunes and rebellion of Canada would have been avoided.

Why did not Mr. Hume say, "if the representations you then
made had been listened to, you would not have thought it
necessary to organize a rebellion?" To be sure it would not
have sounded quite so well, but it would have avoided,
what is quite worth avoiding, *a suppressio veri*. Mr. Hume
assumes in this letter that now at last all is well in Canada,
but upon this point Mackenzie rudely undeceives him,
detailing a list of grievances long enough to dishearten even
Hume. As to the general manner in which the public
business is being conducted Mackenzie says:

> There is no check on the activity of the officials: a
> combination grasps power, seizes the revenue, dispenses
> the patronage, audits its own expenditure, never lays
> out a dollar to profit, holds its four sessions, becomes
> odious, and gives way to another combination founded
> like its predecessor upon the distribution of the spoils.

If Baron Metcalfe of Fern Hill[5] had still been living, one
can imagine the faint, indulgent smile which might have
irradiated his suffering features, had this letter fallen under
his notice. But Sir Francis Head, Sir John Colborne (Lord
Seaton), and Sir Peregrine Maitland were all still living to
make their comments. A story *ben trovato* is generally
better than one simply *vero*; and, had it been alleged that
the bluff Sir Francis had exclaimed, "Well, that little rascal
Mackenzie has read the puzzle of 'responsible government'
at last, has he?," the thing would have been more than
credible, it would have been convincing.

A few days before writing this letter, in moving the
second reading of his bill for rendering sheriffs elective – a
proposal which was supported by his old sworn enemy,
H. J. Boulton, who had returned from Newfoundland to
Canada and been elected to the assembly, – Mackenzie stated
that "immediately after the Haldimand election a new batch
of magistrates had been appointed with no other qualification
than that they had voted for Brown." Referring to the
same subject in an address to his constituents of about the
same date,[6] he says that, although he saw the members of
the government daily, they gave him not the slightest
intimation of their intention. He had the preposterous idea –
preposterous at least from the modern standpoint, and never
more so than today – that because he represented the county,

he should be consulted in such matters. "As Mr. Brown," he continues.

> was the government candidate twenty new magistrates out of twenty-six that voted are chosen from among his supporters. A merchant in Dunnville wrote me that he would accept the agency for issuing marriage licenses: I sent the application to Mr. Secretary Leslie, who instantly found an agent in a returning officer who had voted for Brown. Thus it is that popular responsible government is worked, the freedom of election interfered with. To the victors belong the spoils; . . . honours, civil and military, are exclusively conferred on those who vote for the *Brown* of any political combination that can obtain a majority in the assembly. . . . Situations in counties are bestowed less on account of fitness to discharge important trusts than because a candidate has shown that he possesses a talent for electioneering on behalf of the Draper-Viger or Baldwin-Blake managers of the machinery here. Such results of a system for which I struggled hard in your district long before half your population were born grieve me.

Mackenzie was not the first reformer, nor the last, who has had to lament that *plus çela change, plus c'est la même chose*. There is a terrible constant in human affairs, and that is human nature.

But while Mackenzie was giving vehement expression to his sense of the evils of the time, it cannot be said that he himself always rose to a very high level of statesmanship in his new parliamentary career. There is a strong touch of the ancient demagoguism in a speech which he delivered in the assembly on the eleventh of July, 1851, against the adoption of a report of the committee of the whole on the incorporation of Trinity College. Travelling quite out of the record he went back to the first, long abolished, charter of King's College – just as in his complaints to Lord Goderich he had gone back to the long repealed Act of 1818 on the subject of unlawful assemblies – and recited in the assembly such portions of the Thirty-Nine Articles of the Church of England as were most adapted to give offence to the Roman Catholics, whose political support, as already mentioned, he was at this time cultivating. Mr. Hincks in the same session moved a resolution in favor of an appeal to the judicial committee of the Privy Council on the question of the legality of the creation of the rectories. Mackenzie said the whole thing was a farce: "it was ridiculous to send to Mr. Blake, chancellor, to decide the question if Mr. Blake, rector, was legally possessed of his rectory." In the first place it was not proposed to refer any such question to Mr. Blake, chancellor; in the second it was most characteristic of Mackenzie to assume that *no man, save himself*, could rise superior to pecuniary interest. He showed himself in advance, not only of his own times, but of ours in objecting to the bestowal of places on members of the legislature except after a decent delay, and on the sixth of August he moved the second reading of a bill to prevent members from accepting offices until after the first session of the succeeding parliament. According to the published report,[7] "he went over several appointments of judges, namely, Messrs. Blake, Sullivan, Draper, Smith and Aylewin, characterizing them all as jobs." Of Aylewin in particular he said that "he might have been heard to bellow out patriotism loud enough to be heard a great way off; but that was for the public. In private he could chisel places for his friends, and last of all, by the grossest job of all, chisel himself into a judgeship."

Neither this bill, nor that for rendering sheriffs elective, carried: party does not willingly surrender any means of consolidating its power. Of course it is responsible to the people; but it likes to have as many ways of persuading the people as possible, and as few barriers as possible to doing what it may find convenient. The bill which Mackenzie introduced for doing away with the court of chancery was also lost; but, to the surprise and chagrin of Mr. Baldwin, it was supported by a majority of the Upper Canada members and the court on the perfecting of which he had bestowed his best endeavours [and] was only saved by the votes of Mr. Lafontaine's followers. Mr. Baldwin took the matter so much to heart that he resigned, though, somewhat singularly, he retained the office of attorney general for some time after he had ceased to be a member of the cabinet.

Whether Mackenzie manifested any unholy glee on this occasion is not recorded; it is safe to say he did not sorrow over the event. In the previous year (1850) he had had some correspondence with Mr. Baldwin on the subject of

his claim to compensation for services rendered in connection
with the Welland Canal investigation of 1835-36, for which
the House of Assembly had voted him £250; and also in
regard to the supposed surplus proceeds of a sheriff's sale
of his property in York under civil process by his creditors
after he had fled the country. Two letters of Baldwin's in
reply have been preserved; both are decidedly frigid in tone.
"In the opinion you quote," writes Mr. Baldwin on the
twenty-third of August, 1850,

> that the most exact and respectful attention is due to
> the position of the humblest individual, I entirely
> concur. But I do not conceive that it is at all essential
> to that end that lengthened epistolary correspondence
> should be entered into by the different members of the
> government with parties setting up claims upon the
> province. It forms certainly no part of my duty to do
> so. . . . Neither does it form any part of my official
> duty to advise persons upon the nature or extent of
> their claims, either at law or in equity, upon public
> bodies or others, whether corporations or individuals.
> And I adhere to the view which I took when you
> applied to me for an opinion in June last, that, con-
> sidering my official position and the claims set up by
> you upon the government, it was not for me to become
> your private counsel in the matter. . . . Ministers in
> this country not being provided with the means of
> securing the assistance of private secretaries, your
> acquaintance with public business will convince you
> how impracticable it would be to undertake to answer
> all the letters that may be addressed to them throughout
> the year. I do so as often as it is in my power. . . . I
> make this remark as I have received some letters from
> which, for the reason I advert to, have not been replied
> to.

A later letter – dated twenty-fourth of September, 1850,
is as follows:

> Sir, – Whatever was done by sheriff Jarvis was, I
> suppose, done under the authority of civil process; and
> I do not see how since the general amnesty, the Crown
> has any interest that would give it a right to interfere

in the matter. Though were all the facts before me, it might prove otherwise. – I remain your obedient servant, Robert Baldwin.[8]

What appears to be a final communication from Mackenzie has been preserved amongst the Baldwin papers. It is dated thirty-first of December, 1850, and begins as follows:

> This is the last day of the year. I have already lived longer than one out of every twenty of the inhabitants of this continent do, and probably may not see another year close. Thro' life however, I have openly pursued the course my judgment and inclination dictated, and am therefore puzzled to find a reason for the course you are now taking with me.

He proceeds to detail the circumstances of his employment upon the Welland Canal enquiry, and how he had lost the £250 voted him by the assembly, through the refusal of Sir Francis Head to sanction the money bills of that body, after it had refused supplies for the purposes of civil government. The decision to withhold the supplies, Mackenzie says, was taken, chiefly through his own exertions, as a sanction to Baldwin's course in resigning. "At last," he continues, matters were brought to a crisis, and all I had in the world was sacrificed." The passive voice is sometimes most conveniently employed for the active, when it is not particularly desired to call attention to the action; and, "were brought to a crisis" is a neat example, for Mackenzie could not have been charged with egotism had he said "At last I brought matters to a crisis." "When told," he continues,

> that my demand would, if brought before the assembly in March 1849,[9] cause excitement and do you injury, I offered no objection, but . . . waited another year, and last summer you would neither pay me, which you could have done in five minutes, nor arbitrate, nor allow the matter to go to a committee, nor promise to pay me after the session, nor hear me in council. It seems as if you supposed that, as I was not wealthy you would harass and vex me. I would not say so if you had decided any way, but you do nothing.

Some remarks follow as to the kind of appointments the government is making, and he concludes in words which may possibly have made the statesman wince:

> If to be a leader in politics, if to have influence, if to secure success to party, such a course of conduct as I complain of (that is if I see and view it through a true medium) is needful, it is fortunate for me that my responsibilities in that way are light. . . . Am I entirely beyond the pale of justice? Must frank and fair dealing ever bend at the shrine of a temporary expediency? Must the question ever be, Will doing this strengthen the party? God forbid.

After all, what is the answer to these questions? When the pleading patriarch exclaimed "Shall not the judge of all the earth do right?" he felt that there was but one answer to his question. But when the question is, "Shall we (a government) do for a people – on the ground that we believe it to be right – that which they would not do for themselves, and would be angered at our doing for them?," the answer is not perhaps so obvious or inevitable. The problem which popular government continually presents to an honourable man in power is, how far he will consent to make himself the instrument of policies, positive or negative, which jar upon his own sense of right and of public expediency in the broadest sense. Let the man, it may be said, who does not agree with public opinion step aside and make room for some one who does. Who does? Or who sacrifices his own principles in *pretending* that he does? Or who has no principles of any kind to sacrifice? To drive a faithful servant from power is the first step towards getting an unfaithful one. The region of politics must ever be, to some extent, the region of compromise; but the man who has a true sense of responsibility to the people at large will dare much on behalf of what he conscientiously believes to be true and right. In this case, Robert Baldwin might well have dared a little more.[10] If Mackenzie's relations with Baldwin were lacking in cordiality, even more so were his relations with Lafontaine. On the second of August, 1850, he addressed a long letter to that gentleman complaining bitterly of the treatment he had received at the hands of the reform government. In it he dwelt upon the sympathy he had always manifested towards the liberals of Lower Canada in

their days of struggle. Now he was "forgotten and treated
with ingratitude: whether it was Viger, Papineau (D. B.),
Draper & Co., or Lafontaine, Sullivan, Baldwin & Co., all
alike agreed to ostracize me." The general amnesty by
which he had profited was, he hints, "a necessary prelude
to the Rebellion Losses bill, as it prevented too close an
enquiry into the antecedents of those who were to benefit
by the new grant." He says he could "point out men who
were unwearied in their efforts to secure the revolt" who
had been "successful applicants for part of that grant." "It
chills me," he continues,

> when I see you, a Lower Canadian, withholding a paltry
> $1000 and interest from me who risked all to aid and
> strengthen your countrymen. . . . I seek no rebellion
> losses – I only ask to be paid or else to be heard before
> your council. You, Sir, have prevented my petition to
> the assembly from being referred; you have joined
> with others in refusing my petition to the executive
> council to be heard in person on behalf of my claim:
> you have excluded my just debt, though powerfully
> advocated by Mr. Hincks, your finance minister; you
> have rewarded my long and active and unwearied
> attachment to your countrymen with impoverishing, as
> far as you could, my family. . . . Have you forgotten
> your remonstrances to the government and parliament
> when, instead of being the leader of a successful party,
> you was [sic] the inmate of a prison. Apply them to
> my case. Is there not a pleasure in acting nobly when
> we have power? What pleasure does power bring us
> that equals the weariness attached to its exercise?

The correspondence, unfortunately, does not exist entire.
Mackenzie apparently returned to the subject, or entered
on some other topic, in June of the following year, for
there is a letter from Lafontaine to him dated Toronto,[11]
21st June, 1851, written in a most unamiable mood. It was
short and may be given entire.

> Sir, – I beg to inform you that your letter dated
> Thursday morning, 19th, insta., was handed to me last
> evening on my return to Toronto. I do not feel myself
> called upon, nor have I the time nor inclination to
> enter into any such correspondence as that which your

communication is intended to invite. I see, however, with pleasure that the rule which requires that 'no member shall speak beside the question in debate' has at last attracted your attention, and I have no doubt that your observance of that rule for the future will much contribute to your comfort and leisure. – I have the honour to be, Sir, your obedient servant, L. H. La Fontaine.

The power-polished sarcasm could not much further go.

Light is thrown on the relations between Mackenzie and his Haldimand constituents by certain letters which have been preserved amongst his papers. One of his correspondents was a Mr. Thomas Tipton, who published the *Haldimand Independent*, first at Cayuga and later at Dunnville. In a letter dated 21st April, 1851, this gentleman, who affected no small measures of philosophy as well as of high patriotic sentiment, describes the opening of the assizes. It is a little surprising, considering the happy days on which the country had fallen at this time, to find him speaking almost as if the family compact and its retainers were in full possession. "There were a great many present," he says, "the whole swarm of government supporting officials and office seekers were there, strutting before the astonished public in all the pomp of authority and rank." The language reminds one of Mackenzie's own in days gone by, when every office holder was a sycophant and a parasite. Mr. Tipton finds that "human nature works in a peculiar manner: men in general are indifferent to measures that make for the good of the country at large, and can only be roused by some appeal to the spirit of faction." Such being the said limitations of human nature, Tipton explains that his main object in writing is "to urge the necessity of raising some cry that would create a party in Canada previous to the general election." Mackenzie's reply is not on record; but a month later Tipton, who has been applying his great mind to the question of a cry, writes again and recommends getting up a petition on the subject of the clergy reserves, to head off one which he understands Bishop Strachan has in preparation. He wants to be in the field, "as there are a great many loose fish in the community who can be led aside by any plausible story, and these would sign the first petition brought them." If "the people" only knew it, the flattery which is lavished on them in public is offset by many such a sneer in private.

In regard to the important question of a cry the sagacious Mr. Tipton gives Mr. Mackenzie his choice of three. These are: the clergy reserves, the increase (extention?) of the suffrage, and the lowering of the price of crown lands. "Whether either of these questions," he says, "can be used to wake up the people, I leave to your consideration." Then, either the rebellion had not waked up the people, or they had fallen asleep again in the very dawn of their liberties. Morning naps are sometimes very alluring. It must not be supposed that Tipton had any sordid ends in view. Listen to him: "Even if we should not succeed, some benefit would be done: whatever draws off men's attention from their every day affairs and animal desires tends to elevate and expand their ideas." We must assume that Tipton's ideas were elevated and expanded, and his animal desires held in check, by his efforts to get up a cry and to catch the "loose fish" before Strachan had a chance at them. "You know," writes Tipton in a letter a little later in date, "what a motley mass we had to deal with at the last election" (the one at which Mackenzie was returned). Then a few days later again:

> I see that the *Examiner* advises the people not to waste their energies in petitioning. . . . If he knew the sort of people we have to deal with in this county, he would counsel differently. Petitioning itself will serve to awaken the minds of the people. If we were to call public meetings to choose anti-clergy representatives,[12] very few would attend them. Some political characters might, but the mass would look on with apathy. . . . I have talked to a Baptist preacher, a friend of mine, and he has consented to preach a little on the voluntary principle, and perhaps others may be inclined to do so too.

And all for what? to obtain a just settlement of the clergy reserves question? Not primarily, if at all; but to "rouse" the people. The clergy reserves question was only one of three available "rousements."[13] The thing was to get people roused and then to "keep them in play."

On the third of July this gentleman has heard of Baldwin's resignation, and refers to him as "the least liberal member of the cabinet, and the most in favour of retaining the clergy reserves for religious purposes." He has also something more to say about the masses: "Among the great part of the population very little high feeling exists. There are a few, however, of nature's noblemen scattered here and there, who are exceptions." It may be assumed that Mr. Tipton would not have had to go far to find one of these exceptions. Three weeks later he writes: "I think the Roman Catholic party will support us very well, if they are managed right. We must sow a little dissension between them and the church of England. I do not like religious differences, but circumstances require these things." One must sympathize with this noble soul positively compelled to sow religious discord – against his principles – in order to gain votes for his candidate. Mackenzie himself had bowed, in a measure, to the same necessity in the speech already referred to, which he delivered in the legislature just about a fortnight before the date of this letter.

The member of Haldimand had another correspondent in the county, a Dr. T. S. S. Harrison, who is fully alive to the same necessity of fomenting discord between catholics and English churchmen. "I have been thinking," he says, "of writing some rabid article in the *Patriot* against Catholics, and then answering it through the *Mirror,* for the purpose of widening the breach between High Church and Pope. However it requires consideration, and must be done well; for I think the editor of the *Mirror* is a man of more talent than the other." On the 22nd July he writes to say he has done the deed, and that the *Patriot* has swallowed the bait; even his own family do not know that he is the author of the article. Whether he answered himself with equal virulence in the *Mirror* does not appear. Such were the cards that practical politicians were playing in the year of grace 1851, and in the year 11 of responsible government, that is to say if we date it from the year of the Baldwin resolutions.

There is no trace of political manoeuvring in a letter which Mackenzie wrote from the house of assembly at Quebec, in the month of August, to the first number of his friend Tipton's paper, the *Independent*. The tone is extremely moderate, and the advice given eminently practical. "The great question before the legislature at present," he wrote, "is the line of railway proposed to be opened from Halifax, via Quebec, Montreal, Kingston, and Hamilton to the Detroit

river near Sandwich." His advice in connection with the
approaching dissolution of parliament was as follows:

> Bid your supporters to beware of discord about creeds
> and churches, and to push forward for a common
> education to all, freedom in trade, an equalized elective
> franchise, an improved system for the public lands, law
> reform, and thorough financial retrenchment. Persever-
> ance effects much, and if you're certain you're right,
> keep straight ahead.

The resignation of Baldwin was tendered on one of the
last days of June. Lafontaine about the same time took the
very unusual course of signifying that he meant to resign
before long. He did not do so, however, till about the middle
of October. The ministry having thus been broken up, its
reconstruction was entrusted by Lord Elgin to Mr. (afterwards Sir) Francis Hincks. The latter associated himself
with Mr. A. N. Morin as leader of the Lower Canada
section of the cabinet; and amongst the new men taken in
was Mr. John Rolph, who became commissioner of crown
lands. Early in the year 1852, we find Rolph and Mackenzie
in correspondence. On the 2nd of January, 1852, Rolph
acknowledges a letter in which Mackenzie had apparently
complained of the failure of the government to consult him
in regard to matters in the county of Haldimand, for which
in the general election he had been again returned. Rolph
assures him that

> no such neglect as you advert to shall ever take place
> with my consent. . . . You ought to be, and will be,
> consulted on all matters relating to your county.
> Besides local, I shall thankfully receive your suggestions
> upon all public questions, and be most happy to
> promote in every way your private interests.

Nothing certainly could be more amicable than the tone of
this letter, and it must be assumed that the relations of the
two men at this time were entirely friendly. On the 24th
February Rolph refers to some application or petition
Mackenzie had sent in – probably relating to the claims he
had unsuccessfully prosecuted under Lafontaine-Baldwin
administration – and promises that the government will do
what it can in the matter, though he hints that it may not
be able to meet his views fully. "You advert," he says,

at some length to the history of the past and the services you have rendered. I am certainly fully alive to the events you mention, and can be no stranger to the part you acted in them; nor am I insensible to your merits as a public man. Your narration shows me that circumstances . . . have not afforded you that justice to which you are entitled. . . . Whenever the state of things may favour your personal advancement, it will afford me much pleasure.

A letter dated the 4th May shows that Rolph, who had been returned for Norfolk, was having some trouble with his local committee, who were claiming absolute control of appointments, which he considered was going too far. A few days later he speaks of having had to vindicate against the local association the right of individual constituents to address him directly on the subject of their wants. He tells Mackenzie that he had received a letter from the chairman of the association "in these or nearly these words: 'Herewith you have the names of the persons you are to insert in the commission of the peace.' " Advanced liberal as he was, Rolph seemed to consider this dose of reform principles a little too strong. The local machine was showing itself a real infant Hercules and preluding to noble achievements in the future.

On the 7th of June Rolph broaches a more interesting subject. He puts the question directly to Mackenzie, who, since his return from the states, had been in great financial straits, whether he would like an office under the Crown Lands department. "You know," he says,

something of the nature and extent of the duties of this department, and how much there is abroad demanding a care and attention which no one can bestow from his own chair amidst the routine and other internal duties thrown upon him. Now have you, if I can so arrange it, any objection, throughout Canada West, to discharge for me, from time to time, such external duties as I cannot possibly discharge myself. The duties will of course embrace everything I want to do, and ought if possible to do myself, through wide spread (and almost irresponsible) agencies, besides enquiries, the correction of abuses, and the saving to the public the, no doubt, large sums of money yearly lost. The remuneration will,

I think be satisfactory, and certainly all I can do consistent with my public duty.

In a postscript Rolph added "It will not vacate your seat."

Three days later Rolph wrote: "I am enjoying some leisure moments in looking into the interesting and instructive fragments you so obligingly sent me." Mackenzie, in addition to his other activities, was indefatigable in making clippings from newspapers; and it was a collection of these, accompanied doubtless by observations of his own, that Rolph was now acknowledging.

What Rolph's precise object was in making Mackenzie the offer he did is hard to determine. Accounts seem to agree that he was naturally of a benevolent disposition – Mackenzie himself held that opinion of him strongly in earlier years – and he may simply have been moved by a desire to come to the assistance of a man whose means were painfully narrow. However this may have been, Mackenzie took the offer very seriously, and wrote two letters in reply one of which he did not send, and the other of which he did send. In the first he expressed himself as prepared to take the situation, provided "my work is promptly paid for by my employers, and no personal independence bartered for gain." He also commented on the actual methods of the government: "The patronage you *waste* upon the press and printing is truly enormous – no one seems to heed it – there is no attempt at prudence or economy, which though it may be carried too far, yet on the other hand should never be lost sight of – and this under 'responsible government.' " The letter actually sent ran as follows:

Dear Sir, – No man who is poor, and has a large family dependent on him for support, should be unwilling to labour for their subsistence. I therefore accept your proposal of the 7th inst., mailed on the 8th, and only received by me on the 12th, Saturday. Had it been made six or eight months since, I could have readily perceived how it might have been useful to me, but what work can I perform in Upper Canada on the eve of a session to be held five hundred miles hence it is not quite so clear. You, however, wish to serve me, for I asked nothing of you; and therefore, as my seat will not be affected, nor my independent action in or out

of the legislature interfered with, I stand ready to fulfill
your orders when received.

One can imagine the scorn and gibes with which the writer
of this letter would have received a statement made by a
member of the legislature in the olden time to the effect that
his independence as a legislator was not affected by the
fact of his holding a well-paid government office. The thing
in those days appeared to him absolutely unthinkable – at
least he absolutely refused to think it – but now he was going
to show how it could be done: he was going to be a kind
of general agent of the commissioner of crown lands at a
good salary, and an independent legislator at the same time.

As it happened, however, the thing was not to be. Having
drawn Mackenzie so far, Rolph wrote on the 19th June
thanking him for his expressed willingness to undertake the
duties referred to, but alleging reasons why, for the present,
nothing should be done in the matter. "I shall rely," he said,

> upon your co-operation as soon as anything effective
> can be done. Perhaps so immediately before the coming
> session it might subject you and myself to some unjust
> suspicions and animadversions, and impair your useful-
> ness and *apparent* independence of office during legis-
> lation. It might, too, lead to a discussion in the House
> about the vacating of your seat; and if the matter of
> employment were fully carried out, it might give a
> colourable objection against you.

We read in a venerable book about a certain supple as well
as subtle beast of the field, who inviting the first parents of
mankind to transgress, gave them the assurance, "Ye shall
not surely die;" but we do not read that, after they had
done his bidding, he drew their attention to the very doubtful
light in which their conduct must appear: he seems to have
spared them that. Mackenzie did not enjoy this letter; and,
after thinking over the matter for a week, he drafted a
letter, dating it the 28th of June, rejecting the whole proposal. This letter, however, *he did not send*; and, strange
to say we find Rolph writing on the 20th July, acknowledging
a letter received from Mackenzie that day, and thanking him
for "the spirit in which you regard the sincerity of my
intention to serve you and through you the public." "Be
assured," he says, "there was no jobbing about it. . . . I

never will deal in jobs. I will never propose anything
derogatory to your political standing or my own." The date
of this letter is somewhat of a puzzle for, there is a note in
Mackenzie's handwriting to this effect: "Wrote Dr. Rolph
July 17th in answer to his letter of 21st, 22nd, and 19th of
June, animadverting on them and on the proposition as
made known by Postmaster General Morris, and telling him
I had instantly scouted the proposition when I found what
it was, of which he had given me no knowledge." The
instant scouting is not very powerfully illustrated by the
withholding of the rejection from the 28th of June to the
17th of July. Of the letter written on the latter date no
copy has been preserved; but reasons for rejection are given
in the draft letter of the 28th of June, and these are of the
flimsiest kind, visibly adapted, for lack of better, to cover
retreat from a position felt to be as it really was, untenable.

The session opened at Quebec on the nineteenth of
August, and was marked by a furious explosion of wrath on
Mackenzie's part against Rolph. The occasion was a dispute
that had arisen between the latter and Mr. G. S. Boulton,
in the course of which Boulton had referred to the flag of
truce incident in connection with the Upper Canada rebellion
and the testimony of Lount.[14] Rolph defended himself as
best he could and courted investigation. Then Mackenzie
plunged into the debate. He affirmed that all that Lount had
said, and more, was true. "How," he said,

> a man who evidently feels keenly the black dishonour —
> at least the deadly dislike and distrust that all honour-
> able men must have of him after so vile an act — could
> be such an errant fool as to risk an investigation into
> it, upon so slight a ground for ultimate acquittal as the
> certificate of this man Carmichael,[15] I cannot conceive.
> . . . Why did he hypocritically smile in Sir Francis
> Head's face, and pledge his sacred honour to the people
> of Toronto that he was against the rebellion. . . . Miser-
> able, degraded, false-hearted sneak, you are caught.
> You have put on record what will provoke enquiries
> which will sear you as with a rod of iron. Yes, and it is
> left for you to be not only the despised of honour,
> loyalty, and truth, but to be a detested recreant to your
> brother criminals. Go, however, and dine and smile and
> advise with Lord Elgin. He has helped to make you the

guardian of Britain's chivalry and loyalty in America, and he at least should have all the honour of it.[16]

This was a strange tirade to come from a man who not so long before had expressed a desire for the return of Mr. Rolph to parliament, who quite lately, had been in friendly correspondence with him, plying him with newspaper extracts and suggestions of one kind and another intended to be of service to him, and had consented to accept an office at his hands. The side blow at Lord Elgin was most characteristic. In former days governors *chose their advisers*; and this was precisely the system Mackenzie had assailed. In Lord Elgin's time governors did so no longer; for the era of responsible government had been ushered in, and Lord Elgin had been obliged to accept Mr. Rolph at the hands of Mr. Hincks, who vainly hoped that the appointment of that gentleman would propitiate the "clear grit" section of the reformers, and attach them to his government. Vainly – because George Brown, stronger in his uncouthness than a score of Rolphs, all suavity and urbanity, – was now commanding that spartan band. Mackenzie knew all this, and yet he must have his fling at Lord Elgin. He was quite prepared to blame ministers; but he was not going to let responsible government, or anything else, deprive him of his old time luxury of blaming the governor as well.

Once more Mackenzie attempted to appeal to the country through a journal of his own. From January, 1853, to the autumn of 1860 he published, though not with great regularity, a weekly paper entitled *Mackenzie's Message*. The principal message that Mackenzie had at this time for the country was that its public men were in great part corrupt; that responsible government was a fraud, and that under the union Upper Canada was being sacrificed to Lower Canada. It is best, however, to allow him to speak a little for himself, as he is so able to do. In one of his first numbers he prints a letter he had written to the Earl of Aberdeen, then prime minister of England, in which he says that profligacy is staring him in the face everywhere; that there is no way of comprehending how the finances of the province are managed; that the governor virtually controlled the whole situation, and that "his ministers must yield to him or quit their berths, made immensely lucrative by the patronage and power of a country twice as popular and

thrice as wealthy as Scotland when united to England." Next
we find him complaining that Mr. Hincks is about to reward
a certain person with a registership for his faithfulness to
his personal interests," when another person has far superior
claims on the score of long residence and enterprise in the
section of country concerned. "Is this," he asks, "public
opinion?" Who said it was? Mackenzie never could get the
true formula of responsible government into his head. He
had helped to create a form of government that depended
absolutely on votes for its existence; and yet, when it shaped
its course to get or keep votes, he was dissatisfied. "As
matters go," he says again, "Upper Canada will soon insist
on a repeal of the Union rather than submit to distant and
unsympathizing legislation and perpetual pillage, and then
Lower Canada must shoulder half the debt her profligate
politicians are so fond of creating." He describes the way
in which things are done:

> A wharf or a light house is to be built – a canal or a
> railway is to be built – public printing is to be given
> out – large purchases are to be effected – townships are
> to be surveyed – Indians out west to be tranquillized –
> this commission is to be filled up or that . . . a hundred
> things I need not mention are to be performed. Who
> shall be Queen's counsel, and who shall have the fattest
> pickings of such jobs as the above? Who but members
> of the assembly and their near relatives? See how a sop
> of this kind has tamed editors at times and how the
> shutting off of the huge trough has set them roaring
> again.

He admires the fine roads in the neighborhood of Quebec,
but suspects that Upper Canada pays for them. "Upper
Canada seems to be a sort of milch cow for the brethren
down here. . . . Lord Elgin would seemingly sanction all
these things: when was there a bill injurious to the public
interest that he did not sanction?" In spite of all his talk
in former years about responsible government, Mackenzie
could not, or would not, get it into his head that Lord
Elgin's ministers were responsible for the bills he sanctioned.
Speaking of a general union of the British colonies in
North America he says: "The more I see of this country,
the more impracticable do I view any such scheme, and
am therefore compelled to adhere to an authority not seldom

cited, that of Chief Justice Robinson in his letter to Lord John Russell, 1839, where he affirms the thing to be impracticable." In a letter from Quebec to his constituents dated June 13th, 1853, he says:

> We have been assailed with such a host of officials and office beggars today and Saturday as would weary any living creature. Our time is wasted by a constant scramble for more pensions, more salaries, more plunder, and if any one complain all who have axes to grind howl at him in course. Our Lower Canada brethren seem to have no sense of shame in such matters. From a province of patriots, when out of place, they have been transformed into a province of placemen.

In the summer of 1853 Lord Elgin paid a visit to England. Noticing his departure Mackenzie credits him with "great tact in the management of cabinets and legislatures, and no want of ability in the choice of fit instruments for his purpose." It would have been fairer to say "no want of ability in making the best of such materials as the existing system of government compels him to use." In a letter to Hincks dated Toronto, November 8th, 1853, he speaks of having been "spared to see you squeezing enormous annual revenue from the yet slender resources of an agricultural people, and squandering it as even the old family compact could not have dared to do; for where they exacted one dollar of tax from society, you demand eight or ten." Mackenzie had decidedly a sense of humour. In July 1854, he published a short article entitled "The Assembly's Tradesmen" in which he gives a list of the goods furnished to the legislature by tradesmen in Quebec. Amongst these articles were a couple of rat traps upon which he remarks:

> Rats enough we certainly had among us – but if the people do not catch them at the polls Cardinal's[17] traps will never do it. John Langton, J. Price, J. Rolph, J. Hartman, Francis Hincks, Malcolm Cameron, George Crawford, Pierre Chauveau, Morin, Morrison, Sherwood, Lyons are much addicted to ratting, and now is the time to catch them if ever. Musson, the apothecary, charges the house three dollars for twenty pounds of

chloride of lime; and less would never have neutralized the odours from Hincks, Cameron & Co.'s rattery. We had bugs also in the legislature, and Musson demands one dollar for Smith's Exterminator. The election purge would be more apt to work a cure.

Mackenzie's affections were really harking back to old times and old associations. In the session of 1851, noticing in a letter to his constituents the absence of Sir Allan MacNab from the House owing to illness, he said that though opposed to him in politics he likes to see him in his place and missed him when absent; and now, in noticing the arrival of Sir Edmund Head, he wonders "whether he will prove more wise in his generation than the indiscreet Sir F. Head, or the generous and prejudiced but really kind and benevolent Metcalfe." "Indiscreet" is truly a mild word in Mackenzie's mouth as applied to Sir Francis Head. Imbedded in his nature was more toryism than he was aware of. In 1856 his opinion of the people was not improving, as the following may testify: "What the elections may do in New Brunswick I know not; but I much fear that the mercenary, servile, craven spirit abroad here would curse Canada with a fresh crop of clever, supple, yielding, selfish knaves, the fit representatives of a people careless of liberty, ignorant of its worth." In June 1856 we find him uttering the following strangely-worded caution: "Canadians! join no secret society; unite in no conspiracy; confide not in noisy politicians; destroy all papers that might injure your unsuspecting neighbor; *prepare for stormy times*; studiously avoid all expression, even in jest, of a desire for forcible independence or annexation by violence." It looks as if stress was meant to be laid on the words "forcible," and "by violence." Mackenzie was not the only one, at this time, [who] was led to despair of the Canadian constitution. Mr. Isaac Buchanan, in declining a nomination for the county of Huron, made the following grave statement:

Both the great principles for which I contended (responsible government and the secularization of the clergy reserves) have in name been yielded to the people and the practical good effect of them found to be nothing at all. It seems that, in a new country, there is not a class of men in circumstances to be trusted with the working of British institutions.

This was what former governors and colonial secretaries used to say, and what reformers abused them for saying. Mr. Buchanan concluded in favour of a written constitution for Canada, and in this he was strongly supported by Mackenzie, who recommended "going to work in earnest to have it carried into effect." Whatever he thought of Buchanan's political ideas – and there is reason to believe he adhered to them to the end – he soon lost faith in Buchanan himself, and spoke of him as "a base political cheat." He joined the *Globe* in its strong condemnation of the coalition government of 1854, characterizing it as "a band of political highwaymen led by gouty MacNab and orange Macdonald, renegade Scotsmen, slouches who have done oppression's dirty work, sanctioned too by the poor old defunct Robert Baldwin for the sake of John Ross[18] since September 14th, 1854."

This last outburst bears [the] date, November 27th, 1857. In the following year, harrassed by poverty and more or less failing in health, he resigned his seat in the legislature, but continued intermittently to publish his paper for a couple of years longer. To alleviate his position, some of those who regarded him as having rendered valuable services to the country in years gone by raised a fund amounting, Mr. Lindsey says, to £1250 for his benefit, out of which £950 was invested in the purchase of the house in Bond street, Toronto, in which his last days were spent. More might have been raised but for a disagreement between Mr. Mackenzie and the committee, which caused the former to insert a notice in the public journal in 1859 refusing to allow any more subscriptions – of which there were about $1500 outstanding – to be collected.[19] This led to a breach between Mackenzie and Lesslie, and the former said some hard things about one who had through life been his staunch friend and frequent benefactor.[20] It is not difficult to imagine the condition of mind to which a man of Mackenzie's temperament would be brought by the varied disappointments, anxieties, and miseries which crowded upon him in these later years. Finally the brain which in the past had performed such prodigies of toil, and responded to almost impossible demands, began to give way. Hope had deserted him, and when hope dies, the light of the soul goes out. During his last illness, his biographer informs us, "he would take no medicine, take no stimulant, obey no medical

directions." .Periods of prolonged unconsciousness super-
vened, and on the twenty-eighth of August, 1861, the sadly
perturbed spirit quitted the exhausted frame.

There is a hush by the bedside, and a hush must possess
the mind that has followed from its opening to its close
the troublous career of him who lies there, set free at last
from care and toil, from outward struggle and inward strife,
from the clamour of the world and the mutiny of self. What
strange peace may flow around him now, who knows? Has
the riddle of life been read? Have its discords been keyed
into harmony? Has its confusion felt the touch of a divine
law of order? To us at least who live, with work as yet
unfinished, with some portion of our destiny yet to accomplish, there comes a message from the passive face of the
dead – a message interpreted by one as "What phantoms
we are, and what phantoms we pursue!," but which perhaps
may lend itself to a better reading. No message can be
authentic which tends to reduce the value of significance
of life. The true message of death is that we take a larger
view of life, and strive more for self conquest than for
victory over others. One would not dwell needlessly on the
errors of the dead; but in thinking of the broken, passion-
swayed, tempest-tossed and self-tormented career of him
whose life has been our study, it seems, as a whole, wonderfully to enforce and bring home the counsel delivered by
the best and wisest friend of mankind:

*"Judge not that ye be not judged; for with what judgment
ye judge ye shall be judged, and with what measure ye mete
it shall be measured to you again."*[21]

The character of Wm. Lyon Mackenzie – the true quality
and significance of the man – has, it is trusted, been set
forth dispassionately and not altogether inadequately in the
preceding pages. A man is best judged by his own facts and
utterances, not by the opinions of friends or adversaries,
and still less by the second-hand generalities of hack-work
historical summaries. The reader of this work will at least
know what the man said and what he did, what virtues he
attributed to himself, and what faults he acknowledged,
what he accomplished, and what he repented of. His was
not a complex character in the least, though it certainly was
a self-contradictory one. There were no dark corners in his
mind. All his faults were conspicuous, which was a moral
advantage at least. 'Cleanse me,' the Psalmist prayed, 'from

secret faults.' He had neither the subtlety of Rolph, nor the reserve and reticence of Robert Baldwin, nor the caution of Bidwell. His instincts were generous, and in spite of a singular readiness to pervert facts in his public statements, there was in his nature a fundamental veracity. Why *would* facts be obstinately *so* when he wanted them otherwise? Wasn't it their fault? He had no gifts of concealment however: while he could say things that were glaringly untrue, he could not act with calculated duplicity.

As to his influence on the political development of Canada very different views have been expressed; but the best opinion of today, unless the writer of this volume is wholly in error, is that it was retardatory rather than otherwise. Even his old friend, Joseph Hume, as we have seen, thought he had thrown things back. Rebellion, if unsuccessful, is always followed by reaction – sometimes even if successful – and it is not difficult to trace in the policy of the three governors who preceded Lord Elgin, and even in the early policy of Lord Elgin himself, a less favourable disposition towards responsible government than the Colonial Office had begun to manifest in the days of Sir Francis Head. The problem of Upper Canada, as it presented itself to the home authorities, was complicated, it should always be remembered, by the companion problem of Lower Canada. The two provinces had similar constitutions, and it was difficult, therefore, openly to apply different principles in the administration of one of them from those applied in the administration of the other. Lower Canada had taken the bit in its teeth in a way that Upper Canada had not. There the government was face to face with a permanently hostile majority of the legislative Assembly. In Upper Canada the government had from time to time the support of the Assembly, and was strongly supported in that body for over a year before the rebellion broke out; this it was that made Mackenzie so furious. It is easy to see how the home government would be restrained to some extent in its treatment of the upper province by the policy imposed in the case of the lower. Mackenzie – we have his own word for it – had pledged himself to support a rising in Lower Canada by a similar movement in Upper Canada; and thus it was that the latter province was most needlessly dragged out of a course of steady and peaceful, if not very rapid, constitutional development.

Character is destiny, or, as an ancient sage has it, 'Ηϑος ἀνϑρωπω δαιμων. Mackenzie played his part according to his nature and the influences by which he was surrounded. He threw the cards into confusion, and broke in upon the better plans and clearer purposes of other men; he committed grave errors and even great wrongs, on which he passed sentence himself with all the severity that history demands. But in the broadest sense he preserved his integrity; his aims were not commonplace or selfish; and however fully we may confirm his own condemnation of his political course, the judgment we pass will not be unmitigated by a touch of sympathy with what was essential in the man, and with his ultimate aims.

NOTES TO TEXT

Those notes enclosed in brackets have been added by the editor. All others are those of the author. Certain attempts have been made to make LeSueur's notes consistent in style, and the editor has used the terms "ibid." and "op. cit." where appropriate; otherwise the notes have been left in the form originally used.

– A. B. McK.

Chapter One

1. [Sir Peregrine Maitland (1777-1854) was Lieutenant-governor of Upper Canada from 1818 to 1828 and of Nova Scotia from 1828 to 1832. For biographical details see D. B. Read, *The Lieutenant-Governors of Upper Canada* (Toronto, 1900).]

2. [In LeSueur's typescript these figures were not provided. The figures given here are from the page-proof version on microfilm in the Public Archives of Canada. (p. 15)]

3. A committee of which Mr. Mackenzie was chairman, appointed by the Upper Canada Assembly in the year 1831, to consider that state of the representation of the people, made a report, doubtless drafted by Mackenzie himself, in which the statement occurs that "It (the Constitutional Act of 1791) lacks the animating principle of the British Constitution by which the loss of public confidence insures the loss of office and power." This was practically the ground taken by Sir Frances Bond Head in his controversy with the reform party in 1836.

4. "On the breaking out of the war of 1812 between Britain and the United States the settlers in Upper Canada were generally on the highroad to prosperity,

cultivating a land as any under heaven outside the
valley of the Nile, and with less waste land than in
any country of like extent." Thomas Conant, *Upper
Canada Sketches*, p. 44. This testimony is of value as
derived directly from ancestors strongly in sympathy
with political reform.

5. Mr. Conant, in the work already cited, page 26, tells
how three brothers Conant, ancestors of his in
Massachusetts, met during the war "behind blinded
windows and closed doors. On canvassing matters
thoroughly they came to the conclusion that the
colonies would never succeed. . . . Britain's name
carried with it a sense of power and unlimited
resources, and Roger Conant could not make himself
believe that she would ever let the colonies go."

6. Robert Gourlay saw very little need at this time for
a legislature in Upper Canada at all. "Sure I am,"
he says, "that it would have been better both for
Canada and the parent state had there been no
attempt to transplant the British Constitution – much
better for Canada to have had no parliament up to
the present time (1821). Had ministers simply and
sincerely considered that all of government which is
required to make people happy and contented in a
young country, is only security for person and
property; had they, with this single object in view,
chalked out certain rules to be observed by a governor and council; and devised right plans for the
disposal of the wild land, the provinces might have
flourished far beyond what they have done, been free
of all discontent, and run no risk from invasion."

7. i.e. One seventh as Clergy Reserves and one seventh
as Crown Reserves.

8. "It is generally supposed at home that all the first
settlers were loyalists who sought refuge from the
American rebellion. It is true that a great proportion
were so; but, even in the very commencement of
Governor Simcoe's administration, it was clearly
observed that many of those who sought his protection, and obtained large grants of land by stating
that they preferred to live under a monarchy, did so
with the sole view of obtaining those grants, and then

cared not to conceal that they were Americans at heart. . . . In the outbreak of 1837 the portions of the province that displayed disaffection were precisely those in which the first American settlers located themselves." *Canada, as it was, is, and may be,* by Lieut. Col. Sir Richard H. Bonnycastle, Royal Engineers, London, 1852. The author resided in Canada for several years before and a few years after the rebellion. [Gore was Lieutenant-Governor of Upper Canada from 1806 to 1811, left on leave just prior to the War of 1812, and returned to the colony for two years of service commencing in the autumn of 1815. See G. M. Craig, *Upper Canada; the Formative Years* (Toronto, 1963), p. 43.]

9. [Peter Hunter (1746-1805) was Lieutenant-Governor of Upper Canada from 1799 to 1805, during which time he also held the position of commander-in-chief of British forces in Canada. See: E. A. Cruikshank, "A memoir of Lieutenant-General Peter Hunter," Ontario Historical Society, *Papers and Records*, 1934; Read, *op. cit.*]

10. See Note D on "The Political State of Upper Canada in 1806," in the Report on the Dominion Archives for 1892, which throws much light on the proceedings not only of Thorpe, but of Willcocks, Wyatt, and John Mills Jackson, all importations from the British Isles.

11. [John Charles Dent, *The Story of the Upper Canadian Rebellion; largely derived from original sources and documents* (Toronto: C. B. Robinson, 1885). For biographical information on Dent, see Donald Swainson's introduction to Dent's *The Last Forty Years* (Toronto: McClelland and Stewart, 1972).]

12. William Lyon Mackenzie himself says in the first number of his *Colonial Advocate*: "The majority of those who have witnessed his (Gourlay's) proceedings here think he much lacked discretion. We think so too. What then? Oppression often drives a wise man mad." The latter remark is not very relevant as the proceedings which showed lack of discretion *preceded* the oppression.

13. 59 George 111, chapter 11.

Chapter Two

1. [Charles Lindsey,] *Life and Times of William Lyon Mackenzie*, Toronto [: R. R. Randall], 1862.
2. *Ibid.*, Vol. 1, p. 16.
3. At the present time one daughter only, survives.
4. Vol. 1, p. 39.
5. "The great drawback to progress in Upper Canada was her incapacity to control the imposition of duties by the St. Lawrence, owing to the non-possession of a sea-port. The revenue laws of the Province applied only to the imports from the United States." [William] Kingsford, *History of Canada*, Vol. X, p. 222.
6. It may be well to record the exact language used by the Lieutenant-Governor: the occasion was the opening of the legislature on the 12th October, 1818 – "You will, I doubt not, feel a just indignation at the attempts which have been made to excite discontent and to organize sedition. Should it appear to you that a convention of delegates cannot exist without danger to the constitution, in framing a law of repression, your dispassionate wisdom will be careful that it shall not unwarily trespass on that sacred right of the subject to seek redress of his grievances by petition."
7. D. B. Read, Q.C., *The Lieutenant-Governors of Upper Canada and Ontario*, Chapter IX.
8. The *Gazette* was the official paper, but a section of it was non-official.

Chapter Three

1. See *ante*, page 24.
2. "It is a fact worth mentioning," says Mr. Dent (*Story of the Upper Canada Rebellion*, Vol. 1, p. 96), "that attorney general Robinson was the only member who recorded his vote against the repealing statute." This is a surprising statement considering that Mr. Robinson was not a member of the house at all at this time – he was elected for the first time in the follow-

ing summer – and that the vote for repeal was as above stated, unanimous. Mr. Robinson's elder brother, Peter, was a member of the house, and it happened that he was the seconder of the motion. Mr. Dent appears to have got his notes mixed: attorney general Robinson was, in 1829, the only member of the house who opposed the repeal of the statute of 1804 "for the better securing the province against seditious attempts &c." – the one under which Gourlay was banished.

The Colonial Secretary, Lord Bathurst, was somewhat disconcerted at the passing of this bill and hinted to Sir Peregrine Maitland that he should have reserved it for the significance of his Majesty's pleasure. Sir Peregrine under date May 7th, 1821, replied with some little spirit that he could not see why it should have been so expressed in the Act of 1791, or else in his instructions, and that two similar preceding acts had not been reserved; nor had any question been raised on the subject. He pointed out, moreover, that forty was a very moderate number of representatives for the population of Upper Canada, which was now in excess of that which Lower Canada possessed in 1791 when the Act fixed the number of members of his Assembly at fifty. His Lordship did not return to the charge. Canadian Archives, Q. 329, p. 151.

3. *Life of Sir John Beverley Robinson*, by Major General C. W. Robinson, C.B., pp. 150-51.

4. The one which Mr. Robinson had been influential in getting passed in 1822.

5. Quoting from the *Colonial Advocate* of January 10th, 1828, a declaration by Mackenzie in favour of "such a change in the mode of administering the government as would give the people an effectual control over the action of their representatives, and through them over the actions of the Executive," Mr. Lindsey, Vol. 1, p. 140, note, says: "These sentiments he claimed to have enunciated in the first number of this paper; but, if so, the utterance was not very distinct."

6. "Of Upper Canada politicians we are entitled to place Mr. Mackenzie among the very earliest advo-

cates of responsible government. It is doubtless true
that others afterwards made the attainment of this
principle more of a specialty than he did; for where
abuses grew up with rank luxuriance, he could not
help pausing to cut them down in detail." Lindsey,
Vol. 1, p. 179. To this it may be added that Mackenzie did not possess the instinct for party leadership; Robert Baldwin did. The one was an idealist;
the other a doctrinaire.

7. The difficulties which had arisen in connection with
the government of Lower Canada had led the British
Government to consider the advisability of uniting
the two provinces. A bill for that purpose was in
fact proffered in the year Mr. Robinson went to
England (1822) but was withdrawn on account of
the strong opposition which, it became evident, it
would encounter in both provinces.

8. ["If so, it will always remain so."]

Chapter Four

1. [A word was obviously missing here in the original
typescript, and "interest" has been inserted. It seems
to convey LeSueur's meaning.]

2. Lindsey, Vol. 1, p. 67.

3. *Story of the Upper Canada Rebellion*, Vol. 1, p. 110.

4. *Ibid.*, p. 104.

5. ["Opt for a just and unbending man."]

6. *Colonial Advocate*, 27th January, 1825.

7. *Ibid.*, 3rd February, 1825.

8. *Ibid.*, 11th April, 1825.

Chapter Five

1. *Life and Times of William Lyon Mackenzie*, Vol. 1,
p. 126.

2. May 23rd and June 16th, 1825.

3. Some four years after this the Attorney General,
Mr. Robinson, was made chief justice, and Mr.

Boulton was advanced to the attorney generalship. Sir John Colborne was lieutenant-governor at the time, and we find him writing to the colonial secretary, Sir George Murray, as follows: "Mr. H. Boulton, the attorney general is *very* unpopular, and I regret to add that his conduct in many instances, as a professional man, appears not free from blame. The local government, therefore, will be rather embarrassed by his promotion." Canadian Archives, Q. 352, p. 28.

4. He hinted, it will be remembered, that their conduct was almost enough to drive Mr. Robinson to suicide.

5. There were two bills on this subject. The second, which was introduced by the attorney general, was entitled "An Act to conform British subjects in their titles to real estates in this province derived through aliens." It has not been thought necessary to narrate the passage of this bill through the legislature.

6. "The attorney general having carried every measure he wanted to carry and put behind every measure he wished to leave untouched (either with the connivance or from the carelessness of the movers) obliged the tamed legislators to sum up the supplies, roads, contingencies and a hundred other things in a word on a day, and be off about their business. Mr. Rolph as a leader is not quite a match for the minister, who is full of finesse and always succeeds." *Colonial Advocate*, 22nd February, 1827. Mackenzie had not in reality a vast amount of respect for the special tribunes of the people in the Assembly. That has already appeared; and is further shown by the expression applied to them in the *Advocate* of the 14th June, 1827, "The speech-makers, haranguers and popularity hunters of the commons house of parliament."

7. These words certainly do not imply any deep sense, at the time, of political wrong or even of defect in the system of government.

8. Brother of the celebrated bishop of Exeter.

9. Father of Sir Allan MacNab. (The name was variously spelt in those days.)

10. [The phrase is Italian, meaning "within his breast."]

11. *History of Canada*, Vol. X, p. 229.

Chapter Six

1. *Colonial Advocate*, 12th January, 1826.
2. Peterborough took its name from the Christian name of this gentleman. See Captain Basil Hall's interesting and highly favorable account of this settlement, which he visited in July, 1827, *Travels in North America*, Vol. II, chapter 10.
3. *Colonial Advocate*, 13th April, 1826.
4. [Certain words in the original typescript had somehow been omitted; the phrase "is questionable" seems to convey the author's intended meaning.]
5. This appears to have been the only reference made by Macaulay to Mackenzie's family. Though most objectionable, it hardly bears out Mackenzie's statement in the *Advocate* that the design of Macaulay's communication was "to scoff and mock my mother, an old woman of seventy-five years, to drag my unoffending wife and children before the public to be jeered at about their poverty"; nor yet Mr Lindsey's allegation (Vol. 1, p. 142) that Macaulay made "jeering remarks in reference to Mr. Mackenzie's mother, an aged woman of seventy-five years." If Macaulay said anything else about Mr. Mackenzie's mother neither Mackenzie himself nor his biographer has quoted it.
6. ["Far from the matters (or business) at hand."]
7. Instead of "O lymoges! O Austria!" The home of the Robinson family before the American Revolution was in Virginia.
8. Nothing but a sense of obligation to historical truth could have induced the author of this book to deface his pages with the long-forgotten scurrility which follows. But just because it has been long-forgotten, and because from the very nature of the case, every one at the time of its production was only too willing to let it pass out of remembrance, the true posture of affairs in Upper Canada from 1826 onwards has not been properly understood, save by a few. The *Colonial Advocate* of the 18th May, 1826, fixed irrevocably the attitude of Mackenzie to the higher society of the province, and of that higher society to

him. It is not too much to say *"Hoc fonte derivata clades/In patriam populumque fluxit."* [The phrase is from Horace: "The damage was derived from this source/And it has flooded upon the people and the country."] – The *clades* [damage] of the rebellion.

9. Mr. Robinson's mother became Mrs. Beman by her second marriage in the year 1802.

10. Why this economy of letters it is hard to imagine, but so it is in the text.

11. The following is the roll-call of the principal [of] these early practicioners of lynch law in Canada: Charles and Raymond Baley, sons of Mr. Baley the inspector general; Henry Sherwood, son of Judge Sherwood; John Lyons, private secretary to the Lieutenant Governor; Samuel P. Jarvis; Charles Richardson, brother of the author of "Wacousta"; James King, a student in the office of solicitor General Boulton; Charles Hervard, son of the auditor of land patents; and Peter Macdougall, a business man of the town. The party was said to consist of fifteen altogether, but the evidence against the others appears not to have been conclusive.

12. Lindsey, Vol. 1, p. 99.

13. [See: Charles Lindsey, *Life and Times of William Lyon Mackenzie* (Toronto: P. R. Randall, 1862), Vol. I, pp. 78-107; William Kingsford, *The History of Canada* (Toronto: Rowsell & Hutchison, 1898), Vol. X, pp. 240-244.]

14. The columns of the *Advocate* afford very little clue to what this provocation consisted of; and Mr. Lindsey himself gives no particulars whatever apart from his reference to the Macauley correspondence, which was followed almost immediately by Mackenzie's outburst. From the pamphlet published by Macaulay, in which the whole matter was resumed, he quotes only half a dozen words, presumably the most offensive to be found in it. These are given above. What the Robinsons had to do with the business is past finding out.

15. Vol. 1, p. 96.

16. Pamphlet "On the Destruction of Mackenzie's Press," Ancaster, U.C., 1828 (In Toronto Public Library).

Chapter Seven

1. [Literally: "Nothing was ever so unequal to (or unlike) itself."]
2. Of Collins Mr. Lindsey has the following mention: "Free speech met small encouragement at the hands of the executive. Francis Collins, who had been the official reporter of the legislature for five years, in an evil hour, in 1825, commenced the publication of a newspaper, the *Canadian Freeman*, and in that year the lieutenant governor cut off his remuneration." Mr. Mackenzie's account of him is less sympathetic: "Mr. Collins began by offering to defend the acts of the present executive, loving the wages of sin better than truth, but finding his services despised, he turned round and abused them. . . . He has lost the esteem of the country and his cloven foot can no longer be had." *Colonial Advocate*, 13th and 27th March, 1827. Mackenzie was strong on "the cloven foot."
3. *Colonial Advocate*, June 14th, 1827.
4. Speech reported in *ibid.*, March 13th, 1828.
5. *Ibid.*, April 26th and May 7th, 1827.
6. *Ibid.*, January 25th, 1827.
7. *Ibid.*, March 15th, 1827.
8. *The Autobiography of John Galt*, Vol. I, p. 319.
9. *Ibid.*, Vol. II, chapter 2.
10. There were two letters written by Galt to Mackenzie, the second dated May 1st, 1825, again thanking him for his civility and ordering the paper to be sent to the Canada Company, London.
11. *Colonial Advocate*, January 3rd, 1828.
12. In this very year, 1828, this whole question was discussed at some length before the committee of the House of Commons appointed "to enquire into the state of the civil government of Canada." One of the chief witnesses examined was Mr. James Stephen of the colonial office – the same official who was so strongly denounced by Sir Francis Head on account of his democratic properties. That gentleman's opinion was that the grievance alleged on this head was "merely imaginary," and that much more substantial evils would ensue, in a country like Upper Canada, if the judges were independent of the Crown.

The Crown could act in restraint of many forms. of misbehaviour which would not support a case for removal by the action of parliament; while the danger of a judge's being removed by the Crown "without the most grave and sufficient cause is surely very inconsiderable." In a small colony, he said, or even in a large one, "people are exceedingly united to each other, by domestic, social, and party ties; and such unions exercise the most powerful influence in the legislative bodies. When a judge is dependent on them there will always be a danger lest he should make unworthy and unbecoming concessions to conciliate their good will or avert their displeasure." Questioned as to whether there was not some danger that a judge dependent on the executive might not become its partisan in any difficulty between it and the representatives of the people, the witness frankly acknowledged that such a danger did exist; "but," said he, "you must make your choice between opposite dangers, as in all human affairs." The time for constituting independent judges would come, he finally said, when the country had developed to such an extent as to give a sufficient controlling force to public opinion.

13. *Colonial Advocate*, April 3rd, 1828.

Chapter Eight

1. Mr. Dunn died in May, 1854. Mr. Mackenzie, who was then publishing his "Message," devotes the following notice to him a few words of which we venture to underline: "Mr. Dunn was both able and honest; he was a faithful guardian to the public purse, fond of encouraging public improvements, yet utterly averse to all kinds of peculation. He generously aided not a few of the members of the legislature and many others when in a pecuniary difficulty; powerfully supported the Welland Canal; encouraged the commencement of the St. Lawrence Canals; was a great advocate for good roads, and often risked his office and its emoluments to promote reform and progress.

To colonial oppression he was an unvarying enemy; and as a bank director none could be more liberal and impartial. . . . Mr. Dunn has been called to his last audit at the early age of sixty-two years, and his memory will remain sweet and pleasant in the recollection of the early settlers of Canada, for he was the pioneer of the forest, a true and unchanging friend and his heart soon warmed to the Canadian soil." *Message*, May 26th, 1854. It is not generally supposed that the "Family Compact" kept men of this kind in office. Mr. Dunn was made receiver-general and a member of the legislative council under Sir Peregrine Maitland in the year 1821, and retained the office till the union of the provinces twenty years later.

2. It may be safely asserted that there was never any dependence of either branch of the legislature on the executive in the old province of Upper Canada comparable to that which exists in Canada to-day under the system we call "responsible government." The parliamentary majority by which a government is supported must continue their support on risk of seeing the most substantial benefits *in esse*, and in many cases most enticing ones *in posse*, withdrawn from themselves. The mere money indemnity paid to members – in Upper Canada it was $2 per diem – is in the great majority of cases a powerful dissuasive against bringing on a general election under the auspices of another party; while the patronage and other privileges they enjoy, with possible reversions in the shape of senatorships, judgeships, commissionerships, &c. all tell in the same direction. On the other hand we have the testimony of Lord Sydenham that the "placemen," as he called them, "generally voted against the executive." See his life by Scrope, p. 149. [LeSueur here refers to George Julius Duncombe Poulett Scrope (ed.), *Memoir of the Life of the Right Honourable Charles, Lord Sydenham* (2nd ed. London: J. Murray, 1844). G. Poulett Scrope was Sydenham's brother.]

3. This was an Act passed in the year 1774 (the year of the Quebec Act), its object being to provide a revenue out of which the expenses of civil govern-

ment in the province could be, at least in part, defrayed. The duties levied were chiefly, almost exclusively, on spirits and molasses, and the proceeds, arising as they did under an imperial statute, were appropriated by the executive government, subject to the sanction of the Lords Commissioners of the Treasury, and not by the provincial legislature. This Act was not abrogated by the Constitutional Act of 1791.

4. See above.

5. *Colonial Advocate*, November 13th, 1828.

6. Speaking of this address, Mackenzie (*Colonial Advocate*, November 24th, 1828) says: "Among the 1440 signatures appended to this address were perceived very few crosses indeed. The signatures afforded on the average as fair a specimen of an educated and intelligent population as could be met with in any part of his Majesty's Dominions." We may take this as one of many indications that Upper Canada was doing very fairly in those days. Amongst the signatures is that of the unfortunate Samuel Lount, afterwards hanged for treason, as well as that of Mackenzie himself, who eluded that fate.

7. Mackenzie's bill as rendered by sheriff Jarvis was put in evidence and was as follows:

Wm. L. Mackenzie
To Election Expenses.
(To ¼ share of hustings, stationery

1st day(	printing and constables	£4, 7, 6
	(To fee of returning officer	1, 3, 4
	(To " " poll clerk	1, 3, 4
	(Constables	15, 0
2nd day(	Returning Officer	1, 3, 4
	(Poll Clerk	1, 3, 4
	(Constables	5, 0
3rd day(	Returning Officer	1, 3, 4
	(Poll Clerk	1, 3, 4

£12, 7, 6

Mr. Lindsey states that Mackenzie's expenses in this election amounted altogether to over £500.

8. A younger brother of Dr. Rolph, George Rolph, had

been returned in the general election for the county of Halton.

9. Canadian Archives, Q. 351, p. 29.

10. This visit was made shortly after the close of the session of 1829. Referring to it, Mr. Lindsey (Vol. 1, page 161) says: "The alarming sound of a threatened dissolution of the Union even then fell upon his ears; he could detect in them nothing but the complaints of discontented faction." Circumstances *do* alter cases, and standpoints have much to do with conclusions.

11. Gourlay, who was quite a bit of a thinker – very much more so than Mackenzie –, was strongly of opinion that taxes in Upper Canada were too low. Generalizing, he says: "The people fairly represented will not endure that degree of pressure (in taxation) required to put industry to its full stretch; and while there is not sufficient necessity to goad, there is want of ambition to lead on." He praises greatly the English system of taxation, but says it never could have been carried into effect but by "a corrupt representation of the people." The rotten boroughs were as "the handspikes which squeezed from the grape the wine which itself would not yield." *Statistical Account of Upper Canada*. Introduction, page ccclxxx.

12. *Colonial Advocate*, April 1st, 1830.

13. [The word used here in the original typescript was "indefence," but it was obviously a typing error.]

Chapter Nine

1. Charles Lindsey, *Life and Times of William Lyon Mackenzie*, Vol. I, p. 180.

2. [LeSueur spoke here from personal experience: from 1856 until his retirement in 1902 he had worked for the Post Office of the government of Canada.]

3. Mackenzie sounds a note of rather savage triumph over the change: "Now we shall have good government assured to Upper Canada; the right men are at the helm of affairs in England, and the base, mercenary hirelings who, to serve their own private ends,

have so long kept the province in strife and confusion, will follow their arbitrary master into oblivion." *Colonial Advocate*, January 13th, 1831.

4. In the previous session he had sent down, in compliance with the wish of the House, a statement of the receipts under various heads and of the total expenditure of the fund for the five years 1825, 1826, 1827, 1828 and 1829, but had not shown in detail how the money had been applied.

5. When Sir Francis Head came out in January, 1836, he had instructions to arrange for handing over the casual and territorial revenue to the province in consideration of a moderate increase in the permanent grant for the expenses of civil government. The matter was discussed in the legislature, but the necessary bill was not passed; and things remained on the old footing till the Union.

6. The contract was in the name of his brother-in-law and foreman, James Baxter.

7. "We have in our possession a portrait of the late Mr. Canning which bears a striking resemblance to that of Mr. John Rolph; also another engraving, which the Bostonians affirm to be a correct likeness of General Jackson, the President of the United States, taken at a more youthful period of his life, but which every one who has seen it declares to be as much like the head and countenance of General Sir John Colborne, our most excellent lieutenant governor, as 'one pea is like another'." *Colonial Advocate*, March 18th, 1830. Sir John had then been over sixteen months in the province.

8. This is precisely what happened. Baldwin, to gain power for the Upper Canada reformers, who were in a decided minority at the time of the Union, made an alliance with the great body of the French Canadians who, like his own party, had been in strong opposition, armed or unarmed, to the government. The union was wholly factitious, as George Brown, not to speak of Mackenzie himself, soon perceived; and not only factitious but likely to be very injurious to Upper Canada. Under Brown's leadership the Upper Canada reformers regained what they had lost, or were in danger of losing,

under that of Baldwin – a true consciousness of their own aims and ideals; and just as they did so they fell away from the Lower Canada alliance. Thus was brought about that opposition between the two sections of "united" Canada which resulted in the "deadlock" of 1864, out of which an exit was found in Confederation.

9. The French Canadian *habitants* always objected to being called "peasants," the word being in some way associated in their minds with social and political inferiority.

10. [John McGregor, *British America* (Edinburgh: W. Blackwood, 1832), 2 Vols.]

Chapter Ten

1. Vol. 1, p. 202.

2. Professor Adam Shortt, "Municipal Government in Ontario, an Historical Sketch," p. 20. Published in University of Toronto Studies, History and Economics, Vol. II, no. 2.

3. The division list was as follows: Yeas – (Attorney-general H. L.) Boulton, Berczy, (G. S.) Boulton, Brown, Burwell, Elliott, (A.) Fraser, (R.) Fraser, Ingersoll, Jones, Lewis, McMartin, MacNab, Macon, Morris, Mount, Robinson, Samson, Shade, (Solicitor-general) Hagerman, Thomson, VanKoughnet, Warren, Werden. Nays – Beardsley, Bidwell, Buell, Campbell, Clark, Cook, Duncombe, Howard, Ketchum, Lyons, McColl, Perry, Randall, Roblin, Shaver.

4. [Sir Thomas Erskine May (1815-1886), an English constitutional jurist, author of several works on British parliamentary practice, as well as *Constitutional History of England since the Accession of George III, 1760-1860* (1861-63) and *Democracy in Europe* (1877).]

5. *Parliamentary Papers*. Seventh edition, pp. 60, 62.

6. [Frederick] Bradshaw, *Self-Government in Canada* [1903], p. 119.

7. The Ontario constituency of North Renfrew, vacant from June 1st, 1902, to December 7th, 1903.

Chapter Eleven

1. Judge Macaulay, says Mr. Lindsey (Vol. I, p. 249), "showed the greatest impartiality on the trial, though there might be a question about the adequacy of the punishment awarded." Mr. Mackenzie, in a letter from London to the *Colonial Advocate*, says that the judge "might just as well have amerced him in two pence."

2. How kindly Mackenzie could write of people at times, even when they belonged to a class with which in general he was not wont to sympathise is shown in a passage found on page 228 of the book referred to, where he speaks of the suicide of Sir John Colborne's private secretary, Mr. I. Mudge, which occurred at York in the month of June, 1831. The passage is interesting in itself and deserves to be quoted: "Mr. Mudge, as I learn, was nephew to the lady of Sir John Colborne – he appeared to be about five or six and twenty years of age – held the rank of lieutenant in the British army, and filled with honour to himself and advantage to all who had business to do with the head of the government the important office of confidential secretary to the lieutenant Governor. As a man of business he was methodical, prompt, and decisive; and in his habits sobriety and love of order were distinguishing characteristics. Benevolence was visible in his actions; it is understood that for a long period before his death he allowed a former servant who had fallen into a lingering disease the same wages as when in health in his service."

   If Sir John Colborne was a hypocritical governor, as Mackenzie elsewhere alleged, he had at least chosen a good secretary. The administration generally had a pestilent habit of employing good executive officers.

3. One of John Galt's novels.

4. [Joseph Hume (1777-1855), radical member of the British House of Commons from 1818 to 1855. A Benthamite "philosophical radical." Hume was also a free trader and a dogged believer in "retrenchment" in the area of expenditures from the public purse.]

5. [William Cobbett (1763-1835), "radical" journalist

and author, whose writings reflected and described the way of life and the problems of the English "common man." *Rural Rides* (1830) was a major account of a decade of travels around the English countryside; his weekly *Political Register* (1802-1835) was an articulate, graphic, and forceful account of popular grievances. Daniel O'Connell (1775-1847), the greatest Irish political leader in the House of Commons during the first half of the nineteenth century; a major force behind the Emancipation Act of 1828 and leader of the movement to repeal the union of England and Ireland.]

6. [Henry George, third Earl Grey (1802-1894). These letters were later published as *The Elgin-Grey Papers, 1846-1852*; edited with notes and appendices by Sir Arthur G. Doughty (Ottawa: King's Printer, 1937).]

7. The "worst markets" here referred to are simply the English market. From that market all goods could be imported (under Imperial Act, 6 George IV, Chapter 14) free of duty. On goods imported from foreign markets duties varying from seven and a half to thirty per cent were imposed. For far the larger part of the goods which the province required to import the English market was the *best* market.

8. Letter of "Guy Pollock" in *York Courier* of December, 1832, replying to one by "William Tell" in the *Colonial Advocate*.

9. It had been summoned for the 31st October.

10. Strange to say, neither the date nor even the fact of his arrival at York is directly mentioned in his own paper. In the vulgar sense Mackenzie was never a self-advertiser.

Chapter Twelve

1. [This sentence in the original typescript made little sense: "Prudential considerations than, if no other, made it necessary that Mackenzie's views and statements should be brought publicly to the notice of the Upper Canada executive; how best to do it became the practical question."]

2. ["Simplicity is blameless!"]
3. Further light is thrown on Colborne's views by the following summary of a letter from him to Hay, under secretary of state for the colonies, dated 16th January, 1833, taken from the Canadian Archives *Report* for 1900, page 421: – "Has received the voluminous correspondence resulting from Mackenzie's visit. . . . Many of his statements and insinuations are against the Assembly and Council; believe, therefore, that the production of the despatch before prorogation would cause much irritation. Several of the subjects spoken of by Mackenzie had been laid before the colonial secretary by the Assembly and lieutenant governor, and two of the most respectable and opulent gentlemen had been sent to London to urge payment of the war losses without effect, but as soon as a persevering imposter gives his version the claims are taken into consideration. . . . If it is understood that a demagogue makes an impression, while those who, in times of emergency, are looked to for support continue to be overlooked, the reputation of the demagogue must rise in the estimation of his fellows and enable him to increase his factious party. . . . The province is tranquil and many of Mackenzie's supporters are not sorry he is absent."
4. The discussion of the Council is announced in the first paragraph of their address in the following words: "Having perused this despatch, we comply with your excellency's desire in returning it to your excellency, taking it for granted that the only reason for laying it before the legislative council was the direction contained in the despatch that it should receive publication."
5. [In LeSueur's revised and re-written version of 1915 there were fifteen pages of new material added at this point. The two paragraphs which conclude both original and revised versions were virtually identical. The new material used by LeSueur in his revised version consisted mainly of detailed description and quotation from correspondence between the Colonial Office and Sir John Colborne. Among the letters quoted are Stanley to Colborne, April 2, 1832 concerning the expulsions of Mackenzie from the

Assembly), in acknowledgement of Colborne's letter of 31 January, 1832; Colborne to the Colonial Office, June 18, 1832, in reply; Goderich to Colborne, 6 March, 1833 (dismissing Boulton and Hagerman); Colborne to Goderich, 30 April, 1833. The gist of LeSueur's use of this material is given in the first paragraph of the new material: "It will be instructive to do here what has not hitherto been done, namely, to present somewhat fully the correspondence that took place on this matter between the Colonial Office and the provincial Executive, as it will exhibit their respective points of view, and afford evidence that good intentions were not wanting on either side, but that each in its own way was anxious to safeguard the interests of the colony." *William Lyon Mackenzie* (microfilm version in page-proof), pp. 281-295; Public Archives of Canada.]

6. Mr. Lindsey writes (Vol. 1, p. 276): "An article appeared in the *Upper Canada Courier*, attributed to the pen of the attorney general containing direct threats of rebellion." Would it not be well to banish from history such phrases as "attributed to the pen of," unless some information is forthcoming as to *who* did the attributing and *on what grounds*? Certainly it seems highly improbable that Boulton, on the eve of setting out for England to justify himself, should have penned such an article – necessarily entrusting certain persons with the secret of it. There is nothing moreover to show that he ever entertained such sentiments. Mr. Mackenzie himself always attributed the article to Gurnett, editor of the paper.

Chapter Thirteen

1. *Colonial Advocate*, November 25th, 1833.
2. i.e. In addition to having an elective legislative council, referred to elsewhere in the letter, which bears date 19 Richmond St., 10th September, 1833.
3. His study of the question could not have been very profound, seeing that a short residence in the United States served to reverse the opinion here announced,

which is also greatly at variance with the newspaper extracts he had furnished to Lord Dalhousie.

4. "Bank rags" that were good for gold after repudiation had become general in the United States.

5. "Mr. Ketchum was one of the most benevolent and beneficient of men." *Toronto of Old* [1873], by the Rev. Henry Scadding, D.D., p. 102.

6. The four ridings were constituted as follows:

    1st Township of York (with peninsula), Etobicoke, Vaughan and King.

    2nd Township of Caledon, Chinguacousy, Toronto, Gore of Toronto and Albion.

    3rd Townships of Scarboro, Markham, Pickering and Whitby.

    4th Townships of East Gwillimbury, North Gwillimbury, Scott, Georgina, Brock, Reach, Whitechurch and Uxbridge.

7. *Colonial Advocate*, December 31st, 1833.

8. The Act of 1791, as the British North America Act does to-day, gave the King power to disallow any act of the provincial legislature within two years after its receipt by his Majesty. In this case the two years from the date of the receipt by the King had not yet expired.

9. The phraseology of this address is deserving of attention. It is far from suggesting that the provincial legislature felt itself destitute of influence or power. A contrast is manifestly intended between his Majesty's ministers four thousand miles away, whom the legislature could not control, and the local executive on which it could at least bring a strong influence to bear. There is nothing here that points to an *irresponsible* local government.

10. It was now about 350,000.

11. i.e. As *alderman*: one of the common councilmen in the same ward received 150 votes.

12. The view taken of his election by some of his political sympathizers is shown by the following quotation from an article in the Niagara *Reporter*: "This is a punishment deservedly inflicted upon the aristocracy, and we sincerely hope and are well assured that he will be re-elected to that office until the pride and haughtiness of mushroom nobles are reduced to their

proper level, and until the insulted majesty of the people is avenged." The hope thus expressed was not destined to be fulfilled. He held office until the end of the calendar year (1834) and was not re-elected. His successor was Mr. R. B. Sullivan.

Chapter Fourteen

1. The paper in question was written by the Hon. Toussaint Pothier, a member of the legislative council. It has not been published. The original is preserved in the Dominion Archives.

2. Ketchum had had enough of political contention and did not come forward.

3. These sentiments did not differ materially from Fothergill's, but it seems strange to find them uttered by Rolph who, only three years later, was so deeply implicated in Mackenzie's revolutionary schemes that he had to flee the country. His presence at the Jarvis dinner shows that he had gravitated in some measure to the conservative side. Since his defeat for the Assembly in 1830 he had been practising medicine in Toronto, and had probably been brought into personal relations that had diminished his ardour for "reform."

4. See Dr. Ryerson's pamphlet, "The Affairs of Canada, 1836."

5. *Canada as it was, is and may be*, London, 1852, Vol. I, p. 142. By the "leader of the radical party" Mr. Bidwell is meant.

6. Mr. Allan MacNab, Afterwards Sir Allan); who was president of the Gore Bank, was just at this time erecting a very fine house for himself at Hamilton.

7. [On August 6, 1835, a riot occurred in Baltimore, Maryland, as a result of the fear that the trustees of the Bank of Maryland, which had collapsed early in 1834, had been guilty of fraud. See Richard Hofstadter and M. Wallace (eds.), *American Violence* (New York: Random House, 1971), pp. 122-26.]

8. The date is significant. He had published the "baneful domination" letter in June; and the strong demon-

strations of public disapproval which followed seem
to have placed a certain restraint for a time upon his
utterances.

9. "With the impatience of an enthusiast," says Mr.
Lindsey (Vol. I, p. 346), "he published his discoveries
before the time came for making his official report."
As Mr. Mackenzie was responsible only to the house
of assembly in which his party had a majority he
could afford to indulge his "enthusiasm."

10. Vol. I, p. 350.

11. Quoted by Lindsey from the Montreal *Vindicator*,
Dr. E. B. O'Callaghan's paper.

Chapter Fifteen

1. *A Narrative*, by Sir Francis Bond Head, Bart.
London, 1839.

2. ["In his own manner."]

3. *Canada as it was, is and may be*. Vol. 1, p. 180.

4. *The Emigrant*, by Sir Francis Bond Head. London,
1846, p. 47.

5. [This sentence originally contained the following
words which followed "province": "assigned seemed
to call for immediate action."]

6. Mr. Baldwin seems thus to have recognized Mr. Perry
as the leader of the reform party in the legislature.

7. The two unbending tories were G. S. Boulton of
Durham and Edward Mulock of Carlton.

8. The fact was that Mackenzie had been very much
occupied since the beginning of the session in hunting
down Merritt in connection with the Welland Canal
enquiry; and in spite of the usefulness of his labours
in bringing irregularities to light, had not increased
the estimation in which he was held for good judgement or balance of mind. Merritt declined in a
committee of the House to reply to a torrent of
invectives Mackenzie had directed against him, con-
tenting himself with imputing his violence to insanity.
Commenting on the incident, the *Patriot* (February
23rd, 1836) said, " 'Insanity' is a word powerless to
express the fever of his rage."

9. The point was a very minor one into which it is not worth while to enter. The colonial secretary, on being fully informed of the facts, stated to Sir Francis that his defence was "satisfactory and conclusive." Despatch of 25th July, 1836, published in British Parliamentary papers relating to Canada, 1839, Vol. II.

10. The explanation of the earlier vote is, probably, that the executive council as Sir Francis Head constituted it, consisting, that is to say, of three old councillors and three new ones, commanded sympathies *on both sides of the House.* The Council as a body complained that they had not been treated with due consideration by the lieutenant governor, and quite possibly they had not. The word "responsible" may be used with greater or less exactness; and the conservative sense on this occasion may have been, as applied to the Council, *a body having responsible duties to perform* and therefore entitled to respectful and considerate treatment. The reformers would use the word in its more technical sense.

11. A somewhat striking example of this phase of opinion is found in a passage of Christie's *History of Lower Canada,* (Vol. 1, pp. 350-51), written twelve years after these events. After describing the arbitrary proceedings of the official class under Sir James Craig (1807-1811) the author proceeds: "Whether the scheme of responsible government on which Canada now (1848) prides itself, will prove a better speculation, posterity, which there is every probability will pay well for it, will determine better than we of the present day can possibly pretend to do. It differs from the former in this; that *they* were of the appointment of the crown solely, independently of the country; whereas *these* are named at least with the concurrence of the representatives of the people . . . for the mutual advantage, as pretended of the governing and governed, but on a basis always of corruption, and consequently no more than a bureaucracy of another and still baser kind. Certain principal officials or heads of departments are it seems to retain their offices with the large salaries appertaining thereto and constitute the executive coun-

cil or provincial ministry so long only as they can preserve seats in the Assembly and secure a majority in it of partisans or adherents – no matter by what means, that being their affair. . . . In other words that while they can secure their dominion in the Assembly – in that body intended to be the constitutional check upon them, and to whom they are supposed responsible – they shall be responsible ministers, with the treasury at command and its attendant influences; and theirs the spoils of office as the reward of corruption, and the means of perpetuating it. A fair understanding in fact, that corruption shall be legal, and the people pay, provided always the representatives have their share; and this is responsible government! A more perfect inversion whereof, nevertheless, it is difficult to conceive. . . . It is in fact, but another and more plausible scheme to monopolise the people's treasury among the few supposed to possess their confidence, or adroit enough, by corruption or otherwise, to make it appear so."

Chapter Sixteen

1. [*A Narrative*,] Vol. I, p. 377.
2. The account referred to is quoted in the *Patriot of* July 8th from the *York Courier*. The following evidence bearing on the point was given by Dr. John King of Toronto before a committee of the new House: "I voted against W. L. Mackenzie at the last election. . . . Was present at the closing of the poll on Wednesday evening, and heard Mr. Mackenzie say, in addressing the people, that he was perfectly satisfied with the conduct of the returning officer, or words to that effect; and if he was left out, he was left out fairly. He was then in a minority. Witness requested the people to mark and remember what Mr. Mackenzie had said." There was afterwards a family connection between Dr. King and Mr. Mackenzie, a son of the former marrying a daughter of the latter.
3. Vol. I, p. 382.

4. The reference is to the Montreal election riot of May 21st, 1832, when a detachment of the Fifteenth Regiment, after repeated warnings had been given to the mob, who were pelting the soldiers with stones, received the order to fire. Three of the rioters were killed. See Kingsford, *History of Canada*, Vol. IX, pp. 480-84. The charge against Sir Francis Head of defaming the catholic religion is founded on remarks made in one of his books with reference to certain respects of catholicism in South America.

5. "The principle of responsibility," he said, "though long before the country, has never yet been practically acted on." So far he agreed with Sir Francis Head.

6. These words are very significant as showing how impossible the colonial office felt it at this time, *more than a year before the rebellion broke out*, to oppose any continued resistance to the clearly expressed will of the province.

7. Mr. W. H. Draper's election to the Thirteenth Parliament was his first introduction to political life. He sat for Toronto, having defeated the previous member, Mr. J. E. Small.

8. The prophecy was really a remarkable one; for Sir Francis "put the question" and swept the country.

9. Mr. Mackenzie summed up the matter thus: "Words cannot express my contempt at witnessing the servile, crouching attitude of the country of my choice." Quoted by Lindsey, Vol. I, p. 395.

10. Lindsey, Vol. I, p. 382.

11. This passage is not taken direct from *The Constitution*. It is quoted in Ryerson's second letter to Hume and Roebuck.

12. [Maria Monk was the nominal author of the greatest piece of anti-Catholic nativist literature in nineteenth century North America, *Awful Disclosures of the Hotel Dieu Nunnery of Montreal* (New York, 1836), which charged that life within the convent in which Monk had taken vows (in fact she had not) was characterized by orgiastic proceedings and infanticide. The controversy which resulted is described at length in R. A. Billington, *The Protestant Crusade, 1800-1860* (Chicago: Quadrangle Books, 1964), pp. 99-108.]

13. [Archibald Acheson, second Earl of Gosford (1776-1849) was governor-in-chief of British North America from 1835 to 1837. He was appointed by the Melbourne ministry also as a royal commissioner to enquire into the affairs of Lower Canada. His policy of "conciliation without concession" to the French-Canadian *patriotes* led by Papineau was deemed a failure by British authorities and he resigned his commission shortly before the 1837 rebellion broke out in Lower Canada.]

Chapter Seventeen

1. Mr. Ridout was also deprived of his commission as colonel of the second regiment of East York militia.
2. This building, a frequent meeting place of the extreme party, was only removed, to make way for a better structure, in the summer of 1906.
3. Dent, *Upper Canada Rebellion*, Vol. I, p. 365.
4. *Ibid.*, p. 367.
5. Lindsey, Vol. II, p. 24.
6. *Ibid.*, p. 35.
7. Dent, *op. cit.*, Vol. II, p. 352.
8. Lindsey, *op. cit.*, Vol. II, p. 53.
9. On the arrival of Sir F. B. Head, Sir John Colborne, whom it was intended to recall to England, and who had proceeded as far as New York on his homeward journey, received orders to return to Canada as commander of the forces in both provinces. On the recall of Lord Gosford, Sir John was sworn in as administrator of the government (February 27th, 1838).
10. The italics are not in the original. Such language would emphasize itself sufficiently at the time.
11. Lindsey, *op. cit.*, Vol. II, p. 73.
12. *Upper Canada Rebellion*, Vol. II, p. 46. Mr. Dent refers to certain unpublished "Gibson, M.S.S." for the facts in connection with this interview.
13. Lindsey, *op. cit.*, Vol. II, p. 87.
14. The only European officer on the field was Van Egmond.

15. Lindsey, *op. cit.*, Vol. II, p. 92.
16. Dent, *op. cit.*, Vol. II, p. 126, and footnote pp. 135-38.
17. *Ibid.*, Vol. II, p. 134. See also Mackenzie's *Narrative.*

Chapter Eighteen

1. Lindsey, Vol. II, p. 126n.
2. ["One is safest in the middle."]
3. Lindsey, *op. cit.*, Vol. II, p. 163.
4. A small detachment of royal artillery had by this time been sent to expedite matters.
5. Mr. Lindsey, Vol. II, p. 183, refers to an unpublished letter of Van Rensselaer's, dated February 24th, 1840, withdrawing "all charges whether express or implied against his (Mackenzie's) moral integrity or honesty of purpose."
6. This certainly suggests a period of retirement, and therefore bears on the question of the writer's return to Navy Island after seeing Mrs. Mackenzie safely to Buffalo.
7. "Farmers of America, we abhor war. But how stands the case? I imagine a township full of sheep farms with a forest of wolves behind it. The owners must either expel the wolves, or they will increase and multiply, and never cease to devour the sheep. So it is with you; the wolves who are devouring Canada and threatening your choicest settlements must be expelled, or they will make as bad neighbours to you as the wolf does to the sheep. After removing the wolves you may have peace on your borders, but not before. Never will life or property be safe on this extended frontier till the flag of England has ceased to wave over the North American continent." *Mackenzie's Gazette*, 16th March, 1839. Mr. Lindsey (Vol. II, page 258) mentions a fact which plainly shows that Mackenzie was embarrassing, or at least believed he was embarrassing, the relations between the United States and the British governments; namely that some time after his imprisonment, he offered in a memorial to the President to cease the

publication of the paper during the remainder of his term, if certain ameliorations were granted in the conditions of his confinement.

8. Amongst a number of papers lately transferred by the Durham family to the Dominion Archives are two letters from one Thomas Handcock, who speaks of himself as having been at one time on the staff of Sir Peregrine Maitland. In the first, dated New York, June 7th, 1838, and addressed to Mr. Weir of the Montreal *Herald*, the writer states that he had had a conversation with Mackenzie and O'Callaghan (a Lower Canada rebel) on the subject of the burning of the *Sir Robert Peel*, and that both spoke of it as part of a general scheme to bring about a war between England and the United States. "When Mackenzie," the letter proceeds, "opened the paper containing the account of the outrage, he laid his hands on the counter and jumped and kicked with frenzied triumph." The second letter, dated October 10th, 1838, is addressed to Dr. Bartlett of the New York *Albion*. It contains the information that the writer was employed for a time in Mackenzie's newspaper office, and that he there saw "the most perfect plan of the fortifications of Fort Henry, Kingston, and a map of great correctness of the different points of attack." See, in regard to this, Lindsey, Vol. II, page 181. It was in Mackenzie's office that the conversation respecting the *Sir Robert Peel* took place. Handcock may, or may not, have been a trustworthy person, but there is nothing in his story that taxes belief. The letters must have been transferred to Lord Durham.

[LeSueur was aware of recent manuscript acquisitions by the Public Archives of Canada because in 1907, while he was writing the biography, he was asked by Arthur Doughty, Dominion Archivist, to manage the archives. One of the tasks he seems to have performed was the organization of the Durham papers. See W. D. LeSueur to the Honourable Rodolphe Lemieux (Minister of Labour in Laurier's administration), 1 October, 1907. Papers of the Members of the King Family. John King Papers, Vol. 4; in the W. L. Mackenzie King Papers, Public Archives of Canada.]

9. In Major Richardson's *Eight Years in Canada* there is a very interesting and pathetic account of a visit paid by him to Van Shoultz in his prison at Fort Henry (Kingston). "His whole demeanour and attitude," the author says, "were such as could not fail to command respect. . . . There was, moreover, a placidity and quiet resolution about his fine countenance that could not fail to interest; while the glance of a moment was sufficient to satisfy the beholder that, whatever his political faults, the man was a gentleman and a soldier." He was rather startled by his visitor's enquiry, "How he, a Pole, and in all probability a refugee, who had often shared her bounty, should have armed against England, a country that had effected so much in amelioration of the conditions of his exiled countrymen." Collecting himself, however, he replied that he really thought he was doing England a service, as he had been given to understand that the whole Canadian people were anxious for independence, and that thousands would join him in a few hours. "He added that he bitterly regretted having embarked in the Canadian disturbances into which he had been committed by false promises – that, however, he knew his fate and was prepared to meet it. . . . He politely thanked me for having been interested enough in him to pay him a visit, and remarked with a faint attempt at a smile, that it would soon be all over with him." (Pages 67, 68).

10. Dufort was a trusted emissary of the Lower Canada rebels, and had visited Toronto before the rebellion broke out to make confidential communications to certain reform leaders in that city.

11. See Kingsford, *History of Canada*, Vol. I, p. 499, and Richardson, *Eight Years in Canada*, p. 69.

12. This was for a time the headquarters of the refugees.

13. Montgomery, proprietor of the hotel (burnt by order of Sir Francis Head) at which the rebels had gathered, was now keeping an hotel at Rochester, N.Y.

14. The original of this letter, with a large quantity of other matter relating to the rebellion, is in the Dominion Archives at Ottawa.

15. Thus Lord Melbourne is "cruel and lewd;" Lord John Russell "clever and unprincipled, therefore fit for such company;" the Earl of Minto, first lord of the Admiralty, is "like Earl Grey, a perfect *leech*, greedy for office for himself and his relations;" while another member is charged with an intrigue of which particulars are given.

Chapter Nineteen

1. Had there been more dignity and restraint in Mackenzie's character, he might possibly have passed for its Brand, the man who by his uncompromising absolution led others to their ruin.

2. [Sir George Arthur (1784-1854), lieutenant-governor of Upper Canada from 1838 to 1841.]

3. Even Dr. Kingsford represents Arthur as a thoroughly unfeeling man, and it has been alleged that his experience in the convict colony of Van Dieman's land had rendered his nature hard and severe. The following passage from a well-known work presents him in a very different light: "Colonel Arthur's administration of Van Dieman's land lasted for twelve years, and was marked throughout by a rare combination of humanity with firmness and courage; and above all by a shrewd common sense and practical judgment, which secured for him alike the respect of the colonists and the confidence of statesmen at home." – D. B. Read, Q.C., *Lieutenant Governors of Upper Canada and Ontario* page 194.

4. Lindsey, Vol. II, p. 186.

5. There is a batch of letters (copies) in the Dominion Archives from the prisoners belonging to the Van Shoultz expedition, in confinement at Kingston, some under sentence of death. These unfortunate men and lads were far from sharing Mackenzie's opinion of his own non-responsibility.

6. [Lajos Kossuth (1802-1894), Hungarian patriot and leader of the revolution of 1848-49 in Hungary; an exponent of popular reforms such as complete

emancipation of the serfs and taxation of the nobility.]

7. Lindsey, *op. cit.*, Vol. II, p. 224.
8. He meant grandfather, George the Third.
9. See Mr. Lindsey's interesting account of the trial, Vol. II, pp. 244-52.
10. See above.
11. Lindsey, *op. cit.*, Vol. II, p. 188.
12. *Ibid.*, p. 258.
13. See a letter from the sheriff of Monroe county quoted by Lindsey (Vol. II, p. 266) which also indicates that Mr. Mackenzie was not the most manageable of prisoners.
14. *Ibid.*, p. 261.
15. *Ibid.*, p. 272.
16. *Ibid.*, p. 279.
17. This does not tally very well with the affidavit taken by Mackenzie in 1839 that, as early as June 1838, he had tried to dissuade the patriots from attacking Canada.
18. The reader will certainly be reminded of Van Rens-salaer's account of Mackenzie on a previous page.
19. A word omitted here in the original. It is not quite clear who washed the sow, or when, or how, the operation was performed.
20. There is perhaps more concentrated gall in this than in anything Mackenzie ever wrote. What follows indicates the source from which some of Mackenzie's ideas might have been drawn, if they were not original with himself.
21. Why did Brown not come and destroy it himself, instead of sunning himself down in Florida? A man who talked so glibly about stringing people up should not have been afraid of the gallows.
22. Ellice was a son-in-law of the second Earl Grey, and brother-in-law to Lord Durham. He was in Canada with Lord Durham and had extensive property in county Beauharnois. Brown and Ross must have been tories, but the memory of their misdeed seems to have perished.
23. He probably means Lord Durham.
24. He was not altogether alone in this opinion. In Mr. Hannay's *Wilmot and Tilley* ("Makers of Canada"

series) we read: "Mr. Robert L. Hazen, an eminent lawyer, who was a candidate for the representation of the city of St. John, declared in his nomination speech that he had never met with anyone who could explain to him satisfactorily what responsible government meant," p. 64. Mr. Humbert, a candidate for the county said: "Very few people understood what responsible government meant. He hardly understood it himself." This was in the general election in 1842.

Chapter Twenty

1. Whether his Lordship who, as Lord Howicke, was under-Secretary for the Colonies when Mackenzie was in England, "well knew" of the "insults, injuries and oppression" to which his correspondent referred may be doubted. Certainly his chief, Lord Goderich, did not seem to be very distinctly aware of them when he penned his despatch of the eighth of November, 1832.

2. How would it have suited Mackenzie's purpose to quote that?

3. The italics here are Mackenzie's own. The preceeding pages have, it is hoped, made it clear that there was a very near prospect of desirable constitutional reforms at the very moment chosen for the insurrection. It has been claimed for Mackenzie that he hastened these changes; it will be observed how far he is from making such a claim for himself.

4. Mr. F. Bradshaw, M.A., in his *Self-Government in Canada, and how it was achieved: the story of Lord Durham's Report*, London, 1903. "This volume," Mr. Bradshaw says in his preface, "is the result of research work carried on in the seminar of the Director of the London School of Economics and Political Science." Such a work ought to be reasonably free from party spirit.

5. In point of fact no "large mass of the people" did unite for any such purpose. Mackenzie's followers, all told, were not a large mass, and numbers of them

declared that they had hoped to accomplish their object by a mere "demonstration."

6. [Harriet Martineau (1802-1876) wrote on a variety of social and historical subjects. She popularized the classical economics of Malthus and Ricardo, translated Auguste Comte's *Positive Philosophy*, advocated religious liberty in general, and was an ardent exponent of the anti-slavery movement. Her major historical work, very popular in the nineteenth century, was *The History of England during the Thirty Years' Peace, 1816-1846* (1849).]

7. [See Chapter Eight, note 2, above.]

8. The Province being in a state of rebellion its constitution had been suspended by an imperial Act passed on the tenth of February, 1838. Limited legislative powers were vested in the governor and a Special Council nominated by him.

9. The official head was the Hon. R. B. Sullivan, President of the Council, and a member of the Legislative council, who retained his place in the reconstruction.

10. In one of his letters to Mackenzie E. B. O'Callaghan thus speaks of Viger and D. B. Papineau: "I have great confidence in Mr. Viger's love of Canada. I know Mr. D. B. Papineau personally, and a purer, more single-minded, and honourable man does not live."

Chapter Twenty-One

1. A couple of years later the same writer, in the same paper, made some serious qualifications as to Baldwin's fidelity to the cause of reform.

2. The good relations between Mackenzie and Lesslie did not, unfortunately, continue to the end. See Dent's *Story of the Upper Canada Rebellion*, Vol. II, p. 325.

3. *The Examiner*, which supported Mackenzie, recorded the result thus: "The great Globe, the Georgium Sidus, was totally eclipsed yesterday. Visible in Haldimand." The Georgium Sidus, however, passed

out of the shadow in the general election that took place in December of the same year, when Mr. Brown was elected for the county of Kent.

4. See Toronto *Examiner* of 5th August, 1851. Hume's letter was dated 21st April, 1851. Mackenzie did not reply till the 29th of July.

5. Sir Charles Metcalfe was raised to the peerage by this title before he left Canada.

6. See Toronto *Examiner* of 23rd July, 1851.

7. *Ibid.*, August 13th, 1851.

8. The original of these letters is amongst Mackenzie's papers.

9. Just at that time the Rebellion Losses Bill, the signing of which by Lord Elgin produced the serious riot of the 21st April, 1849, was under consideration.

10. Mackenzie was paid shortly after Mr. Hincks became premier.

11. Toronto was then the seat of government.

12. In preparation for the general election, which took place in November of that year.

13. A colourful evangelist, asked on what principle he made his sermons, is said to have replied: "First I explain, den I spounds, den I puts in de rousements." The Haldimand gentleman seemed to have little confidence in anything but "rousements."

14. See above.

15. Carmichael, the flag-bearer, had made a statement in Rolph's favour.

16. The incident occurred in the house of assembly on the 2nd of November, 1852. The report is taken from the Toronto *Examiner*.

17. Cardinal was head messenger or office-keeper to the assembly.

18. The Hon. John Ross was a son-in-law of Mr. Baldwin.

19. Lindsey, Vol. II, p. 298.

20. Dent, *Upper Canada Rebellion*, Vol. II, p. 324.

21. [Thus ended the original manuscript of LeSueur's *Mackenzie*. In the version which reached the page-proof stage, the author added three new paragraphs. Added here to the original text, they represent a summation of his views on Mackenzie, his character, and his legacy.]

SUGGESTIONS FOR FURTHER READING

The departure marked by William Dawson LeSueur's interpretation of William Lyon Mackenzie and his times is best judged by comparing it with Charles Lindsey's *The Life and Times of William Lyon Mackenzie* (Toronto: P. Randall, 2 vols., 1862) and J. C. Dent's *The Story of the Upper Canadian Rebellion* (Toronto: C. B. Robinson, 2 vols., 1885). William Kilbourn's *The Firebrand: William Lyon Mackenzie and the Rebellion in Upper Canada* (Toronto: Clark Irwin, 1956) tells a story and interprets a character, as it set out to do, but omits much that would have provided a more balanced, if less compelling, account. David Flint's *William Lyon Mackenzie: Rebel Against Authority* (Toronto: Oxford University Press, 1971) also provides an entertaining survey of Mackenzie's career.

Two collections of Mackenzie's writings deserve special attention. *The Selected Writings of William Lyon Mackenzie* (Toronto: Oxford University Press, 1960), edited by Margaret Fairley, draws from a variety of sources including newspapers, pamphlets, broadsides, and letters. Significantly, however, it does not deal with the post-rebellion years, which revealed much about Mackenzie's character not fully apparent before 1837. This gap was filled in part by Anthony W. Rasporich, whose edited collection, *William Lyon Mackenzie*, in the Canadian History Through the Press series (Toronto: Holt, Rinehart and Winston, 1972), contains a thorough selection of Mackenzie's newspaper writings and provides an excellent introduction that surveys interpretations of Mackenzie and places his eclectic mind in a European context.

Upper Canadian scholarship in the last two decades has tended to offer the sort of interpretative revision first suggested in LeSueur's *Mackenzie*. Gerald Craig's *Upper Canada: the Formative Years* (Toronto: McClelland & Stewart, 1963) was the first major work of serious scholarship in a half century to rehabilitate the Family Compact and to suggest that the support offered them by Upper Canadians was possibly warranted. Craig was also highly critical of Mackenzie, concluding, like LeSueur, that Mackenzie had indeed "greatly injured" the cause of reform. His views were supported by the work of S. F. Wise who, in several important and suggestive articles, examined in detail the thought of and support for the Upper Canadian Tories. See in particular: "God's Peculiar Peoples," in W. L. Morton (ed.), *The Shield of Achilles* (Toronto: McClelland & Stewart, 1968); "Sermon Literature and Canadian Intellectual History," in J. M. Bumsted (ed.), *Canadian History Before Confederation* (Georgetown: Irwin-Dorsey, 1972); "The Conservative Tradition in Upper Canada," in *Profiles of a Province* (Toronto: Ontario Historical Society, 1967). Wise's introduction to Francis Bond Head's account of his experiences in Canada, *A Narrative* (Toronto: Macmillan, Carleton Library No. 43, 1969) is both sympathetic and critical; it invites comparison with LeSueur's treatment of Sir Francis.

Several recent studies have been built upon this rehabilitation of the conservative tradition in Canada. Notable in this regard are J. E. Rea, *Bishop Alexander Macdonell and the Politics of Upper Canada* (Toronto: Ontario Historical Society Research Publication No. 4, 1974) and Terry Cook, "John Beverley Robinson and the Conservative Blueprint for the Upper Canadian Community," in *Ontario History*, LXIV (1972), reprinted in J. K. Johnson (ed.), *Historical Essays on Upper Canada* (Toronto: Macmillan, Carleton Library No. 82, 1975), pp. 338-360.

Interpretations of the nature of Mackenzie's thought abound. The student may perhaps best be introduced to these views by consulting the following articles: F. H. Armstrong, "William Lyon Mackenzie: the Persistent Hero," *Journal of Canadian Studies* (August, 1971); Lillian F. Gates, "The Decided Policy of William Lyon Mackenzie," *Canadian Historical Review*, XL (September, 1959); J. E. Rea, "William Lyon Mackenzie – Jacksonian?" *Mid-America*, L (July, 1968); R. A. Mackay, "The Political Ideas of William Lyon Mackenzie," *Canadian Journal of Economics and Political Science*, II (February, 1937).

For examinations of the general state of Canadian historical writing in Canada in the late nineteenth and early twentieth centuries, see Kenneth N. Windsor, "Historical Writing in Canada to 1920," in C. F. Klinck (ed.), *Literary History of Canada* (Toronto: University of Toronto Press, 1965), Donald Swainson's introduction to the Carleton Library edition of J. C. Dent's *The Last Forty Years*

(Toronto: Macmillan, Carleton Library No. 62, 1972), and Carl Berger's *The Writing of Canadian History* (Toronto: Oxford University Press, 1976). William Dawson LeSueur's entire career as essayist and historian is examined in A. B. McKillop (ed.), *A Critical Spirit: The Thought of William Dawson LeSueur* (Toronto: Macmillan, Carleton Library No. 104, 1977).

Note on the Editor

A. B. McKillop was born in Winnipeg and educated at the University of Manitoba and Queen's University. He has taught at Dalhousie University, Queen's University, and the University of Manitoba, where he is Assistant Professor of Canadian History. His publications include "Nationalism, Identity and Canadian Intellectual History" (*Queen's Quarterly*, 1974), articles on aspects of the political climate of Winnipeg during the depression, and *A Critical Spirit: The Thought of William Dawson LeSueur* (The Carleton Library No. 104, 1977).

Related Titles in the Carleton Library Series

3. LAURIER: A Study in Canadian Politics, by John W. Dafoe, with an introduction by Murray S. Donnelly.

4. CHAMPLAIN: The Life of Fortitude, by Morris Bishop, with a new introduction by the author.

8. LORD DURHAM'S MISSION TO CANADA, by Chester New, edited and with an introduction by H. W. McCready.

10. POLITICAL UNREST IN UPPER CANADA, 1815–1836, by Aileen Dunham, with an introduction by A. L. Burt.

20. JOSEPH HOWE: Voice of Nova Scotia, compiled and with an introduction by J. Murray Beck.

21. LIFE AND LETTERS OF SIR WILFRID LAURIER, Volume I. by O. D. Skelton, edited and with an introduction by David M. L. Farr.

22. LIFE AND LETTERS OF SIR WILFRID LAURIER, Volume II, by O. D. Skelton.

24. FRONTENAC: The Courtier Governor, by W. J. Eccles, prepared for republication by the author.

26. LIFE AND TIMES OF SIR ALEXANDER TILLOCH GALT, by O. D. Skelton, edited and with an introduction by Guy MacLean.

42. THE COLONIAL REFORMERS AND CANADA, 1830–1849, compiled and with an introduction by Peter Burroughs.

43. SIR FRANCIS BOND HEAD, A Narrative, edited and with an introduction by S. F. Wise.

44. JOHN STRACHAN: Documents and Opinions, edited and with an introduction by J. L. H. Henderson.

46. ROBERT LAIRD BORDEN: His Memoirs, Volume I, edited and with an introduction by Heath Macquarrie.

47. ROBERT LAIRD BORDEN: His Memoirs, Volume II, edited by Heath Macquarrie.

52. MONCK LETTERS AND JOURNALS: Canada from Government House, 1864–1868, edited and with an introduction by W. L. Morton.

63. LAURIER AND A LIBERAL QUEBEC: A Study in Political Management, by H. Blair Neatby, edited and with an introduction by Richard T. Clippingdale.

70. RENEGADE IN POWER: The Diefenbaker Years, by Peter C. Newman, with an introduction by Denis Smith.

71. CUTHBERT GRANT OF GRANTOWN, by Margaret A. McLeod and W. L. Morton, with a new introduction by W. L. Morton.

72. STATISTICAL ACCOUNT OF UPPER CANADA, by Robert Gourlay, abridged and with an introduction by S. R. Mealing.

80. PHILIPPE DE RIGAUD DE VAUDREUIL, Governor of New France, 1703–1725, by Yves Zoltvany.

82. HISTORICAL ESSAYS ON UPPER CANADA, edited and with an introduction by J. K. Johnson.

104. A CRITICAL SPIRIT: The Thought of William Dawson LeSueur, edited and with critical commentary by A. B. McKillop.